A Very Bad Wizard

D0162568

In the first edition of *A Very Bad Wizard: Morality Behind the Curtain—Nine Conversations*, philosopher Tamler Sommers talked with an interdisciplinary group of the world's leading researchers—from the fields of social psychology, moral philosophy, cognitive science, and primatology—all working on the same issue: the origins and workings of morality. Together, these nine interviews pulled back some of the curtain, not only on our moral lives but—through Sommers' probing, entertaining, and well informed questions—on the way morality traditionally has been studied.

This Second Edition increases the subject matter, adding eight additional interviews and offering features that will make *A Very Bad Wizard* more useful in undergraduate classrooms. These features include structuring all chapters around sections and themes familiar in a course in ethics or moral psychology; providing follow-up podcasts for some of the interviews, which will delve into certain issues from the conversations in a more informal manner; including an expanded and annotated reading list with relevant primary sources at the end of each interview; presenting instructor and student resources online in a companion website (www.routledge.com/cw/sommers).

The resulting new publication promises to synthesize and make accessible the latest interdisciplinary research to offer a brand new way to teach philosophical ethics and moral psychology.

Tamler Sommers is Associate Professor of Philosophy at the University of Houston. His research focuses on moral responsibility, revenge, honor, and the philosophy of punishment. He is the author of *Relative Justice: Cultural Diversity, Free Will and Moral Responsibility* (2012) and co-host of the Very Bad Wizards podcast. He is currently writing a book in defense of honor.

"The study of morality is the most exciting game in town, and when people ask me why I think so, I always refer them to Tamler Sommers's extraordinary book, *A Very Bad Wizard*! This new edition even tops the first edition, and it brims with witty, insightful, and fascinating conversations with the best moral psychologists and moral philosophers of our times."

Edouard Machery, *University of Pittsburgh, USA*

"Sommers's interview style cuts straight to the heart of a wide range of issues in morality and psychology. Not only does Sommers offer clear and crisp challenges to many of philosophy's leading figures, but he manages to do so in a way that brings these issues to light for any intelligent layperson. Sommers covers topics ranging from free will, justice and objectivity in morality, to meaning in life, honor, and the morality of violence. In doing so, he is providing an invaluable service to philosophy and related areas like social psychology by pushing today's best thinkers to answer the tough questions, and all the while bringing philosophy to life for a wider audience. Tamler Sommers is not just a very bad wizard, he is a very badass wizard!"

Michael McKenna, *University of Arizona, USA*

"Sommers' interviews are easygoing but sharp and critically engaged. He knows how to bring out what's most interesting in his subjects, and he also presses them in just the right ways. The line-up of interviewees includes many of the brightest lights in moral philosophy, each with a rich and provocative body of work to discuss, and this second edition's additions are first-rate. While this would be excellent background reading for students in a variety of ethics courses, it's actually entertaining and enlightening reading for anyone interested in gaining access to some of the very best contemporary work in moral philosophy."

David Shoemaker, *Tulane University, USA*

"This clever and thoughtful book makes ethics come alive by ditching dry philosophical prose and opting instead to let real human voices speak for themselves. The range of topics is impressive, the interviews are probing yet accessible, and the author is an eminently likable guide to the terrain. I teach this book in my intro to ethics course, and the only disappointment is not having time for my students to read the whole thing. It allows students to see thinkers in the process of thinking, and to appreciate what charitable and constructive philosophical conversation looks like."

Neal Tognazzini, *Western Washington University, USA*

A Very Bad Wizard

Morality Behind the Curtain

Second Edition

Tamler Sommers

Routledge
Taylor & Francis Group

NEW YORK AND LONDON

First published 2016
by Routledge
711 Third Avenue, New York, NY 10017

and by Routledge
2 Park Square, Milton Park, Abingdon, Oxon, OX14 4RN

Routledge is an imprint of the Taylor & Francis Group, an informa business

© 2016 Taylor & Francis

The right of Tamler Sommers to be identified as author of this work has
been asserted by him in accordance with sections 77 and 78 of the
Copyright, Designs and Patents Act 1988.

All rights reserved. No part of this book may be reprinted or
reproduced or utilised in any form or by any electronic, mechanical, or
other means, now known or hereafter invented, including photocopying
and recording, or in any information storage or retrieval system,
without permission in writing from the publishers.

Trademark notice: Product or corporate names may be trademarks or
registered trademarks, and are used only for identification and
explanation without intent to infringe.

First edition published by McSweeney's 2009

Library of Congress Cataloging in Publication Data
Names: Sommers, Tamler, 1970- author. Title: A very bad wizard :
morality behind the curtain / Tamler Sommers. Description: Second
Edition. | New York : Routledge, 2016. Identifiers: LCCN 2015044502 |
ISBN 9780415855723 | ISBN 9780415858793 Subjects: LCSH: Ethics.
| Psychology and philosophy. | Philosophers--Interviews. Classification:
LCC BJ45 .S64 2016 | DDC 170--dc23 LC record available at
http://lccn.loc.gov/2015044502

ISBN: 978-0-415-85572-3 (hbk)
ISBN: 978-0-415-85879-3 (pbk)
ISBN: 978-0-203-70890-3 (ebk)

Typeset in Times New Roman
by Saxon Graphics Ltd, Derby

MIX
Paper from
responsible sources
FSC
www.fsc.org   FSC® C013056

Printed and bound in Great Britain by
TJ International Ltd, Padstow, Cornwall

Contents

CENTRAL ARKANSAS LIBRARY SYSTEM
LITTLE ROCK PUBLIC LIBRARY
100 ROCK STREET
LITTLE ROCK, ARKANSAS 72201

Researchers Interviewed

Kwame Anthony Appiah is Professor of Philosophy and Law at New York University. His research spans many topics in ethics and political philosophy, often pulling from both African and African-American intellectual and literary work. Most recently, he has focused on the role of ideals and idealization in politics. His most recent book, *W. E. B. Du Bois and the Emergence of Identity* synthesizes many of these themes.

Simon Blackburn is Distinguished Research Professor of Philosophy at the University of North Carolina at Chapel Hill and Fellow of Trinity College, Cambridge University. His research in ethics typically defends metaethical quasi-realism and neo-Humean moral psychology. In his most recent book, *Mirror, Mirror: the Uses and Abuses of Self-Love*, he tours the history of philosophy to evaluate themes of narcissism, vanity, and self-love.

Paul Bloom is the Brooks and Suzanne Ragen Professor of Psychology at Yale University. His research focuses on developmental and moral psychology, especially of children and adults navigating the world of values. *Just Babies: The Origins of Good and Evil*, his most recent book, argues that infants have an early sense of goodness, empathy, and justice, as well as hostility toward strangers, parochial tendencies, and bigotry. He expands the account of reason by focusing on how it affects moral deliberation.

Alan Fiske is Professor of Anthropology at the University of California, Los Angeles. His research focuses on the psychology, anthropology, and neurobiology of human social and moral relationships. His most recent book, *Virtuous Violence: Hurting and Killing to Create, Sustain, End, and Honor Social Relationships*, co-authored with Tage Shakti Rai, analyzes the many motivations of violence in literature, across cultures, and in contemporary contexts.

Joshua Greene is Professor of Psychology at Harvard University. His research focuses on issues in moral psychology, especially as informed by neuroimaging studies. His recent book, *Moral Tribes*, combines research from psychology, neuroscience, and philosophy to analyze moral conflict.

Jonathan Haidt is a social psychologist and Thomas Cooley Professor of Ethical Leadership at the NYU Stern School of Business. He is the author of The Happiness Hypothesis and The Righteous Mind.

Joseph Henrich is joint Professor of Psychology and Economics at the University of British Columbia. He also directs the Centre for Human Evolution, Cognition, and Culture. He researches evolutionary approaches to psychology and decision-making, pay special attention to the effects of culture. His most recent books are the 2014 *Experimenting with Social Norms: Fairness and Punishment in Cross-Cultural Perspective* and forthcoming *The Secret of Our Success: How Culture Is Driving Human Evolution, Domesticating Our Species, and Making Us Smarter.*

William Ian Miller is the Thomas G. Long Professor of Law at the University of Michigan. He is the author of numerous books including *Why is Your Axe Bloody? A Reading of the Njal's Saga, Eye for an Eye, Humiliation,* and *The Mystery of Courage.*

Tage Rai is Post-doctoral Research Fellow at the Ford Center for Global Citizenship at Northwestern University. His work explores the effects of society and culture on moral judgments. In his most recent book, *Virtuous Violence: Hurting and Killing to Create, Sustain, End, and Honor Social Relationships,* co-authored with Alan Fiske, analyzes the many motivations of violence in literature, across cultures, and in contemporary contexts.

Michael Ruse is Lucycle T. Werkmeister Professor of Philosophy at Florida State University, where he also directs the History and Philosophy of Science Program. Ruse draws extensively from the work of Charles Darwin, as in his 2008 book *Reflections on the Origin of Species,* and he extrapolates the implication of evolutionary theory for morality and religion, as in his 2006 book *The Evolution-Creation Struggle.*

Nancy Sherman is University Professor of Philosophy at Georgetown University and Fellow of the Kennedy Institute. Her research explores the implications of ancient Greek philosophy on contemporary topics like war and moral psychology. Her most recent book, *Afterwar: Healing the Moral Wounds of Our Soldiers,* argues that philosophy and moral analysis should supplement medical and psychological services to help veterans heal after war.

Peter Singer is Ira W. DeCamp Professor of Bioethics at the Princeton University's Center for Human Values. His research focuses on many issues in ethics, from applied utilitarian philosophy in the domains of animal rights and the alleviation of world poverty to moral psychology. His most recent book, *The Most Good You Can Do: How Effective Altruism Is Changing Ideas about Living Ethically* challenges the reader to enact effective change to a maximal degree by donating money, organs, and expertise.

Stephen Stich is the Board of Governors Professor in the Philosophy Department at Rutgers University. He is the author of numerous books including *The Fragmentation of Reason*, *Deconstructing the Mind*, and *Knowledge, Rationality and Morality: Collected Papers*.

Galen Strawson is Professor of Philosophy at the University of Texas at Austin. His research explores metaphysical and moral psychological topics in the philosophy of mind, often borrowing insights from Locke, Hume, Kant, and Nietzsche. His most recent books are *Locke on Personal Identity*, and a second edition of *The Secret Connexion: Realism, Causation, and David Hume*.

Valerie Tiberius is Professor and Chair of the Department of Philosophy at the University of Minnesota, Twin Cities. She researches many themes in moral psychology, focusing especially on theories of wellbeing and reflection. In her book, *The Reflective Life: Living Wisely with Our Limits*, she develops an account of wisdom tied to moral reflection that analyzes the things that make life valuable, our own intrinsic limits, and how we can live well by reflecting on the right things, just the right amount.

Frans de Waal is C. H. Candler Professor of Primate Behavior at Emory University and Distinguished Professor at the Utrecht University. He researches primate behavior to elucidate the foundation and formation of moral emotions and religious belief, as in his 2009 book, *The Age of Empathy: Nature's Lessons for a Kinder Society*, and his 2013 book, *The Bonobo and the Atheist: In Search of Humanism among the Primates*.

Susan Wolf is Edna J. Koury Distinguished Professor of Philosophy at the University of North Carolina at Chapel Hill. Her research in ethics usually connects with interests in philosophy of mind, political theory, and aesthetics. Her most recent book, *The Variety of Values: Essays on Morality, Meaning, and Love* exhibits her philosophical range.

Liane Young is Associate Professor of Psychology at Boston College. Her work confronts many topics in moral psychology, mostly pulling from contemporary neuroscientific and experimental psychological studies. Her most recent studies have looked at various aspects of cognition, evaluation, and norm violation in cases of purity, disgust, and sexuality.

Philip Zimbardo is Professor Emeritus of Psychology at Stanford University. He conducted the Stanford Prison Experiment and has investigated psychological theories of madness, manipulation, and authority. His book, *The Lucifer Effect: Understanding How Good People Turn Evil*, chronicles his experiments and explores these themes. Most recently, his work has focused on time, as in *The Time Paradox: the New Psychology of Time that Will Change Your Life*, and the effects of technology on manhood, as in *Man (Dis)connected: How technology has sabotaged what it means to be male*.

Foreword to the Second Edition
by David Pizarro

Sometime during the winter break of the 2009/10 academic year, I was browsing the philosophy section of a Barnes & Noble in southern California. There, sitting next to books about existentialism and New Age, I came across a copy of the first edition of *A Very Bad Wizard*. By that time I had known Tamler for a few years already, and considered him a friend (we had first met a few years before, when he was still a graduate student in North Carolina). So, basking in reflected glory, I pulled out my phone, snapped a picture of the book on the store shelf, and sent it to Tamler.

Only after taking the picture did I bother to browse through the actual contents. I hesitate to say that I was envious, but that's only because such an admission would require that I swallow my pride. But, yeah, I was envious. The authors Tamler had lined up were a dream team for any ethics nerd. These were people whose work I not only admired, but who had shaped the way I think about morality. And here Tamler had gotten to speak to all of them personally about their work. (Seriously, how did a young philosopher convince Phil Zimbardo—as close to a rock star as psychology will ever have—to actually agree to be part of his book way back then?)

But the book also represented something else that made me pretty happy—it was a sort of sign that moral psychology was finally "official." You see, when I was a graduate student morality was not a very respectable thing to study (not in any serious psychology PhD program, at least). It had come to be viewed as, at best, a cottage industry of folks churning out fairly narrow research in specialized journals, mostly about the theories of moral development that the psychologist Lawrence Kohlberg had proposed decades before. Aside from that, it was a pretty dead topic. So choosing to study morality in grad school, at least for a psychologist, was a pretty good way of lowering the already-low odds of ever actually landing a job in academia. Luckily for me, right around the time I actually needed a job, that all changed: morality exploded onto the scene in a great big, glorious, interdisciplinary mess. Suddenly it was what was hot in the streets. This happened largely because of the emerging work of a handful of scholars that, I think, are best characterized by their willingness to step out of the narrow confines of their discipline, and who took steps toward doing real interdisciplinary work on the topic of morality. And hence my happiness—this book is full of those scholars. Honestly, if you want to understand where the great morality explosion of the early "oughts" came from, there are very few places that might serve as a better starting point.

But there's something about this book that goes beyond just simply being a great collection of discussions with some of the top scholars in the field. To describe what that something is requires me to go on a bit of a personal tangent (I promise I'll bring it back to a wonderfully insightful point about the book itself). When Tamler wrote this book, he initiated a chain of events that led to a pretty big change in my own personal and academic life: he and I started co-hosting a podcast on the philosophy and psychology of morality (very un-creatively entitled "Very Bad Wizards"). Why does this matter? In the last three years we've released about 100 hours of audio, and have probably spent at least twice as much time talking, texting, and emailing each other off the air. Let's just say I know the dude pretty well. It's only from those many hours of conversation (conversations which blend the personal and the professional in the most awkward of ways), that I've come to appreciate this book for what it really is.

I don't mean that it's *not* an entertaining collection of great scholars talking about their ideas concerning the nature of human morality. I really do believe that's an accurate description. It's a great book, in that pretty much any individual chapter serves as a great introduction to a particular theoretical or empirical approach to ethics. For this reason alone, I would recommend it as a great resource for instructors to use in any course that deals with ethics/moral psychology (I've used it for this purpose, and can tell you that students love it).

However, now that I've come to know Tamler I also see this book as another, bigger thing: the expression of a single, specific view about what ethics is and how it should be done. It might seem odd that a book with so many different voices and ideas (some that are even in direct conflict with each other) could represent a single viewpoint about ethics. But it's not so odd if that viewpoint is that human morality is best represented as a messy plurality of ideas that can only be understood by taking a fundamentally *inter*personal approach. Despite Tamler's self-reported antipathy toward big theories, I think this is pretty close to the theoretical approach he actually endorses. And in that much, I think I agree. Ethics are about the messy problems we face as social creatures that have to navigate a social world where people have different desires, interests, priorities, values, metaphysical beliefs, opinions, food allergies, and favorite baseball teams. To even attempt to derive a single set of abstract, universal principles to determine what we *ought* to believe, or to try to "boil down" human morality to some singular, universal psychological formula, seems to sacrifice the richness and diversity of the real ethical decisions that human beings make in their everyday lives.

These points get made pretty well when you get a group of top scholars in the field and actually talk to them in a real, personal way. Seriously, doing it this way makes a difference. There's just less chance to cheat here—scholars were not given the chance to submit chapters that neatly encapsulate their ideas, or to review evidence that tends to favor their views and downplay the rest; they didn't get a chance to spend hours editing their own words for consistency and clarity. On top of that, Tamler's prompts and questions are ones that are coming from a fellow scholar, so the normal set of filters we academics pop on so easily and automatically when talking to journalists really aren't there in these discussions. It's as if—*just for a bit*—people forget that this might be going in a book.

As a result, tongues seem a bit looser, and examples can get a bit more colorful. For instance, we get to hear some good old-fashioned trash-talking from the likes of Steve Stich (Chapter 16), who says that a vast amount of moral philosophy "belongs in the rubbish bin," and Galen Strawson (Chapter 1) who similarly expresses that philosophers "have made a truly unbelievable hash of all this." We also learn idiosyncratic details about the lives of these scholars (especially when those little details seemed to have played a role in shaping their ethical views), such as when Valerie Tiberius (Chapter 3) brings up Tamler's Springer Spaniel's desire to hunt when discussing the Aristotelian approach to virtue, or when Susan Wolf (Chapter 4) admits to realizing that she wasted a year of her life playing Sudoku. And then there's just some bits that may have nothing to do with anything, but somehow serve to humanize the authors—like the not-so-subtle way Simon Blackburn (Chapter 10) communicates that he's probably not a big supporter of (English football team) Arsenal, or the way Frans de Waal (Chapter 11) kindly makes Tamler feel normal after Tamler reveals his habit of pulling out pictures of Bonobo sex for the guests at his party.

This is also evident in some of the uncomfortable moments. This format reveals that difficult topics are ... difficult to talk about. Visceral and distressing examples like terrorism, rape, or honor killings are much harder to discuss in person without the tools of abstraction one might normally use when writing. But that's good—one would want in a researcher studying such uncomfortable topics to be sensitive to their distressing nature. So if I didn't sense some discomfort in Alan Fiske and Tage Rai (Chapter 15) when they bring up some of these examples, I'd honestly wonder if they really understood the nature of the topics they were studying.

In short, after god-knows-how-many hours of talking to Tamler in the last few years both on- and off-air, I've now come to see this book for what it is at its core: the sneaky manifesto of a moral pluralist who believes that ethics are fundamentally messy. But, if so, it also mounts a compelling positive argument: that if we have real conversations with real people—and set the bullshit aside—we might get a little closer to understanding exactly what *kind* of mess we are faced with. If I'm right, this book is probably the most hopeful expression I've ever heard Tamler make.

Ithaca, Cornell University
New York
February 19, 2016

Preface to the First Edition

Questions for the Interviewer

Why interviews? Don't philosophers write articles and books?

Yes, and that's a good thing. But the interview format has its advantages too. In books and articles, the arguments are worked out beforehand and then presented to the reader in digested form. Interviews allow for the ideas to be challenged and developed during the piece itself—and that's exciting stuff for a philosopher. There's a reason Plato only wrote dialogues. Questions, objections, responses to objections—these are the things that make philosophy move forward. But even in philosophical dialogues the authors know where the debate is heading. Dialogues are constructed to reach conclusions arrived at beforehand. I was able to ask questions without knowing what the answers would be. I never knew what direction the interview would take until it was happening. Like I said, exciting stuff for a philosopher.

What's up with the title?

The title refers to a scene at the end of *The Wizard of Oz*, when Dorothy and friends return to the Wizard's palace to claim their reward after making short work of the Wicked Witch of the West. The Wizard—in the form of an enormous floating green head—stalls, telling them to come back the next day. The group starts to protest and the green head fulminates about the dangers of arousing the wrath of the Wizard. Meanwhile, little Toto runs off to a booth by the side of the hall and pulls back a curtain to reveal that the Great and Powerful Oz is really just a balding carnival barker from Kansas. The green head, explosions, fire, and smoke are mere illusions produced by a machine. Dorothy is outraged.

"You're a very bad man!" she tells him.

"Oh no, my dear," the Wizard replies, "I'm a very good man. I'm just a very bad wizard."

And he is a good man. Because now that the illusion has been exposed, the Wizard can show our heroes that they've spent the movie searching for something they already have. The Scarecrow's brain, the Tin Man's heart, the Lion's courage, and Dorothy's ability to return home have been inside them all along ... naturally. Wizardry not required. I think the same is true for all of us when it comes to morality. We don't need a lot of smoke and mirrors, we don't need illusions. We have what we need, naturally.

So the guiding figure of this book is a Cairn Terrier?

Hey, Toto does what every philosopher and scientist tries to do: he uncovers the truth about how something in the world actually works. As a philosopher, my aim is to understand the kind of morality and freedom we really have, not the kind we want to have. And I've been drawn to work in other disciplines that can shed light on this question. This book has allowed me to go straight to the source, to talk with the researchers who are using technology and scientific techniques never before available to make thrilling advances in the science of human nature. The goal of every interview is to pull back part of the curtain that conceals the inner workings of our moral lives.

Isn't that a little dangerous?

It's true that some people feel threatened by the prospect of naturalizing morality. They think morality has been underwritten by God, or some equally mysterious understanding of Reason with a capital *R*. Science, they worry, may reveal ethics to be a sham. I think this fear is misguided, as misguided as the Tin Man's belief that his heart couldn't be made of tin. Learning what makes a car run doesn't stop it from running. Morality is out there—what could be more exciting than discovering the true origins and mechanisms that lie beneath it? We shouldn't be scared about what we'll find. All we need to do is ...

... follow the yellow brick road?

You said it, not me.

Preface to the Second Edition

More Questions for the Interviewer

So you're back for a sequel. Does it have a tagline like "This Time It's Personal"?

There's no tagline, but now that you mention it, I have become more interested in the personal side of philosophy. Some of the new material will reflect that.

What exactly is new for this edition?

Eight brand new interviews with leading researchers in philosophy and moral psychology: anthropologists Alan Fiske and Tage Rai, psychologist Paul Bloom, and philosophers Anthony Appiah, Simon Blackburn, Nancy Sherman, Peter Singer, Valerie Tiberius, and Susan Wolf. With all the interviews from the first edition also in the line-up, this is a murderer's row of talent for anyone interested in the nature of morality.

I have to agree. What else is new about this edition?

For each interview, I included questions for discussion and a list of suggested readings that would make a good pairing for people who want to learn more about that topic. There will also be online resources for instructors who want to use the book in their courses.

What about you? Have you or your views changed since the first edition?

Absolutely. It's been 12 years since I conducted the first of these interviews with Galen Strawson. I've changed my position on free will and moral responsibility multiple times since then. And that's just one example.

Did you go back and revise your chapter introductions accordingly?

No, I left all the chapter introductions from the first edition as they were. I think it's more interesting to see how a philosopher's views can evolve and shift over the years.

In other words, you're too lazy to go back and revise them?

No! Ok, maybe a little. But I have reorganized the order of the interviews into four parts and rewritten the introductions to the parts.

I hear you have a podcast called Very Bad Wizards. Is 'Very Bad Wizard' your brand now?

Don't ever use the word "brand" in my presence. But yes, I co-host a biweekly podcast with Cornell psychologist David Pizarro. We talk informally about many of the topics in this book. Readers may find it helpful as a supplement to the interviews in this text. We also have some of the people I interviewed on the podcast. Valerie Tiberius and Joe Henrich have joined us. And Paul Bloom is a frequent and popular guest. At the end of each chapter, I suggest some "podcast pairings" that would go well with the interview.

It says "explicit" on iTunes.

If you're offended by bad language or questionable humor, the podcast is definitely not for you. My daughter explains that in her disclaimer at the beginning of each episode.

You said earlier you've become more interested in the personal side of philosophy. Do you mean their private lives?

No, not their private lives. I was referring to one of the ways that my views have shifted over the years. I've grown suspicious of the more systematic, abstract, impersonal theorizing that goes on in philosophy and moral psychology. Many of the new interviews reflect this change of heart. But more abstract, theory-driven approach to philosophy and moral psychology is well represented as well.

Seriously—"More Questions for the Interviewer"? Couldn't think of a new gimmick for the prefaces?

Not just the prefaces, the introductions to the parts too. I'll see you over there.

Acknowledgments

Although I didn't know it at the time, this project was launched in late 2002 when Vendela Vida offered me the chance to interview a philosopher of my choice for the inaugural issue of the *Believer*. I was in graduate school at Duke University planning a dissertation on free will, and thought immediately of Galen Strawson, a celebrity in the field. Over the next five years, Vendela continued to allow me the freedom to select more researchers whose work I found fascinating and relevant to my own pursuits. I'm grateful to the people at the *Believer* and McSweeney's for making the first edition of this project possible.

I owe a big debt of gratitude to Andrew Beck and Routledge for giving me the opportunity to do a second edition with eight new interviews. Without Andy's patience and encouragement, I never would have completed this project. Grants from the Research Enhancement Fund at the University of Minnesota, Morris, and the Small Grants Program at the University of Houston provided funding for some of the travel for the interviews. I am grateful to my colleagues for their enthusiastic support of what some might (misguidedly) consider to be a nonacademic project.

Big thanks to Jared Smith for his excellent work transcribing the interviews in the second edition. I'm grateful to Jared and Boomer Trujillo for helping assemble study questions and supplemental readings. Thanks to Ami Palmer for compiling the glossary, and thanks also to Christopher Richards for his help with editing and transcribing my interview with Philip Zimbardo in the first edition. And although there is no consensus over whether *A Very Bad Wizard* is a good title, I'm grateful to Eddie Guzelian and Ethan Pines for helping me (over beers and oysters) come up with it at the last minute.

Thanks to David Pizarro for contributing the foreword and for co-hosting the Very Bad Wizards podcast with me over the past three and a half years. The podcast allows us to engage with a large audience and David to pursue his true love, composing beats. After 84 episodes, I still love listening to his opening song, sampled from *The Wizard of Oz*.

As usual, my wife Jennifer Sommers provided invaluable editing advice and had to put up with a lot of ranting and hot-tempered resistance in the process. I don't know how I could have completed the project without her assistance.

Thanks to my daughter Eliza for the wealth of stories she provides me and for changing my mind about free will and moral responsibility when she was 2½ years old. I dedicate this book to Jen and Eliza.

Finally, my deepest gratitude to Anthony Appiah, Simon Blackburn, Paul Bloom, Frans de Waal, Alan Fiske, Josh Greene, Jonathan Haidt, Joe Henrich, William Ian Miller, Tage Rai, Michael Ruse, Nancy Sherman, Peter Singer, Steve Stich, Galen Strawson, Valerie Tiberius, Susan Wolf, Liane Young, and Philip Zimbardo—the distinguished researchers featured in this book. All were exceedingly generous with their time, energy, and assistance. Putting together this book has been an education and a pleasure. I hope the reader enjoys it too.

A Note about the Interviews

The interview chapters are grouped by theme into four parts. Each part begins with a brief introduction, and each chapter begins with a more detailed introduction covering the interviewee and his or her work.

The interviews with Galen Strawson, Michael Ruse, Jonathan Haidt, and Frans de Waal previously appeared in the *Believer*. I have updated the affiliations of interviewees from the first edition. Otherwise, I have left all the introductions from the first edition intact.

Part I

Free to Be You and Me? Maybe Not

Introduction

Samuel Johnson once said that "all theory is against the freedom of the will; all experience is for it." Do you agree with that?

For the most part, yes. Philosophers and scientists have mounted strong theoretical arguments against free will for thousands of years.

And for thousands of years people have remained unconvinced

Right, because we *feel* free. We *feel* responsible.

That may be true, but it also feels like the earth is flat and that we're at the center of the solar system. In almost every other field we allow logic and science to trump experience—why not here?

Some people worry about the ethical implications of denying free will and moral responsibility. They think it would drain our lives of meaning and purpose, and maybe lead to a world where "everything is permitted" and no one is held accountable. So if free will is an illusion, maybe it's one we're better off embracing.

Is that what the authors you interviewed believe?

Not at all. In Chapter 1, the philosopher Galen Strawson argues that we cannot freely create our characters, and therefore that we are not ultimately responsible for our behavior. But he still thinks that we can deny free will and lead moral and fulfilling lives.

You used to defend a similar view.

That's true, Strawson was a huge inspiration for my early work. I still agree with him that we can't spin our characters and personality out of thin air. But now I side more with his father—the great philosopher P. F. Strawson—who argued that blame and responsibility can be grounded in our emotional responses. We talk a bit about his view in the interview.

You also interviewed Philip Zimbardo. Isn't there a movie about him?

Yes, it's called *The Stanford Prison Experiment* and it's a fictionalized retelling of his famous 1971 experiment. Billy Crudup plays Zimbardo.

The guy who played 'Dr. Manhattan' in Watchmen?

That's him! And in Chapter 2, the real Philip Zimbardo discusses that study and several others that show how situational factors—our social and physical environment—can exert tremendous influence over our behavior. We discuss a whole tradition in social psychology that reveals our characters to be less stable than we think. According to Zimbardo, having a better understanding of the causes of our behavior can lead to a more just and effective approach to education, foreign policy, and criminal justice.

1 Galen Strawson

You Cannot Make Yourself the Way You Are

> "You sound to me as though you don't believe in free will," said Billy Pilgrim.
> "If I hadn't spent so much time studying Earthlings," said the Tralfamadorian, "I wouldn't have any idea what was meant by 'free will.' I've visited thirty-one inhabited planets in the universe, and I have studied reports on one hundred more. Only on Earth is there any talk of free will."
> —Kurt Vonnegut, *Slaughterhouse-Five*

Imagine for a moment that it was not Timothy McVeigh who destroyed the Alfred P. Murrah Federal Building in Oklahoma City, but a mouse. Suppose this mouse got into the wiring of the electrical system, tangled the circuits, and caused a big fire, killing all those inside. Now think of the victims' families. There would, of course, still be enormous grief and suffering, but there would be one significant difference: there would be no resentment, no consuming anger, no hatred, no need to see the perpetrator punished (even if the mouse somehow got out of the building) in order to experience "closure." Why the difference? Because McVeigh, we think, committed this terrible act of his own free will. He chose to do it, and he could have chosen not to. McVeigh, then, is morally responsible for the death of the victims in a way that the mouse would not be. And our sense of justice demands that he pay for this crime.

Humans have an undeniable tendency to see themselves as free and morally responsible beings. But there's a problem. We also believe—most of us, anyhow—that our environment and our heredity entirely shape our characters. (What else could?) But we aren't responsible for our environment, and we aren't responsible for our heredity. So, by extension, we aren't responsible for our characters. But then how can we be responsible for acts that arise from our characters?

This question has a simple but extremely unpopular answer: we aren't. We are not and cannot be ultimately responsible for our behavior. According to this argument, while it may be of great pragmatic value to hold people responsible for their actions, and to employ systems of reward and punishment, no one is really deserving of blame or praise for anything. This answer has been around for more than two thousand years; it is backed by solid arguments with premises that are consistent with how most of us view the world. Yet few today give this position the serious consideration it deserves. The view that free will is a fiction is called counterintuitive, absurd, pessimistic, pernicious, and, most commonly, unacceptable, even by those who recognize the force of the arguments behind it. Philosophers who reject God, an immaterial soul, and even absolute morality, cannot bring themselves to do the same for the dubious concept of free will—not in their day-to-day lives, nor even in books, articles, and extraordinarily complex theories.

There are a few exceptions, however, and one of them is Galen Strawson, Professor of Philosophy at the University of Texas, Austin. Strawson is one of the most respected theorists in the free-will industry and, at the same time, a bit of an outsider. Two main philosophical camps engage in a technical and often bitter dispute over whether free will is compatible with the truth of determinism (the theory that the future is fixed, because every event has a cause, and the causes stretch back until the beginning of the universe). But if there is one thing that both sides agree on, it's that we do have free will and that we are morally responsible. Strawson, with a simple, powerful argument that we will discuss below, bets the other way.

Strawson's was not always such a minority view. Enlightenment philosophers like Spinoza, Diderot, Voltaire, and d'Holbach challenged ordinary conceptions of freedom, doubted whether we could be morally responsible, and looked to ground theories of blame and punishment in other ways. Strawson is a descendant of these philosophers, but still incorporates the British analytic tradition into his work. His views are clear and honest, and there are no cop-outs—quite unusual in a literature mired in obscure terminology and wishful thinking. And his essays are always deeply connected to everyday experience. One of the main issues Strawson addresses is why we so instinctively and stubbornly see ourselves as free and responsible. What is it about human experience that makes it difficult, maybe impossible, to believe something that we can easily demonstrate as true?

Galen Strawson is also the son of perhaps the most respected analytic philosopher of the past century, the great metaphysician and philosopher of language, P. F. Strawson.[1] Though not primarily concerned with the topic of free will, P. F. Strawson has written one of the classic papers of the genre, an essay called "Freedom and Resentment." Galen (not from oedipal motives, he assures us) is one of its most effective critics.

March 2003

1   The Buck Stops—Where?

TAMLER SOMMERS: You start out your book *Freedom and Belief* by saying that there is no such thing as free will. What exactly do you mean by "free will"?

GALEN STRAWSON: I mean what nearly everyone means. Almost all human beings believe that they are free to choose what to do in such a way that they can be truly, genuinely responsible for their actions in the strongest possible sense—responsible period, responsible without any qualification, responsible *sans phrase*, responsible *tout court*, absolutely, radically, buck-stoppingly responsible; *ultimately* responsible, in a word—and so ultimately *morally* responsible when moral matters are at issue. Free will is the thing you have to have if you're going to be responsible in this all-or-nothing way. That's what I mean by free will. That's what I think we haven't got and can't have.

I like philosophers—I love what they do; I love what I do—but they have made a truly unbelievable hash of all this. They've tried to make the phrase "free will" mean all sorts of different things, and each of them has told us that what it *really* means is what he or she has decided it *should* mean. But they haven't made the slightest impact on what it really means, or on our old, deep conviction that free will is something we have.

TS: That's true. Biologists, cognitive scientists, neurologists—they all seem to have an easier time, at least considering the possibility that there's no free will. But philosophers defend the concept against all odds, at the risk of terrible inconsistency with the rest of their views about the world. If it's a fact that there's no free will, why do philosophers have such a hard time accepting it?

GS: There's a Very Large Question here, as Winnie the Pooh would say. There's a question about the pathology of philosophy, or more generally about the weird psychological mechanisms that underwrite commitment to treasured beliefs—religious, theoretical, or whatever—in the face of overwhelming contrary evidence. But to be honest, I can't really accept it myself, and not because I'm a philosopher. As a philosopher I think the impossibility of free will and ultimate moral responsibility can be proved with complete certainty. It's just that I can't really live with this fact from day to day. Can you, really? As for the scientists, they may accept it in their white coats, but I'm sure they're just like the rest of us when they're out in the world—convinced of the reality of radical free will.

TS: Well, let's move on to the argument then. There's a famous saying of Schopenhauer's that goes like this: "A man can surely do what he wants to do. But he cannot determine what he wants." Is this idea at the core of your argument against moral responsibility?

GS: Yes—and it's an old thought. It's in Hobbes somewhere, and it's in Book Two of Locke's *Essay Concerning Human Understanding*, and I bet some ancient Greek said it, since they said almost everything.

Actually, though, there's a way in which it's not quite true. If you want to acquire some want or preference you haven't got, you can sometimes do so. You can cultivate it. Perhaps you're lazy and unfit and you want to acquire a love of exercise. Well, you can force yourself to do it every day and hope you come to like it. And you just might; you might even get addicted. Maybe you can do the same if you dislike olives.

TS: But then where did *that* desire come from—the desire to acquire the love of exercise ... or olives?

GS: Right—now the deeper point cuts in. For suppose you do want to acquire a want you haven't got. The question is, where did the first want—the want for a want—come from? It seems it was just there, just a given, not something you chose or engineered. It was just there, like most of your preferences in food, music, footwear, sex, interior lighting, and so on.

I suppose it's possible that you might have acquired the first want, that's the want for a want, because you wanted to! It's *theoretically* possible that you had a want to have a want to have a want. But this is very hard to imagine, and the question just rearises: Where did *that* want come from? You certainly can't go on like this forever. At some point your wants must be just given. They will be products of your genetic inheritance and upbringing, in which you had no say. In other words, there's a fundamental sense in which you did not and cannot make yourself the way you are. And this, as you say, is the key step in the basic argument against ultimate moral responsibility, which goes like this:

1   You do what you do—in the circumstances in which you find yourself—because of the way you are;
2   so if you're going to be ultimately responsible for what you do, you're going to have to be ultimately responsible for the way you are—at least in certain mental respects;
3   but you can't be ultimately responsible for the way you are (for the reasons just given);
4   so you can't be ultimately responsible for what you do.

TS: I suppose it's the third step that people have the most trouble accepting.
GS: Yes, although the step seems fairly clear when you look at it the right way. Sometimes people explain why (*3*) is true by saying that you can't be *causa sui*—you can't be the cause of yourself, you can't be truly or ultimately self-made in any way. As Nietzsche puts it, in his usual, tactful way:

> The *causa sui* is the best self-contradiction that has been conceived so far; it is a sort of rape and perversion of logic. But the extravagant pride of man has managed to entangle itself profoundly and frightfully with just this nonsense. The desire for "freedom of the will" in the superlative metaphysical sense, which still holds sway, unfortunately, in the minds of the half-educated; the desire to bear the entire and ultimate responsibility for one's actions oneself, and to absolve God, the world, ancestors, chance, and society involves nothing less than to be precisely this *causa sui* and, with more than Baron Münchhausen's audacity, to pull oneself up into existence by the hair, out of the swamps of nothingness.

There's lots more to say about this basic argument, and there are lots of ways in which people have tried to get around the conclusion. But none of them work.

2   Viewing Hitler Like the Lisbon Earthquake

TS: I notice that the argument makes no mention of the theory of determinism. But historically the debate over freedom and responsibility has revolved around the truth of determinism, and the question of whether free will and moral responsibility are compatible with it.

GS: Yes, many people think that determinism—the view that the history of the universe is fixed, the view that everything that happens is strictly necessitated by what has already gone before, in such a way that nothing can ever happen otherwise than it does—is the real threat to free will, to ultimate moral responsibility. But the basic argument against ultimate moral responsibility works whether determinism is true or false. It's a completely a priori argument, as philosophers like to say. That means that you can see that it is true just lying on your couch. You don't have to get up off your couch and go outside and examine the way things are in the physical world. You don't have to do any science. And actually, current science isn't going to help. Ultimate moral responsibility is also ruled out by the theory of relativity. Einstein himself, in a piece written as a homage to the Indian mystical poet Rabindranath Tagore, said that "a Being, endowed with higher insight and more perfect intelligence, watching man and his doings, [would] smile about man's illusion that he was acting according to his own free will."

TS: And the illusion that he and others were morally responsible for their actions?

GS: Yes, but I just want to stress the word "ultimate" before "moral responsibility." Because there's a clearly weaker, everyday sense of "morally responsible" in which you and I and millions of other people are thoroughly morally responsible people.

TS: I suppose your lazy unfit man who acquires a love for exercise is responsible for his choice in this weaker everyday sense. He made the choice, and he acted on it. On the other hand, it seems that in order for this man to be *deserving of praise* for his decision, he would have to be morally responsible in the deeper sense, in the ultimate sense. And in fact, isn't that an implication of your argument—that no one is truly deserving of blame or praise for anything?

GS: Well, *truly* is a flexible word—again I think *ultimately* is better—but yes: no one can be ultimately deserving of praise or blame for anything. It's not possible. This is very, very hard to swallow, but that's how it is. Ultimately, it all comes down to luck: luck—good or bad in being born the way we are, luck—good or bad—in what then happens to shape us. We can't be ultimately responsible for how we are in such a way as to have absolute, buck-stopping responsibility for what we do. At the same time, it seems we can't help believing that we do have absolute buck-stopping responsibility.

TS: You're right that many people find this hard to swallow. As you write in one of your essays, if it all comes down to luck, "even Hitler is let off the hook." So how should we regard Hitler and Stalin and other villains of history? Should we view them like we view the Lisbon earthquake, or the Plague?

GS: In the end, and in a sense: yes. Obviously it's wildly hard to accept. For some people I think it's impossible to accept, given their temperaments (they might not be able to make sense of their lives anymore). As I said, I can't really accept it myself—I can't live it all the time. If someone harmed or tortured or killed one of my children, I'd feel everything almost anyone else would feel. I'd probably have intense feelings of revenge. But these feelings would fade. In the end, they're small and self-concerned. Only the grief would last.

Maybe one way to put it is this: people in themselves aren't evil, there's no such thing as moral evil in that sense, but evil exists, great evil, and people can be carriers of great evil. You might reply, Look, if they're carriers of evil they just are evil, face the facts. But I would have to say that your response is, in the end, superficial. After all, we don't call natural disasters evil.

There's another thing to say about the Hitler case. Our sense that he must be held utterly responsible for what he did is both cognitive and emotional, and it usually seems to us that these two factors can't possibly come apart. The cognitive part, the sense that it is just an absolute objective fact that he is wholly responsible in the strongest possible way, seems inseparable from the non-cognitive part, the moral nausea, the disgust, the anger, I don't know what to call it. They seem inseparable in the way that blood is inseparable from a living body (that was Shylock's problem). And since the non-cognitive emotional part is plainly a completely appropriate reaction it can seem that the cognitive part must be, too.

Nevertheless, I think they can come apart. Many of our emotional responses can stay in place when we confront the fact that there is no ultimate moral responsibility. We don't stop retching involuntarily when we realize that there is nothing objectively disgusting about a smell of decay. No doubt some of our emotional responses are *essentially* connected to belief in ultimate moral responsibility. But I think even the most emotionally intense desires for revenge and retribution, say, can be felt in a way that does not presuppose ultimate moral responsibility.

TS: I don't know. Take the case of Timothy McVeigh—his execution was shown to the families of the victims on closed-circuit TV. Why? So that the families could experience "closure." Don't you think that kind of retributive impulse presupposes a belief in moral responsibility? If a malfunctioning computer, or a mouse, had caused the death of their loved ones, would they have had to watch the destruction of the mouse (or computer) in order to attain this closure?

GS: What you say sounds right, so what can I say in reply? It's not enough for me to say that a hated human is just not the same as a hated mouse or computer. Quite so, you'll say, and that's precisely because we take a human to have ultimate moral responsibility. I'm sorry about repeating "ultimate" every time, but I think it's important. Let's just call it deep moral responsibility from now on, DMR for short. (It sounds like some exotic psychotropic drug.)

So I guess you're right. These desires for revenge and retribution are just not going to be the normal human thing if they don't involve the belief that the hated person has DMR. They're going to be unusual. So why did I say what I said? Partly because I was thinking of a remarkable book called *Revenge*, by Laura Blumenfeld, in which she describes cultures in which the whole business of revenge and vendetta gets ritualized. I don't think the Mafia has to believe in DMR to feel intense desires for revenge and retribution. And desire for retaliation doesn't require anything of the sort.

Which reminds me of something interesting: the old rule, older than the Old Testament, that says "Life for life, eye for eye, tooth for tooth, hand for hand, foot for foot, burning for burning, wound for wound, stripe for stripe" is almost universally misunderstood. It's not an intrinsically vengeful idea. It was intended as a counsel of restraint, of moderation in retaliation. Take an eye for an eye, it says, but no more. Measure for measure. No escalation. At one point Blumenfeld goes to the Roman Catholic region in northern Albania and asks a member of the local "Blood Feud Committee" about turning the other cheek. The guy just laughs—they all do, in the room, they titter—and says "In Albania we have 'Don't hit my cheek or I'll kill you.'" One feels they really got the hang of Christianity.

TS: So in your view, then, the idea of retaliation can play an important pragmatic role, but actual *belief* in deep moral responsibility isn't necessary to function as a human being.

GS: Not only isn't it necessary, it may even be harmful. I like what the psychologist Eleanor Rosch said in a talk she gave in San Francisco last August called "What Buddhist Meditation Has to Tell Psychology about the Mind." At one point she was discussing the Buddhist doctrine of the endlessly ramifying interdependence of everything, and observed that "an understanding of [this] interdependence has clinical significance. It can provide people who suffer from guilt, depression, or anxiety with a vision of themselves as part of an interdependent network in which they need neither blame themselves nor feel powerless. In fact it may be that it is only when people are able to see the way in which they are not responsible for events that they can find the deeper level at which it is possible to take responsibility beyond concept and (depending upon the terminology of one's religious affiliation) repent, forgive, relax, or have power over the phenomenal world."

Trouble is, this is very, very hard to do. And it needs some explaining. Seeing the way in which you are not responsible for events in the manner that Eleanor Rosch describes certainly doesn't mean that you become an irresponsible person. Also, while some of us are fiercely self-critical, and would do well to ease up on—ourselves—for self-criticism is another form of self-indulgence—we don't particularly want Hitler & Co. to "relax." It takes reflection to see the truth in what Eleanor Rosch is saying.

TS: Buddhist meditation and Buddhist philosophy in general appears in much of your work. Do you practice some form of meditation yourself?

GS: I tried meditation when I was an undergraduate (and putative flower child, with hair to my waist) at Cambridge in the UK in the late 1960s and early 1970s, but I've never managed to keep it up … I tried again last year, after a 25-year gap, using Patricia Carrington's utterly dogma-free method of "clinically standardized meditation." It was pretty interesting, but I lapsed again.

TS: Did you feel, when you were doing it, that meditating made the denial of free will and DMR easier to accept—I mean on more than just a theoretical level?

GS: Well, the denial of DMR didn't come to mind when I was actually meditating, or trying to, though I think it would have seemed pretty natural if it had. But perhaps you're asking whether meditation made a discernible difference to my attitude to DMR in the rest of my daily life. The answer is that I don't think so, though it might well have done so if I'd been better about it, or gone on for longer.

So can I live the denial of free will and DMR rather than just accept it theoretically? Well, if I think I've done something bad, I feel wholly responsible—I feel remorse, regret, and so on. So, no. But perhaps the remorse doesn't endure for too long. I think that if such feelings persist too long, they become self-indulgent in some deep way. I think, in fact, that all guilt is self-indulgent—it's all about self—while things like remorse and contrition are not, although they can become so if they get ritualized.

But to get back to your question: I'm pretty sure it's not meditation that has got me any closer to living the fact that there's no deep moral responsibility. Insofar as I have got closer, it is just living a life, and the long and devoted practice of philosophy. I think philosophy really does change one over time. It makes one's mind large, in some peculiar manner. It seems to me that the professional practice of philosophy is itself a kind of spiritual discipline, in some totally secular sense of "spiritual"; or at least that it can be, and has been for me. It would be very surprising if intense training of the mind didn't change the shape of the mind as much as intense training of the body changes the shape of the body. It does.

Here's an odd confessional passage from a paper I wrote 15 years ago that I'd forgotten about until someone mentioned it recently.

> My attitudes on such questions are dramatically inconsistent. For (*a*) I regard any gifts that I have, and any good that I do, as a matter of pure good fortune; so that the idea that I deserve credit for them in some

strong sense seems absurd. But (*b*) I do not regard others' achievements and good actions as pure good fortune, but feel admiration (and, where appropriate, gratitude) of a true-responsibility-presupposing kind. Furthermore, (*c*) I do not regard bad things that I do as mere bad luck, but have true-responsibility-presupposing attitudes to them (which may admittedly fade with time). Finally, (*d*), I do (in everyday life) naturally regard bad things other people do as explicable in ways that make true-responsibility-presupposing blame inappropriate. I suspect that this pattern may not be particularly uncommon.

TS: Interesting you say that; I would think it *is* pretty uncommon. The idea that we don't deserve credit for our achievements and good deeds? It seems to go against some core American ideals, anyway.

GS: Well, perhaps it's uncommon, but I don't think it's that rare. I agree that it may be pretty un-American, but I don't think it can be that unusual worldwide—or am I the weird one here? One can certainly get a lot of pleasure or happiness from having done something, but taking credit for something does seem absurd, like taking credit or responsibility for one's height or one's looks (putting cosmetic surgery aside). People sometimes say that one can take credit for effort even if one can't take credit for natural talent, but in the end being the kind of person who's got determination and who perseveres and makes an effort—that too is a gift, a piece of luck. It just so happens that we particularly admire it, in the same way that we find some people or landscapes particularly attractive.

TS: And how about (*d*)—the idea that blame is inappropriate for the bad actions of other people?

GS: As for that, I realize that when I wrote it I was thinking of everyday life, not of monstrous acts. (*d*) involves taking what my father called the "objective attitude" to others, and that's certainly how it is for me when it comes to others' wrongdoing in everyday life—at least after the heat of the moment.

3   "It's Very Hard to Imagine the Word 'Schmuck' Issuing from My Father's Mouth"

TS: Let's talk about the objective attitude for a moment. In 1962 your father, P. F. Strawson, wrote a famous paper that continues to haunt anyone working on free will today. In the paper he claims that when you adopt the objective attitude toward another human being, you lose some essential features of interpersonal relationships. You'll start to see this person as an object of social policy, a subject for "treatment"—some Orwellian scenarios come to mind—but you can no longer see them fully as a person. But if we're going to accept the belief that there is no free will, no DMR, it seems we'll have to take the objective attitude toward *all* people, including those closest to us. Are the implications of this as cold and bleak as your father suggests?

1   "We Got off on Being Puppeteers"

TAMLER SOMMERS: What was the original purpose for doing the Stanford Prison Experiment? What did you want to demonstrate or discover?

PHILIP ZIMBARDO: It was 1971 and a time of enormous social change in our country, especially in California, where a lot of social movements started. The hippies, the love-ins, the be-ins, the beat poets—all of it was here. There was a strong antiwar movement; I was heavily involved in that. I was involved when I was at NYU, and then again when I got to Stanford. And one of the big issues was questioning authority, rebelling against it. Don't trust authority, don't trust anyone over 30—you know, the big signs: FUCK AUTHORITY, OINK OINK: AGAINST THE PIGS. And the question is: how much of that is rhetoric? Do we have a new generation of independent free thinkers?

A little less than a decade earlier, at Yale, Stanley Milgram demonstrated the enormous power that situations can have on seducing ordinary people into a role where, although they thought they were teachers, they really ended up almost *executioners* of a stranger. Milgram's study, though it was really important, was about authority's pressure on an individual. My reasoning is that this rarely happens in the world. Authorities dictate, give general orders, or an ideology, and it filters down through systems in various ways, and then low-level people carry it out. But most of our lives are in institutions, in families, in schools, in hospitals, in armies, in teams … and institutions have a different kind of power. It's an institutional power, systemic power.

TS: Higher-level influences?

PZ: Yeah, it's not people telling you to do this bad thing. It's creating a general ideology, a general orientation, a way of thinking about things. And there're sets of rules and laws and a focus that moves people in a certain direction, and you have group conformity, and you have group-think. That's the reason I did the Stanford prison study. In a sense, it was like Milgram's study, in that it was an attempt to demonstrate how powerful social situations can be when pitted against the individual will to resist, the individual's sense of willpower and freedom. In that sense, they're really bookends of what's come to be known as "the power of the situation." His is one-on-one; mine is institutional power.

TS: And this experiment could broaden our understanding of the power of situational elements.

PZ: It's really to broaden his message and put it to a higher-level test. In Milgram's study, we don't know about those thousand people who answered the ad. His subjects weren't Yale students, though he did it at Yale. They were a thousand ordinary citizens from New Haven and Bridgeport, Connecticut, ages 20 to 50. In his advertisement in the newspaper he said: college students and high-school students cannot be used. It could have been a selection of people who were more psychopathic.

For our study, we only picked two dozen of 75 who applied, those who scored normal or average on seven different personality tests. So we knew there were no psychopaths, no deviants. Nobody had been in therapy, and even though it was a drug era, nobody (at least in the reports) had taken anything beyond marijuana, and they were physically healthy at the time. So the question was: suppose you only had kids who were normally healthy, psychologically and physically, and they knew they would be going into a prisonlike environment and that some of their civil rights would be sacrificed. Would those good people put in that bad, evil place— would their goodness triumph? It should have!

TS: You mean, given our conception of human behavior?

PZ: Right. They should have had some inner sense of character and integrity, not to get seduced into mindless obedience and mindless conformity. To be able to say, "Hey, that's the role, it's not me. I'm this other person, I'm this college student, I'm this antiwar activist, I'm this civil-rights activist."

TS: But as it turned out …

PZ: Even when we preselect for intelligent, normal, healthy, young men, that doesn't minimize the power of the situation.

TS: I read that the focus of the study was going to be mostly about the prisoners, more than the guards. Since then, interest in the study has in large part shifted to the guards.

PZ: When we got the idea to do the study, yes. More about the prisoners. To prepare for the research, I taught a course in the psychology of imprisonment with an ex-convict, a guy named Carlo Prescott, who later became the consultant for this study. He had just been released from prison after 17 years. In our course we brought in ex-convicts and guards and prison chaplains. And so my sympathies were heavily with prisoners. I was antiprisons, anticorrections, etc. We really wanted to understand the socialization of becoming a prisoner; what's happening. Essentially, we were, at some personal, Hollywood level, pulling for the prisoners to be able to resist.

TS: Hoping that they'd all be Cool Hand Luke, to one degree or another.

PZ: They'd be Cool Hand Luke, or they'd pretend to go along with it. When we bugged the cells we could say, "Oh, we're faking this thing." After the first day, we were ready to call it quits, because nothing was happening. Everybody felt awkward. But then what became apparent was the ingenuity of the guards. It was the guards that were going to make this thing work or not work. The key was the morning of the second day, when the prisoners rebelled. They were saying "Fuck you," they were cursing at the guards, they were ripping off their numbers, you know, "We're people!" It was like all those protest marches. "I'm a man," that kind of thing. I was really happy. The guards came to me and said, "What are we gonna do?" I said, "It's your prison; make the decision." They said, "Well, we need support." So they called in the other shifts. But now the guards on the morning shift started dumping on the other shift—"How did you let this happen?" So suddenly egos are involved, and the whole shift is embarrassed. So now that they have 12 guards, they break down the doors, they strip the prisoners naked. There was some physical struggle, and they got the ringleaders of the rebellion and put them in solitary.

TS: And that was when all the degradation started?

PZ: Normally, there were only three guards and nine prisoners. But each shift realized that [the rebellion] could happen again on their shift. The first thing they said was, "I realize now these are dangerous prisoners." So they were going to have to use tactics. They organized a good cell and a bad cell. The prisoners in the good cell were going to get privileges. Then they said, "Everything is a privilege," short of breathing air. Food is a privilege.

TS: Was there a sort of taste of having this power over someone else, this authority?

PZ: I think that came secondarily. I think it was the fear first, that this could happen at any time. It took us by surprise, and it was embarrassing for that shift. Then all the other guards thought, "It could happen on my shift, then I would be responsible." But saying that they were dangerous prisoners meant that they were no longer experimental subjects. I think the sense of power came after they began to ratchet up the control. To say, "Okay, now, we're going to have these counts go on for hours on end. We're going to arbitrarily show that we're in control. I tell a joke, you laugh, I punish you. I tell a joke, you don't laugh, I punish you." I think the sense of power came after the display of domination and control, in that guards began to feel that, "Yeah, I can do this, I can get away with it." And then once the prisoners gave in even slightly, then they just kept amping it up.

TS: This is jumping ahead, but didn't you quote Charles Graner [the Abu Ghraib ringleader] as saying something like: "Part of me thought this was terrible, that what I'm doing is humiliating another person, but part of me just likes to see a prisoner piss his pants"?

PZ: In fact, Graner said that the Christian in him knew it was wrong, while the other part ... wanted to see a guy pissing his pants. There's a movie called the *Human Behavior Experiments*, by Alex Gibney. He's the one who won the Oscar for *Taxi to the Dark Side*. And he looked at the Milgram study and the Stanford prison study, and he interviewed some of the participants from the Stanford study. He interviewed the guard they called John Wayne, who's now a mortgage broker in the suburbs someplace. So Gibney asks John Wayne about Abu Ghraib. John Wayne says, Given the time, we could have gotten there. You know, we were almost there. And then he says something like, "We got off on having them be our puppets," or "We got off on being puppeteers." It really was that sense of total control. It's like *Pinocchio*. It's frightening, but it's also insightful to say, "Look how far we came in five days."

2   Taking on the Roles We're Assigned

TS: Another really interesting part of your book is your fairly detailed description of the situation's impact on *you*. Philip Zimbardo as the prison superintendent. My favorite example in the book is after one of the prisoners broke down and you had to release him, and you thought he was going to lead a prison break-in. So you started to get obsessed with this prison break-in and you're trying to reach the chief of police. The officer thinks you're a nutcase.

PZ: Right, the "psycho psychologist."

TS: A visiting colleague later asked you a normal question for a psychologist: What's the independent variable here? Let me read this; this is great. You get angry. "Here I had an incipient riot on my hands. The security of my men and the stability of my prison were at stake, and I had to contend with this bleeding heart, liberal, academic, effete professor whose only concern was a ridiculous thing like an independent variable. You effete liberal academic, I have a break-in on my hands, what are you talking about, 'independent variable'?"

PZ: And that was only the third day! Of course, it was all a rumor, there was no break-in. But see, I had been doing research on rumor transmission. And now there was a rumor of a break-in. I was the psychologist! I should have said, "Great, we're gonna study this." And if there *was* a break-in, that would have been a very dramatic thing: what would happen, and how would you deal with it? But at that point I had become the prison superintendent, and the only interest you have is your institution. The administrator cares about the institution, the integrity of the institution, and its staff. That's where, you know, I really switched over to being focused more on the institution, the agenda, the itinerary, and the guards.

TS: So you brought the prisoners up to the classroom ...

PZ: The fifth-floor storage room, actually. It was terrible. It was this dark room. There were bags over their heads for hours and hours. I was sitting there, too, so it was wasting time. Nothing happened. We didn't collect data on the rumor transmission, we just wasted all this time. But did we all realize how stupid we were? No, we blame it on the prisoners. We thought that somebody must have spread that rumor to get us upset. So then the guards said, "Okay, we're going to ratchet up the abuse of the prisoners. We're going to keep them up longer, counts are going to be two hours at a time, pushups will be doubled, and so forth. Put them in solitary confinement for longer periods for any infraction." That was transformative for me, but I still didn't realize it. It's not like I stepped back and said, "Oh, my god, look at you."

TS: At any point did you have a kind of awareness that you were getting sucked into it, or did that only come afterward?

PZ: No. Well—it came out partially when prisoner 819 ... he was beginning to have an emotional breakdown. When the chaplain was interviewing him among the others, he started crying, you know, hysterically, and at that point I thought the chaplain was going to say, "Blow the whistle, look, this is out of control." In fact, he told me later, he said, "Oh, that's a first-offender reaction, that is, they're all very emotional initially and they have to learn not to do that because they're going to look like sissies, they're going to get abused." But then 819 went ballistic, he started ripping up his pillow, his mattress and shit, and they put him in solitary confinement. And his cellmates got punished for not limiting that. He's now hysterical and one of the guards comes and says, "We think he's breaking down." So I brought him up to a recreation room for the cameramen and observers. When prisoners were going to be released we brought them there to settle down before we took them to student health. So I bring this guy there, 819, and I'm saying, "Okay, 819, look, time is up, we're going to pay you for the whole time," and so forth, and just then the guards line up the prisoners and get them to chant: "819 is a bad prisoner. Because of what 819 did my cell is a mess. I'm being punished for 819."

Now this guy starts crying again and says, "I've got to go back! I've got to go back and prove I'm not a bad prisoner." And so that was a shock. And so I said, "Wait a minute, you're not a prisoner, you're not 819, this is an experiment, you're a student, your name is Stewart." And at that point I said, "And I'm Phil Zimbardo." He said, "Okay, okay." And I escorted the student out. But saying: "I'm not the superintendent. I'm this other person ..."

TS: It was almost as much of a discovery for you as it was for him?

PZ: Yeah, so it was ... But then you get sucked back in.

TS: Even the peripheral people, right? The parents, the chaplain ...

PZ: Yes. The chaplain was there because he came to see me, he wanted some references for a paper he was doing on violence or something, and then he told me he had been a prison chaplain. And I said, "Hey, I'm going to do this experiment, could you come down and give me a validity check?" So he was in my office and he came down and he's treating me like I'm the superintendent. And so he was really at fault—he definitely should have blown the whistle at that point.

TS: At fault in one sense, right? Like everyone else, wasn't he also just sucked into his role?

PZ: Yeah, he was sucked into the role. The kid was breaking down; this was after three days. And the chaplain says, "Oh, it's very realistic, what you're doing. Good simulation." The amazing thing with him was that during meetings with the prisoners, he asked them: "What're you doing when you get out?" And they said, "What do you mean, sir?" "Well, you're in a prison." So he actually reinforced it, because he was an outsider. And he told them they would need a lawyer if they wanted to get out. And one kid said, "Well, you know, I'm gonna go to law school. I can defend myself." And the chaplain says, "Lawyers who defend themselves have a fool for a client." And then he says, "Would you like me to get you help?" And the kid says, "Yeah." The kid gives him his mother's name, and he calls. So there was this bizarre thing. He calls the mother and says, "Your son needs a lawyer." Now that he's trapped in his priest role, he made a promise to the kid. Rather than calling to say, "Hey, your son is in this experiment, he's having a hard time dealing with it, maybe you should take him out." In one sense, the ethics of the priest should have been, you know, he told the kid he would help, but he was so narrowly focused on what he said—"I will get you a lawyer"—that he told the mother to get him a lawyer. The mother calls a cousin, and this public defender actually comes in.

TS: The parents went along with all of this as well, right?

PZ: Yes. One of the rules was that on visiting days, visiting nights, parents had to see the warden first, and then the superintendent on their way out. The reason we did this is because we wanted to bring their behavior in the situation under control. So essentially, these were good middle-class parents, and they were following the rules. They signed in, they sat down, they saw the warden, they went in, they saw the superintendent. And they just fell into it.

The other story, which was very moving, was this couple who came out after seeing their son. He was in really bad shape. The mother began right off: "I don't mean to make trouble, sir"—that's the other thing, the "sir." You see, usually they'd say "doctor" or "professor," but "sir"—"but I've never seen my son looking so bad." As soon as I heard, "I don't mean to make trouble," a red light went on in my head: She's going to make trouble. So she's trouble—not to the experiment, to the prison. And so I said, "What seems to be your son's problem?"

TS: Your *son's* problem.

PZ: Yes, right, so here the whole experiment was about the power of the situation over the dispositional personal attributions. She's saying, "There's something bad about this situation." As an administrator, I'm saying: "What's wrong with your kid?" She says, "Well, he doesn't sleep." I said, "Does he have insomnia?" So I'm putting the problem onto *him*, not the situation. And she says, "No, no, they wake them up every few hours." And I said, "Oh, that, that's called the counts." I run through this whole thing, and I tell her why it's essential, and the husband's just sitting there, real quiet and really upset because his wife is challenging authority. She says again, "I don't mean to make trouble." And so I think she's going to blow the whistle. I automatically did something that is so horrific, and against all my values: I just turn to the father and say, "Don't you think your boy can handle a little stress?"

TS: Ah, so that he'll …

PZ: What's he going to say—"My boy's a sissy"? He's gotta say, "Of course. He's a tough guy, he's a leader." I stood up immediately. He stood up. We shook hands. I said, "I'll see you next visiting hour. Good work, sir."

TS: So you played on the father's fear that it would be his son's weakness, rather than the situation, if he had to quit.

PZ: Essentially what I did was say, "Here's this woman who's soft. And we men have to stick together." And yes: What does it say about your son, and therefore what does it say about his father? I mean, you want to say that your son is a sissy? He can't handle it? But it was automatic, it wasn't a strategic thing. I mean, this was instantaneous. We have all that knowledge stored. So we did the handshake thing. The son broke down that night and the next day I got a letter—I think I have it in the book—I got a letter the next day from the mother saying, "Thank you very much, it's really very interesting, I'm still concerned about my son." Meanwhile, he had broken down. So she was right on.

TS: Another fascinating description from the book is Carlo. Carlo was himself a prisoner on parole, right? He was a consultant for the study, and then you had him leading the parole board. You'd think that if anyone would be sensitive to the sort of suffering that goes with being in front of a parole board, it would be Carlo. And yet he jumped into the role with both feet.

PZ: It's interesting. Nobody's really mentioned Carlo. Nobody cared for that. And it's a really powerful thing. Here's a guy who'd had his parole denied for 17 years. That means every year you come up, once a year, you have three to five minutes to plead your case, you do your thing, and you get turned down. And you don't know why. They don't tell you why. Just— you got turned down. So he'd recently been paroled, and his sympathy should have been with the prisoners, no question about it. But now he's the head of the parole board. And it was brilliant. I think we have a little bit of it on video. He had a blank pad, and he picks it up and says "I see here from your rap sheet that you're a troublemaker." He was reading from it, he was very creative and very eloquent. All the dialogue from the book is actually from the audio tape. Again, here was a guy who hated prisons, who went into a rage about what prisons did to him. In prison, he saw people break down. And we put him in that role, and he says, "You're a troublemaker. It says here that you said this and this about this guard and that. You're a threat to the community. I don't see how we can release you. What do you expect to do when you get out?" The kid says, "I want to be a teacher." He says, "I wouldn't want you teaching my children." Carlo didn't have kids. And so, in one way it was this brilliant improvisation but it was horrendous because he was as evil as a parole officer. And for each one, he said, "Forget it. There's no way. Get out. If it was up to me, I'd leave you here forever." One kid came back in; he went out and came back in and begged him, said, "You know, I'm sorry, I was too flippant," and so forth.

TS: What did Carlo say to that? Something really cutting, I remember that.

PZ: It was an Asian kid. Carlo said something like, "We don't usually get people of your race here." And that day this kid got a full psychosomatic rash, you know, over his whole body. We had to release him.

TS: This is also amazing—the parole board lasted two days, and Carlo felt terrible about it the first night. So then, you'd think, Okay, finally, he realizes ... But then he was back full force the next day.

PZ: Again, you're physically out of the situation. You're saying, "Oh my god, was that me?" But the next day I think was the more hard-core part. He just went right back into it. He told me afterward, when the whole thing was over, "When I think back it makes me sick." But it's exactly like [Abu Ghraib guard] Chip Frederick. I don't know why he did it. You can't verbalize it, you can't say, "Oh, I was being given that status of power, I was showing off to the other people there." Really what Carlo had encrypted was all of the power, the authority. The same way he hated it when he got turned down. And now you give him the power and what does he do?

3   Learned Helplessness

TS: So, let's turn to the prisoners for a moment. We talked about how the guards got off on having control of the prisoners. From the interviews of the prisoners afterward, it seems like the worst part of the experience for them was the *loss* of control, being at the arbitrary whim of these guards— the arbitrariness of what would happen to them. They'd be in the good prison cell if they did bad things, the bad prison cell if they did good things. Can you elaborate on why that's such a horrible thing?

PZ: You know, I just realized this for the first time. The last book I did was called *The Time Paradox.* And it's really about how people divide the flow of their experience into time zones: past, present, and future. And I just thought, for the very first time, I don't know why, that is what happened to the prisoners. They got into this "present fatalism" mode.

TS: Present fatalism?

PZ: Nothing I do makes a difference. My life is controlled, fated. My life is controlled by the guards. And it's totally arbitrary. So there's a sense of learned helplessness. That's the underlying concept. The original study was by Marty Seligman of the University of Pennsylvania. You put dogs in a situation where they get shocked until they press up a bar on the door, the door opens, then they escape. But then you change the situation. Now when they press the bar, nothing happens. And sometimes when they stop pressing, the door opens. So now nothing they do makes any difference. They can escape without pressing the bar, they press the bar, nothing. And what happens is: they give up. They just stop. They lay down and they take the shock. It's a learned helplessness. It's not built into the system, not genetic. We're genetically designed to survive. But once you learn that your behavior does not control important consequences, you stop behaving. And that's essentially what happened there. The guards—and they never all got together, they all did it in various ways, different shifts. They created an arbitrary environment where there was no predictability; you couldn't predict what was the right or the wrong answer. It's that sense of fatalism: I don't control outcomes. And one of the most central aspects of human nature is the perception that I have reasonable control over my life, that if

I do *a*, then *b* is gonna follow in a reasonable amount of time. And the more I do *a*, and *b* doesn't happen, then I try *c*. So I keep changing my behavior to get the desired outcomes. If nothing I do ever gets a desired outcome, I stop doing anything and I stop desiring the outcome. I stop desiring freedom, or whatever. It's a horrendous condition.

TS: One of the striking things—I guess this is analogous to the dogs finally not even taking steps to get out—was the prisoners accepting the judgment during the "parole hearings." You even asked them: "Look, if, *if* I offered you the opportunity to leave, but you had to forfeit your money, would you do that?" A lot of them said yes! They forgot that they could do this *at any time* and probably still get the money, any time they wanted. And yet, when the judgment didn't go their way …

PZ: They stood up, they put their hands out, put their handcuffs on. And here now, again, the parole board, we purposely did it … it was on a different floor, it was in a big laboratory classroom, there were people not connected with the experiment on the parole board, so it wasn't like the prisoners were locked in that chamber, but they carried the situation around in their heads. And so, once we said "We'll consider your parole," when Carlo said, "Take 'em away," it was just this automatic thing. They put the bags over their heads. When they *should* have said, "Hey, the only reason I'm in this study, and the only reason people said to be in it, was for the money." It wasn't that they were interested in prison life; they weren't psychology students. And the guards took them away. Also, at that point, the guards were at their worst.

TS: You focus a lot of criticism in the book on your role in the experiment. Here's a sort of emblematic quote: "Only a few people were able to resist the situational temptations to yield to power and dominance while maintaining some semblance of morality and decency; obviously I was not among that noble class." Why are you so hard on yourself?

PZ: Well, yeah, because I deserve it! I was the adult, they were kids. I had done lots of research. I should not have allowed myself to get so trapped in that role. The whole study is about the power of the situation; I mean, that abstract concept should have been there to say, "Hey, look, here's that thing you're studying, and here you are caught up in it." And I kept coming close to it, with 819, with the prison break, but I kept being drawn back in. When one of the prisoners broke down, I should have said, "Look, that's enough." The mother was right. And I humiliated her.

One day Christina Maslach came down and saw the guards line up the prisoners for the toilet run at ten o'clock. The guards chained the prisoners' legs together, the prisoners have their bags over their head, their arms on each other. The guards are cursing and yelling at them, the prisoners are shuffling along. I look up and I have the day's agenda—and I check off *ten o'clock toilet run*. That's all it is. She looks at it and says, "This is horrendous! This is dehumanization. This is a violation of everything that humanity stands for. And you're allowing this to happen, essentially." So that was a really critical thing. I wasn't being cruel, I was just being totally indifferent to suffering. And indifferent to suffering because what was happening is what usually happened at ten o'clock. If it didn't happen, *then* I would have been concerned: "Where's the ten o'clock toilet run?" The toilet run didn't have to be with chains, it didn't have to be with bags, it didn't have to be with all this other stuff. But that got to be the routine. So we're following a routine, it's nothing more than a checking off, for me. For her, it was nothing less than a violation of humanity.[2]

4   Putting the Situation on Trial

TS: This experiment and a lot of others in social psychology expose something that's called the "fundamental attribution error." Can you explain what that is, exactly?

PZ: In all individualistic societies, our analyses tend to be focused on individual personality. Character is what's important, free will is what's important. Characters in novels, characters in movies. We have heroes and villains. We identify the person as the instigator of the action, whether good or bad. And this is true through all of our institutions, so individuals get credit for success, individuals get blame for failure. Law deals only with individuals. Medicine, aside from public health, deals only with individuals. Religion, sins of individuals. So all of our institutions deal with individuals. Even economics is the "rational man theory," which proves to be totally irrational.[3]

So because of that, we're conditioned from early childhood, in those societies, that when we're trying to understand the cause of any given behavior, we attribute the cause to something inside the person. Motives, values, beliefs, genetics. And when we want to change undesirable behavior, we focus on changing the individual. And so if the behavior is undesirable, we reeducate, we imprison, we medicate, we segregate, we sterilize, we execute individuals. And at the same time—the fundamental attribution error has two parts—we underestimate the power of the social context, the social situation. So we overestimate how important the person is, we underestimate how important the situation is. That's the fundamental attribution error.

TS: You say that this is a problem particularly in an individualistic country like the US. Would you say that more collectivist cultures—in Southeast Asia, for example—have a more accurate understanding of human behavior precisely because they take social context more into account?

PZ: Yeah, I think a collectivist orientation simply says, you have to be aware that individuals are always impacted by others, by the family, by social mores, by social rules of being. So when understanding any behavior, collectivists are not primed to say, "Let's look at the individual." There are lots of very simple studies that, you know, show animation of fish swimming, and there's a school of fish, and then there's one fish that's separated, either swimming ahead or behind. When Americans look at that, they focus on the isolated fish, and say he's falling behind. Asians focus on the school of fish, and say they slowed down to let him catch up.

TS: Let's talk about this issue of responsibility. And here I'm almost certain that I'm going to come at this from maybe another side than you normally get. It seemed in other interviews that people were worried about your work being a *threat* to moral responsibility and free will. And often, it seems, you assured them that it isn't. You say a few times in the book, "I'm not saying they're not responsible, this isn't 'excusology'—they're still responsible for their immoral behavior." In one interview I think you even used the phrase "ultimately responsible." My take here is the opposite. It seems like your work *does* undermine moral responsibility.[4] I mean, look at the Stanford Prison Experiment. It was a coin toss that led the guards to be where they were. How can we hold people responsible for bad luck, for a bad coin toss?

PZ: It's really a very complicated and central issue that needs to be dealt with more. I think philosophers have to deal with it more—it's really a philosophical and legal issue. In the extreme case, it really is a matter of "the situation made me do it." So are we going to put the situation on trial? Well, we don't have a mechanism. I gave a talk at Harvard Law School and [Harvard psychologist] Jon Hanson said that these ideas should provoke a revolution in legal theory because we have no way of putting the situation on trial. In a sense, international tribunals put the system on trial. They have individuals, but that's the real importance of international tribunals for crimes against humanity. They say that even though within your system it was acceptable for you to do this—to kill Jews, or to kill Tutsis—there's a higher international standard of humanity, of justice, that applies, and so it's that ultimate system which dominates your parochial system, your Nazi system, your Communist system, etc.

TS: As you say, though, it's the individuals who are being tried.

PZ: Yes, even there, you know, what comes out of that is the guilt or innocence of each of the leaders. So tribunals say "We have the power to put leaders on trial, even though none of them actually killed anybody—it's just that they created a policy, they created a system." But I would hope they would go to the next level and make it explicit: "In punishing this person, we are publicly declaring that this ideology produced the crimes against humanity. And so we, as an international body of humanists, of jurists, decry the horrors of this kind of system." So you're really sending out a message: it's the system that's wrong, and these people helped create it. Hitler helped create it, and Pol Pot … But once it's created, once the Stanford Prison Experiment was created, I'm irrelevant. If I had died during the thing, it would have gone on. The guards would have been happier. If Hitler had been killed, the whole thing would have gone on only because it had already corrupted the legal system, the educational system, the business system. With all these mechanisms in place, he became irrelevant. In fact, he would have been a big martyr.

TS: That's interesting—you know, there's a philosophical view of punishment that's called the "expressivist theory of punishment"—they say that the goal of punishment is not to give people what they deserve, which is hard to make sense of, and not just to deter future crime, but to publicly express your condemnation of an act. Punishment is the only way to express moral condemnation of an act or a system. If you don't punish the culprits, you're sending an implicit message that the act is morally acceptable. And I suppose you could apply that to responsibility, that that's the new way to look at responsibility, as expressing our condemnation.[5]

PZ: Yeah, most punishment does not deter, except for a very short time. There are so many multiple factors that go into producing any kind of crime that a deterrent effect can't have that much influence. In fact, most people don't even know that someone got arrested in New Hampshire, or Arizona, or Alaska for something and is on death row. So how can it be a deterrent for me here in San Francisco? But the notion that we as a society want to express our revulsion about this kind of act makes sense—that it's an expression of a public consensus that this is wrong and that we will not tolerate it. And that's what I'm saying. International tribunals should make explicit that what we're expressing is this revulsion about a system that could create these crimes against humanity. And the way we're doing it is by singling out people who were instrumental in carrying out the policies of that system.

5   "Free Will Is an Illusion"

TS: Let's talk about the free-will question for a moment. In the interviews I've heard, you seem to try to dodge questions about free will.

PZ: Yes.

TS: On the other hand, you say repeatedly that we have this infinite capacity for good and evil, but that who we are is shaped by our situation and circumstances. This relates also to the question of the different levels of situation and system. So where would our free will be in all of this? I know that some people will say that free will is located more in deciding what kind of situations we create for ourselves and others. But aren't those decisions then also determined by other situations, other circumstances?

PZ: There could be an infinite regress. I can see what you're getting at. I mean, free will is something that people really want to believe in. It's the inner individual's control over his or her fate. Certainly individualist societies really want to believe in it. We want to believe—that's the most fundamental motivation. I did it because I chose to do it. In fact, one reason the book doesn't sell[6] is that nobody wants to hear this argument. It's just alien to what it means to be a citizen, to be a person. We say we act out of free will. In fact, in Chip Frederick's trial, I'm sure the prosecutor at some point asked: Do you mean they didn't *choose* to perform these acts? The prosecutor couldn't even understand what the situationist argument meant.

It violates everything ... how could a soldier not have free will? So I think that's the problem. We place such a high value on the belief that individuals act out of free will, act out of personal choice, that their behavior is not determined by anything outside of them ...

But I think it's an illusion. I just read a great quote this morning—something like, "I don't believe in God, but I miss him."[7] I don't know who said that, but it's like ... I don't really believe in free will, but I can't live without it. I can't live without the belief. I think it's about the dignity of individuals.

TS: But it's an illusion nevertheless.

PZ: I think I would have to say free will is an illusion. A lot of control is an illusion. Advertisers give you an illusion of control: You're choosing Kellogg's Corn Flakes over another brand because ... Or take all the cigarette companies. Their whole thing was freedom of choice—that the anti-smoking fanatics are taking away your freedom of choice, and you have the freedom to choose to smoke whenever you want, wherever you want. So it's giving people an illusion of choice. I did a whole set of research in dissonance theory, where we got people to take painful electric shocks, really painful electric shocks. And we said, "Of course, you don't have to do it. If you choose to go on, remember, it's your free choice." I think we used those words. And they said yes. They're strapped into this thing, I'm standing with a lab coat over them, they're in a little cubicle, I'm the professor, they're the student, it's an experiment. Half of them refused, but the other half said, "Yes, I'll go on." The truth is there was no choice. That's the way we manipulated it. But if they agreed, thinking they made a free choice, then they psychologically perceived the shock as less painful.

TS: It doesn't hurt as much as it would have if they hadn't thought they made the choice?

PZ: Right. And physiologically, they react as if it were less painful. And we have control groups where we lower the shock by 20 volts and physiologically they lower the shock by 20 volts. They have no free choice. We arrange it so that they're going to go on. We know they're going to go on. And just saying "Remember, you have a free choice, you don't have to do it, right?"—as soon as they say "Right," then they change. They say, I don't have to do this. And they're taking electric shocks and "Gee, it's not so bad." So the dissonance is: you agree to do something which you know is not good for you. But if you believe you chose to do it, then you perceive, you rationalize why it should be good for you.

TS: Rationalizing at the physiological level—that's fascinating. I read about another experiment like that where they gave two groups a very tedious task. One group got paid a lot, the other hardly anything. The people who got money for it droned on about how boring it was. The people who got almost nothing didn't complain ...

PZ: That's Festinger and Carlsmith. That's one of the very first experiments in dissonance theory. So if you got a lot of money for it, then you were extra-aggrieved. You complained. If you only received ten cents, and nothing in later studies, then you said, "Oh no, it was interesting."

TS: You have to justify it to yourself.

PZ: And you believe it. I did a lot of that research. I have a whole book called *The Cognitive Control of Motivation*, which has all these studies. We've done things with hunger. You become less hungry if you agree. You have people who say, "You can't eat anything for 24 hours." Then you come in, fill out some questionnaire, then you say, "Okay, now, in some conditions, we're asking some people to go another 24 hours. You don't have to do it if you don't want to. I can't even give you any more money to do it." But if they agree to do it they become less hungry. I mean, physiologically measured they become less hungry. The moment they agree to do something they don't really want to do.

TS: It's also interesting because it seems like there's a sort of misperception of the kind of control that we actually want. The prisoners in your experiment were upset about their lack of control over the situation. But what they wanted wasn't this illusory kind of control that probably doesn't exist. They just wanted to make decisions that led to outcomes they could predict. And we normally have that. That's the kind of control we hate to lose, and maybe we misinterpret that as a kind of ultimate control.

PZ: Ultimately, you want control of outcomes. You want to be able to say, "Here's what I'm going to do today. I'm going to do this and this and this and this, I'm going to go and buy something." I don't expect to go down to the store and say "I want to buy something" and the guy says "I don't want you in my store, you look dangerous," or "I'm going to call the police, don't touch the food." Suddenly you're not controlling the outcomes, because here's some things you didn't expect. I guess what I'm saying is that we do want to have real control, and in the absence of that, we're willing to accept illusions of control. We're willing to accept the belief that we are controlling, and then psychologically we do control. We say "I'm less hungry," "It's less shocking," "It's not going to hurt so much," "I feel really good about that." And that's where we become manipulable by advertisers, by salesmen, by wheelers and dealers. Because it's so important for us to have control. And where we don't have real control somebody can just say, "Hey, by voting for me, you're exercising your control." "By smoking Camels, unfiltered, that shows you're a real man, you're in control."

TS: *You're* making the choice.

6 "You Can't Win a War on Nouns"

TS: This talk of responsibility and control reminds us of the quote by Condoleezza Rice you cite in the book. She's explicitly denying the power of situationist elements to influence people like terrorists. She puts it all on them, on the wickedness of their characters: "When are we going to stop making excuses for the terrorists and saying that someone is making them do it? No, these are simply evil people that want to kill."

PZ: Right—I was furious! Here's this supposed intellect, and she says "They're just evil people." And you guys [the Bush administration] aren't evil, you guys are saying, Rice especially, "We don't want the smoking gun to be a mushroom cloud." She's saying if we didn't do this [the war on terror] we could have a nuclear bomb go off in the US.

TS: You're very hard on her in the book. The whole Bush administration really, and Rumsfeld and Cheney especially.

PZ: God, yes!

TS: I want to play devil's advocate and ask whether in their own way, they were trapped in the situation as well. Which led them to institute their policies. It's a little harder to figure out the details of their situation because there's so much we don't know, but isn't it reasonable to assume that they were in one just as much as—

PZ: No, but in their case, they helped create the situation.

TS: That's true, but in doing so, weren't they also part of a larger situation that led them to create the situation in Abu Ghraib?

PZ: The abuses in Abu Ghraib are one thing. But I'm saying they were the principals in creating the whole—I don't know what the broadest context is—the war on terror. That is, Cheney primarily, and Bush and Rumsfeld and George Tenet. For very conscious, aware reasons, they decided to label the global challenge of terrorism—which it should have been called—a *war* on terrorism, so that Bush could be the active commander in chief, so they could have martial law, so they could suspend lots of rights. That's why it's called "the war on terror." And you can't win a war on nouns! We lost a war on drugs, we lost a war on poverty, we're losing a war on terror. It's not clear if verbs win or adjectives win. So I hold them responsible because they set up the system; they are the Hitler and Goebbels and Goering. Each of them said, "Here's my domain, and I'm going to run it this way, and we're not allowing alternative views." Saying that anyone who criticizes us is putting our boys and soldiers in harm's way, anybody who criticizes us is unpatriotic. They set up all these mechanisms, to say, you know, you're feeding the enemy—you're killing the soldiers by protesting against it. And then they essentially instituted—because of this unique power base—the NSA secret thing, they're spying on us, they have these renditions, torture things, a whole set of things that are alien to everything, all basic American values. The Military Commissions Act, which they pushed through, overturns two hundred years of Anglo-American law. I mean, they gave up habeas corpus. Simply redefine someone as an [unlawful] enemy combatant; that means they have no rights. And essentially anyone in the world who's suspected of terrorism can be arrested anyplace in the world, brought to an undisclosed place without a charge, and kept there indefinitely. There are people in

Guantánamo who have been there for seven years with no charges against them except that they're "suspected of terrorism."

For me, it's not that the administration was "trapped in the situation." I'm saying they *created* the situation. They created a system in which each of these parts fall out. I'm saying they're responsible.

TS: In that expressive sense?

PZ: I like that expressive view, yes. But you know, if we were to be the losers of the war on terrorism, they would be brought before a war crimes tribunal. If there was in fact a real war, and we lost in Iraq, the Iraqis would say, "Okay, you invaded our country under false pretenses, you did all these things, all these people died. We're going to put you on trial."

7   Heroes in Waiting

TS: Let's conclude, as you do in your book, on a more optimistic note. You talk in your book about some ways to avoid some of the problems of succumbing to the situation. Knowing the power of the situation can help us resist when we ought to.

PZ: Yes.

TS: But I'm wondering how that's supposed to work in practice. Take the Asch conformity experiments.[8] It seems that the subjects there are operating with this heuristic: "If everyone else is perceiving something, and I don't have any reason to think they're lying, then they're probably right and I'm wrong." Under normal circumstances, that seems pretty reasonable. How are we supposed to know when a situation is corrupting or illusory?

PZ: That's a good point. You said it right. Our life is organized around a bunch of heuristics to say "Under ordinary circumstances, when the majority of people see something a certain way, it's probably the way to see it." And in fact, in the real world, more often than not it is that way. Similarly, the majority of times when an authority says, "Here's what I believe, and here's what you should do," and you do it, it's for your advantage. Your parents, the priest, your teachers, the rabbi. The problem is that we aren't really taught to be sensitive to the exceptions to the rule. That is, parents abuse kids, priests abuse kids, authorities are sometimes false authorities, authorities are sometimes evil. In the Milgram study, it's all about somebody who starts off being a totally just authority and transforms to become totally unjust. At some point, they'd say: "I don't care if the guy has a heart attack, I don't care if he's dead in there. You have to keep shocking." At that point, you're an adult, and you should say "This doesn't make sense." Except that you've been so conditioned to be obedient to authority.

It's like the elementary school teacher who didn't let you get out of your seat unless you raised your hand to go to the toilet. And it didn't matter if you peed in your pants. I still remember in first grade, a little girl raised her hand and said, "I have to go to the bathroom." The teacher said, "No, put your hand down." The kid peed all over herself. Everyone laughed at her.

We carry these sets of heuristics and we never get trained to be wary of the exception to the rule. Because that's where the danger lies. Sometimes the majority is wrong. In Nazi Germany, the majority was wrong to say, "We gotta kill Jews." In Rwanda, the majority among the Hutus were wrong to say, "We gotta kill Tutsis." But that's the hardest thing. How do you, as an individual, become situationally savvy enough to say, "Wait, this situation is the exception"?

TS: Exactly. What should we do?

PZ: Part of it is having a certain level of skepticism, of cynicism, in the back of your optimism. So optimism is "I love the world, I love most people," but if I grew up in the ghetto, I developed street smarts, street savvy, which means I'm never fully trusting. I never trust anybody 100 percent. The Mafia thing. You always sit with your back to the wall. Nobody's ever going to come and take you from behind. Whenever you walk into a situation, the first thing you do is look for the exits, because you know if there's a fire, everybody's going to go to the exit they came in through, and you'll be crushed. And you're going to walk out the other one. It should be part of our basic training of being situationally sensitive, situationally savvy.

TS: Basic training at the parental level or the school level?

PZ: The school level, because again, most people are good most of the time, but there's always a bad apple. There's always the bully in the class. There's always the hustler. There's always the wheeler-dealer. There's always the pimp who's trying to get women to do what he wants.

TS: You can always stumble in a bad barrel.

PZ: Yeah, you can just make the wrong turn. And then you're in this bad thing. The terrible thing is by accident of birth. People grow up in inner cities, people grow up in war zones, people grow up in places where there's 200 percent inflation. And their lives are going to be powerfully impacted by those situations. But we still want to believe that they have individual freedom of choice to rise above it. And the interesting thing is, some few do. Most of them don't. If a guy gets released from prison and goes back to the neighborhood he came from, the chances of him having recidivism are enormous. If you put him in a different situation, give him a place to live, give him a job ... They do this here, something called the Delancey Street Foundation. Instead of going to prison, they give you a job and an apartment immediately. And there's social support. They never break the law again. I don't know what the recidivism rate is, but it's probably 10 percent. It's as simple as that. If I have a job, if I have respect, and I have a place to live that's away from the bad situation, then I can exercise free choice and I can be a good person.

TS: So, in your skeptical sort of way, you think we can rise above our situations, or at least create situations which allow us to rise above bad ones?

PZ: My argument is in fact that most people are good most of the time. But evil makes the news. Evil is dramatic, evil is swift. So some kid spends hours making a sandcastle and another kid comes and steps on it in a second and destroys it. Somebody spends years making a sculpture and someone comes with a hammer and breaks the arm off. So evil, graffiti, and all these kinds of things—destruction is swift and powerful—if it bleeds, it leads. All the news organizations, they want the stories about evil. They want the death and the violence, the incest and the rape. I'm saying most people, most of the time, don't do anything bad. Maybe they cheat on their income tax and feel guilty about it. The last chapter of my book is not only about how you resist, it's also a celebration of heroism as the real antidote to evil. And that's the main thing I'm doing now. I'm starting the Heroic Imagination Project. To be consistent, I say most evil is done by ordinary people put in certain situations. And it's the *act* that's really evil—most people are really not. Most heroes, most heroic acts, are also done by ordinary people who aren't special in any way. They just happen to be put into a certain situation of emergency, of evil, of immorality, of corruption, that gives them the opportunity to act on it.

TS: Joe Darby, the Abu Ghraib whistle-blower, for example. You discuss him in your book.

PZ: Yes. Most heroes are ordinary people put in a situation, often only once in their lifetime, that gives them the opportunity to act. So what I've been trying to do has been to democratize heroism and demystify it. There're two kind of heroes. There are impulsive heroes, and there are reflective heroes—people who blow the whistle on Enron. Sherron Watkins and others. Christians who helped the Jews. But what I'm saying—Gandhi, Nelson Mandela, Martin Luther King Jr., Mother Teresa, they're exceptional. The reason we know their names is that they organized their whole lives around a sacrifice. And it's great that they did it. I'm not gonna do it, I'm not going to give up my whole life to any cause. But in fact, I think Obama said his grandmother was the unsung hero. Most people who do heroic things, sacrifice for others, they do it in silence. Every single person who's identified as a hero always says, "How could I not do it?"

TS: So there's the banality of evil and the "banality of heroism."

PZ: The banality of heroism. I think that's a reasonable expression, and it really says that it's the heroic act that's extraordinary because it's rare. And so if we can have more and more kids think, "I'm a hero in waiting," and if we can have hero resources in schools and summer camps where kids learn situational savvy, these kinds of street smarts, they can learn social influence skills to form a network. So you want them to say, "I'm a hero in waiting," and then "I have to be prepared. I have to learn first-aid skills, I have to learn social influence skills, I have to learn a set of things, and that when the time comes, I will act!"

Notes

1   See Chapter 12 of Philip Zimbardo's *The Lucifer Effect* for a more detailed and dramatic account of the Milgram experiments.

2   Zimbardo and Christina Maslach were married the next year.
3   See my interview with Joe Henrich (Chapter 14) for more on the "rational man" or Homo economicus model of human behavior.
4   See my interview with Galen Strawson (Chapter 1) for some thoughts on why this might not be such a terrible implication.
5   Note that if you viewed moral responsibility in this manner, it would not be vulnerable to the argument Galen Strawson presents in Chapter 1. People would not have to be responsible for who they are in order to be responsible for their actions.
6   Zimbardo's *The Lucifer Effect* did, however, make it to number 11 on the New York *Times* best-seller list.
7   The quotation appears in Julian Barnes's *Nothing to Be Frightened of* (2008).
8   In these studies, a subject was asked to evaluate the length of lines in the presence of other "subjects" who were really in collaboration with the investigators. When these "subjects" unanimously gave obviously wrong answers, the real subject started to give that answer as well, conforming with the rest of the group.

Questions for Discussion

1   Briefly describe the "Stanford Prison Experiment," the different roles available in the experiment, and the role Philip Zimbardo himself played.
2   What is situationist theory in social psychology? What does it say about human behavior?
3   Describe the changes that began to take place in the participants and Zimbardo himself. How are these changes perceived by those outside the experiment?
4   What role does Carlo specifically play in the experiment, and what do his actions potentially show about situationism?
5   What is the "fundamental attribution error"?
6   Is the outcome of the Stanford Prison Experiment an argument in favor of moral responsibility and freedom of the will, or an argument against it?
7   Describe Zimbardo's view of free will and how situationism fits into such a view.
8   What is a 'Hero in Waiting' and how does Zimbardo see situationism playing a role in this phenomenon?

Suggested Readings

Zimbardo, Philip. *The Cognitive Control of Motivation: The Consequences of Choice and Dissonance*. Scott, Foresman and Co., 1969.
——. *The Psychology of Attitude Change and Social Influence*. New York: McGraw-Hill, 1991.
——. *The Lucifer Effect: Understanding How Good People Turn Evil*. New York and London: Random House, 2007.
——. *The Time Paradox: The New Psychology of Time that Will Change Your Life*. New York: Random House, 2008.
Haney, Craig, Curtis Banks, and Philip Zimbardo. "Interpersonal Dynamics in a Simulated Prison." *International Journal of Criminology & Penology* (1973): 69–97.

Milgram, Stanley. "Behavioral Study of Obedience." *Journal of Abnormal and Social Psychology* 67(4) (1963): 371–8.

Nelkin, Dana K. "Freedom, Responsibility and the Challenge of Situationism." *Midwest Studies in Philosophy* 29(1) (2005): 181–206.

Benjamin Jr. L. T. and Simpson, J. A. "The Power of the Situation: The Impact of Milgram's Studies on Personality and Social Psychology." *American Psychologist* 64 (2009): 12–19.

Manning, R., Levine, M. and Collins, A. "The Kitty Genovese Murder and the Social Psychology of Helping: The Parable of the 38 Witnesses." *American Psychologist* 62 (2007): 555–62.

Assorted Media and Podcast Pairings

The Stanford Prison Experiment website. www.prisonexp.org

Philip Zimbardo. "The Psychology of Evil" (TED talk) www.ted.com/talks/philip_zimbardo_on_the_psychology_of_evil

Very Bad Wizards, Episode 9 "Social Psychology, Situationism, and Moral Character." (Warning: even more explicit than most) http://verybadwizards.com/episodes/9

Part II

The Big Questions

Virtue, Honor, Meaning, and the Good Life

Introduction

I don't remember this section from the first edition.

It's almost entirely new. Aside from William Ian Miller (Chapter 6), none of these interviews appeared in the first edition. These are the interviews that best reflect the change in my philosophical interests.

How so?

I've always thought that academic philosophy—and ethics especially—is far too technical and inaccessible to the ordinary reader. I used to attribute this to bad writing and way too much jargon. There's plenty of that, but over the last few years, I've started to think that the problem is rooted in the whole approach that philosophers take to moral philosophy. Many philosophers want ethics to be modeled after mathematics or the hard science. So they try to devise logical proofs, universal principles, and systematic theories for concepts like 'moral reason,' 'goodness,' 'obligation,' which they expect to be immune to every conceivable counterexample.[1] They test these theories against idealized, fantastical thought experiments and then refine and refine them long past the point where anyone remembers why (or whether) it's important to do so. But morality isn't like math or physics. It's messy, and our philosophy needs to reflect that. There's a limit to how precise we can make our moral theories without getting further and further detached from the real world. And ethics has to be about the real world or what's the point?

Any plans to come down off that soap box and talk about the actual interviews in this part?

The authors in Part II inspired a lot of these reflections. And their work addresses real-life issues with important practical implications. In Chapter 3, Valerie Tiberius discusses the biggest question of them all, Socrates' question: how should we live? What is a good life, a valuable life, and how can we do better at attaining it?

That's what you call a practical question?

In a way it's the most practical question there is. I think students come to college with little certainty about their values, about the kind of life they want to lead. They see their courses exclusively as a means of achieving that life. (As one of my students put it, college is too expensive to use for self-examination.) But sometimes it's worth questioning and reflecting on our values, our beliefs about the good life. Tiberius offers one way of doing that.

Chapter 4 addresses another practical question (in a certain sense)—what is a meaningful life or activity? That's the topic of my interview with Susan Wolf. Wolf presents her account of meaningfulness, and explains why it matters that an activity is meaningful when we're deliberating about what to do. She also gives a qualified defense of the kind of ethical theorizing I'm worried about. Her own theory of meaning is a model for how to be rigorous without being overly systematic.

What about Chapter 5?

Nancy Sherman's work is probably the best example of how philosophy can have huge practical implications for our lives. She tells the story of Admiral James Stockdale, how he relied on Epictetus' stoic philosophy to help him survive his experience as a POW in Vietnam. Sherman explains both the benefits and costs of embracing stoic ideals for military personnel on active duty. Sherman is also a leading Aristotelian scholar, and she describes the advantages of Aristotle's virtue-based approach over contemporary ethical theories that focus only on acts and universal moral principles.

The last two chapters are about honor and vengeance. Hasn't our civilization finally moved beyond those primitive ideals?

Not according to William Ian Miller and Anthony Appiah. In Chapter 6, Miller defends the nobility of cultures that emphasize the importance of honor and revenge, and argues that these values still pervade our lives whether we admit it or not. Appiah agrees that a sense of honor is part of human nature, but he's more ambivalent about its effects. We discuss his new book which examines the crucial role that honor has played in promoting moral revolutions. We conclude by considering some ways to harness honor-based values to bring about further moral progress.

3 Valerie Tiberius
The Good Life

The Greek philosopher Socrates was like that guy who corners you at a party and gets you into conversations you don't feel like having. Except that he didn't just do it at parties; he cornered people on the streets of Athens and interrogated them about their beliefs and values. By the year 399 BC, the Athenians had had enough. They brought Socrates to trial on two trumped-up charges: impiety and corrupting the youth. In his famous defense (dramatized in Plato's Apology), *Socrates denied the charges and claimed that he was simply urging Athenians to reflect on the deepest questions human beings face: how should we live? What is the best kind of life? To Socrates, the citizens of Athens had things backwards. They focused only on the most practical questions—how to make money, how to gain power—but they never asked themselves why they wanted these goods in the first place. Socrates was not corrupting anybody, just asking them to spend at least as much time thinking about their souls as they did about their bank accounts. He thought it made sense to focus on the question "what is the best sort of life?" before you worry about the practical ways of attaining that life. The jury didn't buy it. Socrates was sentenced to death by hemlock.*

Socrates' question was the dominant topic in ancient philosophy, but after that it receded into the background. Moral philosophers have been more concerned about reasons, obligations, autonomy, and justice. Maybe it's fear of hemlock, but in the last one hundred years philosophers reflecting on the best lives (rather than morally right or wrong actions) have been the exception rather than the rule. Valerie Tiberius, Professor and Chair of the University of Minnesota Philosophy Department, is one of those exceptions, and an exceptional one at that. Starting with her dissertation, she has devoted the bulk of her research to questions about wisdom, reflection, well-being, and the good life. Our conversation covered many of them. Do human beings have a function? What about dogs? What role should reflection play in the good life? What about emotion? How can we make our values more consistent and attainable? How much control over our values do we have? In contrast to some philosophers, Tiberius takes the empirical research on happiness in psychology and economics seriously, albeit with an appropriate measure of skepticism.

Tiberius is the author of two books: Moral Psychology: A Contemporary Introduction *(Routledge, 2014) and* The Reflective Life: Living Wisely with our Limits (Oxford University Press, 2008). *I interviewed her over Skype on a bad connection, which she handled with a lot more wisdom than I did.*

March 2015

1   The Mother of all Questions

TAMLER SOMMERS: Most of your recent work tackles what's likely the most important philosophical question of all, the one that Socrates devoted his life to answering. How should I live? What makes a good life? There's a sense in which it's the first question, the one you'd want at least a rough answer to before moving on to any others. Yet it's rare to find philosophers working on this question these days. Why do you think that is?

VALERIE TIBERIUS: Well, it's becoming somewhat more fashionable lately. I have a suspicion that philosophers are noticing empirical psychologists suddenly working on happiness, welfare, virtue and thinking to themselves: "hey wait a minute that was our topic!" I don't know if that's true, but I have that suspicion that the psychology work is motivating philosophers to get more into it. And, of course, there have always been some philosophers who work on these big questions—Julia Annas, Susan Wolf, and Bernard Williams are a few who come to mind.

TS: So most philosophers just forgot about the question, and then the psychologists reminded them?

VT: It's more that the psychologists' research has annoyed them. A lot of philosophers read what psychologists are doing and think that it has nothing to do with the question of the good life as we understand it.

TS: But why did philosophers cede the territory in the first place?

VT: One thing I've heard from philosophers who have a bit more of a sense of the history (by which I mean philosophers who are older than me) is that we might be coming out of a moment where the kind of philosophy that's rewarded is very abstract and disengaged. As one of my friends called it: "epicyclic engineering."

TS: That's great, I like that.

VT: I know, it's really good. So, pondering these huge questions which philosophers used to do was not rewarded anymore.

TS: Because the question is so massive and broad, it's hard to break down with simple, straightforward arguments or cases?

VT: Yeah, I'm inclined to think that's part of it, especially since the best things that I've read on the good life and well-being are all book length. Not that there aren't good articles, but the articles tend to be: "here's a theory, let's fix this problem," whereas the stuff where you read it and think "this actually progresses the debate" or "this is a really cool contribution"— they tend to be books. And it's hard to write a book. There must be something else to it, though.

TS: Part of it seems to be that philosophers tend to shy away from messy problems and topics, and this is definitely one of them. How do you even approach the topic of a good life? Do we need some sort of shared conception of what you're talking about to get the ball rolling? How do you approach a question of that complexity and size?

VT: One thing I've started to think is that there isn't just one question or one subject matter here. That comes from my way of thinking about how you should do normative ethics as a Humean naturalist (which I am).

TS: What do you mean by that?

VT: I call my approach 'constructivist.' The hallmark of the constructivist approach is that you start with the practical problem that you're trying to solve. So you think about normative ethics as practical problem-solving rather than as discovery. And then you ask: "well, what are the judgments that we start with?" And then: "what are the norms, the kind of procedural, rational norms of improvement for those judgments?"

TS: Well, let's start there. When it comes to the good life, what is the practical problem that we have to solve?

VT: Well, there's more than one problem, and that leads me to think there's no single subject matter about the good life. The problem that I'm interested in is: how do you help people improve their lives without sacrificing the interests of the community that they belong to? How do you help people live happier, better lives for them, and also recognize that they're social creatures who have to get along with each other? How can I live my own life better without screwing over everybody else?

2 The Problem with Aristotle

TS: What are some other relevant problems?

VT: A different question you might have is how to raise children, where you're essentially trying to create a functioning adult. If you're interested in helping already grown-up persons improve their lives, your recommendations or theory will be constrained by concerns about coercion and paternalism. Also concerns about motivation: the ideal of the good life for a person shouldn't seem alien to that person. But if you're focused on children, a lot of those concerns are absent. And so it might be a different kind of project. And it might not be that every theory of well-being fits equally well no matter what your practical interest is.

TS: That's an interesting distinction, not one I've ever thought about. But it's important.

VT: I think Aristotelian theories, which I don't care for personally, make a lot of sense when you think about raising children. But it's not so useful when you're making recommendations to adults who already have their own goals and projects.

TS: This was something I wanted to ask you: why you reject Aristotelian theories? Because at first glance, there would seem to be a lot of similarities in the way you deal with questions about the good life. He was practical too—at least for a philosopher. He focused on character and dealt with actual real-life situations.[2] Can you just give a brief summary of Aristotle's approach?

VT: The Aristotelian view is that living a good human life is flourishing as a member of the human species. So the normative recommendations are species-based. And in the contemporary Aristotelian literature there's a lot of talk about what it is to be a good human being *qua* member of the human species. Most Aristotelians think that virtues like courage, wisdom, temperance, justice, are not just means to your own happiness. The virtues are constitutive of a good human life. That means that a life lacking virtuous activity just can't be a good life. So virtuous activity isn't a means to some other good; it just is the good—and, for Aristotle, the point is that it's the good *for you*. (As opposed to being a morally good thing that might or might not be good for you.) You can't live a flourishing life without developing the virtues. So the approach collapses the moral and the prudential.

TS: And that's why you're not on board?

VT: It's more that I find the idea of grounding virtues in human nature totally uncompelling.

TS: So it's not that you don't care for his particular virtues.

VT: No, it's more abstract than that. I find the virtues compelling. But I think that if you're going to recommend those virtues to people—"Tamler, you should be more courageous, or more temperate"—what justifies those recommendations are the goals that *you* [Tamler] have, or the values that you hold dear. They're not grounded in the fact that you're a human being. According to Aristotle, the oak tree hasn't fulfilled its function unless it grows tall and produces more acorns. Similarly, you won't have fulfilled your function as a human being unless you develop these virtues. It's the function argument that I don't sign on to.

TS: I agree with you about that. But here's one way of understanding the Aristotelian approach that might be more appealing. I used to have a dog—well, I still have dogs, but this one was a purebred. Her name was Tess, she was a Springer Spaniel, and she was bred to flush out birds for hunters. That was the function of her breed. Now I'm not a hunter so that wasn't her function for me. But knowing the breed's function was an interesting clue as to what activities she would love and the different ways she could flourish. I'm sure she would have been ecstatic if we had gone hunting. But instead we did things that were close enough. I took her on long hikes in the woods and she would dart around like crazy chasing shadows and barking at chipmunks and squirrels and birds. She probably enjoyed those hikes more than I've ever enjoyed anything in my life. Even in our yard, she could just chase bird shadows for seven straight hours until she collapsed.

What I'm trying to say is that maybe you can think about function more naturalistically, not in that teleological way. We're human beings. We enjoy friendship, social and political engagement, deliberation, and so forth. These are the activities and traits that tend to fulfill us in the deepest possible way. Would you be OK with that?

VT: Absolutely. And in fact in my own work I'm always talking about the value of friendship and relationships with other people. That's why the kind of disagreement I have with Aristotle is farther back. It's over the theoretical justification for his conclusions. I guess where things would come apart is if you think about this: What if you happen to have a Springer Spaniel who doesn't give a crap about hunting and would rather lie around in the windowsill and chew on rawhide? Are you going to say: "look Snoopy, get your ass out there and go hunting because that's your function and you're not fulfilling it!" Sometimes contemporary Aristotelians really say things about human beings who are different and have different capabilities from the norm—they say things like "it's a shame that you're not like the rest of us," essentially. It's a shame you're not living up to your human nature or that your psychology doesn't allow you to flourish in a way that's natural for human beings.

TS: Right, good point. You might think that certain people are defective as human beings. It might even serve to justify coercion. The thought would be that if you force people to be a certain way, you'd actually make them happier, according to your conception of *eudaemonia*.[3] You might see coercion as more like Lasik surgery, correcting their vision or something.

VT: Yeah, the word 'defective' is a good word, because I think that's the part of the Aristotelian program that bothers me. Human beings would count as defective because they deviate from a species norm. That's the bit I don't like. But a lot of Aristotelians these days are changing … they're bending in good ways.

3 How to Live Well

TS: So let's turn to your own account of well-being.

VT: My approach to thinking about a good life and well-being is what I call value-based. To put it in a nutshell: to live well is to live a life in accordance with your coherent and sustainable set of values. It is to fulfill a sustainable set of values over time. Our values bring with them standards of success, so succeeding in terms of your values, the coherent and sustainable set of values—that's living well.

TS: Let's try to break down each part of that account. The first part states that you live in accordance with values that you have. How do you find out what values you have, exactly?

VT: None of these things is very simple. The first question is: what's a value? As I'm sure you know, there's a split between philosophers who identify values with beliefs and philosophers who identify them with desires or something affective. I like a view that's kind of a hybrid. To say that you value something as opposed to merely wanting it or merely thinking it valuable is to have the cognitive and the affective line up.

TS: What would be an example?

VT: I think all of us value certain relationships in our lives. Like your relationship with your spouse or your children. It's not just that you want to have that person in your life. You also believe it's a good thing to have them in your life. And you take success in terms of that relationship to be a standard for assessing how well your life is going. That's the cognitive dimension to it.

TS: OK, what about the second aspect of your account—that our values should be coherent and sustainable?

VT: I often use the word 'appropriate' for values. You can have values that aren't good for you to have, because they're not part of a coherent or stable set.

TS: What would be an example of that?

VT: You could value a particular relationship that's harmful to you. So, if your wife is a horrible person who insults and criticizes you all the time …

TS: You know, she does insult and criticize me a fair amount …

VT: But, you know, there are always competing reasons.

TS: Yeah, she would consider herself fully justified.

VT: Another example that's familiar to people like us are undergraduate students who think their career path is going to med school. They want to be a doctor partly because their parents have always instilled that in them. And, if you talk to them about it, you might guess that it is something they genuinely value. But it could be dysfunctional or inappropriate value if in fact they have no passion for it, if they were to move along that career path, they'll end up being bored or killing themselves …

TS: So that's the 'coherent' part of it—a good life won't have values that will be destructive to the other things that you value in life.

VT: Yes, given that almost all of us have multiple values, they have to fit together in some way. But they also have to be sustainable because you're going to change, your circumstances are going to change. There are some commitments, projects, goals, and values that will serve you better over time than others.

TS: Serve you better in what sense?

VT: They'll allow you to live up to them more successfully. So, if you take athleticism. Let's say you're a marathon runner or triathlete and what you value is being the best. You do the sport because you're very competitive and you want to win contests and events. You will have more luck in your life (unless you die young) if you shape that value over time so that the things you care about are more like doing your best and being competitive with other people in your age group. But if the value is always put in terms of being an Olympic-level athlete, you're just going to fail.

TS: Right, and of course many athletes have unrealistic expectations in the first place, no matter what age they are.

VT: I would say that for most normal people, there's some sort of basic core set of general values like relationships, meaningful work, success, things like that that don't really change at the most general level of description. What does change is how you instantiate that value with sub-goals. For example, everyone values friendship and that is very unlikely to change over the course of a lifetime. But what the value means to you and how you plan to realize it may change. When you're young, you might think "the more friends the better!" But then as an adult you might realize that a few good friendships are more important than many superficial ones. Or, at one stage of life you might pursue friendships with people who like the same sports as you, but later in life you might pursue friendships with people who have kids the same age as yours and similar parenting styles.

TS: So you want values that aren't too specific, then, so that they can be realized over time.

VT: What's important is recognizing that the specific ways that you try to live up to your values have to flex with changes in circumstances and changes in you. So the specific way that friendship is realized changes, but the basic, abstract value doesn't.

TS: How much of all this is in our control? One thing that Aristotle probably got right is that there's a lot of luck involved in whether we're going to live a good life. I know you agree with that to a certain extent. But how much control do you think we have in getting our values to mesh, to be sustainable and coherent? How much of it is due to early training, natural talents, accidents, even something like appearance?

VT: I agree with you that Aristotle is right about the role of luck. The luck that's a particular problem for my view is the luck involved in choosing the right values or setting the right goals for yourself.

TS: Interesting. Choosing values isn't something that is obviously luck-based, right?

VT: On my view, you don't have that much control over what your values are. It's something I worried about because people spend decades in therapy trying to nudge what they care about in healthier directions. And often they fail. This is one of the areas where it's really important to know your empirical psychology. A lot of that research should get us to recognize how little control we have over things that we have historically thought we have lots of control over.

Now I've never been persuaded that we don't have *any* control. If what you're talking about is trying to live a better life, you have to do what you can do. But a lot of the things we value and care about are rooted in our childhoods. And you can't go back and have a different set of parents or a different upbringing. But there are various ways to try to move the goals that you have in healthier directions. That's a problem that no theory is going to sidestep.

TS: It's just a problem with being human.

VT: It's a problem with being human, exactly.

TS: Humans are also different, as you pointed out earlier. How does your account handle individual or cultural differences in conceptions of the good life?

VT: This is one of the main reasons I like this value-based approach. People value different things in different ways, so it's easy for my account to accommodate individual differences. But if you want to go from talking about individual good lives to making generalizations about good lives for people, or eventually to policy recommendations, you have to start talking about groups of people and what groups of people value. It's important to recognize that these are empirical questions. So the claims have to be justified in terms of what's good for *most* people, given that most people are like this. But what you don't get on this kind of view is an 'everyone must do this' or a 'you're a defective human being unless you proceed along this path.'

4   Reining in the Charioteer

TS: One potential source of control that philosophers have appealed to is our capacity for reason. The idea is that as rational creatures, we can use our reason to make our values the right values, sustainable and coherent. In your book, you talk about Plato's idea of the soul. It's divided into three parts: the desiring part, the spirited (emotional, courageous) part, and the reasoning part.[4] The good person, according to Plato, has reason running the show, reason as the charioteer guiding the other two aspects of our souls. That's always been a tempting image for philosophers. You're skeptical though that reason can give us that much control over our values.

VT: Yes, I'm skeptical about this view that might be described as rationalism. I spend a lot of time in *The Reflective Life* trying to rein in rational reflection.

TS: Rein in the charioteer.

VT: Now I do think reflection is important. It's important to think about what matters to you, and how those things fit together, and how successful you are living up to those things. But I also think that when you do that kind of reflection, you should pay a lot of attention to your emotional responses. And I also think you shouldn't do that kind of reflection all that often. If you're always reflecting, then you're not actually engaging with the things that you care about. And you're not learning from experience about what works and what doesn't work.

TS: I know there's no simple answer to this, but what role should reflection play in a healthy life?

VT: It's because there's no simple answer that it would be very hard to respond to your question. So let me start here. One role that I think reason does not have is the role of dictating what ends we should pursue. That's one of the things that makes me a Humean.[5] It's what I reject about Kant. I don't think there are rational principles that tell us we must value X on pain of irrationality.

TS: Because you're sane.

VT: Yes! Although I know some pretty nice people who take Kant's view on this.

TS: I do too. They're very nice and yet they're Kantians. That's what's weird about them.

VT: Anyway, once you get away from that part of the Kantian picture, you start thinking about reflective capacities as psychological capacities along with all sorts of other psychological capacities. They're not magic. And they're not divorced from the rest of our psychologies.

TS: If we want to make tasty dinner we have to ask: 'OK, when can I go to the store, what do I need to buy?' There's no difference in kind between that kind of reflection and reflection about the values. Is that the idea?

VT: Yes, although one thing that could be hidden in your question: am I endorsing the view that all reasoning and all rational processing is instrumental?

TS: It sounds like you are, right?

VT: You know, I find that to be one of the hardest questions. There's a sense in which I endorse that view, but I also think that we do a lot of thinking about things we value for their own sakes. I agree that reason can't tell us to value or not to value friendship and happiness. There is no rational principle that's going to lead you there. But often there are particular relationships in our lives that we value as ends—we don't merely value them for the pleasure or financial security they bring us.

TS: But even if we value things for their own sake—that doesn't mean there are reasons to have those values.

VT: Yes, but what I wanted to say further is that you can engage in reflection about whether the things that you value for their own sakes are the right things to value for their own sakes.

TS: How does that work exactly?

VT: I think there's a difference between rationally evaluating an end by some kind of coherence method and evaluating it instrumentally. So, in other words, let's say there's something you value for its own sake. You can't ask: is this a good means to a further end that I value because you're admitting to yourself that you value it for its own sake. But you can ask how the value fits in with the rest of your life. I take it that isn't quite instrumental reasoning.

TS: It certainly isn't simple instrumental reasoning.

VT: If the choice is between instrumental or categorical imperatives, then it's instrumental. But it's a lot more complicated than what you get in economics, where we're just always deliberating about how to satisfy a preference.

TS: Let's take a concrete example in which we value something for its own sake, but then, after reflecting in this way, we realize that maybe it's not the right value to have.

VT: It could be something like reputation. I think this happens even in Philosophy where people really care about recognition and standing and accolades and being loved by their peers.

TS: Maybe especially in philosophy.

VT: That's the kind of value where, if you care about it for long enough, it's no longer instrumental. It's not really just the pleasure that you're after. It is the standing. It's like fame. You want to be famous. And I think those kinds of positional goods where your success depends on other people failing are generally not good for people. And it's the kind of thing that upon reflection you can see isn't good for you.

TS: I just want to understand how this works. I don't think I chase reputation too much, or if I do, I'm not very good at it. But let's say I was overly concerned about it. In what way could I see that this wasn't a good value for me to have?

VT: This goes back to what we were just talking about. A person can only see it in relation to the other things they care about. Even if you don't value fame as a means to feeling happy, a lot of people who value those sorts of positional or relational goods end up feeling stressed and frustrated frequently. So you can notice that about yourself.

TS: You can notice that you're more resentful, you have these negative emotions like jealousy. And you value not having a bitter or envious existence.

VT: Yes. You can notice that the things that you do to promote your reputation are bad for your relationships. You know, most people don't notice these things. But that's not to say that they're unnoticeable.

TS: Even if you notice it, there's a gap between that and being able to do anything about it.

VT: Yeah, exactly. And you know, this is what therapists do. One of the main functions of cognitive behavior therapy is to give us a technique to change what we care about. If you care about things that are ruining your life, you try to retrain your paths of judgment and belief.

TS: One worry about relying too much on rational reflection is how prone we are to biases. Our deliberation can get distorted in many different ways. In your book you talk about positive illusions. And there's all the research in behavioral economics and social psychology, which shows how irrational we can be when deliberating about what's good for us.

VT: Once you've abandoned Kant and you see that reflective capacities are just a subset of all the psychological capacities we have that work together in various ways, then you start asking yourself: what are the heuristics, the strategies we can use to deal with that? These biases definitely are obstacles to self-knowledge. So one thing that's important is to pay attention to the feedback you get from other people, whether it is explicit or sort of tacit.[6] But that's not easy either, because a lot of other people you deal with in life have their own agendas. And their feedback isn't always trustworthy.

TS: Your perception of their feedback can be distorted too, right?

VT: Yeah. I suppose you can moderate these things a bit by paying for feedback from a professional, but often it's not that hard to figure out what people's agendas are. It's not like people are completely opaque. If you have a colleague who's in competition with you, and he says something mean to you, you can see he's being a jerk because he's feeling competitive. It's not easy, but I think it's doable.

5 Conflicting Values and Shifting Perspectives

TS: So what about when our values conflict? They often do conflict, even values that we've reflected upon and endorsed as good values. Independently, they might be good values to have but they push against each other. Does your account give us a way to prioritize values or at least a process for addressing these conflicts?

VT: Next question [laughs]. I've thought about that a lot but I don't know that I have anything great to say. On a more theoretical level, one big concern is that I don't want to defend the view that people are better off if they only have one value, or very few of them that don't conflict. That just seems implausible. It's something I've written about. For most people, it's better to have values that are not easy to put together than it is to have a simple set of values where there are never any conflicts.

TS: Because in the former case, you'll have a richer life, a more textured life?

VT: Yes. For most human beings, there are diminishing returns with the pursuit of consistency.

TS: Can you explain what you mean by that?

VT: You can increase value fulfillment of one value by decreasing the variety of values you have, but this is not likely (for most of us) to result in greater value fulfillment overall. Partly that's because value fulfillment isn't on an arithmetic scale. It's not like for each source of conflict you eliminate, you'll get one more unit of fulfillment. Here's an easy kind of example: a parent who quits his job, abandons all his hobbies, and ignores his relationship with his partner, is going to have lots of time to devote to being a great parent, but he's quite unlikely to be a good dad if he's bored (and possibly miserable and resentful).

But again, people are different. I think some people really are perfectly well off being workaholics, valuing work above everything. That is a good life for them.

TS: Do you mean that that's the best they can do or that it's actually good?

VT: It is actually a good life. I do talk about the importance of shifting your perspective in living your life between the things that you value. Oh, I hear a dog!

TS: That's my big basset mutt Charlie. A UPS truck must be somewhere in the neighborhood. His original function must have been to let out deafening barks whenever anyone is trying to deliver something. But let's talk about shifting perspectives. I thought the discussion you had in the book was really interesting, but I didn't connect it to value conflicts.

VT: Well, the kind of conflict that most people in our culture experience is a kind of work/family conflict. I think it's a part of wisdom to be able to shift your perspective, essentially shift your attention, which includes your emotional dispositions, from one activity that is constituted by a certain part of your values to a different kind of activity. So when you finish work on Friday and you're going camping with your family on the weekend, you're not thinking about work all the time. You're getting the good family stuff.

Now I don't think philosophers have any particular skill here. I'm never going to be able to tell people how to do that. Philosophical expertise doesn't help us. What I'm concerned to say is that this reflective capacity is part of wisdom, which is not at all Kantian and not particularly rational in the strict sense.

TS: So in what sense is it a reflective capacity then? Because I often find that I don't shift perspectives like that enough. I reflect on that, but still struggle to achieve that form of wisdom. And when I do start shifting attention in that good way, it doesn't seem to be a result of reflection. More often it's something intangible, maybe like flow or something …

VT: Yeah, that might have been careless. What I want to say is that it's part of being wise. I should probably restrict 'reflective capacity' to the things where you're actually reflecting. But I do want to say that it's part of wisdom.

TS: So that's one example of shifting perspectives. There was another interesting example in your book. It's from a novel about a woman in Congo.

VT: Yes, *The Poisonwood Bible*.

TS: In that example the shift in perspective is different—it's a question of how you handle misfortune. You talk about this character Leah whose younger sister died and on the same day that there was some massive upheaval or revolution in Congo. And she spends the anniversary of that day grieving for her sister. And Leah has another sister who used to get very upset over trivial things, like spilling something on her dress. And Leah thinks: "that's probably how people see me. I'm mourning my sister on this day when all of this horrible stuff happened to Congo." You use this example to talk about all the different perspectives you can take toward misfortune. It's associated with all the times we think: "you need to have perspective," or "put X in perspective."

VT: Exactly, yeah. What I was worried about is the idea that it's virtuous to have this kind of perspective, as you just put it, to have your reactions be in line with your views about what actually matters. If you follow that line of thinking far enough, you could believe there's a ranking of how much things matter. And you should never be as aggrieved by a thing that matters at number 10 as you are about number 8. My concern was to forestall a conclusion that Leah shouldn't feel sad about her sister's death because worse things have happened.

TS: You wanted to rule that out.

VT: I wanted to rule that out. And on the flip side, I also think it's true that being completely overwhelmed and overwrought by the fact that you have a hole in your dress, that's genuinely lacking perspective. And there's a sense in which the person who thinks that way is lacking some virtue.

TS: So what's the wise way of dealing with this issue? Because we can tell ourselves to put things in perspective, and sometimes that helps and sometimes it doesn't. You know, if you're on the job market, it's probably all you think about, all you care about, the only thing that matters. Even though you know there are worse things, more important things, going on in the world than your job search. What's the wise way to handle something like that?

VT: So there's one question of whether it's effective and then there's a different question about which perspective is appropriate at what time. I think for people who are on the job market, it actually would be appropriate for them to think, 'my child could have cancer, or I could be living in a genocidal country.' Those things are much worse than having trouble on the job market. But when you're a young person and you're that stressed, those techniques are likely not to be effective.

I think we don't rank these things in a fine-grained way, so that having a loved one die, for example, just maxes it out. And you're allowed to be sad, and you're allowed to grieve appropriately. And an anniversary of a death is an appropriate time to grieve somebody that you've lost. There is a utilitarian sense in which a million people dying is worse than one person dying, but in terms of what matters to you, your sister or family member's death is at the top of that scale.

TS: Some might worry that we're just going with our gut feelings about what's appropriate. People like Singer, for example.[7] What if the little sister with the hole in her dress feels the same way? I know there's something fishy about this question, but how are we supposed to know that the little sister has lost perspective whereas Leah hasn't?

VT: Optimistically you could think if you were to get the sister in a calm, cool moment she would see that people dying is worse than having a hole in your dress. If she's the kind of person who can never come to see that, well then you're stuck. But I think a normal human being in that situation who's freaking out over something trivial, usually they can recognize that they're freaking out over something trivial. They may not be able to do it at the time, but as soon as they aren't freaking out they'll acknowledge that it isn't that important.

TS: And they'll feel embarrassed about their behavior.

VT: Right. You can try and train yourself so that in the future you won't react like that, but then the question becomes: what about the person who just can't see it, and who thinks their little concerns are more important than other people dying? If you're a Humean and you think there are neither rational principles that prescribe sets of values to us, nor are there values woven in the fabric of the universe, nor is there a God to punish us if we get it wrong, all you can say is that those people have lost a considerable motive to virtue, as Hume says about the knave.[8]

TS: There's nothing more we can do to convince him.

VT: I think that's a big problem with moral philosophy—wanting the fool, or the sensible knave, to suffer.

TS: I interviewed Simon Blackburn recently, and he quoted Bernard Williams saying that philosophers are always looking for "that argument that will stop them in their tracks as they come to take you away." That's such a great line.

VT: Exactly, yeah. A point that I often make in my writing is that we don't have the argument that stops people in their tracks. But people think it's so much worse not to have that than it really is.

TS: I couldn't agree more.

VT: Because we're related to each other in all of these important ways. If you're the kind of person who has a set of values that are totally peculiar and alien, so that no one else can understand—you hear their criticisms and they bounce off your head like it's nothing—well, you've got to be pretty weird.

TS: It's the exception, not the rule.

VT: Yes.

6   Do We Reflect Enough?

TS: How common do you think that serious reflection about this topic is? I talk to my students and I don't get the sense that they put that much thought into questions about the good life. I'm not sure they ask themselves: what kind of life do I want to lead, what will be the most fulfilling path for me? Their goals and ends are more localized, they're focused on their careers. And that's a shame. But then I was talking to my wife this morning, and we realized that we don't spend much time thinking about those things either. We don't spend much time reflecting about our values, and how we can more effectively realize them.

So how common do you think it is to do this kind of reflection, not for a philosopher working on this question, but for the ordinary run of humanity?

VT: Well, first of all, I don't think it's very common for philosophers working on this issue either.

TS: Right.

VT: Really, you get caught up in maybe chairing your department, publishing, walking the dogs, trying to make dinner, visiting your parents.

TS: The more immediate, pressing things.

VT: Yeah. So I don't think it's all that common, and that's not necessarily bad. But there are things that can happen in your life where it would be good to have cultivated some habit of thinking about what you value. You lose your job and you're confronted with the possibility of having to change careers. Your spouse dies. Something happens to the health of someone you love—any crisis where you have to decide whether to do something. In those cases, I believe people are better off if they've had some kind of conversation with themselves about what matters in life.

What I definitely don't believe is that it's the purview of academics to be good at this kind of thinking. I think academics are some of the most self-deceived, personally unreflective bunch of people! Myself included.

TS: Yeah, that's very true. It's the old Kissinger quote: because the stakes are so small.[9] But since we can notice this about ourselves, would it be valuable to try to integrate this kind of thinking into our lives a little more? Not obsessively, not pathologically. But it would be good for me to have conversations with myself, not just in these crisis moments, but periodically.

VT: Yeah, and that's what I meant about having a habit to rely on. If you've done it when you weren't in crisis, then you have some substance there to rely on. I wonder about college students. On the one hand I think they're too young. Of course their concerns are going to be local, and nothing bad has happened to most of them. Many of them haven't had to think about this stuff, and that's sort of as it should be. But then on the other hand, they are starting their adult lives. I'm changing my introduction to ethics class in the fall and we are going to talk about happiness, the good life. And then I might get them to do some journaling or reflection narratives about what they think a good life is.

TS: That sounds like a great idea. You're right that in college, at that age, it's just natural to be unreflective. But it may be a little worse now than it used to be, probably because of the economy. Most of my students have jobs and sometimes families to take care of—it's hard to worry about the more abstract or long-term goals.

VT: I have several colleagues, some in psychology, one in business school at Michigan, who do these kinds of narrative reflection writing in their classes and they think it's great for their students. Interestingly, and a propos of the kind of reflection you're asking about, I've recently been participating in a group of corporate leaders, business school professors, social scientists, and philosophers (called the Society for Progress, believe it or not) that has really given me some optimism about business people. There's a lot of reflection among at least some business leaders about what really matters in life and how business can contribute positively.

7 The Wisdom of Humility

TS: I've asked this question of a lot of the people in this book: How much has your research on this topic affected your life? You work on this big question, you study wisdom. Do you feel that this has made you wiser? Or if it hasn't made you wiser, has it affected your life in tangible ways?

VT: Maybe the most tangible things have come from reading all of that work on unreflective processing, the literature on biases, and how reflecting on your reasons for things can make your choices worse. That had quite an effect on me. But I think the major effect has been that I've become more forgiving of other people, and of myself. When you think about how much of what we do is not under our control—you know, you can have this naive picture which maybe a lot of philosophers still have: "I do things for reasons that I endorse and so almost all of my actions have that kind of form" ...

TS: Reason as the charioteer ...

VT: Yes, and when you start really reflecting about what all the other forces are, it makes you a lot less certain that you understand why you do what you do, and why other people are doing what they're doing. And this makes you more forgiving if what they do hurts your feelings. It also makes me a lot more humble when I think about what's good for other people. Maybe because I'm an oldest sister, but I have a certain reputation in my family for being a little bit bossy. Some of this research has made me think that people are really complicated. There is so much going on that we should always be very cautious when we make judgments about what would be good for somebody to do.

TS: Do you think that's part of living a good life, to recognize that you're not an expert about other people's intentions? You're not an expert about what's good for them and what's the right thing to do for them?

VT: I do think that's part of living a good life because I think it's an important component of being a good friend.

TS: So it sounds like your work made you more laid-back about other people and yourself.

VT: Yeah, yeah, I guess that's right.

TS: Your writing has that kind of laid-back quality to it, in a good way.

VT: Really? Thanks! I don't know if this is correlated with being more empirical and being more interdisciplinary, but it's really important to me that what I write is not only accessible to philosophers.

TS: It's so important. I wish more philosophers agreed with you. I had this troubling thought recently that novelists and now filmmakers have shed more light on living good lives than philosophers have. Do you agree with that? If so, why would that be?

VT: That's very interesting. I haven't thought about it though so I don't really have an answer. I've been wondering more whether psychologists are shedding more light on these questions with the positive psychology kind of research that they've been doing. Do you have an example of a kind of film or novel?

TS: Maybe it's not fair to invoke Tolstoy because he's such a philosophical novelist but you can learn so much about life, about struggles, about how to conquer them, how to handle not conquering them, just from reading Tolstoy.

VT: It's true that I'm always using literary examples from novels.

TS: Right, I noticed that in your book. But OK, here's an example from a film. I was reading a lot of philosophy before I got engaged, but the thing that made me realize I was ready to get married, that I wanted to get married, was seeing this series of movies by François Truffaut: *Stolen Kisses* and *Bed and Board*. Those two movies made me understand that being married could be fun, even for young people. Honestly, I saw them and about a week later I decided to propose. There was a direct causal link. I would have proposed eventually anyway, but those movies pushed me over the edge at that point. No theories about marriage, no arguments, no psychological research either—nothing could have made it as salient to me as seeing that movie.

VT: It's not true that I never get it from philosophy. I've had that experience reading Williams where I just think "*Yes!*" But it's true that you don't often get that feeling with philosophy.

TS: I get that from Williams, too. But it's usually because he's trashing some overly systematic or abstract approach to moral philosophy.

VT: Right! That's true. So, I'm just purely speculating, but part of what happens when you engage with literature is that you can see the value of something that you don't currently value—like your case of marriage. Or you can see that there's something you value and there's a way of doing it that wasn't on your radar. It's important that our values are so entwined with our emotional responses, because a film or a novel can engage you in a way that lets you feel it. And feeling is part of what it is to value something. So, the mere assent, the mere cognitive assent isn't really sufficient.

Notes

1 Simon Blackburn makes a similar point at the beginning of our interview in Chapter 10.
2 See my interview with Nancy Sherman (Chapter 5) for a more detailed discussion of Aristotelian ethics.
3 "Eudaemonia" is the Greek word most associated with Aristotelian ethics. It can be translated as "happiness," "flourishing," or "well-being."
4 This image comes from Plato's dialogue *Phaedrus*.
5 Hume believed that our values were ultimately grounded in our emotions, not reason. His famous quote "Reason is, and ought only to be the slave of the passions" from the *Treatise* captures this idea.
6 Nancy Sherman makes a similar point in Chapter 5. Aristotle believed that friendships were an important check on our values and attitudes.
7 See my interview with Peter Singer (Chapter 9). Singer is skeptical of using our feelings or intuitions as guides to what we ought to care about most.
8 I describe Hume's example of the sensible knave in the introduction to Chapter 10.
9 The quote that's commonly attributed to Henry Kissinger (but may have first come from Woodrow Wilson) is: "academic politics are so vicious precisely because the stakes are so small."

Questions for Discussion

1 Why does Tiberius reject the Aristotelian account of well-being? How does her example of Snoopy the Springer Spaniel illustrate her objection?
2 How does Tiberius define a value?
3 What role do values play in Tiberius' account of well-being?

4   In what ways does Tiberius think that values can be inappropriate? Why is this important for her account of well-being?

5   What makes a value like "cultivating friendships" coherent and stable, but a value like "beating everyone at triathlons" incoherent and unstable?

6   How much control does Tiberius think we have over our values and how to shape them?

7   Why does Tiberius think that just reducing the number of values you hold to make them consistent ultimately has diminishing returns? Why might this be a problem for her account? How does the idea of shifting perspectives help to address this problem?

8   How can literature, film, or art help us to understand our own values, the values others have, or values we might need as a community?

Suggested Readings

Tiberius, Valerie. "Well-Being: Psychological Research for Philosophers." *Philosophy Compass* 1(5) (Sept. 2006): 493–505.

——. *The Reflective Life: Living Wisely with our Limits*. Oxford: Oxford University Press, 2008.

——. "Constructivism and Wise Judgment." In *Constructivism in Practical Philosophy*, edited by James Lenman and Yonatan Shemmer. Oxford University Press, 2012, pp. 195–212.

——. "Cell Phones, iPods, and Subjective Wellbeing." In *The Good Life in a Technological Age*, P. Brey, A. Briggle, and E. Spence (eds.). Routledge, 2012, pp.181–90.

——. "Mostly Elephant, Ergo." Interview by Richard Marshall, *3:AM Magazine* (Oct. 8, 2012): www.3ammagazine.com/3am/mostly-elephant-ergo

——. "Recipes for a Good Life: Eudaimonism and the Contribution of Philosophy." In *The Best within Us: Positive Psychology Perspectives on Eudaimonic Functioning*, edited by Alan Waterman. Washington, DC: American Psychological Association, 2013, pp. 19–38.

Assorted Media and Podcast Pairings

Tiberius, Valerie. "Episode 77: Valerie Tiberius: Wisdom and Well-Being." Interview by Luke Muehlhauser, *Common Sense Atheism* (Nov. 7, 2010): http://commonsenseatheism.com/?p=10552

——. "Simon Keller and Valerie Tiberius." Interview at *Philosophy TV* (31 Oct., 2010): www.philostv.com/simon-keller-and-valerie-tiberius

Very Bad Wizards, Episode 78 "Good Philosophy, Better Lives (With Valerie Tiberius)" http://verybadwizards.com/episodes/78

4 Susan Wolf

Meaning and Objectivity

Imagine that you've made a promise to your friend Isabella, but then the day comes and you back out. Now think of two different scenarios for why you didn't keep your promise. In one scenario, you're tired, hungover, and you just want to close the curtains and watch five straight hours of Law and Order SVU. *In the other, you bail because your favorite filmmaker is coming to a local arthouse movie theater for a special screening, followed by a Q&A. You used to work at this theater, and the manager can get you into the private reception afterwards. How should we (and Isabella) evaluate your behavior in these scenarios?*

In both cases, it's clear that you owe her an apology and that you should try to make it up to her in the very near future. But the first scenario seems a lot worse, doesn't it? Isabella would likely be a lot less angry in the second case, and depending on the promise, she might not hold it against you at all. What accounts for these different reactions?

Philosophers often frame cases like these as conflicts between morality and self-interest. But that won't explain the difference here. Your reasons for backing out in the second scenario seem more legitimate, but it's hard to call "I might be able to meet Martin Scorsese" a moral reason. So how can we explain the different responses? In her recent book, Susan Wolf offers a compelling answer. According to Wolf, we react more leniently to the second case because the activity in question is meaningful, whereas the first is not. Watching Law and Order *may be a good way to get through a hangover, but it's not a meaningful way to spend your time. But if you're a film student, or even just a film lover, the chance to meet your favorite director, while not moral, is definitely meaningful.[1]*

Wolf argues that the simple framework dividing human behavior into selfish and moral actions ignores the important dimension of meaning. Her new book, Meaning in Life and Why It Matters *offers an analysis of this dimension. What makes an activity or a life meaningful? Is meaning ultimately subjective? Can we be wrong about finding something meaningful? Can doing Sudokus be meaningful? Wolf discusses all these questions in her book, and we talk about them in the interview.*

If we had the time, we could have talked about plenty more. For over 30 years, Wolf has been writing on the deepest topics and questions that philosophy has to offer: freedom, responsibility, blame, virtue, personal identity, and love to name just a few. She is also the best philosophical writer that I know: clear, elegant, rigorous without being fussy or technical. She has an uncanny talent for getting readers to question their deepest convictions. Her work has caused me to change my mind on several occasions, and it happened at least once in our conversation. Wolf is the Edna J. Koury Distinguished Professor of Philosophy at the University of North Carolina. I interviewed her in her office at UNC.

December 2014

1 The Role of Theory in Moral Philosophy

TAMLER SOMMERS: Before we talk about your new book, let's talk briefly about your famous and wonderful paper "Moral Saints."[2] You introduce this notion of a moral saint, who always does the morally right thing. You point out that this ideal would leave no room for us to develop our characters in interesting ways, and is therefore not an ideal we ought to strive for. At the end of that article, you write that your aim isn't to criticize moral theories like utilitarianism or Kantianism. Rather, it is to put moral theories like them in their place. Can you explain what you mean by that?

SUSAN WOLF: Well, most simply I was just pointing out that the question 'What's the morally right thing to do' or even 'what's the morally right way to live' isn't the last question for practical reason. Because even if we can identify an answer to what's morally right, there is still the question of how much moral rightness or goodness (depending on your favorite way of thinking about morality) should weigh into who I am and what I should do.

TS: And since we have this further question, we'll look for a way to answer it. You write that the philosophical temperament will naturally look for some kind of metatheory that will tell us 'OK, here is where you work on being a great cook or tennis player, and here is where you act morally.' Philosophers especially are going to want a set of principles that can determine when to be moral and when to develop their character and abilities.

SW: Right.

TS: But you say you're pessimistic about the existence of that kind of theory.

SW: Well, I wouldn't call it pessimistic in the sense that it makes me sad or I wish it were different. But I am doubtful, skeptical, that there is any kind of systematic answer to how much morality should count and how much other stuff should count. And that is related to the meaningfulness issue as well.

TS: Do you think moral philosophers place too much emphasis on moral theorizing in general?

sw: What I really want to say is that philosophers need to step back from the assumption that there will *be* a correct moral theory. But I think it's a worthy activity to figure out what a good moral theory would look like, and even ask whether there is a correct moral theory. Let's try and do the best we can inside of moral theory. That's an excellent way of thinking hard about ethics. But the idea that I'm going to come up with an answer—that seems highly unlikely to me. We have a desire for there to be a correct moral theory—we like systems, we like answers. It's part of a philosophical temperament, and it's not just philosophers. Many people in general have a hard time living with the idea that there's nothing more to say, we just have to use our judgment. So I'm not even against having that temperament. But, it does tend to make us push our views against what evidence and wisdom would suggest.

ts: Let me see if I get this, because it sounds a bit weird to say both "I think we should work on theories," and also "we shouldn't think that a theory will be correct." But on the other hand, maybe I do understand. I love film, I love movies, I'm a huge fan. Let's say I tried to come up with a theory about what makes a great film. I know from the start that there's no chance I'll come up with a successful systematic theory that will determine whether a film is great or not. But it would make me think harder about the different aspects of filmmaking and push me to question and sort through my assumptions. So the theorizing might help us delve deeper. Is that the idea?

sw: Good question. In the case of art, it seems to be a deep feature of that inquiry that you'll never get a theory that will be able to give necessary and sufficient conditions that predict or explain what makes a great work of art great.

ts: So it seems more obvious in the case of art?

sw: Well, not to everyone. But it does seem obvious to me. In the case of ethics I don't think it's quite as obvious. But maybe it is the same idea for why it's a good exercise to think hard about ethics. What I mainly want to say, and I don't see the relation to aesthetics here, is that if you don't believe there's a moral theory out there, then you might think that we should just go with our moral intuitions. We might say that this reasoning stuff, it's just philosophers playing games and rationalizing.

I don't agree with that. I do think reason has a lot to say about ethics. I don't mean pure reason, devising principles out of thin air. I just mean that reflecting as a responsible, intelligent, and perceptive human being can give you better conclusions about ethics than just going with your intuitions. So I do think there are ethical truths and that you get better as you think harder about them. In that respect I think theory is just kind of an extreme and rather particular way of thinking about how these truths will look. Now in the end, the theories are probably going to be false. But as an activity or an exercise of moral reflection, looking for moral theories, seeing what's right and wrong about them and how far you can get is very useful for giving us some insights.

TS: I get what you're saying. But having said that, I was kind of hoping you would say "Yes, absolutely philosophers are putting too much emphasis on theory!" Because moral theorizing has its downside too, right? The downside is that it can become a game: theory, counterexample, refining theory, new ridiculous experiment as a counterexample. And that can distract rather than inform how we should approach real-life moral problems.

SW: Well it depends. It depends on what kind of counterexamples we are talking about and what we are doing with them. The variations on 'trolleyology', or similarly arcane or science-fictional examples do really seem to have left real life behind. But there are also good thought experiment counterexamples, like George and the chemical biological warfare factory.[3]

TS: You're right, that's a great example. But that's a counterexample that Williams designs to criticize overly systematic and theoretical approaches to ethics, right? Whereas trolley problems are sometimes used to establish certain normative principles. I used to be a fan,[4] but trolley problems seem like they've gotten to a place where they're doing more harm than good to ethics—in spite of the good intentions. Sort of like Frankfurt cases for free will.[5]

SW: Yes, right, it is!

2   Understanding Meaningfulness

TS: Okay, let's transition into the new book. One way to look at the book is that it's an extension of "Moral Saints."

SW: Well, it's certainly continuous with it. When I wrote "Moral Saints," the idea of meaningfulness was nowhere in my psychology. It wasn't as if I saw this coming. But both my new book and "Moral Saints" show a kind of preoccupation with the idea that moral value is not the only value. And also that we shouldn't turn questions about value into a dichotomy between self-interest and morality. In that sense, they are clearly coming from the same sensibility.

TS: In "Moral Saints," you contrast two points of view, the moral and non-moral. Do you see the new book as a way of trying to bring them together? Can your conception of meaningfulness serve as a guide for how we should negotiate the terrain between the two points of view?

SW: My immediate answer is no. Do you see a way in which it could serve as that?

TS: I guess meaningfulness would be in some ways a conception that encompasses both the moral and the non-moral point of view and might even allow us (in a non-systematic way) to shed light on which point of view to take?

SW: Right, so there must be a problem with the book, I think, because Nomy Arpaly's commentary actually picks up on this too.[6] And I'm wondering whether your questions are coming from the same place. My claims are that meaningfulness is a dimension of the good life and that a lot of philosophy seems to not notice it. I offer an analysis of this dimension. But the idea that the analysis creates an independent point of view—that was not something that I meant to suggest. I don't think reasoning from the point of view of what would be most meaningful, for example, is a natural part of a person's everyday reasoning. In deciding what career to take, for example, 'is this a meaningful career' is an important question. But is it the *most* meaningful career? That's not something we ask ourselves.

TS: So take that example. Imagine someone is deciding whether they want to be a schoolteacher in an impoverished community, or they want to go into hedge funds. Many people might look at this as a battle of self-interest versus living a life where they're doing something for others. I know you want to resist that dichotomy. But maybe reflecting on which course of action is going to be the most meaningful—would I find meaning in hedge funds, or is it just for the paycheck?—could help me decide. Or could it?

SW: Anything's possible. But I'm certainly not defending the view that when there's a choice between X or Y, and X is more meaningful, then you should always do X.

TS: So it's not supposed to be a trump card or tie-breaker.

SW: No, I didn't mean to suggest that meaningfulness is now supposed to be our answer, to approach everything with the idea of what's going to be best from the point of view of making, or maintaining, my life as meaningful.

TS: Okay, let's get to the details of your analysis of meaningful activities and meaningful lives. I guess the label for it is the "fitting fulfillment" view. And the main point is that a meaningful life has to satisfy two different criteria, right?

SW: Suitably linked.

TS: Suitably linked, right. Can you talk about the first one, being fulfilled?

SW: OK. So, one aspect of a meaningful life is that you, the subject, finds yourself engaged, gripped, excited, caring deeply, about an activity or project or your relationships within it. That's what I'm talking about. Something that fulfills you.

TS: So what would be a paradigm example of satisfying this criterion, of leading a fulfilling life?

SW: Well it's doing something you love and doing in a certain way that you identify with. It's easier, actually, to start with the paradigm of the absence of it. The alienated housewife is one of my initial examples, because she feels alienated from what she spends most of her time doing. She thinks "I don't care about this, I don't love this, this isn't who my best self is. I don't get any sense of self-realization out of it." That's the opposite of being fulfilled by an activity.

TS: I was just reading this article this morning about Tom Brady. For him, being a quarterback is his life, it's what he devotes all his time and energy to, the thing he cares about most. His studies, training, diet, are all geared toward improving and maximizing his capacities. And he loves it and it's what defines him. He takes so much pride in excelling and feels shame on the (rare) occasions he fails. So, is that an example, just from the subjective point of view, of a perfect match between the person and his activity. Is this a paradigm case of someone meeting the fulfillment condition in your account of meaningfulness?

SW: Short answer, yes. Slightly longer answer, the two things in your description that clench the yes are that he loves it and that it is a source of great pride.

TS: And the other stuff is …?

SW: Well, the fact that all of your life is geared toward an activity isn't necessarily a guarantee that it's fulfilling. I love movies too, and there are several that tell the story of athletes whose lives are devoted to their sport but they don't love it. The opposite of the Tom Brady story. Maybe it's a tennis mom or a hockey dad who made them participate. There are various pressures. Same thing happens in medicine. Some people go into medical school who don't love it. But they might still have dedicated their entire life to succeeding at it. It informed everything they do but it's not fulfilling. That's like the alienated housewife, or the alienated swimmer.

TS: So just because you're good at an activity and it informs your life, it doesn't mean you're fulfilled.

SW: No. They commonly go together, but not always.

TS: OK, so I think almost everybody would agree that being fulfilled captures some part of our conception of meaningfulness. So let's move on to the second criterion, which is a lot more controversial: objectivity. On your view being fulfilled is not enough. It's not enough for us to find it meaningful. The activity also has to be, in some sense, objectively meaningful. Can you explain what you mean by this?

SW: It's actually easier to explain when you explain them together. The idea is that meaning does involve fulfillment but it also requires fulfillment by things that are worthy of the kind of interest you give to them.

TS: Worthy in what sense?

SW: The things that fulfill you—let them be activities—have to be valuable. So you're not wasting your time by engaging in them. You're doing something valuable or something that connects you to value in some positive, affirming way.

TS: You give a couple of examples, and this is probably another good one where it helps to start on a case where the criterion is *not* fulfilled. One example is the person who devotes their time to crossword puzzles or Sudokus. By the way, you seem to have a grudge against Sudokus. Is there a history?

SW: Yeah, I'm definitely down on Sudoku. I must have spent a year or so doing Sudokus. And you get better at them so you do harder ones and they take longer. Having done this for a significant amount of time, a point came when I thought "This is such a waste of time!" It's not even that satisfying to get it right. So the reason I am down on Sudoku is partly because I feel like I know from firsthand experience what it's like to really be gripped by doing them and therefore feel like I have a lot more authority than I would about some other things to say that this is a waste of time. I wasted my own time that way.

TS: I know the feeling. For me it was Candy Crush, which is worse.

SW: That is probably worse.

TS: It was awful, I'm not ready to talk about it. So then the idea for Sudokus is: "Well I know it's not objectively meaningful because I realize now it was a waste of time." But let's talk about your examples of other unworthy activities in which people are fulfilled and maybe never come around.

SW: A lot of the examples that I discuss are somewhat bizarre.

TS: So here's the one I want to ask you about. The case of Sisyphus fulfilled.[7] It's an example from Richard Taylor. Sisyphus is condemned to push this boulder up this hill and watch it fall down for all eternity. And it's just miserable and boring. But then someone injects him with a drug and all of a sudden he finds the activity to be the most thrilling, exciting, fulfilling experience of his life. And your point with this example is that even though the activity now feels fulfilling to Sisyphus, we wouldn't say that he's truly engaged in a meaningful activity.

SW: Right. We wouldn't say he's living a truly meaningful life.

TS: So here's my challenge. I agree with that judgment, but I think what drives the intuition is not anything about the activity but the fact that he was injected with a drug. Once he's on the drug, he's not really Sisyphus anymore. He's a lobotomized Sisyphus, he's Jack Nicholson at the end of *One Flew over the Cuckoo's Nest*. So my intuition is not that his *life* isn't meaningful, it's more that it's not *his* life anymore. Because we know that the "real" Sisyphus wouldn't be fulfilled in that activity.

Just to press that point, imagine if Sisyphus is more along the lines of how Camus portrays him. No drug, but at some point he says, "Okay look this is my life right now. I'm going to try and make the very most out of this. I'm going to be constantly aware of how that boulder feels, take in every aspect of the mountain, pay attention to every sensation, every muscle, when I'm pushing it up, and how it feels when I get to the top. And then as the boulder rolls back down, I'll enjoy the rest and the view all around me as I walk down after it." Now I no longer have the intuition that it's a meaningless activity.

SW: You're totally right, I agree completely. But I don't take that as a challenge—I take that as the truth. It shows that the important thing is not the activity you're doing, but how you relate to it—that's what makes it meaningful or not.

TS: But isn't how you relate to the activity something better captured by the subjective rather than the objective criterion?

SW: Oh, no, I don't think so at all. Okay, so here's where we have to work this out. As an aside, there is this wonderful article by Joel Feinberg in his book *Freedom and Fulfillment* in which he talks about a variation of Sisyphus who juggled the boulder.[8] He can't keep it up at the top but he finds ways to *make* it a challenge. He makes challenges for himself in connection with it. It's a variation on the kind of thing you're thinking about.

TS: Like what an only child does to entertain himself.

SW: Yes, right! If all goes well. Yes, if he's raised properly. It's a great example, Feinberg's case, a great variation. Now, the issue is, what did we learn? What have we discovered? I suggested, and you agreed, that it's not the activity itself but the way you relate to the activity. You interpreted that to mean, 'so it could be subjective after all! It's not objective.' And I think that's wrong.

TS: But Sisyphus found a subjective feeling of fulfillment.

SW: But he's found fulfillment by doing something worthwhile, which is facing his fate and responding in an intelligible and (to capture what Camus was saying) a kind of courageous way. So, it was an exercise of some kind of intellectual or human virtue in his approach. Here is this guy who is fated to do these horrible things, and yet he finds a way to make it not a waste of time.

TS: So that's where the objectivity comes in—in the virtues he displayed …

SW: Well, in *this case*, yes. So that's the thing—objective value is such a broad category. It includes products—he created a beautiful temple—or just the realization of virtue or deep achievement of wisdom, and many other things as well.

TS: I want to make sure I understand this. There are two different ways that you could describe the Sisyphus case. The first is that an authentic, genuine Sisyphus (not drugged, lobotomized Sisyphus) has found fulfillment in his activity and this is still part of the subjective fulfillment criterion. It doesn't bleed into the objective criterion because we're only concerned with the question of whether Sisyphus—*real* Sisyphus—feels a deep sense of fulfillment. But you reject that description. You agree that real Sisyphus is fulfilled, but what makes his activity truly meaningful is the virtuous way he faced his circumstances. Without that, his life would not be meaningful in this more objective sense.

SW: Yes, that's right.

3   Cults, Impartial Observers, and Daughters Watching *Jessie*

SW: Here's another example of how someone might feel fulfilled but not lead a truly meaningful life. This is a difficult case. At some point in the book, I talk about people who are in some way deluded or deeply mistaken about the objective nature of what they're doing. Someone who is in a cult, for example, and thinks they are dealing with a supreme leader. She devotes her life to the leader but in fact he's a scam artist, right? If she never learns the truth or is never disillusioned, she might spend her whole life believing this is a really meaningful way to spend her time—to make the leader more powerful, to protect him from his enemies. But in fact, she is not creating value at all.

Now, you might think it's not totally meaningless. I mean, there are a lot of aspects to deal with in this case. But it's certainly not a paradigm of a meaningful life, to be in that situation. And it's another case in which, yes, there is intellectual activity going on. It's not a lobotomized person at all, just a deluded person. And it's just not right to say this is as meaningful as life would get.

TS: This seems like a big reason that you want to hold onto the objectivity criterion. You want to retain this notion that people can be mistaken about how meaningful their activity is, right? If we have loved ones who are doing something that they find meaningful, we might have a legitimate reason to want them to do something else.

SW: Yes we can say that, right. And about ourselves—we can worry about our own activities and ask, "I know I love doing this, but is it really meaningful?"

TS: Okay, just to press a similar challenge as before, couldn't you also capture entirely this idea without appealing to anything objective? For example, my daughter Eliza—I've raised her to watch great movies …

SW: I did the same!

TS: It's so important. She's been watching classic films, screwball comedies, noir movies, since she was 5 or 6. And great TV shows. *Arrested Development, The Simpsons, Fawlty Towers, Louie,* we even started watching *The Americans* but realized that wasn't appropriate. Too much sex for a 10-year-old. But Eliza also has friends. She has friends and they watch these horrific Disney Channel shows like *Jessie* and *Life with Boys.* I'll come home sometimes and she'll be watching *Jessie* with its ridiculous laugh-track—it seems like a betrayal of everything I've raised her to appreciate. And I say something to that effect and she always says: "Leave me alone! I like this show, *I* think it's good. Just because you don't like it doesn't mean that I can't!"

SW: Good for her!

TS: Yeah, I agree—she shouldn't take that crap from me. But anyway, when she watches those shows, I *know* she's not doing the most meaningful thing that she could be doing. Now I could be thinking about this in objective terms. Those shows are objectively bad. They're not worthy of her attention. Or I could think—and I do—that *she* would ultimately find it more fulfilling to watch *The Simpsons* or whatever.

So maybe when we say to people "that activity isn't meaningful," we're not making a judgment about its objective value, even if it might sound that way. Rather, we're saying that *they themselves* would be more fulfilled by a different activity. In other words, the claims about meaningfulness are still tied only to the agent and our prediction about what the agent will find most fulfilling.

SW: Right, so the challenge is that we have these intuitions about which lives or activities are more or less meaningful. My explanation is some of the time it's because they have more or less objective value. And yours is: no, your daughter's nature being what it is, she would actually have a better psychological relationship to a different object.

I have a few things to say about that challenge. Number one, empirically I find it dubious in many cases that she would be even more fulfilled, that there would be a psychologically better state of her qualitative experience if she did something else.

TS: Well it's sometimes true at least.

SW: Yes, that's right. Sometimes.

TS: But all I am trying to explain is the feeling that someone can be mistaken about the meaningfulness of their activity. I don't always have to be *right* that it's a mistake. Just like you won't always be right about an activity being objectively valuable.

SW: So you're thinking that if she just tried *Fawlty Towers*, she would like that more and it would be a better experience for her. And it follows that *if* you were convinced you had a false empirical belief, that she wouldn't be more fulfilled watching *Fawlty Towers*, then you would say: "OK, go ahead, watch *Jessie*."

TS: I guess that follows, right.

SW: Well ... I doubt that really. I don't think you would say that.

TS: Oh, good point! You're probably right. I'd still think it was a waste of time even if I thought that she found deep fulfillment watching *Jessie*. I'd still think she should be doing something more meaningful.

SW: Right, so if a person is just as fulfilled doing a patently absurd activity rather than something worthwhile, do we always want to say then, "OK , I guess it's a meaningful thing to do"? If you're hesitant to say yes, then ask yourself why. Isn't it because even if it were true that she's fulfilled, there's still something missing from it, namely that their time is spent doing this absurd thing.

TS: That seems like a natural way to describe it.

SW: And there's another thing, probably the more important point. I take it that a good account of meaningfulness should answer not only our intuitions about *which* activities are meaningful (and it can only answer it to a degree, not perfectly), it should also make sense of why people might care about meaningfulness. And why they care about it in a different way from the way they care about happiness. So, I offer an answer: because we care about connecting to our world in a way that would make our lives seem good from some point of view other than our own. Whether it's God or our next-door neighbor, or an imaginary viewer, we want to be able to be proud of ourselves. That's where pride came in with the Tom Brady story. The fact that "Oh, I feel even more interested in this TV show than that TV show" doesn't give you any basis for feeling proud of yourself. Unless you think, "This is a better show—I'm getting more out of it." Right? And then we're back to objective value.

TS: OK, I agree that when I question the value of my activity, I'm not only asking whether I find it personally fulfilling. I do want my activity to be valued by other people.

SW: Well, we want it to be the sort of thing that other people ought to value.

TS: But when you bring in this "what they ought to value"—and you mention at some point the "impartial observer"—

SW: What other people would "appropriately value" is probably the weaker, and better, thing to say.

TS: Yeah, so you write:

> By living in a way that is partly occupied and directed toward the preservation or promotion or creation of value that has its source outside of oneself, one does something that can be understood, admired, and appreciated from others' point of view including the imaginary point of view of an impartial, indifferent observer.
>
> (p. 28)

I agree with everything in that passage except the impartial and indifferent observer part. And that's what grounds the 'ought to value' or the 'appropriately value,' right? Now I was trying to think about this honestly. Your work does a great job of making people introspect.

SW: Yeah, good!

TS: I was thinking that if I'm writing a book or article, it's the people I respect and admire—I want *them* to value it. But I don't care at all about an impartial, indifferent observer. I don't think about that for a second. I don't say, "Hmm, I wonder whether an impartial and indifferent observer would find this meaningful ..."

SW: Right, who cares? Good. That was perhaps a misleading way of saying what I want to say, which is a few things. First, when you talked about the people you want the approval from, you talked about people you respect. By saying you respect them, you're already saying they have what you take to be good perspectives on value, right?

TS: Right.

SW: Here's the kind of case I had in mind here. You might have contempt for everybody around you with respect to a particular thing. You think: "they don't understand my painting." And so you don't want *their* approval. In fact, you might think that their approval means nothing, because they just approve of whatever the *New York Times* tells them to approve. What you want is for your painting to be *good.* That's the way you would normally put it. And if there isn't anybody around, perhaps if you're Van Gogh, who can tell you whether it's good, you have to go to the imaginary. If there were somebody with good taste I would want *them* to approve of it. So the impartial and indifferent is not so important, it's just a way of saying this is somebody you can respect.

TS: I see. So the challenge for somebody who wanted to do away with the objectivity criterion, then, is: how do you explain someone like Van Gogh? Nobody is appreciating his stuff, but he was devoted to it and it was meaningful anyway. Why? Because he thought he was doing something good. And it was good.

SW: Or, alternatively, there's the commentary by John Koethe about the riskiness of trying to be a great artist, poet, writer, and so forth. It's risky because you might not know whether it's good. You hope it's good and you think it's good. The fact that other people don't recognize it to be good isn't decisive for you. So, are you fulfilled by it? Fulfillment is probably the wrong word there because you're so uncertain of whether you're being a success. But, you have the right attitude toward it such that, if in fact it is good, then your life will have been meaningful. Fulfillment isn't all about success. It's about being gripped, or into something, being excited about it, tracking something that you regard as worthy.

TS: Something that you personally regard as worthy. And you might be wrong.

SW: And you might even know it's risky and therefore not be fulfilled in the ordinary language sense that involves a level of satisfaction.

TS: Writing can sometimes be like that. You have no idea if what you want to write is valuable or just totally worthless. And it's a bad subjective feeling too, staring at the screen, it's torture. In that sense, the meaningful activity doesn't have to meet the subjective fulfillment criterion, right?

SW: Well, some other people have pointed out something similar, Robert Adams in the commentary but some others too. Fulfillment is an imperfect word for what I am talking about because it seems to assume success in what you're aspiring to do. Whereas I'm more interested in success in the sense that I'm really engaged by the thing I am doing in a way that makes me think that what I'm valuing about it is correctly valued.

TS: For me, fulfillment doesn't entail that you're successful or that you even think you're going to be successful. It's a subjective experience of "I love doing it, I find it meaningful."

SW: The example Adams uses is the example of the guy who is trying to assassinate Hitler, and somebody who is engaged in a political movement and is not succeeding. And he's getting the feedback that it's unsuccessful, he's aware of it. The news comes out and it keeps getting worse rather than better. So to say he's fulfilled by that is to my ears funny.

TS: Right, because subjectively he'd feel frustrated, like it's all for nought. Well, we don't have to argue over how to correctly define fulfillment, but I do think it's one of the best words for capturing a sense of *eudaemonia*.[9] 'Fulfillment' and 'flourishing' are good ways of capturing this subjective feeling that can't be reduced to these other categories.

SW: I'm glad you like the word since it's the word I do use. And I agree that it captures all of those things. It is a subjective way (feeling has perhaps a little more content) of relating to what one is doing. Like flourishing, it's good as the paradigm of the best-case scenario. If your life is meaningful and going really well qua meaning, then you're feeling fulfilled. But it also seems like your life could be very meaningful but not going so well. You're engaged in projects of positive value. Yet they are projects that also make you very unhappy. Your loved one is dying, for example, or your candidate is losing. So it's still giving meaning to your life and subjectively it is giving meaning to your life. But fulfillment is not the right word.

TS: Like caring for a sick relative. It's a fairly miserable experience but still meets both criteria for meaningfulness.

SW: It might *not* be meaningful, by the way. It could go either way.

TS: Right. It's funny, I never thought I would question the fulfillment criterion for meaningfulness but a case like that makes me question it. Do you see fulfillment as necessary?

SW: When I wrote the book I did think there was a subjective condition that is a necessary element, but fulfillment might be the word that only captures the best-case scenario. But there's still something very important about people who are meaningfully caring for a sick relative. Their subjective attitude toward what they are doing is still essential.

TS: It's essential that they find it meaningful, even if they don't find it fulfilling.

SW: Yes, I guess the point is, the subjective experience of finding something meaningful can't be completely identified with being fulfilled by it.

TS: So the subjective condition is like a spectrum. The minimum is that you find it meaningful, even if it is very frustrating and not something you enjoy. And then the best case is *eudaemonia* or flourishing or flow.

SW: Right, exactly.

4 Objective or Intersubjective?

TS: When Jon Haidt talks about meaningfulness in his commentary, he emphasizes its intersubjective nature. He doesn't see it in terms of objective value, but rather intersubjective value. How far apart are you and Haidt on this issue?[10] Is your disagreement a substantive one, or are you offering two ways of describing essentially the same thing? From a practical perspective, does anything hang on which conception of meaning I embrace: yours or Haidt's?

SW: I don't know how to separate the philosophical from the practical here, but I think it's a pretty deep difference. I suppose the practical aspect might be this. Even if you get the confirmation and approval from your community, there's still some point in stepping back and saying, "Yeah but maybe we're *all* wrong."

A good example is analytic philosophy. Take some people in certain places, Oxford for example. Now some of my best friends teach at Oxford and there are many good philosophers who teach at Oxford. But their community is big enough for them to keep each other affirmed that what they are doing is worth doing. That's not enough. According to Haidt's view, that would be enough for meaning. I think that's a scary thing. A big cult would do the same thing. So there's that on the one side. On the other side, what about the lonely artist whose work everyone says is worthless? Should he give up? A very difficult question, I think.

TS: That's a tough one because I'm singing hallelujah when you talk about the Oxford people. You're right that they have a community and they endorse some of that really technical, abstract theorizing that honestly might be worthless. So the idea is: if they were convinced by your view rather than Haidt's, they might want to take a step outside of themselves and ask: "What are we all doing here? What is this all about?"

SW: Right, they would try and articulate the value of what they are doing. It might help.

TS: Couldn't they also widen their intersubjective circle a little bit? So now it's not just their immediate community, but people outside of it?

SW: The imaginary community of possible reasonable human beings!

TS: Well not quite that wide maybe, but outside of their immediate community. Widen it to the broader philosophical community that includes people like you, Blackburn, Bernard Williams who do question the value of some of that stuff.

SW: It may be, empirically, that we would get to the same place. But I think you're using that idea because you want to avoid this imaginary community. Because, with other philosophers, how do you know we're not idiots?

TS: It's funny because I'm about to talk to Simon Blackburn.[11] I could see him pressing this same kind of point.

SW: Actually, since you mention this, I say that my sense of objective is 'soft.' But what I mean is not that intersubjectivity would do. That would be one form (very soft). What I meant is I have no desire to be defending a kind of G. E. Moore[12] "values are part of the fabric of the universe" view. I'm not defending the view that there are values out there independent of human beings, or that there is some kind of metaphysical value space. A lot of people think objective value means that it's out there, it's mind independent and human nature independent. But I have no inclination to think any of that is true.

By objectively valuable, I just mean *really* valuable. My thinking it valuable doesn't make it so. But I also think that *our* intersubjective community thinking it, no matter how broad the actual empirical community is, doesn't make it so either. It might be evidence that there's something to it. But it's not confirmation.

TS: So would you say the same thing about other domains of evaluation? Take aesthetics …

SW: That's the same kind of value. The word objective is perhaps misleading in that it makes people think objective must mean something independent of us, but that's not how I mean it. I would like another word, something that just means *real value*! I don't think Blackburn has any reason to disagree with me about this.

TS: That makes me think that a "soft objectivist" and a "sophisticated subjectivist" might converge in terms of how you thought about these things. But maybe you have a more natural way of describing the idea, because we don't have to go into contortions to decide what community matters ...

SW: Haidt and I would have to sit down and talk a long time. But he does say some worrisome things, like that marching example. He gives an example from someone's memoirs about hive mentality and how marching with his fellow soldiers gave him a feeling of fulfillment. Well that's very scary. Jackboots. When you think of the Nazis marching you think: "yeah they were all personally fulfilled by marching to the Führer."

TS: But it wasn't meaningful.

SW: It was pretty horrifying. You would hope they would step back and say, "Why are we doing this?"

TS: Right. And that's another way that your views might make a practical impact. You write that "attention to the category of meaningfulness may help us to better understand our values and ourselves, and may enable us to better assess the role that some central interests and activities play in our lives."

If we have this category of meaningfulness, how is it going to help us better understand our values and ourselves?

SW: At least one way is negative, it will keep us from distorting the way we understand our values by trying to push it into the dichotomy of "it makes me happy" or "I'm doing something morally good." We can just leave it for what it is. I'm doing it because I love this person, I'm doing it for her, not for the world or for me—for her.

The same with philosophy. We're always challenged with the question "why is doing philosophy valuable?" And there are a couple of unsuccessful ways of justifying philosophy. One is to talk about how much good you're doing for the world. You're doing a little good, but let's be real, right? When you see people thinking "this is the way I can make the best contribution to the world" I think they should get over themselves.

TS: For me it's more that I would be homeless otherwise. I'm not capable of doing anything else for money.

SW: Right, right. Well there are lots of reasons why we do these things. But you could say—it's not the best thing I could be doing from an impersonal point of view, but it's a good thing that I'm doing. And it better be a good thing if it's going to count as a justification.

On the other hand you can say, "Look I just enjoy it and why isn't that enough?" Well, to spend your whole life doing something *just* because you enjoy it doesn't seem enough. But I think those are the alternatives most people will naturally flock to.

TS: Is this where you'd bring in Bernard Williams? His critique of utilitarianism is that it can require you to do things that shatter your integrity as a whole person. Our projects rarely maximize the world's happiness, but they can be central to our identity. You mention his critique when you say that utilitarianism can demand that we sacrifice the things that make life worth living in the first place. And then you say that your view about meaning allows us to see his critique in a different light. Can you explain how?

SW: I was thinking about people who find Williams' idea unacceptable because they think he's saying "so as long as you find something really important to you, this is who I am, this is my project," that would trump anything. Or then morality can't really touch it. And that seems to be totally open ended in terms of what gives meaning to your life. If you're a pederast or something, that might define you, but morality shouldn't have to cave just because this is the most important thing in a pederast's life. Now if meaning has an objective component too, then the idea that morality should, in some way, take note of whether the issue is a meaning-enhancing issue for someone or not, has different implications. It doesn't say that morality has to accept *anything* that means a lot to them. But morality should accept valuable things that mean a lot to them, things that give meaning to their lives.

TS: Morality should take into account that they are objectively worthy activities.

SW: Right, and the value might not be moral value, but we want to make room for people to live meaningful lives, understanding meaning the way I understand it.

TS: This is what Nomy Arpaly in her commentary was getting at: It sounds like your idea is "well you can live a life that you find valuable and ignore moral concerns … within reason." And then the other way too, "you can live a moral life, devoting most of your existence to morality … but within reason." Is the idea of meaning that this gives you these "within reason" endpoints?

SW: No, it isn't. So in this respect, Williams and I are in the same place fighting against the philosophical temperament to systematize. If there is a conflict between morality and what gives meaning to your life, there isn't a formula for saying which one should win, right?

TS: But what you said with the pederast case is, I guess.

SW: The point of the pederast case is that it doesn't give meaning to his life, he just thinks it does.

TS: Right … so we can no longer take it as an acceptable alternative to morality.

SW: My idea is that morality ought to be concerned with whether its dictates are compatible with a moral agent's living a meaningful life. But morality doesn't have to be concerned with whether it's compatible with a pederast being a pederast.

Now, I'm not saying that if the meaning of a person's life depends on X then morality can never trump it, that morality always has to step aside. That's not true even when the activity *is* meaningful in my sense. Sometimes you just do have to throw your manuscript over the side of the lifeboat. But I think ethics, and our moral intuitions, support the idea that we should give more leeway to people in their ability to pursue meaning-enhancing projects than we do in their leeway to pursue pleasure-enhancing, or happy-enhancing projects.

TS: Can you give an example?

SW: In some early papers I have a couple. Imagine that a professor has office hours and learns at the last minute that her philosophical heroine is in town to give a paper and that there would even be a place for her at dinner. Should she go even though she can't tell her students she won't be at office hours? I'm sympathetic to the idea she should go hear Iris Murdoch! It's a chance of a lifetime! Even though there isn't really a moral justification for that. It connects to one's identity as a philosopher and one's passion for philosophy in a certain way. Whereas if you compare it to, "Oh I just want to soak in a hot tub for an hour" which might more securely be giving you a lot of pleasure, you can't do that if you have office hours. Suck it up and go to your office! So it's not like this much for yourself and this much for morality. It's that morality should have a different response to what you do in the pursuit of maintaining your meaning-enhancing activities than what you do in response to pleasure or avoidance of pain.

TS: Great example. I think you're absolutely right. We feel like, in the Iris Murdoch case, the student would be more forgiving and we would be more forgiving from the outside. And from the inside, we might feel a lot less guilty ...

SW: Apology is owed either way.

TS: Right. But we look at those two kinds of cases differently. You're giving us this moral distinction between things you do for yourself that are meaningful and things you do for yourself that aren't meaningful, even though both are ultimately for yourself.

SW: That's right.

Notes

1 Wolf describes a similar case at the end of our interview.
2 *Journal of Philosophy* 79(8) (Aug. 1982): 419–39.
3 Wolf is referring to Williams' famous example (from the "against" section of *Utilitarianism: For and Against* co-authored with J. J. C Smart) of an antiwar chemist who is offered a job to manufacture chemical and biological weapons. The example aims to show that utilitarianism could alienate us from our moral feelings and our identity as integrated beings.
4 I talk about trolley problems with Josh Greene and Liane Young in Chapter 17.
5 Here we're referring to Harry Frankfurt's justly famous counterexample to the idea that we can only be morally responsible for an action if we could have acted otherwise (see "Alternate Possibilities and Moral Responsibility," *Journal of Philosophy* 66(23) (1969): 829–39). This case became a near obsession in the philosophical literature on free will. In my humble view, it has received enough attention and has now entered the "epicyclic engineering" phase, as Valerie Tiberius put it in Chapter 3.

6 Wolf's book features four excellent commentaries, including one by the Brown University philosopher Nomy Arpaly.

7 The philosopher Albert Camus famously used the case as an illustration for how to face up to life's absurdity.

8 Feinberg, Joel. *Freedom and Fulfillment: Philosophical Essays*. Princeton, NJ: Princeton University Press, 1992.

9 An ancient Greek term to describe a deep sense of happiness or well-being. See also Chapter 3 (Valerie Tiberius) and Chapter 5 (Nancy Sherman) for more discussion.

10 Haidt's commentary criticizes the objectivity criterion in Wolf's account. My interview with Haidt took place long before this, but we discuss some related matters about objectivity (see Chapter 12).

11 See Chapter 10. Blackburn and Wolf have offices at UNC just down the hall from one another. I interviewed them on the same day.

12 G. E. Moore was a philosopher who developed a "non-naturalist" form of moral intuitionism. According to Moore, properties like goodness were not reducible to natural properties and could only be discovered through the use of our intuitions. See http://plato.stanford.edu/entries/moore-moral, for a detailed account of his view.

Questions for Discussion

1   What does Wolf mean when she says that the question "what is the morally right thing to do?" isn't the last question for practical reason?

2   Despite her pessimism that we can discover fully correct moral theories, why does Wolf still think that ethical theorizing is important?

3   What are the fulfillment and objectivity criteria for meaningfulness in Wolf's account?

4   What do the different variations on the myth of Sisyphus by Camus, Taylor, and Feinberg show about meaning in life? How does Wolf analyze Sisyphus?

5   How can people—members of a cult, insulated academics, Nazi soldiers— be wrong about whether they're doing something meaningful?

6   What is the benefit of having both a subjective and objective component to understanding meaning in life?

7   How does Wolf's example of the professor missing office hours illustrate the practical importance of the dimension of meaning?

Suggested readings

The Variety of Values: Essays on Morality, Meaning, and Love. New York: Oxford University Press, 2015.

"Meaningfulness: A Third Dimension of the Good Life." *Foundations of Science*. Published online, December 2014.

"Good-for-nothings." 2010 American Philosophical Association Presidential Address, 107th Annual Eastern Division Meeting, Boston (29 Dec., 2010): http://philpapers. org/archive/WOLG.pdf

Meaning in Life and Why It Matters. Princeton, NJ: Princeton University Press, 2010.

"Moral Obligations and Social Commands." New York University's Graduate School of Arts and Sciences, 8th Annual Lewis Burke Frumkes Lecture. YouTube (30 Nov., 2009): https://youtu.be/e3-1CGZdyKc

"Moral Saints." *Journal of Philosophy* 79(8) (Aug. 1982): 419–39.

Podcast Pairings and Other Media

"Susan Wolf on Meaning in Life." Interview by David Edmonds and Nigel Warburton. Philosophy Bites (July 4, 2010): http://philosophybites.com/2010/07/susan-wolf-on-meaning-in-life.html

Very Bad Wizards Episode 61: "Putting a Little Meaning in Your Life" http://verybadwizards.com/episodes/61

Very Bad Wizards Episode 53: "Moral Heroes and Drunk Utilitarians" http://verybadwizards.com/episodes/56

5   Nancy Sherman
Navigating Our Moral Worlds

Al Swearengen, the character from the criminally under-watched HBO series Deadwood[1] *performs some terrible actions over the course of the show. In the pilot alone, he swindles a New Yorker into buying a "pinched out" plot of land for gold prospecting (the show is set in 1870 South Dakota) and then has his co-conspirator killed to ensure his silence. By the fifth episode, Swearengen has been personally responsible for the deaths of five people, selling their corpses to a local Chinese merchant to serve as food for his hogs. Oh, and did I mention that he runs the town brothel?*

You might think that Al Swearengen is the archetypical western villain, the evil guy who twirls his moustache while exploiting a helpless town for personal gain. Al does have a moustache, it's true, but the similarities end there. In fact, Al is not a villain but rather a complex hero who the viewers grow to love and admire as the series progresses. And not just the viewers: Al inspires loyalty and devotion among many of the show's characters, including his prostitutes, the town doctor, and the disabled woman who cleans his saloon and suffers a constant stream of Al's foul-mouthed insults.

The two dominant theories in contemporary ethics—consequentialism and deontology— have a hard time making sense of our attitudes to people like Al Swearengen. Swearengen has no interest in acting for the greater good of the world. His concerns are far more local and community-focused. Nor does he follow any recognizable moral law. He lies, steals, kills, breaks promises, and fits more curse words in a sentence than some people do in a lifetime. Nevertheless, we don't judge him to be a bad person. Why is that? To answer that question, we have to go back to Aristotle, to a more ancient approach to ethics that emphasizes character and virtues.

Swearengen has plenty of virtues. He's courageous, tough, loyal, well spoken, intelligent and very funny. He has an uncanny sense of the emotional, personal, and ethical stakes in novel situations. And he's a charismatic leader, he's able to get a diverse group of characters—merchants, prostitutes, preachers, outlaws, a former sheriff—to rally in defense of their town against external threats. Aristotle's works offer great insight on the value of these character traits. His approach allows us to understand complex moral cases like this in a way that modern act-based theories cannot.

None of this would come as a surprise to Nancy Sherman, a distinguished university professor and Professor of Philosophy at Georgetown University. For over 30 years, Sherman has been studying and writing about Aristotle's ethics; indeed, she is one of a handful of philosophers who are responsible for the revival of interest in virtue-based approaches. Much of Sherman's work focuses on the role of emotions in Aristotelian accounts. According to Sherman, Aristotle has a keen appreciation for the epistemic value of emotions. He takes them seriously as "forms of moral intelligence." Aristotle believed, and Sherman agrees, that our emotions help us identify the ethically relevant features of particular situations. Consequently, we need our emotions in order to successfully navigate our moral world.

Sherman's work extends well beyond Aristotelian ethics. The daughter of a World War II veteran, Sherman has long sought to better understand the military experience—the emotional and moral challenges that our service members face at war and at home. This interest, and an appointment at the US Naval Academy in the 1990s, led her to study the works of the ancient Stoics. The Stoics, and Epictetus in particular, had acquired a legendary status among officers and midshipmen because of their importance to James Stockdale in surviving as a POW in Vietnam. Sherman appreciates the value of Stoic philosophy for soldiers, but also warns against its dangers.

In her three recent books Afterwar, The Untold War, *and* Stoic Warriors, *Sherman has written directly about the military experience and how ancient approaches to ethics can help us better understand it. These books have garnered praise in both academic circles and the popular press. (David Brooks discussed* Afterwar *in a 2015 New York Times column.)[2] In October 2005, she visited Guantánamo Bay Detention Center as part of an independent observer team assessing the medical and mental health care of detainees. Though our central topic was Aristotle and the Stoics, we began by discussing this visit.*

June 2015

1 The Role of Psychologists at GITMO

TAMLER SOMMERS: Back in 2005 you visited Guantánamo Bay. You were invited as an observer, right? In what capacity?

NANCY SHERMAN: I was brought on board as someone who had done military ethics, so as a military ethicist. I had served at the Naval Academy from 1995 to 1999 or so as Inaugural Distinguished Chair in Ethics. So I was called in in that capacity.

TS: Can you give a brief description of what you witnessed while you were there?

NS: I was with quite a lot of high-level folks—Army Surgeon General, the heads of the American Psychiatric Association, the American Psychological Association. So we all expected a fairly open and informative visit. But it was very cocooned. I've described it in some detail in some of the short pieces I wrote upon returning. We got PowerPoint briefings for a good few hours. And then we were taken to the detention medical area. We could see a few detainees at a distance, behind barbed wire, but we didn't see detainees up close.

TS: In some of those pieces, you were very critical of the role that psychologists and psychiatrists were playing at GITMO. Can you explain why?

NS: I was critical of the role of the psychologists, in particular, because they were involved heavily in the design of interrogation programs that included EIT [enhanced interrogation techniques]—which is code for forms of torture. The APA (psychological) was very slow in distancing itself from those practices. And now with the Hoffman report on the APA that broke in the *New York Times* a few weeks ago, we know for certain that the APA leadership was colluding with the CIA and the Department of Defense in the writing of their ethics guidelines—which they put out in response to charges of involvement in torture and inhumane and degrading treatment of detainees.

TS: That was one of my questions actually. Why has this controversy about the APA just come out given that you were writing these critical reports over 10 years ago?

NS: Many have been critical of the APA for a long time, including the involvement of two contractors in "reverse engineering" the techniques of the SERE program, Survive, Evade, Resist, Escape—originally used to train our Special Forces folks should they be captured and subjected to torture. We were now using these techniques (including waterboarding and sleep deprivation) on the detainees.[3] But the details of the collusion with the CIA and DOD were not previously known until James Risen of the *New York Times* broke the story, long brewing, that the APA hired an independent legal group to lead an investigation in a neutral way. The story is about their 542-page report.[4]

TS: In one essay, you draw a careful analogy with what was happening at GITMO and certain practices in Nazi Germany.[5] Can you elaborate on the analogy?

NS: At the time, I carefully reread Robert Jay Lifton's *The Nazi Doctors* because I was interested in the use of medical professionals in evil, and because of the 50th anniversary of the Nuremberg Trials. One couldn't help but think about the comparisons. It was critical in Nazi Germany to diffuse a sense of personal responsibility by having elaborate bureaucratic divisions of labor that insulated the agents of evil from the evil. Also, there were the euphemisms, not unlike "enhanced interrogation" that were used routinely as a way to "medicalize" horrible practices. Again, this insulated doctors and medical researchers from what they were doing.

TS: Is there a legitimate or morally permissible role, in your view, that psychologists could play, given the political reality of GITMO?

NS: I think psychiatrists and psychologists are now reasonably engaged as experts who are called in by defense and prosecution teams. I know some who serve admirably in those roles. The person I have in mind advises for the defense on what the detainee has suffered: his state of mind, his emotional and pathological conditions. But with regard to the interrogation programs, when there is a torture campaign in place—with the highest authorities in the land putting it in place and keeping it in place, as happened under the Bush torture campaign—it's hard to see how psychologists won't be subject to those pressures "to take the gloves off." And, as we now know, the ethics guidelines put out by the APA in 2005 put more emphasis on the important contribution psychologists can make toward national security than on the tough ethical challenges they would face in the interrogations.

I should add that General Petraeus wrote a COIN [counterinsurgency] manual around the same time. He took time off to write it. The ethics section warns soldiers about the temptations they'll face to harm those they capture far more than APA leadership warned their practitioner psychologists. That says something!

2   The Mark of Educated People

TS: Let's turn to your research on the ancient philosophers. You began your career study studying Aristotelian ethics. What drew you to Aristotle?

NS: It struck me that he was asking interesting big questions like "Is this a life worth leading? Is it a fulfilling life? Is there a sense of thriving in that life?" He wasn't simply asking about the rightness or wrongness of a discrete action, and what kind of criteria we should use to measure that.

TS: That's the big difference between Aristotle and contemporary ethicists, such as Kantians and the utilitarians: the level of analysis. The focus on actions, Aristotle focused on lives and character.

NS: Yes, the focus is on a good life and a good character, both moral and intellectual. And it's a broader interpretation of 'moral' too. It's not only moral as defined by Kant, which involves respect for persons. For Aristotle, morality or goodness can also include your wit, how you relate to others socially, and even certain aesthetic features.

TS: A central feature of modern ethics is the strong emphasis on impartiality. You write that this concern with impartiality isn't found in Aristotle.

NS: Well, I think there's a difference between utilitarianism and Kant on this. Kantianism may be impartial but it's not impersonal. I always think of Kant as first personal, or better, second personal, philosophy, because it has to do with eye-to-eye morality. Respect for persons is the way we stand in relation to others.

TS: But even for Kant, you're supposed to respect persons because they're rational agents, not because they're your friends or your family or part of a specific community. That's more what I mean by partiality.

NS: Right, with Kant, you're respecting persons in virtue of the reason they share with all persons. For Aristotle, ethics is deeply rooted in actual relationships that often have some history. Aristotle is rooted in the *polis* and interactions that are small in scale compared to the cosmopolitanism of Kant and the Stoics. Aristotle didn't think much at all about a cosmopolitan sensibility, this idea of being a citizen of the universe. That comes later. For Aristotle, what matters is being a citizen in almost a face-to-face community. And as a result, his philosophy tends to praise benevolent deeds not to strangers, not in far-flung altruistic actions, but within friendships, for example. His paradigm case is friendships with others who are persons of good character. And you can't have too many friendships because each would get "watery," (diluted), if you did. That's literally his word, in the *Politics*. He even criticizes Plato for having watery kinds of friendships that would, on Plato's view, count as replacements for the family. That won't work, Aristotle says. So that's an example of his keen focus on interpersonal relations. And he focuses on the kinds of virtues you would have to develop in order to sustain those kinds of meaningful relationships.

TS: You said earlier that utilitarianism is impersonal as well as impartial. Can you explain that?

NS: People like Bernard Williams have pointed out that utilitarianism sees persons as placeholders for utility. People are boxes in which you can put utility, and the actual person or relationship you have with that person is secondary.

TS: They're just vessels for the utility you can add to the world.

NS: Exactly. Now it's not that Aristotle ignores the moral considerations that Kantians and utilitarians are concerned with. It would be sad if Aristotle gave no thought to misplaced loyalties, which can arise in friendship, or in any kind of relationship. But Aristotle doesn't formalize the sort of conditions of permissibility that Kant is very worried about.

TS: This idea that he doesn't try to formalize—that's why I like Aristotle's approach so much. My favorite passage from the *Ethics* is the one where he says that it's "the mark of an educated man to look for precision in each class of things just so far as the nature of the subject admits."[6] Philosophers should have to repeat this to themselves 20 times every day before starting work. How do you interpret that passage in the context of Aristotle's ethical thought?

NS: Well, the people who defend particularism[7] have made good use of this passage lately. Particularists say that we can't have top-down moral principles or rules and just apply them to individual cases. That's not how ethics works. Aristotle knew that you have to be pretty street smart[8] in understanding the phenomena that surrounds you. You have to be familiar with the specifics of every situation, and be able to sense their salience. So the passage has probably guided my own way of doing philosophy. I am able to think best about issues when I have very thick narratives.

TS: By thick narratives you mean …

NS: Highly textured, I need to understand the details. I'm not willing to simplify. I'm less interested in the hypothetical cases that come from the philosophical literature, and more in the ones where I'm really puzzled by something in real life. I'm trying to make sense of the phenomena. That's Aristotle. And I'm not trying to give over-generalized rules that will apply over and over again. That doesn't mean there aren't patterns. Obviously there's going to be a lot of generalization, but sometimes the devil is in the details and Aristotle is incredibly useful for reminding us about that.

3 Emotional (Moral) Intelligence

TS: Let's talk about those details and particulars. How does Aristotle help us get these moral street smarts? How does his approach help us appreciate the ethical salience of concrete particulars in a way that other theories do not?

NS: In the last two years or so, philosophers started to worry about how to form general principles that can capture the specificity of the situation. Aristotle just begins there—with the specific situation—and that's very, very gratifying. It makes sense that he would because Aristotle always had an appreciation for the epistemic value of emotions, he took them seriously as forms of intelligence.

TS: So our emotions help us identify the morally relevant details of specific real-life situations?

NS: Yes, Aristotle believed that you can't really navigate in your world morally unless you have fine emotions that are picking up relevant information. And I think that's an incredibly important part of moral growth and moral education. But it gets lost for centuries because of a prejudice that emotions are so much "mist on your windscreen." That's how R. S. Peters once put it in the 1960s. But emotions are not mist on your mental windscreen. Yes, they can distort, but they also can inform and track the salience of crucial details.

TS: This "mist on the windscreen" idea is still around, right? A few people in this book—Josh Greene, Peter Singer, and Paul Bloom for example[9]—they all worry about the distorting effects of the emotions. Paul Bloom wrote an article for the *New Yorker* that attacked everyone's favorite moral emotion: empathy. He says empathy has this distorting feature leading us to favor people we know, people who look like us, or even people we find cute or attractive.[10] I disagree with Paul's conclusions, but there's plenty of evidence to support his concerns. Does Aristotle have a way of addressing them?

NS: Well it's certainly a big worry. We should be concerned about bias in emotional intake. When's he's talking about an emotion like anger, Aristotle often says that if you know you're leaning too far one way, you should self-correct and move in the other direction. It's a very mechanical model for compensation. But it's also part of his more general philosophy that you have to take self-knowledge and self-awareness very seriously. And that may be a project that you can't do on your own. One of the key features and functions of friendship among good persons is that they study each other's characters and that they can be candid with each other. Your friends need to be able to tell you your faults, without enormous shame or timidity. Of course, they should also have diplomatic skills that are characteristic of negotiating the social space well.

TS: So having friends is one possible corrective. What are some other ways of ensuring that our emotions are reliable rather than distorting indicators of moral relevance?

NS: Well, just to be clear: it's not only the emotions that distort. Beliefs can distort as well and lead to all sorts of prejudice. Beliefs may have some emotional shade but they also may come in fairly cold or non-valenced forms, and still be distorting. That's the nature of prejudice. So I don't think we should fully separate these two ways—emotional and cognitive—of processing the world. That's one thing.

TS: Right, I wasn't suggesting that emotions are the only distorting mechanism. Is your point though that we shouldn't even draw this hard distinction between emotions and the other ways of perceiving the world?

NS: I would soften it, I would certainly soften it. Now I'm not saying that emotions are cold in the way that some other forms of perception are. They certainly have a different feel. But Aristotle thinks of practical wisdom as including how wise we are with regard to our emotions. So our emotions, like our beliefs, can always come up for review and revision. He was aware that you constantly have to know thyself, and that your wisdom is not just calculative—even with regard to the ends of good character. When you're angry you have to ask yourself: is it a justified insult that I am reacting to or am I getting hot-headed about things that shouldn't bother me?

TS: So part of moral training is to calibrate our emotions to the reality of the situation?

NS: I think so. Part of it has to do with emotions being apt or appropriate with regard to both the read of the situation—whether they track, if you like that term. But they can also be apt in the sense of showing that you're a concerned individual. I deal with a lot of these cases of irrational guilt. In those cases, guilt is not tracking real culpability. But the fact that you feel it is indicative of your concern for your troops or your concern as a good parent. An absence of guilt would be a kind of callousness, even though it's not grabbing a real wrong or a real transgression in the way that guilt, if it were justified, would. It's giving us and people we know another kind of information.

TS: That's interesting. Even when emotions are distorting in one sense, they can still be evidence of good moral character.

NS: That's all stuff that Aristotle talks about when he says your emotions have to hit the mean.

TS: I don't want to get too systematic here because that would not be in the spirit of Aristotle. But it is in the spirit to think about these things practically. How does this work, training your emotions, knowing when they're appropriate and when they're not?

NS: That's a good question. I think we've only very recently taken seriously the project of emotional regulation in education. Even in psychology. We've tended to think that they happen automatically. But any parent knows that emotional education—anger management is a classic case—is something that needs a lot of work. Walter Mischel has all this work on emotional regulation in children. Usually, it concerns desire and temptation. Being able to delay and defer has enormous pay-off in later life. In those longitudinal studies, if you can hold off on eating one marshmallow right now, you may be an amazing star later on.

That's very Aristotelean in a certain way. Habituation of character—a terrible phrase, I prefer something like acculturation or moral growth—is about training emotions as well as making choices that are prudent and responsive to the environment. Aristotle just doesn't separate these things. Like how do you understand what's really fearful and what we should pity? Well let's look at some plays—and if you were a Greek, you would see many of the greatest plays ever written. And we even show them now. I'm in conversations regularly with soldiers and audiences and talk-backs in public town meetings where they watch Sophocles. Because it's a great way to address questions like 'Was a certain action really shameful?' Or 'How do I respond to what feels like annihilating shame?' These questions are best captured by these plays.

TS: As opposed to in a treatise or a formalized argument, or something like that?

NS: The conceptual apparatus of philosophical treatises is critical for being able to label and sort murky experience. But so too are narratives that help to embody concepts and reach us in a million other ways that cold texts can't. We know that because we go to movies and we learn a lot about the world and ourselves through movies.

TS: I learned most of what I know at the movies. With a lot of things that require a great deal of training, it's best to start while you're young, right? You're probably not going to be a great concert pianist if you start playing piano in your thirties. How much focus is there on the education of children in Aristotle? Does he think it's crucial for developing a virtuous character and a good life?

NS: Well I think he gives you two answers to that. One is: don't come to my lectures unless you already know the '*that,*' because if you don't know the '*that*' you can't know the '*because.*' That's this famous line in *The Nicomachean Ethics* and it means something like "Look, I'm not going to preach to the converted but I do expect some background." So that's one notion. But he also believed (and this is critical for my work and I think it's also been borne out by psychology and neuroscience) that moral growth and moral development continue throughout the age cycle. That is Aristotle. The book on friendship concludes with "and we take the character traits that we approved from each other." The mutuality of the friendship is that you appraise and critique each other throughout your lives. That's really important. The idea of adult moral character friendships is the name of the game. It's really bottom line for him and that suggests development throughout life.

TS: So, while it should probably start when you're young, it certainly doesn't stop when you're an adult.

NS: Yeah, and he doesn't put any lower age limit on it either. The Stoics are more severe in this regard.

4   Stoicism and Control

TS: Okay. Let's move to your research on the Stoics and how it relates to your work with soldiers. First of all, what led you to start applying the lessons of Aristotle and the Stoics to the experience of service members?

NS: Serendipity.

TS: Like so much in life.

NS: Yeah. Well, I got a phone call in the mid 1990s from the Naval Academy saying that they were in the middle of a cheating scandal. One hundred and thirty-three midshipmen were implicated in the compromise of an electrical engineering exam. "We need to think about this," they told me. "Could you brainstorm with us?" One thing leads to another and I ended up staying at the Naval Academy for about two and a half to three years as their first distinguished chair in ethics. So I designed a brigade-wide ethics course. And what I found when I talked to the midshipmen (who are the cadets), and to my TAs (who were essentially very high-level officers), is that they resonated with Stoicism. It just spoke to them.

TS: In what ways?

NS: One way was that one of their own had embraced it. That's Jim Stockdale who is the longest held POW in the Vietnam War. He had been given the Handbook (the *Enchiridion*) of Epictetus when he was a graduate student at Stanford and he ended up memorizing it on a carrier in Southeast Asia. Then when he was shot down in 1968 or so, the book became his salvation. I was teaching in 2007 and these naval cadets and officers, they embraced Jim Stockdale's story that when he was shot down, he was "leaving behind the world of technology and entering the world of Epictetus." The Handbook became his bible. And so his experience and writing about influenced generations.

But also, as soon as many of them read Epictetus on their own, they found a lot of ideas that resonated with them. For example, the idea that there are some things that are within your control and some things that aren't, and you should only worry about the things that are under control. That speaks to them: they're stranded somewhere half-way round the world on a ship. They can't get back for their own weddings, their kids are born, there's often so little control in their lives. But what they can control they want to be able to control really well. It was fascinating, they took to these ideas like a duck takes to water. I wanted to know why. So I did a lot more research. Epictetus is a kind of thin source and I found myself just going back and reading Seneca who I think is remarkably rich, and many of the other Stoics too. I wanted to respect my officers' and midshipmen's affinities, but I also wanted to show them that there were curses in Stoicism as well as blessings. The 'suck it up and truck on, just be Stoic' mentality had its curses too. In turning to the real Stoics, there were more lessons to be learned than they were going to get from their popular version in Epictetus's little Handbook.

TS: I'm the farthest thing from a Stoic scholar, but I recently read and lectured on Aurelius' *Meditations*. My sense is that there are several core elements of Stoicism. First, as you mentioned, there's the emphasis on developing an immunity to the vicissitudes of life, the things that are outside of our control. Second, there's a related idea that we need to take full control of our emotions so that they don't lead us to be either unhappy or non-virtuous. Finally—and you don't talk about this much in your work—there's this emphasis on fate, on determinism. Aurelius repeatedly described this image of human beings as little cogs in a big machine, the universe, that is ultimately aiming for the good of the whole. How accurate is that as a very brief recap of Stoicism as a whole?

NS: To some degree it's quite accurate. It's true that I don't spend much time on the Stoic's notion of determinism because I still find it hard to understand. I've never found Stoic metaphysics particularly engaging. But what is interesting in Marcus Aurelius is this idea that we are part of a larger system. Your reason is part of the reason of the cosmos and somehow part of a whole that is Zeus, or the cosmos, or cosmic reason. That's kind of a Kantian notion. When you imagine yourself being a moral agent in a Kantian world, you are imagining yourself as taking up a perspective of anyone who could be acting. You don't privilege your own point of view and that's a kind of Stoic inheritance.

What I found especially interesting about Marcus is that he's writing these meditations at night when he's on the battlefield, at war. His troops are rolling out these massive gold effigies of him, these huge statues. I saw one in a museum in Geneva. The size and opulence of this thing was unbelievable. And here he is, saying 'all of this means nothing to me.' He's leading the life of the ascetic while he's got the glory of the Sun god. It's remarkable. But that's what he's aspiring toward. His daily life and what he's aspiring toward are very different.

TS: Yeah, that's admirable, I agree. But I wonder about the desirability of some of the stoic aspirations. Aurelius has a line in the *Meditations*:

> look to no other guide even for an instant than reason alone, to remain ever the same in the face of severe pain even after losing a child or during long illnesses.[11]

I agree that it's virtuous to be a stoic about your own suffering and the threats to your safety. It's heroic, Stockdale was a hero. But to be a stoic about the loss of a loved one? About your son or daughter or your best friend dying on the battlefield? That seems much less virtuous. If your kid dies, you should feel sad, right?

NS: Yes, I think that's absolutely right, I come down on the same side as you. I think Stoicism has an appeal especially in times of deprivation and struggle when you're trying to take control of your life. Trying to be somewhat immune to the vicissitudes is fortifying. But when it's an aspiration to be invincible, then there's something wrong in it. And it can veer toward a numbing. One of the more sensitive writers, Seneca, says "I'm not just a doctor, but I'm also a patient and I too grieved when I lost my friend." And then he says that we can make some distinctions between the kind of tears that are overwrought and the ones that fall naturally. Stoics like Seneca are struggling. They want to give Aristotle a big run for his money, they want to limit the role of luck in *eudaemonia*, and go back to a Socratic view that virtue is sufficient. And they want to do that in terms of minimizing our attachments to emotional objects and commitments that would derail you. But then they squeeze it back in in funny places. They talk about 'preferred indifferents.' They're not goods, they're not virtues, but they're things you'd want to have rather than not have in your life— like the good health of your kid! It makes for incredibly interesting reading.

TS: Even that though, this idea that all things being equal, sure, I'd prefer my daughter was healthy and alive rather than sick or dead—that seems wrong. It's much more than a preferred indifferent. It's the most important thing in your life. I guess I side with Aristotle on this. These relationships are central for *eudaemonia*, not something to sneak through the back door of your theory.

NS: I couldn't agree more. I've never endorsed that part of the Stoic picture. I've found it represents an earnest try to figure out the boundaries of agency in a way that very few philosophers have. It's an active struggle and once you start taking Seneca really seriously you can see how active that struggle is. And that's really useful, because there are a lot of people who do take that battle seriously and especially, I've found, service members.

5   Anger, Revenge, and Holding Others to Account

TS: Not surprisingly, the Stoics have a deep distrust of anger and revenge-based emotions. You seem more on board with the stoics on this, although you express some ambivalence about revenge feelings. Can you talk about their views and where you stand on them?

NS: Sure. The Stoics have a fascinating descriptive account of the emotions, essentially a very robust cognitivist view.[12] But they have a much, much less appealing prescriptive view of emotions as we said before. They'd like to drain emotions from much of life but then sneak them back in various ways. The starting place for them is often anger. We have to remember that many of them—Seneca and Epictetus and Marcus—are writing about life in Ancient Rome. In Roman life, anger is totally overused, misplaced, it's unreliable. Think of Nero. It flashes everywhere, much to the detriment of its citizens. If only you could control it and abstain from it, one day, two days, Alcoholics Anonymous style, then you'll do better. In their world, (but of course, not theirs alone) there is a lot of rage that decimates populations and tyrannizes in horrific ways.

So they think that there's no place for the desire that comes with anger, nor for the actions that flow from anger. In fact, when they classify the good emotions, the ones that are hygienic or pasteurized, the perfect ones that a sage would have, there's no slot for anger and distress. So grief and anger have no place. But there are slots for pleasure, desire, and fear (the other basic emotions, on their view).

TS: Do you agree with them about this?

NS: I think certain kinds of anger really are justified. Maybe not moral anger expressed as payback or revenge actions—but rather as moral protest of some kind. And that's a fine line drawing the distinction between bad retributivist emotions and ones that capture a kind of legitimate moral protest. Recently, writers like Martha Nussbaum, have said there isn't much of a distinction and she's willing to 'just say no' to all of these emotions.

TS: It's funny because she's praised anger and outrage in the past. It was Nussbaum who brought to my attention the Elie Wiesel story about the American soldiers who liberated Buchenwald, the concentration camp where he was prisoner. Wiesel wrote that when the soldiers marched in, the look of hatred, anger, and moral outrage on their faces was the first thing that restored the humanity to the prisoners. He said in a speech that he'll always be grateful for that rage.

NS: That's right, that was her view and she wrote about it eloquently, criticizing the Stoics for extirpating anger, including moral anger from their catalog. But she's now argued something different.

TS: You agree with her older stuff.

NS: Yes, because I think that sometimes the only way to record the moral injury, if you can use that term, is through a kind of resentment, or the reactive attitudes as P. F. Strawson would put it, that embody the practice of holding someone to account. This can be true in a different kind of first-person way with guilt or shame. They can be ways of holding yourself to account for falling short of aspired ideals. All of that is very important for a community with individuals that can be trusted and counted on. That's the kind of point Joseph Butler wanted to make. Resentment can help hold to communities together by holding persons to account. Are you there? Yes I'm there. Can I count on you? Yes you can. These forms of moral address are embodied in these emotions, including anger.

Now, should we sit with them and let them linger and fester? No! And that's part of my preoccupation when I talk to service members. They are wracked by some of these emotions. Moral repair is crucial, whether it be through self-empathy or self-forgiveness or certain community forgiveness, as toward civilians whom soldiers may feel have given them a raw deal. So I'm not arguing that it's a good thing to hold onto these emotions for forever and a day. They can be deleterious to the psyche. They can be deleterious to a community.

TS: You say that Stoic philosophy can be helpful for soldiers, but "it needs to loosen itself from the notion that we aspire to be sages or perfect zero-defect warriors." Can you elaborate what you mean by that?

NS: Well the zero-defect mentality is a bureaucratic management style, and the idea is that you can't make mistakes. Now they have a system where lives are on the line, and people carry a lot of weapons—so you get why they have that mentality. But it also can be crippling in that people do make mistakes. Management can be hard and abusive and punish people without allowing them to learn from their mistakes and move on. And individuals can be really hard on themselves, too, when they lose their buddies or there's an accident. And that often characterizes the military community. People have very high expectations of others and of themselves, typically.

Sages rise only as often as the phoenix does, as one of the Stoic writers says. They don't come very often. The notion of the sage is someone who has already arrived and isn't aspiring but actually perfectly fulfills what would otherwise be called aspirational goals. And that's a kind of unreasonable model. It's an ideal model, and the Stoics aren't good at teaching us how to implement it in non-ideal conditions.

TS: So you think they should loosen themselves from even having the aspiration, right?

NS: I'm thinking of it very much in the military, so it's going to be a slightly longer answer. They're very young when they come in, 17, 18, or so, and they often don't have a lot of sophisticated thoughts about the difference between aspirational principles and those that you have to fulfill perfectly. So when they hear things like 'never leave a comrade behind,' 'always cover your buddy's back,' 'bring home all of your troops,' they take all that as duties that have to be perfectly fulfilled. And that's not what war is about. War is filled with gray, one bad choice in place of another, in short, a lot of compromise. None of the warlords they work with are good guys. They're pretty bad. There's a lot of corruption. But yet the folks that go in don't have that kind of willingness to see things in less than black-and-white ways. Nor do they have the notion that morality doesn't always issue commands that can be perfectly fulfilled.

Another thing is that there's often a command structure that allows the people at the bottom to take the fall. And so they often do take the fall hard with people at the top getting protected. And that creates a very bad environment. So if I were revising the military ethic, I would begin by explaining the difference between aspirational goals and ones you perfectly fulfill. And also teach just how gray those choices and situations can be.

TS: From what you've said about the emotions and all the gray areas in war, it sounds like you're endorsing more of an Aristotelian approach than a Stoic one for soldiers.

NS: I think that's right. It's not as glorious and Aristotle doesn't write in little epigrammatic ways like Epictetus, but yes, that is right. The reason the Stoics are so appealing to all of us and not just the military is that they recognize the struggle to define the perimeters of our agency. They realize that sometimes you have to really draw that perimeter in tightly in order to be autonomous and self-controlled. You have to reduce your attachments to things outside of your control. That's kind of a Buddhist way of thinking, if you like. You have to respect the urges that they are working with, because they reflect a lot of our own ways that we deal with life.

6 The Civilian–Military Divide

TS: Let's close by talking about your new book. A central theme you write about is the increasing distance between the service members' experience and the civilian experience. This is a source of a lot of problems when the soldiers come home—especially after these wars in Afghanistan and Iraq. Most people were in favor of those wars in 2003, but now we've come to regard them as a mistake, at best, and a serious moral injustice, at worst. I imagine that soldiers might feel resentful about this, first and or foremost to the politicians who sent them there—the people who put their lives at risk and probably cost the lives of some of their friends. But also resentment to the population as a whole.

NS: *Afterwar* is very much about the military–civilian divide, the burdens on an all-volunteer force, the kind of moral injuries they suffer. These injuries include some resentment toward civilians, this idea that 'I was at war while you were shopping at the mall.' And this idea that sometimes comes up: 'don't thank me for my service; first say please.' Which means: think about what you're sending me to do. Let's have a much more rigorous debate about the causes or the continuation of the mission, about whether we can stabilize governments and nations in the way that you think. We're trying to execute counter-insurgency in population-centric areas where there are murky enemies, children who are militants one moment and not at another. There are far too many compromised partners and unstable successes. Areas you think you've secured get unsecured fast—as in the areas ISIS controls now.

TS: It's easy to see how Congress and the administration need to be held accountable. They made the decision to send the troops overseas. But you write that the civilian population also needs to take some responsibility for this war and what happened. How do you interpret this idea of civilians taking responsibility?

NS: Well one way is that we have moral obligations to those coming home. I interpret it as an obligation to make positive efforts to reach out to service members upon their homecoming and as they reintegrate. And it's not just clinicians who play a role here. We all have a responsibility to do what we can to break down the civilian–military barrier.

Generically speaking, sailors, marines, wingmen, the reserve guard, they come home feeling misunderstood, resentful. And so those moral emotions we were talking about, the ones that register accountability, they're critical to what I'm trying to do. Clinicians are interested in this term 'moral injury' now, but it has a long history in philosophy. It has to do with emotions that express our practices of holding each other to account, and that's really important for us to think about. Acknowledging those emotions is a way to begin a conversation. I don't think there's any better place for that than in the classroom. We're just blessed to be professors in universities where veterans return in big numbers or small numbers. We teach classes where we can have ongoing conversations with people who served and haven't served, people who are genuinely interested in service. I find my 18–22-year-olds really want to serve in some way, whether in the military or not, they're curious. It's a great way, if not to level the playing field, to open the conversation.

TS: I completely agree. I have a number of veterans in my classes, but I also feel conflicted sometimes. I want to talk to them about their experiences, but I also don't want to pressure them into having conversations they don't want to have. It's a tricky thing to negotiate.

NS: I think that's true. But sometimes there are topics that will bring them out in the same way we were speaking about earlier. Interesting texts that you can gather conversation around. Those of Sophocles, or other Greek tragedies, or great novels that have to do with war. And universities are great places for this, as I say, but they are not the only places.

TS: What about our responsibility at the level of policy?

NS: We have to take more accountability for the wars that we send soldiers to. We should be reviewing much more robustly the War Powers Act of 1973, which gives a lot of power to executives to engage in war. We should be also thinking harder about just what the missions are that we want to get involved in. We need to have more people in political places that have served, and know about it, and have skin in the game. I think it's only about 25 percent right now of Congress, and it was 71 percent in 1971.

TS: And it will probably just get smaller and smaller. You give another stat, only a half of a percent of people in the population serve in the military.

NS: Yes, and that's going to get smaller too, because we're not going to engage in as many large land wars anymore. We're going to go in for smaller footprints, tip of the spear, special forces operations. So the obligations going forward will be even more onerous on individuals to break down the mil–civ divide.

TS: I know you're not a policy person, but a big problem does seem to be the small percentage of people with skin in the game, as you put it, both in Congress and in the whole civilian population. That can lead to detachment, because many of us just have no way of knowing what their experiences are really like. Are you in favor of some sort of draft, or, if not a draft, then some other way of increasing the participation of the rest of the population?

NS: Well it is a big policy question. I've thought about it a little bit in terms of economics and the labor market, and also what it was like during Vietnam to have conscription. So I can't say I'm in favor of a draft. Also, given our current needs going forward, and the nature of the kinds of conflicts, it just doesn't make sense. So I'm not in favor of conscription, but I am in favor of national service of some sort. I think lots and lots of our students are thirsting for experience in the public sector to do service of all kinds. Being able to think about service in that more universal way that includes the military, as well as other forms of national service is critical. I think we should have that. It would make people grow up, it would help the nation, it would give people a sense of purpose and responsibility. Right now, some people take on national service in an enormous way, making enormous sacrifices, others don't at all. As I've said, I haven't worked on it at a policy level, but it seems like a very good idea to me, long overdue.

Notes

1 Seriously, you should be put in jail if you haven't watched this show.
2 www.nytimes.com/2015/02/17/opinion/david-brooks-the-moral-injury.html
3 See "Shrinks and the SERE technique and Guantanamo" (www.counterpunch. org/2007/05/29/shrinks-and-the-sere-technique-at-Guantanamo) for a description of the program and the role of psychologists.
4 "Outside Psychologists Shielded U.S. Torture Program, Report Finds" www. nytimes.com/2015/07/11/us/psychologists-shielded-us-torture-program-report-finds.html
5 "From Nuremberg to Guantanamo: Medical Ethics Then and Now." *Washington University Global Studies Law Review*, 6(3) (2007): 609–21.
6 *Nicomachean Ethics*, Book I, 1094. b24.
7 See http://plato.stanford.edu/entries/moral-particularism, for a description of moral particularism.
8 In Chapter 2, Philip Zimbardo uses this term as well to describe how we should train "heroes-in-waiting." This is especially interesting because situationists like Zimbardo are often regarded as opponents of Aristotelian approaches to ethics.
9 See Chapters 9, 13, and 17.
10 Bloom and I debate the value of empathy in Chapter 13.
11 *Meditations*, Book 1.8
12 Cognitivism is roughly the view that our emotions express propositions or make judgments. For example, when I'm angry at you, I'm expressing a judgment that you did something wrong.

Questions for Discussion

1   How does the use of enhanced interrogation techniques at Guantánamo Bay illustrate the danger of the professional psychologists colluding with CIA and DoD to write their own policies and codes of ethics?

2   What makes Aristotle's approach to ethics different from Kant or utilitarians?

3   What is the role of the emotions in Aristotelian ethics? Why is Sherman critical of philosophers who regard emotions as "so much mist on the mental windscreen"?

4   Why does Aristotle think that friends of good character are so important for helping us live a moral life?

5   How would Aristotle and the Stoics differ in their reaction to losing a loved one?

6   How might the Stoic sage be a misleading or harmful idea for soldiers?

7   What actions might help bridge the current military–civilian divide?

Suggested Readings and Media

Sherman, Nancy. "The Role of Emotions in Aristotelian Virtue." *Proceedings of the Boston Area Colloquium in Ancient Philosophy* 9 (1994): 1–33.

———. "A Crack in the Stoic's Armor." *New York Times*: The Stone: Opinionator. 30 May, 2010. http://opinionator.blogs.nytimes.com/2010/05/30/a-crack-in-the-stoic-armor

———. "The Moral Logic of Survivor Guilt." *New York Times*: The Stone: Opinionator. July 3, 2011. http://opinionator.blogs.nytimes.com/2011/07/03/war-and-the-moral-logic-of-survivor-guilt

———. "The Deepest War Wound May Be the Anguish of Moral Injury." *Los Angeles Times*. 24 April, 2015. http://touch.latimes.com/#section/-1/article/p2p-83381730

———. "Don't Just Tell Me 'Thank You.'" *Psychology Today*. 22 May, 2015. www.psychologytoday.com/blog/afterwar/201505/don-t-just-tell-me-thank-you.

Sherman, Nancy and Heath White (2003). "Intellectual Virtue: Emotions, Luck, and the Ancients." In Linda Zagzebski and Michael DePaul (eds.), Intellectual Virtue: Perspectives from Ethics and Epistemology. New York: Oxford University Press, 34–53.

Assorted Media and Podcast Pairings

BookTV. "BookTV: Nancy Sherman, 'The Untold War: Inside the Hearts, Minds, and Souls of Our Soldiers'". Interview by BookTV. 21 Feb., 2012. https://youtu.be/qZtrthgXRhk

———. "Recovering Lost Goodness: Shame, Guilt, and Self-Empathy." Lecture at UC San Diego. Pub. 2 May, 2013. https://youtu.be/cpbq-MEqcYM

Very Bad Wizards, Episode 56 "Moral Heroes and Drunk Utilitarians." http://verybadwizards.com/episodes/56

6 William Ian Miller

Codes of Honor

> Honor above all, Dog. Honor ain't cost-effective, but y'all must do yo' utmost
> 2 preserve it, cuz in tha end, it have tha most value.
>
> —Herbert Kornfeld

One of the most inspired creations of the parody newspaper the Onion *is Herbert Kornfeld, columnist and accounts-receivable supervisor at a regional office-supply company. The joke of the column—which ran for eight years and somehow never got old—is that this impossibly nerdy-looking Jewish accountant talks and acts like a gangsta rapper and all-around badass. Kornfeld's obsession with honor is modeled on what sociologists often call the "honor culture" of inner-city gang life. The term refers to societies or groups that place tremendous importance on acquiring honor and status, and on avenging slights, insults, and offenses. (Kornfeld zealously defends "tha Accountz Reeceevable code," and is quick to whip out his "letta opener of death" at even the mildest hint of disrespect.)[1]*

Over the past 50 or so years, researchers from a wide range of disciplines have observed and studied cultures with honor-based values systems. They span across history (Homeric Greece, medieval Iceland) and exist today all over the world. Their values can be found in smaller communities within a larger society (the Mafia, pockets of the American South), or they can run through an entire country.[2] Many Arab and Islamic societies are thought to be honor cultures, and as a result research on this topic has attracted the attention of political and military strategists. Former US Army Major William McCallister, for example, has attributed the US's initial unpopularity with Iraqis during the Iraq War to, in part, our failure to grasp the pervasive role that the concepts of shame and honor play in Iraqi society; they are as important to the Iraqis as land and water. McCallister, who now consults with the Marines in Iraq, writes that "It has taken us four years to realize that we must execute operations within the existing cultural frame of reference."[3]

When honor cultures are discussed in intellectual or academic circles, however, there is often an implicit assumption that their values, especially their preoccupation with revenge, are primitive, backward, irrational—of scholarly interest certainly, but something we in the civilized West are grateful to have moved beyond. Not William Ian Miller. Miller, the Thomas G. Long Professor of Law at the University of Michigan, has spent much of his career writing about the honor cultures of tenth- and eleventh-century Iceland as they are described in the amazing Icelandic sagas (written one hundred to three hundred years later). He's one of the world's leading authorities on honor cultures, and also their greatest advocate. Far from condescending to these cultures, Miller sings their praises.⁴ He holds up the lives of his saga Icelanders as a model, something to respect, admire, even emulate. Miller belongs to a small but growing number of legal theorists who believe that the distinction between justice and revenge is artificial, a fabrication of philosophers. According to Miller, the concept of justice has its foundation in revenge, in getting even— and if you're looking for subtle and complex analyses of revenge, the Icelandic sagas are second to none.

William Ian Miller has published numerous scholarly articles and eight books, including Bloodtaking and Peacemaking, Humiliation, *and* Eye for an Eye. *His books are scholarly, entertaining, and highly personal, an almost-unheard-of combination in academic writing. I met Miller at the Grizzly Peak Brewing Company in Ann Arbor. For better or worse, we conducted the interview over, well, several beers. Our discussion (only a portion of which can be reproduced here) spanned more than three hours and a wide range of topics, including Miller's experience growing up Jewish in Green Bay, Wisconsin, my near-fight with my landlord, the hypocrisy of the Israeli University boycott, great revenge movies, and, of course, Miller's views on honor cultures in medieval Iceland and elsewhere.*

November 2008

1   What Is an Honor Culture?

TAMLER SOMMERS: At the risk of overgeneralizing things a bit, what characterizes an honor or honor-based culture?

WILLIAM IAN MILLER: It's not an easy question, actually. One characteristic— and this is why you can have honor cultures within a larger culture—is that there's a roughly egalitarian grouping, where people are very anxious about where they stand, relative to each other. And for them, honor makes a big difference because that's how they determine relative ranking.

TS: Why is that so important to them?

WIM: Well, I don't want to make claims about "hardwiring," but we'd always much rather be looked up to than looked down upon. It's very hard to imagine a culture where being looked down upon is a virtue. And, of course, if you make it a virtue, then it becomes that which is honored. So Christianity has this thing—some Hindu cultures, too—where status was conferred by how wretched you could be. Then it just became inverse honor: "Hey, I'm more wretched than you are." Yeah, I can show I'm more wretched, I can fast 20 years longer than you can. I can sit on a flag pole for six months with no clothes on. You could only do that for three months. So no matter what, it's about status and competitiveness.

TS: Aside from sitting naked on flagpoles, what are some typical ways to gain status in honor cultures?

WIM: You know, there's not a set of rules. There're certain people who get the benefit of the doubt. And they get the benefit of the doubt maybe because their ancestors were honorable. What's interesting to me in studying honor cultures is how redeemable *dishonor* is. Honor is never tested if you're not already down; if you don't get knocked down and see if you can reassert it. So some kind of dissing is built into the system, where you've got to experience being up against the wall. Where you're tested.

TS: What are some of the tests?

WIM: There're a bunch of tests. The prime virtue is clearly courage. So test number one kind of resembles playing chicken. You have to show that you don't scare easy. Everybody knows that people are scared, but you have to show that it's not going to interfere with your actions. So keeping a level head under stress—you know, not everyone can be a physical tough guy. And the sagas are so good about this. They show a lot of physical weenies who are dominating. It's because they're smart. And they don't scare easy. That's the one thing you've gotta have—not scaring easy. You've got to keep your cool.

But suppose you've got a lot of courage, you don't scare easy, and then you have one bad day. You run away from battle one time, or you break down and cry. Soldiers tend to be more forgiving about this—they know everyone has their good days and bad days. But in honor cultures? If you have a bad day, that can always be brought up to ridicule you. That might well be commemorated in song. Even though you can redeem it to some extent, it's still there to ... create tension in situations such as feasts. Someone will get up and say, "Everyone thinks you're so brave, but that's not what they said about you at the battle of so-and-so." And then the question is: can you take that kind of "dis"? Are you cool enough to be able to just laugh at it? Or does that guy have to be taken out and whacked?

TS: And you believe that these kinds of attitudes rise out of situations where everyone is roughly on equal ground?

WIM: I'd put it like this. Honor cultures are a necessary condition of roughly egalitarian communities. Because people will compete for precedence that isn't articulated, it's always how you're standing in the jealous eyes of fellow competitors.

TS: You were talking before about being in grade school, where people start out fairly equal. I guess there's quite a bit of honor-culture stuff that goes on in school.

WIM: Right. You know, I remember growing up that the test for little boys would be to not cry. And you would keep pushing yourself. And all you got if you survived this day's test, jumping off a ledge or something, whatever the contest, was to show you weren't a chicken. It didn't prove that you were honorable, it just proved you weren't a coward for the day.

TS: Are there any other attitudes or practices that, broadly speaking, most honor cultures share?

WIM: Not wanting to be laughed at, unless you're purposely playing the clown, in which case *not* being laughed at would be a dis. But not wanting to be the object of derisive laughter shows how much honor is still alive and well, even among types like us: suppose you slip on the ice and take a bad spill. What's the first thing you care about? Whether you were seen, right? Not how much your back is hurting. You'll deal with that later.

TS: Many people hear about these honor-based attitudes and values and they dismiss them as violent, primitive, irrational. Why is that?

WIM: That's because the people who say those kinds of things tend to be academics and clergy—who got beaten up on the playground. And that's kind of dismissive, but it's partly true. Because if they felt they were *winning* at this game ... I mean, where do *they* think virtue lies? In reason, argumentation, disputation! The very things they're good at! Now come on—give me a break! Look, reason's just fine. But these old thuggish warriors that I study, when reason came in, they saw it as a tool of clerics to get land from them. And they weren't wrong! There's a politics of reason, right? You know that's true.

TS: Sure, but ...

WIM: But that's just one answer. Why do honor cultures get dissed? Because the people who are dissing it don't win at it. Kind of a trivial answer. It's Nietzsche's answer. The other answer is— well, I'm not sure *I* want to live in my saga world, I'm not sure I have the nerves to do it. I respect them, I admire them. I think they're *nobler* than we are at some level. I mean, why is it that these guys make stories we still thrill to, whereas us academics, our virtues make for the tediousness of faculty meetings? You gotta say that there's a falling off!

TS: At the same time, it's not all fun and excitement. There's some grisly stuff that goes on too, right?

WIM: But it's not necessarily honor that makes honor cultures get a bad name. It's the substantive issues on which honor is fought out.

TS: The aggression, the violence, the attitudes towards women ...

WIM: Yeah, okay, but what about an honor culture like my saga Iceland guys, who couldn't give a damn about whether their women screwed around? They didn't care. But now take an Islamic one, where you gotta kill the woman [if she screws around]. We think, that's horrible, the honor culture! But it has nothing to do with honor culture. What it has to do with is that the underlying norms about which they decide that honor are at stake.

TS: You say something along those lines in your book *Humiliation*. That in Islamic societies, and in certain Mediterranean cultures, too, honor is linked with shame—and they link shame with women.

WIM: Well, it's linked so tightly with chastity. In the [Icelandic] Northlands they could care less about it. That's an exaggeration, but they put very little store by virginity in comparison with Mediterranean cultures—whether Christian, Muslim, or Jewish.

TS: Which made me think about guys calling each other pussies all the time.

WIM: Yeah, we still do it. In my courage book [*The Mystery of Courage*], I talk about people saying: "He's one tough mother." That doesn't mean—you don't connect toughness with being a woman. It means he's one tough motherfucker. And then, right, "What a pussy," meaning coward. Of course, this gender stuff was alive and well in the Northlands. It's just that it didn't get actualized into caring what their women did. But the language, the insults, were the same.

TS: What do you think accounts for this difference in caring about chastity? Is it a religion thing?

WIM: No, I don't know why. We don't know what the cause and effect was. Was it because the saga people weren't obsessed with virginity that women had more power, or was it because they had more power and that they could demand more sexual freedom?

TS: You say in *Eye for an Eye* that some honor cultures are "well-functioning" and some aren't. And that in some radical Islamic and inner-city gang settings, things aren't well functioning. Can you say more about that?

WIM: This gets more complicated than I can manage in a few words, but let me try. What the inner city is missing is older people with property and power to force violent young men to keep their violence within limits. Now the older generations have nothing to threaten the hot-headed with to keep their violence within bounds. Honor cultures, like any well-functioning culture, have to *keep violence down* to levels people can live with, with *live*, I guess, taking on a literal edge. In a certain kind of Islamic setting, at least the one we fear in the West, it's the old men who have seemed a little too willing to let their young die, while they keep themselves out of harm's way. A culture of martyrdom can get out of hand—as it did among early Christians and Jews in the first century, and medieval centuries, and Islam now. Christianity tried to resolve it by rejecting volunteering for martyrdom. You had to wait until it came to you.

2 Why Are Honor Cultures so Smart?

TS: At the end of *Eye for an Eye*, you write that it's obvious to you that people in these cultures are better psychologists than we are today, and that we're not as smart now as we were when we worried more about honor than pleasure. Can you elaborate on that?

WIM: I think a sub-polemic in all my academic work—all my writing, even the monograph on the Icelandic sagas—is awe and respect for these people, for how smart they are. And why are they so smart? Because they're better than we are at discerning motive in others. And why is that? Because the stakes are so damn high. They get it wrong, they're dead.

TS: Or they're dishonored. Which is just as bad in some cases.

WIM: Right. So it makes them hyperaware of others. I mean, you want fellow-feeling? They have it a hundred times more than our sentimentalized culture of "Oh, I feel your pain." I see a big downturn in smartness about discerning motive, intention, inner states, with the rise of depth psychology. Freud, Lacan—a joke compared to the British moralists of the eighteenth century, a joke compared to my blood feuders, my Icelandic saga writers. A joke compared to Thucydides.

TS: Do you think we deceive ourselves as to what our motives are?

WIM: No, not really. Self-deception is alive and well in all cultures. It's necessary to get from one day to the next. Although we openly promote self-deception now in a way that they never did. The self-esteem movement, stuff like that. But back then, you had to really care more about what others thought about you. I'm not sure that's always a good thing. It can be crippling in some ways.

TS: Would you say that they're pursuing honor, but at least they're open about it? They know they're pursuing honor. We pursue honor. But we tell ourselves we're pursuing something else. I don't know, well-being, intellectual achievement …

WIM: Right—intellectual achievement for its own sake. Or everyone's number one in their own way. So we're a whole society of number ones. What a joke! I mean Nietzsche is right at some point about this. We're a culture of *ressentiment*. We've constructed a world so that a loser can claim they're the winner. But Nietzsche doesn't get it exactly right either. Because at one level, he's whining nonstop about why *his* guys didn't win.

TS: Didn't win?

WIM: They got outsmarted by the Jews! You lost—stop whining about it. Your blond beast got outsmarted by the Jews—who unfortunately got too smart for their own good by developing Christianity, which really screwed the Jews but good.

TS: Yeah, we're still reeling from that … But to get back to how smart honor cultures are …

WIM: There's so much depth and subtlety. For example, the honor systems I'm familiar with didn't want anyone getting too good, because then they became your lord, and it wasn't a roughly egalitarian community any longer. So what you wanted to do—if you were in the running for first, in order to live, to avoid getting gunned down as the fastest gun in the West—was to care about other's people's envy and not make it hurt them too much. You had to cultivate an attitude that didn't make people *feel* your dominance too much. Or else they would gang together and take you out. So there were these built-in leveling mechanisms. Because people were envying you, and envy is a dangerous sentiment. At the same time, envy was the only sign that you'd made it. So you wanted to be envied. But you didn't want their envy to be too painful or they'd take you out.

TS: How do you strike the balance?

WIM: Well, the cultures differ on this. Certain cultures are like the rap style—"I'm the best, no one can touch me"—and even the Icelanders are like this. There's a certain cultivation of poetry, of song, that tells everyone you're so good. At the same time, that's usually delimited to very ritualized domains where everyone knows it's fun that this rhyming self-promotion is going on. Outside of that, you don't want to make people feel the pain of your dominance. You want to cultivate a style of false modesty, graciousness, generosity. Which still is a sign that you're up there. There's a certain style of false modesty where everyone knows it's false. But if you didn't do it, they would hate your guts.

TS: If you rubbed it in their face …

WIM: Yeah, so you want to be very chary of other people's envy, but you want to know that it's there.

3 Academic Weenies

TS: You often talk about how these values and attitudes can be found, sometimes disguised, in environments that we don't associate with honor cultures—academia, for example.

WIM: The difference between honor cultures, like my saga guys, the *Iliad*, and academic culture now, is that the academic weenies will pretend that they are nonviolent and don't believe in any of this "male" type of assertion, when of course they're fighting over who gets what office, who gets what lectureship, who didn't, and the same pecking-order stuff takes place. We're in denial!

TS: In denial of what?

WIM: In denial of just how much envy and relative standing drives our world. You see people fighting over the silliest forms of precedence that have been the subject of moralist derision from time immemorial. Seating arrangements. My uncle at my sister's wedding stopped speaking to my mother, not his blood relative, because he wasn't seated close enough to the bride's table.

TS: Isn't there a saga you talk about where something like that happens?

WIM: Yes. Somebody's got the seat of honor. They rank the seats. One guy puts his fist next to the guy in the seat of honor. He says, "Gudmund, what do you think of this fist?" "That's a big fist." "Do you think it could do much damage?" "Sure." "How much damage?" "It could probably break some bones." "Do you think it could break your bones?" "Sure," he says. "How would such broken bones appeal to you, Gudmund?" "Not at all." "Then get out of my seat." Gudmund exchanged seats with the guy.

TS: So there's a hierarchy everywhere, it's just a matter of degree.

WIM: To what degree it's official and demarcated by badges or medals or formal noble ranking is in one kind of hierarchy. It's different when the hierarchy is unofficial, when it becomes a matter of these little signs—how I look at you when I talk to you, say, or who gets listened to and who doesn't. Those are the little indicators of where people stand.

TS: But what about the violence in honor cultures? That at least seems to be more under wraps in everyday situations in other kinds of societies.

WIM: Here's the thing about that. I wrote about this in *Humiliation*, a chapter on violence. My high school was this working-class high school, it was pretty rough and tumble, at least to my fearful mind. But I was only in two or three fights my whole time in junior high and high school. Nevertheless, my whole life was geared around being in a fight. So if you actually measured the amount of violence that went on in my life, there wasn't that much. But the threat of it was always there, and it governed a whole lot about who you wanted to be friends with, who you dealt with in a certain way. You're always trying to either not offend or to show that you were not afraid in this or that setting. But if you added up the amount of actual violence, there wasn't that much. But it still was the dominating principle in everyone's behavior, to make sure it didn't happen to them, or if it happened to them, to make sure it happened on their terms. But then I became an academic, so this could just be the coward's-eye view.

TS: In the end of *Humiliation*, you say that you want the reader, most likely an educated non-honor-embracing reader, to come away with the psychological complexity, the danger, involving our everyday encounters.

WIM: Like this encounter right now …

4 "Miller Thinks He's the Norm. And He's Nuts!"

TS: So let me ask you this, because I worry about it myself. I've done some work on honor cultures recently, and like you say, it gives you sort of a new prism, a new way of viewing day-to-day encounters. But often when I'm going on about these things, my wife will accuse me of artificially bringing my work into these situations, projecting it on real life. I remember Galen Strawson, in a review of *Humiliation*, accused you of something similar: generalizing from your own experience. And, like you told me earlier, you grew up as one of a few Jewish kids in Green Bay—you grew up in an honor culture, having to fight for respect. But maybe it's not like that for everyone—people with different backgrounds which made their childhood less of a fight, less competitive. Do you worry that you're doing that at least a little bit—projecting your own experience on the rest of the world?

WIM: You know, people accuse me of this. I have a couple of colleagues who joke, you know, "Miller thinks he's *l'homme moyen sensual*, that he's the norm. And he's nuts!" And of course I think, "No, you're an academic weenie, you just haven't grown up normal." Anyone who's grown up normal knows what I'm talking about.

TS: OK, but, you know, even from our conversation, when you said that even our encounter right now is fraught with psychological complexity, honor—I don't know, I might be deluded, but it doesn't feel that way to me.

WIM: No, we're not trying to one-up each other or anything like that. It's more defensive. Neither of us wants to think that the other one is a fraud or an idiot, right? And we would be sick to death if we thought that that was the sense we gave. We'd lie awake at night, wondering if he thought I'm a total idiot.

TS: I guess I see that ...[5]

WIM: I'm always lying awake at night. I'm an insomniac. I'm always thinking: did I get dissed? I didn't think so at the time but ... I'm always thinking about these things to get revenge for. And my students will ask me—they can see I'm hot-tempered: "Professor Miller, did you get drawn to the sagas because you were like that, or did you become the way you are because of the sagas?" I say, "That's a good question." I ask that of myself, and I think maybe it's both. I was drawn to them because they spoke to me. At the same time, they set a standard for me to live up to. Talk about getting totally involved in your research.

TS: Another person working on honor cultures at Michigan, Richard Nisbett, defended the idea that certain values and attitudes might be better suited for certain kinds of environments. So attitudes focusing on defending honor are better suited for scarce environments, lawless environments.

WIM: Material scarcity, yes.

TS: Also lawlessness.

WIM: Material scarcity, mostly. Material scarcity is what raises the stakes. If you're in a rich culture, you can afford to have someone break into your house.

TS: Right, it's annoying, but—

WIM: —But we're not going to be destroyed. Whereas if somebody steals their lamb, it might mean their kid dies. The loss of the lamb reduces the amount of calories available for consumption and so they might well lose a member of the family. So the high hatred, the killing of the thief in those kinds of cultures, it's not that the thief is stealing a marginal dollar from a millionaire, he's close to committing attempted murder, or even murder.

TS: So in that kind of culture, material scarcity, where a single act of theft could cost you your family, it's probably good to cultivate a kind of reputation.

WIM: A reputation of "don't tread on me." I actually think those cultures when they're working right are more defensive than offensive. And they want to control the jerk who's going around picking fights. But they also have to show "don't mess with me." But how do you show "don't mess with me" without being a little belligerent yourself?

But back to the Strawson thing, where he thinks I'm imposing my own experience on the world. I get accused of this all the time—especially when I give a talk to a group with a high number of academic feminists. As soon as I start talking about girls and high school, you can see that they know what I'm talking about, but they'll be resisting. And I'll answer them by saying something like, I have to work hard—I have to work *really* hard to imagine a world where I don't feel that I have to settle a score, or in which I don't care where I stand. I can't imagine what that kind of world would be like, a world of either complete refusal to recognize a wrong, or a harm done to you, or one in which, when you do have a harm done to you, your first impulse is to forgive. But you don't have to take a leap of faith to imagine my world. You've been fighting against it your whole life! You've been openly at war with it. In fact, forgiveness is often its own form of revenge.

TS: But don't you think there's a spectrum, some variation in temperament? This connects to the environmental issue, since different environments can dictate different kinds of attitudes, right? You might be at one extreme, at least in academia, and other people might truly be less interested in status or avenging slights. Maybe they don't care. Why would it have to be so uniform?

WIM: It wouldn't have to be uniform, and some people don't care, yes. And you know, there's the same spectrum in honor cultures; some people care too much. And people don't like them. They're the types that create too much violence. But it's crazy to think that these kinds of attitudes aren't prevalent or that we can repress them entirely.

TS: Sure. And I'm not denigrating them, or calling them primitive. I'm the same way—I'm a hothead. It's the Israeli in me. And I also love rap music, I joke about it with my friends, I joke about it with my students. But it's gotta be a joke, right? I've got to be making fun of myself while I'm admiring …

WIM: Yeah, of course. The idea of me, a scrawny 62-year-old academic playing tough guy with my students … it's, well, it's a joke. So I'm constantly self-mocking.

TS: It has to be a joke, or else *we'd* be the joke.

WIM: Exactly. I actually do worry that I am overly romanticizing these guys, as part of an active and silly fantasy life I've been cursed with since grade school.

TS: I thought of this because in your books—it's actually very funny—you make a lot of self-deprecating references, calling yourself an academic weakling, things like that. I do the same thing in my classes. But underneath that—I genuinely wish I was a little tougher, a little harder. I mean, I don't wish I was dealing crack on the corners of East Baltimore, but at the same time …

WIM: Somewhere I talked about this commercial "Be Like Mike." The commercial was so smart because you don't want to lose the consciousness of you. You want to be *you*, but with Michael Jordan's skills. I want to be *me*, but also as tough as some of these guys I study. But of course, if I were that, then it wouldn't be me.

TS: Here's one thing I was thinking about. It's ridiculous to think that I could be some badass, like Wee-Bey in *The Wire*. And if I tried, I'd be the laughing stock of the world. I'm kind of a laughing stock anyway; whenever I say I like hip-hop, everyone calls me the guy from *Office Space*. But think of the flip side of this. In the West, we want to take people from the other side and convert them to non-honor-culture values. This happens in the inner city, with schools, and to some extent in Iraq, right? So here's my question: Wouldn't it be just as humiliating, just as incongruous, for some people steeped in honor-culture attitudes and values, to try to take on values like humility, shrugging off insults, turn the other cheek stuff? Wouldn't it seem just as ridiculous for them, in their own eyes and in others', as for me to try to be a badass?

WIM: Well, look. Jewish kids and Asian kids. Part of the competition was how smart you were. But that wasn't the whole Jewish story. The Lower East Side of New York ... You know, if you look at the 1920s Green Bay Packers photos, more than a few of the linemen on the team were Jewish.

TS: Really?

WIM: Yeah. The immigrants are the tough guys.

TS: What happened to us?

WIM: Yeah, right, what happened to us? My daughter told me a wonderful story about Bugsy Siegel. Some Haganah guys come to him to ask him for money. And Bugsy, he don't know from nothing about the Haganah. So they explain to him who they are, we need guns, we need weapons. He says "What, you mean Jews are killing people?" They say "Yeah, we need to, we're fighting." He says, "Jews are killing people?" And he writes them a check.

TS: That's very funny, I love that. But it doesn't exactly answer my question. Let me put it like this: you see in reports from Iraq that some officers come back almost bewildered by the honor codes. One former army guy said that honor and shame are their moral currency, and that until we understand that, we're screwed. Do you think a general misunderstanding of honor cultures has led to (honest, in a way) mistakes, like thinking we'll be greeted as liberators, or that we can establish a democracy without too much pain and loss of life?

WIM: It isn't honor culture the officers don't understand; hell, they live in one. It's the particular substantive matters that trigger honor concerns in Iraq— just what precisely they will take as a big offense and what they'll shrug off. That's where the misunderstandings take place.

5 The Sins of the Father

TS: I want to talk about the connection between honor and revenge on the one hand and justice on the other. Many see the two as miles apart, right? First of all, in America we think justice should be blind, administered by an unbiased third party. Juries who have no personal stake whatsoever in the offense. But in honor cultures, justice is very personal. And they think it ought to be personal.

WIM: Well, it is and it isn't. In honor cultures, you consult. Because it's not clear that you're the only wronged person. There's usually a group of people who are wronged; they have to sit down and make a decision. These are usually small communities in which this happens. And you consult with your neighbors to see what will be tolerated because you don't want to offend them. And so, in fact, there's more of a communal decision-making process than the anti-revenge ideology wants to admit. The anti-revenge ideology wants to make revenge a matter of your own rage, but I just have too many sources where people are told, sorry, no, you can't take revenge. It's not politically feasible. They weigh a lot of things that a legal system of justice would weigh, and they weigh even more, like the state of prior relations.

TS: Sort of like going to a Mafia boss, and the boss lets them know how far they can go.

WIM: Yeah, yeah—there's discussion. And in my sources, if someone goes off and takes revenge without consulting his kinsmen, they hang him out to dry. Because, look. If you can die for your uncle or brother's behavior, you have an absolute right to demand that before they go and kill they consult you first.

TS: This was the second difference I was going to bring up. In our tradition—our conception of justice—you're only responsible for what you yourself do. You're not responsible for the actions of your uncle or cousin.

WIM: You see that even in our revenge-genre movies. We isolate the avenger, we give him no kin. He's not responsible to anyone but his own inner lights. It's American Protestantism triumphant. And that's not what any revenge culture looks like. Because when you go out and take revenge, you're hanging out your kids, you're hanging out your brothers, cousins, and they demand a say. Of course, sometimes they'll also demand that you *take* revenge.

TS: And you're obligated to take revenge sometimes on their behalf, to avenge an insult to them, right? But this seems like a real difference, too. We certainly have a view of justice where people can't be blamed or punished for something they didn't bring about, either through intention or negligence. But honor cultures will retaliate against people who didn't even commit the offense, brothers or relatives of offenders, and that seems perfectly appropriate to them. They don't see anything wrong with that.

WIM: No, they don't. It's totally fine.

TS: You talk about one case in a saga, where a man took revenge against the brother of someone who hurt him years ago. And the brother hadn't even been in the country at the time of the original offense!

WIM: Right, that's right—he wasn't in the country. See, there's a bunch of ways these guys conceptualize revenge. One is that it's a juridical act, getting even for past offenses. The other is forward-looking. They're the best of utilitarians.[6] In revenge cultures, it's my turn–your turn, right? So if I kill a guy's brother, I gotta deal with *him*, the *guy*. So why don't I start with *him*, if it makes better practical sense to get him now, say because I would rather not take my turn on defense with him playing offense; so I take him out ahead of time, for his brother who wronged me who may in fact be not as frightening. So they're looking ahead to who they're going to play defense against.

TS: I wonder if there's also a different way of seeing blameworthiness here, the conditions for being truly blameworthy.

WIM: What do you mean by "truly blameworthy"?

TS: To deserve blame, to get what's really coming to you.

WIM: You know, one of the things that drives me crazy about our modern culture is that we medicalize so much, so that you can't hold somebody culpable because they have some syndrome, some disorder. That doesn't stop us from blaming someone for having the syndrome or the disorder. It just postpones the question. Let's say there's an unlucky person, a *schlemiel.* One time being a schlemiel, okay. Two times being a schlemiel, ehh. Three times, we start blaming the guy. We call him a schlemiel. Which means he's culpable, he's a schlemiel!

TS: But we still have this distinction of what you are, and what you're responsible for being.

WIM: We try to trick ourselves, maybe, into the obviousness of that distinction, but ...

TS: Okay, we trick ourselves. There's still a difference, right? Because some of these honor cultures, they don't trick themselves. There's no pretense that you're not responsible for things that don't trace back to something you did, something that you did intentionally.

WIM: Well, that depends. Here you have to look culture by culture.

TS: Take honor killings. Aside from the horrible barbarism of the whole practice, one thing that baffles people in America is that a killing can happen even when the woman was raped. She was raped, she had no intention of having sex, no control over the act, but she's still culpable, she still has to die.

WIM: You end up telling a "they had it coming" story to yourself, perhaps, or maybe it is that being unlucky is itself an offense. Insurance companies think so. They charge you for your bad luck, say if you're accident-prone though never at fault in any particular accident, just always in the wrong place at the wrong time.

TS: You can also tell a story by projecting some kind of weird intention on her—the way she dressed ...

WIM: Or where she was at the time, right ...

TS: Yeah. Or you could think that intention doesn't matter that much. It happened, she's responsible. Period. That seems weird coming from the perspective of people who place so much stock in what we *meant* to do when determining responsibility. But maybe there's a lot of variation in how much intention matters for culpability.

WIM: Here's the thing. It is psychologically and culturally variable when and how we decide to fix what somebody's intention was. We look at a whole range of things, including how happy they were made by the harm they caused you. Did they benefit by it? Fixing intention is a complicated thing. The person isn't a good judge of his own intentions. And third parties can be bad judges, though not subject to the same biases. So we have to make some social judgment as to how to judge intention and when that judgment should be made.

TS: That's definitely one possible explanation for, say, how honor killings are seen from inside. That intention is fixed in some different way. All I'm trying to suggest as another possible explanation is that we're projecting our own obsession with intention on people who simply aren't as concerned about whether people intended to do something or not when deciding about culpability.

WIM: That's right, I think. But they can't afford to have intention matter that much. At the same time, you'll see discussions in the sagas, where they regret having to kill someone—it's too bad, he's a nice guy, whatever—but they'll get the most honor if they hit him. So there are discussions of culpability, but it can be trumped. They have these other issues. Actually, I think we can focus so much on intention and culpability because we have elaborate systems of insurance. They didn't. So in some respects, what appears to us as their lack of concern with intention is really a very deep concern that they be compensated for any harm you or yours bore some kind of causal connection to. Hell, if you didn't mean it. My son is dead and I have lost his support and fighting capability, to say nothing of my honor, if I let him lie uncompensated for.

TS: True, but I still wonder if it's a different view of culpability. Take something like original sin. It's always struck me as bizarre that Adam ate the apple, or Eve ate the apple, and somehow I'm guilty, it's my fault. What did I have to do with it? That was their business! And theologian philosophers will bend over backwards to impute some weird intention on us—we *would* have eaten the apple, or Adam is human nature, and we're human, whatever. But part of me thinks: whoever came up with that story, they didn't care. You didn't eat the apple, too bad! You're still responsible. You're still guilty.

WIM: Whoever thought the sins of the father weren't passed on to the son ...?

TS: Germans today feeling responsible for what their ancestors did. They weren't alive during the Holocaust, but my dad certainly still wants to blame them.

WIM: And Jews, c'mon. We're blamed for everything.

TS: Right, even stuff we didn't do.

WIM: Even things our ancestors didn't do. What nobody did!

TS: So I wonder if we're the weird ones to focus so much on our intentions. And this reaches its apex in the free-will debate, where the conditions for responsibility can sometimes be impossible—you have to self-create, create yourself out of nothing.

WIM: Yeah, I think the ancient cultures got this much better. They don't deny free will, it's just that they're not obsessive about it. They think you can blame people for being sick, for crossing the street at the wrong time. And in fact, in a folk way, we do this all the time. It's just not official. But you know, in the saga book, I actually say the opposite—that they do care about these things—that they're not as *other* as we make them out to be. That's because there are all these discussions about having to whack a guy even though he didn't deserve it. They're aware of the tragedy of these things. They're hyperaware of the tragic side of their way of settling matters. It's not arbitrary, they're not doing this out of lack of self-reflection.

6 "All Revenge Is Comedy. It's a Happy Ending"

TS: You've written a lot about the role of honor and revenge in movies. Is there a movie you think best gets across some of what we're talking about?

WIM: I actually tell my class that if you want to look at maybe the best revenge movie ever made, it might be *The Princess Bride*. Inigo Montoya can bring tears to anyone's eyes. I mean, here you are in the midst of a comedy—a generic shtick Jewish comedy—and the revenge theme comes on, and all of a sudden it becomes powerful, moving, tears. Not tears of sentimentality, but tears because there's some great truth here. You're at the core of the moral universe. It's so brilliant, and this isn't in the book version of *The Princess Bride*, just in the movie—where Inigo says at the end—he's killed the guy, and he says, "Now what the hell do I do? I've been in the revenge business so long, I don't know what to do." His whole being has been consumed with revenge. Auden has a very smart essay where he talks about Hamlet, and how if he were to take revenge, his whole being would be extinguished in the process.

TS: My 4-year-old daughter knows the speech by heart—Montoya's, not Hamlet's. "Hello. My name is Inigo Montoya. You killed my father. Prepare to die."

WIM: It's one of the greatest acting jobs ever. It's wonderful. Maybe the best revenge movie of all time. And it's a comedy. This isn't my idea; some Greek scholar said this. All revenge is comedy. It's a happy ending. It might be a feud that never ends. So then it's a bunch of happy endings.

TS: But what about a movie like *Unforgiven*, which you've written about, too. On the one hand, it's a happy ending, it's satisfying. But …

WIM: Can you imagine *Unforgiven* ending with Eastwood saying, "Okay, it's forgiven? Ah, Little Bill, it's okay, I know you didn't mean it. Ned just died on you, I'll let it go."

TS: Not as satisfying, yeah. Any other good revenge movies?

WIM: Name a movie you really like, and I bet 80 percent of them will have revenge lurking somewhere, giving it its edge. Take perhaps one of the greatest movies of all time: *Sunset Blvd.* Revenge? Sure, Wilder's on Hollywood, Norma's on Hollywood, and on talking itself. I'm stretching it a bit, but being a Clint Eastwood fan, I love his earliest self-directed western, *High Plains Drifter*. But Clint's revenge movies violate the rules of Icelandic feuding practice. In that movie he overdoes it; he vastly exceeds his just warrant for revenge. In Iceland, say, 50 people attack your brother and kill him. You can't kill 50 or even 20 of them in revenge, though all are legally culpable. Anyway, in revenge, as in love, there are no easy answers. It's complex stuff with the local details, and the littlest shadings and nuances matter greatly.

Let's have another beer.

Notes

1 Tragically, on April 30, 2007, Herbert Kornfeld was found dead in his company's copy room, a victim of "white-on-white" violence and the ongoing office-worker turf wars.
2 Of course, the differences between honor cultures and non-honor cultures are a matter of degree, not kind. Values and attitudes related to honor can be found in all societies, but they are emphasized more in those that are classified as honor cultures. As you'll see below, Miller believes that the differences between honor and non-honor cultures are not as stark as some scholars believe.
3 See smallwarsjournal.com/blog/2007/07/coin-in-a-tribal-society-1
4 Miller noted in an email that this is in large part a rhetorical strategy, "designed to shock the complacent view that honor cultures are primitive and not something each and every one of us is familiar with at some level." For a more qualified defense of honor, see Chapter 7 (Anthony Appiah).
5 My wife, when reading this, looked up at me and said, "You guess you see that? You're exactly like that!"

Questions for Discussion

1 Why, according to Miller, do honor cultures emerge in more egalitarian communities? How are honor cultures beneficial in communities with scarce resources?
2 Why do "academic weenies" dismiss honor cultures as primitive?
3 Why does Miller think that honor cultures are better psychologists than most social psychologists are today?
4 What is one feature that Miller argues inner-city honor cultures lack in order to be well functioning? Why is that feature crucial for a well-functioning honor culture?
5 How, according to Miller, do Western revenge stories often get revenge wrong?
6 Why does Miller call honor cultures the "best of utilitarians?" What did they get right about free will and blame?

Suggested Reading

William Ian Miller. "Giving the Gift of Humiliation," Harper's 288 (Feb. 1994): 26–7. (A short excerpt from ch. 1 of *Humiliation*.)

——. *Humiliation: And Other Essays on Honor, Social Discomfort, and Violence.* Ithaca, NY: Cornell University Press, 1995.

——. "Clint Eastwood and Equity: The Virtues of Revenge and the Shortcomings of Law in Popular Culture." In Austin Sarat and Thomas Kearns (eds.), *Law in the Domains of Culture.* Ann Arbor, MI: University of Michigan Press, 1998, pp: 161–202.

——. "In Defense of Revenge." In Barbara A. Hanawalt and David Wallace (eds.), *Medieval Crime and Social Control.* Minneapolis, MN: University of Minnesota Press, 1999, pp. 70–89.

——. *Eye for an Eye.* Cambridge: Cambridge University Press, 2006.

Podcast Pairings

Very Bad Wizards, Episode 4 "Revenge, Part 1." http://verybadwizards.com/episodes/4

Very Bad Wizards, Episode 5 "Revenge, Part 2: The Revenge." http://verybadwizards.com/episodes/4

Very Bad Wizards, Episode 11. "It is Morally Wrong to Kill Morgan Freeman." http://verybadwizards.com/episodes/11

Very Bad Wizards, Episode 13 "Beanballs, Blood Feuds, and Collective Moral Responsibility." http://verybadwizards.com/episodes/13

Very Bad Wizards, Episode 56 "Moral Heroes and Drunk Utilitarians." http://verybadwizards.com/episodes/56

7 Kwame Anthony Appiah
Honor and Moral Progress

Literature and popular culture are full of characters that live by a code of honor. Entire genres are devoted to them: westerns, gangster films, hip-hop, even Jane Austen novels. The landscape of contemporary moral thought is just the opposite. Very few philosophers talk or write about honor at all. On the rare occasions that they do, it's to dismiss it as barbaric, ridiculous, and destructive—a dispensable relic of the old world.[1] In Anthony Appiah's words: honor has been "exiled to some philosophical St. Helena, left to contemplate its wilting epaulets and watch its once gleaming sword corrode in the salt air."

Yet as we saw in the interview with William Ian Miller (Chapter 6), dismissing or neglecting honor is a mistake. Moral theorists are too often blind to the advantages of honor-based values. These values and associated practices can promote virtues like self-respect, loyalty, compassion, integrity, and courage. They cement bonds within a community and act as a powerful motivator, a call to action. Consequently, appealing to honor can be an effective way to combat abhorrent, immoral practices. As Appiah relates in his new book, honor has played a central role in bringing about moral revolutions.

If Miller is honor's number one fan, Appiah offers a far more qualified defense. Like many contemporary moral philosophers, Appiah regards honor values as incompatible with the core ethical principles of dignity and equal worth. He also worries about honor's associations with violence, prejudice, and mistreatment of women. Indeed, in several of Appiah's examples of moral revolutions—such as the end of dueling honor was the source of the problem as well as the solution. At various points in our interview, Appiah even wonders whether he would press a button to rid the world of honor. Of course, he also recognizes that there is no button. Honor is with us whether we like it or not; it is a fundamental part of human psychology. And as he writes: "it is surely better to understand our nature and to manage it than to announce that we would rather we were different ... We may think we have finished with honor, but honor isn't finished with us."

Anthony Appiah is Professor of Philosophy and Law at New York University. He is the author of 10 books, most recently Cosmopolitanism, Experiments in Ethics, *and* The Honor Code. *All of them are a pleasure to read—along with Susan Wolf, Appiah can claim the mantle of philosophy's greatest, most elegant writer. (It was a constant temptation to fill this introduction with direct quotes from his book.) I interviewed him over Skype.*

May 2015

1   How do Moral Revolutions Happen?

TAMLER SOMMERS: You hadn't written much about honor before your recent book, *The Honor Code*. And in that book you explain that you didn't begin the project intending to focus on honor. Your topic was moral revolutions and how they come about. What made you want to research moral revolutions?

KWAME ANTHONY APPIAH: I think there were two ways into the project. My first interest as an undergraduate in philosophy was in philosophy of science. This was in the mid-1970s so we're reading Thomas Kuhn[2] and people like that. And so the way I approached philosophy of science was by thinking about scientific revolutions. It struck me that the history of scientific revolutions had been very illuminating for epistemology and that it might be interesting to think about whether there were moral revolutions as well. And, if there were, then studying them might be revelatory about normative life and ethical questions.

TS: That's interesting, do you see any parallels between the scientific revolutions that Kuhn talks about and the moral revolutions that you began to research?

KAA: Obviously, they're different in many ways, but one thing they share is that we needed to move from thinking about how *individuals* change their beliefs or values to thinking about how *communities* change those things. The great breakthrough that happened in the philosophy of science was the recognition that we shouldn't focus only on individual people coming to know things—the Cartesian model of epistemology—but also on how communities handled knowledge.

TS: So in both the moral and scientific cases, it's a social process. What was your other way into the project?

KAA: The other route into it was that when I was writing my book *Cosmopolitanism*, I got interested in the ways that people in one society can affect the moral life of people in another. And I learned that when people pointed to the end of foot binding in China, they would often say that it had to do with the sense of Chinese honor. And I thought that was absolutely astonishing. It seemed to me there were so many reasons not to torture little girls by crushing their feet. National honor struck me as about 97 on the list.

TS: One possible explanation for moral revolutions like the end of foot binding is that people were persuaded by new and powerful moral arguments. That's an appealing explanation—for philosophers anyway. But you say that this is not really how it works.

KAA: Yes, I don't think that is what happened. Of course, the cases vary, and no doubt if you looked at a wider range of cases you'd get more variation. But in all of them, the good arguments were around long before the changes came about. Now, as I say in the book, I don't think that the moral arguments are irrelevant. It's not that the change would have necessarily happened without them. Very often in the case of, say, national honor, the reason that a practice is dishonorable is because it's wrong. And you have to grasp the way it's wrong to see what is dishonorable about it. So I don't mean that the moral arguments are irrelevant. But if you give me some sound moral arguments against foot binding, I can almost certainly find you an eleventh-century Chinese thinker who already knew it. And the same is true about slavery. Aristotle defended slavery as something that was appropriate for people who were naturally slaves. But people in Aristotle's own day told him he was wrong. So the idea that suddenly new arguments come along—that it's never occurred to anybody that slavery might be wrong or that it might be wrong to cause intense pain to 3-year-old girls—that's not how it was.

TS: So do you think that the arguments are epiphenomenal—that they play no causal role at all?

KAA: No, it's not that I think they're epiphenomenal, I think they're a necessary part of the process. The fact that the arguments are sitting there means they can be mobilized when other conditions arise in which they can somehow be brought to bear.

TS: So the arguments put it out into the realm of possibility that these moral revolutions can happen. But you need other conditions to make it actually come about.

KAA: That is how I think about it now.

2   What Is Honor?

TS: You mentioned that in the case of foot binding, a sense of national honor was crucial to ending the practice. And, in your book, you explain how honor played a big role in causing all of the revolutions you researched. I know this is a tough question to answer, because honor is a tricky, messy concept. Can you give a rough sense of how you define honor in the sense that's relevant to your argument in the book?

KAA: I think that to say that someone has honor is to say that they are entitled to respect according to a code, a code of some group to which they belong.

TS: Entitled to respect in what sense?

KAA: It's a positive respect. It's grounded in a sense that there's a fact about the person in virtue of which it's appropriate to have this kind of positive regard for them.

TS: What are the kinds of facts that could ground this?

KAA: The fact could be that they were born to a prince. It could be a weird fact. It could be a society that respects redheads or whatever. The codes that do this assignment are very local, historically and geographically. Although there are certain things that, for one reason or another, do seem to be in common to almost all honor codes.

TS: What are some of those?

KAA: One is actually there in the piece of etymology. The Latin for honor is *honestas*—that is, truth and lies. Lying, being dishonest, dissembling, is a source of dishonor in a whole range of societies—societies that disagree about lots of other things. And that's not surprising because honor is social. Honesty matters because honor has to do with how other people regard you, how they treat you, and people want to treat you on the basis of what you truly are. Dissembling involves denying them access to the features of the basis of their decision whether to respect you.

TS: So lying can trick people into honoring you when there are no real grounds to do that.

KAA: Yes, especially in societies where people care a great deal about social respect, which is most societies. Even in contemporary societies people who pretend not to care about these things tend to care about them a good deal. In all societies, you don't want to give people rewards if they're not entitled to them, so it's really important that you're responding to what they truly are. It undermines the system if they deceive you, if people can get the rewards without the achievements.

Actually, achievement isn't quite the right word. Pretending to be the son of a prince is a way of getting honor even though, of course, being the son of a prince is not an achievement. So I think that it's important to distinguish between two dimensions of honor. One is the status-based forms of honor, the kind of honor you get from being well born, as they used to say, or for being a man as opposed to a woman, or white as opposed to black in the transatlantic slave system.

TS: For this kind of honor, you don't have do anything, you just have to be born a certain way.

KAA: Right, it's not something you've done, it's a social fact about you that entitles you to a kind of respect that other people are not entitled to. The other dimension is earned honor. It's the honor you get because you've done well at something. It's not a reward for hard work, generally speaking, because if you do well without hard work you tend to get these forms of honor as well. But you do have to achieve something in order to get the rewards.

TS: Just to give an example of the contrast—let's use *The Iliad* which you talk about in your book. The first kind of honor is the honor granted to all the kings who are leading armies into this battle. They're entitled to a certain kind of respect that the foot soldiers aren't, the women aren't, and so forth. The second kind of honor is what Achilles has for being the greatest warrior, or Odysseus for being the smartest when it comes to strategy. The kings, along with everyone else, compete for these honors.

KAA: Yes, that's right. It generally works like this: for anything that's valued in this society, there will be honor associated with significant contributions toward achieving that form of value. If it is a military society, military success will be honored. If it's a society like ours, having lots of money will be honored. And it may not be that everybody agrees about what's honorable. When Horace[3] writes to Maecenas, the richest, noblest person he knows, he says that one of the great things about Maecenas is that he respects people not for their mother and father but for who they are themselves. Horace's idea is that the status-based honor (that Maecenas had in spades) is not real. People say this isn't "true honor." So there's pressure always to push more toward the second kind of honor, the achievement honor, and away from status-based honor.

TS: But even the achieved honor doesn't have to be necessarily something that you have control over, right? As you said before, some of these achievements could be a matter of luck, natural talent, or even divine intervention. In Homer, the gods are always coming in and imbuing strength into the hero. But they get the achievement-based honor anyway.

KAA: This is a contrast between honor and modern moral thought. In modern moral thought, it matters what you put in. Intentions matter. It matters when we make good use of our resources. These things are rewarded by our moral responses. In the ancient world, and actually perhaps still today, some people are honored, for example, just because they're beautiful. Now, of course, there's always a certain amount of maintenance involved in being beautiful. But the fact is that Brad Pitt looks the way he does mostly because of his genes. And this is even more explicit with the ancient Greeks.

TS: I wonder if this is one reason why honor doesn't have "a good odor" in contemporary philosophy, as you write in the book. Or as you put it in another place (I like this), honor is "exiled in some philosophical St. Helena." Sometimes I feel exiled there with it.

KAA: Nowadays we have this idea that rewards should be earned. But there are several other reasons for honor's unpopularity in philosophy. Honor is often associated, not just with forms of status where there's no question of desert, but also with things in which, from a moral point of view, there ought not to be distinction at all. Honor is often very gendered in a way that puts women down. That's not just morally indifferent, that's morally repugnant.

Honor also tends to be associated with something else that I think we rightly repudiate: a tendency to seek violent solutions to problems that should have peaceful solutions. Things that should be settled by argument, reason, procedures.

TS: Honor rewards a quick disposition to violence?

KAA: Yes. In fact, it encourages it. Think about dueling, or for that matter honor killing. Those are both cases where resorting to violence is the honorable solution. Honor doesn't just encourage it, it requires it. If you don't do it, you are dishonored. Honor has a very bloody history, and it has a bloody present in many places and that needs to be regulated by morality.

In cases where honor values things that are morally wrong, I think morality should obviously win.

TS: What's the source of this connection between honor and violence? In principle, there wouldn't have to be this connection. There could be many other grounds for honoring people.

KAA: Yes. Although I think it's really the other way around. It's not that honor leads to violence necessarily, but rather that we notice honor more when it's connected to violence. Honor is a powerful mechanism of social regulation. So it's particularly useful in societies, in which organized military conflict and conquest are important. As I point out in the book, honor can motivate people in contexts where there's very little else that you can use to motivate them. If you're motivated by honor, you'll do these things that are difficult to do. And in those circumstances, the normal reward and punishments that we use to get people to do things aren't available. In general, I think there are four large mechanisms of social control. There's morality, the law, money/economic rewards, and honor/dishonor. In contexts where the first three are not terribly useful, honor rises up as a solution. And I think that's very strikingly true in the case of military societies.

TS: It's not easy to motivate people to overcome their fear and risk their lives in their battle. What's the source of honor's motivating power in these charged contexts? How does it succeed in ways that the other three mechanisms cannot?

KAA: Part of that is just how human beings are constituted, especially if they're brought up in a certain honor framework.

TS: I'm asking more about the psychological mechanisms that honor employs.

KAA: Well a big thing to focus on is dishonor. Especially, again, in small-scale societies or older forms of society, dishonor leads to being shunned. In a really small-scale society that's basically a sentence of death. Colin Turnbull writes in his wonderful book about the Mbuti or Bambuti pygmies of Zaire, the forest people, that they don't have any punishment.[4] But if you do something dishonorable enough people will just stop interacting with you. And you can't live on your own in the forest. You'll die because you can't hunt, can't collect honey. All of these are collective activities. The way in which they live depends upon doing things together. Or imagine the experience of someone who is no longer able to participate in the social life of eighteenth-century England because he has refused to fight a duel. We don't have that experience, but ...

TS: But from their perspective, it might seem worse than death.

KAA: Yes, there is the sense that if I don't do what's required, I might as well be dead, right? Of course, if people do go through public shaming and get out the other side, they discover this is false.

TS: False that they can't live without the community support?

KAA: You can live through shame.

3   Honor's Messiness and the Incommensurability of Values

TS: I wonder if the fear of shame is why people like Lance Armstrong stick to their story until the bitter end. They don't realize that if they just come clean, the dishonor will eventually go away.

KAA: It will eventually go away, yes. Especially in our day. You talked earlier about the messiness of honor. This is one way in which honor is messy. You can evaluate someone on a wide range of respect-based issues. Even if we come up very well on some of them, we're going to come up badly on others.

In morality, the idea of an all-things-considered judgment may make sense. But honor tends to have great difficulty with trying to decide about such things. We see this all the time in a familiar kind of case. Some great university gives an honorary degree to person X. X is indeed worthy of honor in the respect that X was pegged for. X is a great physicist, or a great philanthropist, a great lawyer, or a great public servant. Then it is discovered that X has done something in some other area of his or her life that is dishonorable. Now we say we shouldn't give X an honorary degree. But we weren't honoring her for the domain in which she acted dishonorably. Nevertheless, we sort of lose faith in our honor judgment. There's no formula that says honorable in that direction, .5 here and .7 there, but minus .2 here. Let's add it all up. It doesn't work like that.

TS: This is a constant source of debate in hall-of-fame elections in American sports. Some athletes have done terrible things in their personal lives, and the question always comes up whether to take that into account.

KAA: Honor has a certain kind of incoherence. It isn't in the business of tidying itself up in these ways.

TS: Do you think that's a defect of honor—that it can't be simplified or systematized like contemporary ethical theories? Or is that a virtue?

KAA: There are many things about honor that are wildly unattractive. If I thought that we could displace honor with reasonable social costs, I'd be tempted to. If we could abandon honor, we wouldn't have some of these problems (incoherence, violence, sexism, hostility to outsiders). If I could press a button that would sort of turn it off, I would be tempted to for those reasons, including the incoherence.

TS: I think the messiness or incoherence is one of honor's most attractive features. The messiness encourages continual debate and social exchange. There's great value in that. The debates help us clarify our norms and discover what we really believe. They help us shape and revise our values. The expectation of coherence in ethical theory often leads to oversimplifying things, forcing consistency onto the system when it's not really there. Setting aside the other aspects of honor like sexism, violence, and so forth, would you agree with me about that?

KAA: Okay, I think it's true that there are contexts in which there's no simple way of aggregating things. And honor allows us to have conversations about the things we value and the things we don't value. Your hall-of-fame example brings this out very nicely. As I said, in the world of honor, for any value that human beings can contribute to, some people will contribute greatly to that form of value and people who care about that form of value will honor them for it. That's just part of the psychological normative economy of valuing things. If you care about tennis and you think tennis is beautiful and exciting, then you will just honor great tennis players. You won't have to *decide* whether you honor them. You'll be inclined to treat them with a kind of respect that's grounded in a recognition of a capacity they have and they've exercised to a high degree.

So the messiness of honor reveals to us the incommensurability of our many forms of value. Tennis is a form of value for me because I love tennis. It's not a form of moral value though. It's like Bernard Williams talking about somebody like Gauguin.[5] I don't know what to say when someone asks: OK, so how much moral badness can be justified if it produces aesthetic value, or sporting value? The answer is, well, I don't want to think of it that way—I don't want to be trading them off against each other. But in the real world I am trading them off against each other. Of course, from the point of view of morality, the answer to that question ought to be 'none.'

TS: But that's not the only point of view.[6]

KAA: No, morality matters … it matters that you do the right thing from an all-things-considered moral point of view. But the fact is, we do care about these other forms of value, and sometimes at least we excuse moral failings as we do with Gauguin because we think something else of non-moral value is produced by them.

TS: Do you think morality is the trump card, though—that you can contribute to other forms of value, but only if you're being consistent with morality?

KAA: I may have thought that once, but I don't think it now. And one of the reasons I don't think it now has nothing to do with honor, it just has to do with the relationship between our morality and our own private projects. It can be absolutely clear in certain circumstances what I ought to do morally. But what I ought to do morally can be something that gets in the way of achieving an important personal project. I think it's a kind of moral fanaticism to abandon your personal projects because, say, you have to tell a small lie or break a promise you ought morally to keep and so on.

And if you are a person of honor, you will find yourself tempted in certain circumstances to break with morality and do what's honorable. [James] Boswell quotes in the footnotes of his *Life of Samuel Johnson* a letter from a Guards officer about to engage in a duel.[7] And he begins by apologizing for doing this thing that he knows is wrong, but which honor requires him to do.

TS: In this case, honor takes priority.

KAA: He's saying it takes priority for him, but not denying the force of the moral consideration. In fact, he's stressing it. Nor is he excusing himself.

He's just announcing that there's this other demand that he recognizes and that it's winning.

TS: In the book, you say this about honor killings too. Often the family recognizes that the Koran can't sanction the act, but that honor is more important than religion in this case.

KAA: Maybe some people are confused and some people pretend that they don't see the tension. But they're just cheating or confused. The real person is the person who says look, I understand I ought not to be doing this, don't get me wrong. But the honor of my family or my clan or myself requires it. And that's what I'm going to do.

4   Honor's Role in Ending Foot Binding

TS: Can you give us a brief recap of how honor helped to end the thousand-year-old practice of foot binding in China? That was a fascinating chapter.

KAA: Yes. The short version of that is that by the late nineteenth-century China has suffered a series of catastrophic defeats by European powers and Japan. The Chinese intelligentsia, the literati, the Mandarins, are thinking very hard about what's gone wrong with their society. Why is their society, a great ancient society whose traditions they value and whose intellectual achievements are evident even to the outsiders, why has it failed?

They're thinking deeply about these things and they're conversing about them with friendly foreigners. They discussed these issues with scholars and missionaries who studied Confucian tradition, people who knew Chinese well. And these people kept saying to them, "You know, you're a great civilization but you do this terrible thing to your daughters and we just don't understand how you can do that." And these were conversations with respectful outsiders. The Chinese weren't interested in the people who thought that the Chinese civilization was worthless. Why would you take any notice of the person who thought that? But this was their friends who were saying that.

TS: Which is why they were included in their 'honor world,' as you call it.

KAA: Yes, they were in a web of mutual respect. And these outsider friends who said to them, "Look you're amazing but this is weird." So that Chinese literati came to believe they were doing something that legitimately led these friends to lose respect for them—and therefore lose honor. And they were losing honor as Chinese. It wasn't some random family decision that certain individuals made. Foot binding was a culturally sanctioned thing. So some of them just stopped. Kang Youwei is the protagonist of that chapter, a very bold figure in late-nineteenth/early-twentieth-century Chinese thought, who lived the last part of his life in exile. He didn't bind the feet of his own daughters. And yes, part of it was that he had heard his sister's pain when he was a child. But the outsider perspective and the respectful dialogue freed him enough to want to change.

TS: You write that ridicule and shame played a role too.

KAA: Yes, in one of his memoranda, Kang wrote that "foreigners have been laughing at us ... and criticizing us for being barbarians. There is nothing which makes us objects of ridicule so much as foot binding. I ... feel ashamed at heart." He could see it in the way they saw it, and he could see that it didn't look good. And it looked bad for a legitimate reason.

TS: It was significant that they were losing respect as *Chinese*, right? It was important that people like Kang identified with their nation. Because the outsiders were ridiculing *China* and its practices.

KAA: Yes. You asked me at the start to give an account of honor and one of the things I left out is the centrality of identity to this sort to honor. Because your identity affects what the honor code demands of you. You can gain and lose honor through the actions of people with whom you share an identity. So once Kang chose not to bind the feet of his daughter, the issue was not over for him. Why? Because other Chinese were binding the feet of their daughters, and until they all stopped, he was implicated in the practice as a Chinese person. Just as I feel a kind of pain as an American citizen when I think about Guantánamo or Abu Ghraib. Not because I did it, not even because I think the president ordered it, but because it was done in our name. And this is one of the reasons why, if I had that button to press to get rid of honor, I'd be hesitating. There are moments, especially in national history, where it's critical to have that sense that we have something at stake. Not because of anything I have done but because of something we have done as a group. This sense of identification can mobilize people, it can get them to try to put things right. In a democracy, especially a large-scale democracy, the sense of your own agency is so limited. So you need powerful motivators to get people to make things right.

TS: So honor can encourage a kind of self-policing within a community. Because people in the community don't want to look bad in the eyes of others we care about.

KAA: We don't want to justifiably look bad.

TS: Right, justifiably.

KAA: I don't care if ISIS thinks badly of the United States, because their criteria of judgment are so different from mine—so incorrect I would say—that it doesn't matter to me. But if a respectable Muslim person in the Middle East points to Guantánamo, I have nothing to say except I'm sorry. We shouldn't have done that. We have to stop. So, again, morality matters here, because in these kinds of cases, it's the moral wrongness that leads to the shame.

5 Honor and Women

TS: I'm writing a book in defense of honor right now—in fact, that's the working title. The issue that troubles me most as I do my research is the apparent connection between honor and the mistreatment of women. I know there are exceptions—there are honor systems, honor codes, that don't have objectionable or abhorrent attitudes toward women. But mistreatment of women does seem to be a running theme. There tends to be a strong focus on female fidelity and sexual purity, along with a more permissive attitude toward violence.

Of course honor killings are at the far extreme end of the spectrum. In the vast majority of honor cultures, nobody thinks it's OK to murder their daughter or relative because she's been raped or had extramarital sex. But there are more permissive attitudes concerning violence against women who are suspected of being unfaithful, as well as violence toward anyone who even hints that a wife or daughter has engaged in this behavior.

KAA: Because it makes the male person look bad—it's dishonorable for him.

TS: Right, which is true in all countries to a degree. But what is it that makes the connection between male honor or community honor and a women's sexual fidelity or purity so strong?

KAA: I think at some level this is like the former example with violence. It's just a complex social psychological fact that honor is one of the mechanisms that gets mobilized to police gender and sexuality.

TS: So as with violence in general, honor isn't the source of the attitudes. Rather, it's an effective tool for their enforcement.

KAA: When things are of value or important to you, honor is going to be one of the mechanisms you employ to support them. It matters to people, it matters to men that their women be faithful, it matters to women that they should be faithful to their men in ordinary cases, right? Adultery is one of those things that its practitioners don't usually defend. People understand that what they are doing is wrong. It's just that there is this huge temptation in the realm of sex that leads people to do things that they know to be wrong.

And sex normally takes place in the absence of witnesses. So for the social to be represented, it has to be internalized in some way. And the sense of honor internalizes the social in that context. It's important that we should have an internalized sense of the social when we live in a decent society. The world is full of contexts in which we need people to do the right thing when they can get away with doing the wrong thing.

Now guilt and morality are other mechanisms. But why lose the honor mechanism, since we know from looking around that people will in fact give into temptation a great deal?

TS: Let me just make sure I understand the story. Human beings have a special concern for female fidelity, maybe for evolutionary reasons. Honor itself isn't implicated as the source of this special concern. But honor is recruited as a tool for enforcing it, again because of its motivational power.

KAA: Yes, although this is only the right historical story. Once you have an honor code in place, it may be the main mechanism of gender subjugation. So, the historical explanation may be that honor is not the source, but is instead recruited to enforce attitudes and norms. But that doesn't mean that honor isn't the main problem in a particular case or community.

TS: Right, of course not.

KAA: I was watching an Italian film last night. I don't know Italian but I do know because of my work that the Italian word for shame is '*vergogna.*' This was a story of a family. There are two brothers, in their thirties and forties. The younger one tells the older one that he's going to come out as gay to his family at this dinner and he knows it will be difficult. They go to the dinner but then his elder brother comes out first. And then he can't come out because his father has a heart attack. So it's sort of comical. But what's interesting is that this is a modern film about modern people, set in the year 2010. And there's still this preoccupation with honor and shame. And it reminded me very much of another Italian film, *Sedotta e abbandonata*, that I talk about in the book from the early 1960s that is focused on a rape. It's sort of weird to watch because we think of this in moral terms. The issue here is happiness, unhappiness, right and wrong. And yet the whole focus of the family's attention is on the question of shame.[8]

6 The Fine Line between the Honorable and the Ridiculous

TS: In your chapter on dueling, you describe how this practice ended in England because people came to find it ridiculous. It reminded me a little of the honor codes of baseball or hockey—they're always on this fine line between noble and ridiculous. And it's right on that line, it can go either way even for the same individual. In one frame of mind, I can think that these honor codes are ludicrous. And, in other frames of mind, I can take them as seriously as anybody.

KAA: Right and when you've got an honor system that's endorsing something immoral (like all these forms of gender oppression), sometimes you can push people over the edge toward change by getting them to see themselves more in the absurd frame of mind than in the serious frame. Honor, as you say, is constantly at risk of seeming absurd. It's weird because the worst thing for a person of honor is to be ridiculed. And yet, honorable behavior is itself very often, from many points of view, ridiculous. Too great a preoccupation with your honor can make you seem ridiculous. And I think that that's one of the tools for good. Although it has to be used carefully, because the person of honor whom you ridicule is likely to stab you or beat you up. But, still, I do think that there's a tool there. And yes, I think this is what happened with dueling in England. It became increasingly ridiculous.

TS: At the same time, even when you're fully in the mindset that the codes are ridiculous, they still have a certain appeal. *Don Quixote* is as absurd as it gets. But we don't *just* laugh at Don Quixote, there's something we like about him too. There's something appealing about a lot of people who stubbornly subscribe to a code that's gone out of date. I can't pin down what's at the root of the appeal, but it's there.

KAA: Yes. If someone displays a concern for their honor in that sort of way, you do expect them to be, for example, a loyal friend, an honest person, even if their particular form of honor is something you don't endorse, or that you actively disapprove of. You think of it as flowing from a temperament of a certain sort. That old-fashioned kind of honorable gent is going to have your back. He's going to speak up for you when you're not there because you are his friend and so on. And these are attractive features of the code.

7   Honor as a Tool for Progress in America

TS: I taught your book in a graduate seminar in the fall, and we had a big debate over one question after we finished. We saw that honor was effective in promoting moral change in your historical examples. But we weren't sure how that would work in America. How can we use some of the lessons from your book to end objectionable practices in a country like ours? Because America poses some special challenges. Number one, there's this idea of American exceptionalism that seems expressly designed to make us not feel moral pressure from other countries. And second, for many people, that sense of identification as Americans is pretty weak. You said earlier that you feel ashamed as an American about Guantánamo. I'm not sure if that's the common reaction. It's so easy to say: "that's not my group. I didn't vote for Bush/Cheney. I didn't sign on to their policies." Our country is so big and diverse that it takes a massive event like 9/11 to strengthen that sense of national identity. If that happens, we're all putting up American flags and giving blood. Otherwise, it seems hard or impossible to get people to identify as Americans rather than with the various subcultures they belong to. And this may be even more true for the younger generation. My students thought so anyway.

Given all of that, what lessons can we draw from your book that would help us achieve some sort of moral good in this country? And just to keep it specific, let's take factory farming,[9] which you mention briefly in the book. I consider factory farming to be a moral catastrophe. How could we recruit honor to help change something like that?

KAA: I'll get to your example in a second but I just want to say something about American exceptionalism. We started out as a nation with a "decent respect for the opinion of mankind." Now, that means the opinion of reasonable people. I would like us to hold onto that part of our founding. Seeing yourself in the eyes of your friends can help you to see what you most truly believe in.[10]

As for the factory-farming issue, look, you're right that the sense of national identification is weak. The sense of collective that's needed to get people to be involved in moral revolution and we can't mobilize the nation for this issue. But there are other ways. Iowans live in a state in which large amounts of factory farming goes on. And it's to Iowa's shame that the state legislature does nothing about it. If you could get Iowans to see what they're doing, the people who are rooted there, who think of themselves as

Iowans—if you get them to see the thing reflecting badly on them as Iowans, I think that is one of the places to go.

The other thing is this. To me, the lesson of the anti-foot binding, of anti-slavery, and the anti-dueling cases is that you have to organize. What happens in abolitionism in England is that a very large proportion of the nation joins abolitionist societies. They get together regularly and they form a collective sense of the wrong. And then they try to figure out what to do about it. So they sent petitions to Parliament. It was the first campaign in which there were significant petitions to Parliament. It was the largest subject of petitions to Parliament for the first half of the nineteenth century. So there was that sense that we abolitionists, we're a tribe working to protect national honor. So it matters that we're British. But we're also protecting the honor of Liverpool, the honor of Birmingham, the honor of my small village which has managed to get a hundred people together to sign a petition, and so on.

TS: So while national honor played a big role in stopping foot binding, the identification group can be much smaller. It doesn't have to be a whole nation. Moreover, we can identify with multiple groups to promote the same goal.

KAA: Yes. I don't talk about this in the book because it wasn't a book about social movements. But if you just look at the cases, you can see that the anti-dueling societies, the abolitionist societies, the anti-foot-binding clubs, these were really crucial to forming a sense of a new collective identity: the identity of people campaigning against this thing. It's the sense of yourself as an anti—well, we need something more attractive than the phrase 'an anti-factory-farming person.'

Part of the difficulty in the animal welfare movement is that we're split on certain crucial questions. I think everybody should agree that what goes on at factory farms is morally unacceptable. But we don't agree about the larger question concerning the moral status of animals. No reasonable person thinks that their suffering doesn't matter at all. But a lot of people who are vegetarians are vegetarians because they think that the death of an animal matters. I actually don't share that view. I think what matters is their suffering. So you need a unifying term, maybe humanitarian is the right word. You need some moral identification, as it were.

TS: A term that reflects a consensus about what we're all against.

KAA: Yes. But then you need to remind each other regularly, talk to each other about it, wear pins, sign petitions, do all the things that create a collective sense of a movement.

TS: Would a model for this be something like the civil rights movement, which built this large community among themselves?

KAA: Yes, and then they addressed the nation in a sort of collective way. People addressed their neighbors. Look, think about what just happened in Ireland with the same-sex marriage thing. How did that happen? How in a few years did a country that was in the pocket of the Catholic Church come to be the first country in the world to vote for same-sex marriage—with over 60 percent of the vote? Well, because the 'yes' people were a pretty significant group to begin with. And certainly because they had moral arguments. Again, moral arguments were not irrelevant. The canvassers went door to door with those arguments. And some of the canvassers were gay and some were straight. But the point is there were plenty of straight people who were in this 'yes' movement and gave these arguments. They said look, here's why we think it's important. It's important for the equality of our fellow citizens. It's the civil rights movement of our time. We very much hope you would vote yes. But we also want to hear your argument if you're opposed.

This wouldn't have happened if people had just published the arguments in op-ed columns—even if everybody read them. What was needed was a sense that there was a cumulative social activity here moving in the right direction. You can't do this on every front at once. You have to pick your agenda. I think we're beginning to see a movement like this against mass incarceration. I hope that that will take off in this way. The difficulty, as I say, with the factory-farming thing is that some vegetarians have sort of put off some other people who would otherwise be on their side against factory farming.

TS: Right. There's a need for group cohesion, so it's a problem if vegetarians are lumping together meat eaters who want to abolish factory farms and the people who support factory farms.

KAA: You don't have to agree about everything, but you do have to agree about the broad aspects. Then I think what happens is you get a kind of cycle of positive reinforcement. You and I met at an anti-factory-farming meeting. We see each other on the street, we smile at each other as people who recognize each other as being on the right side. You call me up and say, look we're having this protest outside the factory farm in wherever, somewhere in Texas. I think, OK, we're going. It's a bit inconvenient, I was going to do something else that day, but, hey, because I've got this relationship with this person and these other people in this movement, we'll do things together. And then we get the rewards of looking each other in the face as we stand outside carrying our banners.

TS: We take pride in it.

KAA: We are doing an honorable thing together. We are entitled to each other's respect. It's how I feel when I look at my fellow voters. I think, hey, we're doing something. I know my vote is worth squat, it's not going to make any difference. But that "we" are voting really makes a difference.

TS: Yeah, that's a nice analogy. I took a couple of elections off because of this "my vote can't make a difference" thought. But when I started voting again, I realized that it was fun—a nice community feeling.

KAA: I suppose I'm in favor of online voting, but there's a lot of value in small towns and large cities of physically being together and looking each other in the eye, smiling at each other and the poll workers—this shared feeling of "hey, we're doing this momentous thing which half the people in the world aren't allowed to do in their societies." I think those sorts of feelings are where respect, honor, shame, those things come into play. And if you can get them lined up in the right ways, you can change things.

TS: You know, we just had this big flood here in Houston. The next morning a lot of people went out to survey the damage to the neighborhood. It's an unfortunate thing, but it did generate this feeling of community spirit that rarely happens. We were talking to neighbors and people in the area that we've never spoken to before. And just today I read a story in the *New York Times* that happened to be about our neighborhood. In the story, they talked about trucks that had to get off the highway, and the people in our neighborhood who were giving them bottled water and taking them in. No truckers came to my house, but I felt a great deal of pride just for the neighborhood.

KAA: One thing about those moments is that you might be able to build on them, now that you know each other's names. And next time you walk by each other, you can actually say hello and smile. One of the most difficult things to do in our country today is to talk to each other about politics, except with people we agree with. But our society is in trouble because we don't talk to the people we don't agree with. Because we have preposterous images of each other. It's one thing to disagree about politics, it's another thing to think the other side is evil. And a significant proportion on both sides, both on the left and on the right, in the United States, have this very unpleasant and surely distorted view of what's motivating people on the other side.[11] These moments of crisis can allow people then to maybe cross over into these other conversations, though I agree that may be pie in the sky because it doesn't seem to happen very often.

TS: One last thing about the Ireland case. You mention they were the first nation to vote for same-sex marriage by a popular vote. Do you think that played a role, just wanting to be the first nation?

KAA: I'm sure that the sense of national pride played a role—there's only four and a half million Irish for god's sake, why do we care what they do about anything? Well we do now. People in Australia, you know, the Australian broadcasting networks come all the way around the world to cover this thing. And then the eyes of the world are upon you. You want to do the right thing, you want to be seen to be doing the right thing, you want to be seen as the kind of country that is worthy of respect.

Now, the people who voted against many of them probably had the same thought. But I do think that it made it more likely that people would not do what they felt was the easy thing. They would struggle to figure out what they really thought was right, because in the eyes of the world you want to do that. It's important that there were decent people on both sides of this. I don't agree with the people who voted no, but I don't mean to demonize them. No doubt they struggled too, many of them who came to that conclusion. But that sense of collectively doing something in the eyes of the world can raise your moral game a bit. And that's one of the reasons why I don't think I would push the [honor-banishing] button in the end. Because I don't know of any other way of accomplishing that.

TS: Well I guess it's encouraging how quickly change can happen, because it's been pretty remarkable in our country and in Ireland ...

KAA: In a way it's quite puzzling why this particular change has taken off so quickly in a way that others with much longer histories have not. The movement against animal cruelty is much, much older, though it starts with some of the same people, Bentham for example. But he couldn't say what he thought about homosexuality publicly. We only know that because we look at the notes that he left. He wasn't able to say it. He was able to give his arguments about animals. So it's a bit of a puzzle for me why views on homosexuality have changed so quickly, and even in this very Catholic country, in Ireland.

TS: I think one reason is that we have friends who are gay. We interact with them in real life, we interact with them on TV—and that's not true in the case of factory farms. We don't see what goes on there. We aren't confronted with that on a daily basis or sometimes ever.

KAA: Exactly. And the same is true with mass incarceration. If you're not in one of the communities that have been devastated by it, you don't know what's going on. Even if you do know, you don't know in that way where your face is rubbed in it every day. Whereas, I think the late 1960s gay rights movement was correct. If you could persuade people to come out, other people would end up having gay friends and the contact hypothesis mechanism[12] would operate. And we have come out ... and it's worked.

Notes

1   There are a handful of exceptions, including Anthony Cunningham, Dan Demitriou, Shannon French, Shannon Krause, and Peter Olsthoorn.

2   Appiah is referring to Thomas Kuhn's landmark book *The Structure of Scientific Revolutions* (Chicago, IL: Chicago University Press, 1962).

3   In his "Satires," Horace, who was the son of an ex-slave, addresses Maecenas, one of the richest and noblest citizens of Augustan Rome. Though Maecenas himself says "it's no matter who your parents are, so long as you're worthy," the poet objects that most Romans take the opposite view:

Thus he who does solemnly swear to his citizens to take care of the city,
The empire, and Italy, and the sanctuaries of the gods,
Forces every mortal to pay attention, and to ask
From what father he may be descended, whether he is base because of the obscurity of his mother.

sic qui promittit civis, urbem sibi curae,
imperium fore et Italiam, delubra deorum,
quo patre sit natus, num ignota matre inhonestus,
omnis mortalis curare et quaerere cogit

(Sermones, I. 6, ll. 34–7).

4 Colin Turnbull *The Forest People* (New York: Simon & Schuster, 1968).
5 B. Williams, "Moral Luck." In Daniel Statman (ed.), *Moral Luck* (State University of New York Press, Albany, NY, 1993), pp. 35–55.
6 This is also Susan Wolf's view in "Moral Saints." Wolf and I discuss this briefly in Chapter 4.
7 "It must be confessed, that, from the prevalent notions of honor, a gentleman who receives a challenge is reduced to a dreadful alternative. A remarkable instance of this is furnished by a clause in the will of the late Colonel Thomas, of the Guards, written the night before he fell in a duel, September 3, 1783: 'In the first place, I commit my soul to Almighty God, in hopes of his mercy and pardon for the irreligious step I now (in compliance with the unwarrantable customs of this wicked world) put myself under the necessity of taking'" (*The Life of Samuel Johnson, LL.D. Together with the Journal of a Tour to the Hebrides*, edited by Alexander Napier (London: George Bell & Sons, 1889)), vol. 2: 343).
8 *Sedotta e abbandonata* (*Seduced and Abandoned*) (1964), Pietro Germi, director. Story and screenplay by Luciano Vincenzoni.
9 Thanks to Meg Viers in my seminar for coming up with this example.
10 Nancy Sherman makes a similar point about Aristotelian ethics in Chapter 5
11 I discuss this problem in some detail with Jon Haidt (Chapter 12) and Fiske and Rai (Chapter 15).
12 The contact hypothesis was developed by Gordon Allport in 1954. According to Allport, interpersonal contact is the most effective means of reducing prejudice and promoting tolerance and acceptance.

Questions for Discussion

1 Why does Appiah believe that arguments aren't enough to change the moral attitudes of a community? How can honor help?

2 What role does honesty play in honor?

3 What's the difference between status-based honor and earned honor?

4 What makes honor problematic for contemporary philosophers?

5 How does dishonor regulate the behavior in certain societies?

6 According to Appiah, why doesn't morality trump everything when faced with conflicting values?

7 What role does collective identity play in honor and social change? Why is it also important to understand and interact with opposing people or groups?

Suggested Readings

Appiah, Kwame Anthony. "The Case for Contamination." *New York Times Magazine* (1 Jan., 2006): www.nytimes.com/2006/01/01/magazine/01cosmopolitan.html
——. "The Way We Live Now: A Slow Emancipation." *New York Times Magazine* (18 March, 2007): www.nytimes.com/2007/03/18/magazine/18WWLNlede.t.html
——. "The Art of Social Change." *New York Times Magazine* (22 Oct., 2010): www.nytimes.com/2010/10/24/magazine/24FOB-Footbinding-t.html
——. "Kwame Anthony Appiah on Honour." *Telegraph* (15 Oct., 2010): www.telegraph.co.uk/culture/books/bookreviews/8063931/Kwame-Anthony-Appiah-on-Honour.html

———. "The Best Weapon against Honor Killers: Shame." *Wall Street Journal* (25 Sept., 2010): www.wsj.com/articles/SB10001424052748703989304575504110702939510

———. "Is Religion Good or Bad? (This Is a Trick Question)." Lecture at TED250 (16 June, 2014): https://youtu.be/X2et2KO8gcY

———. "Kwame Anthony Appiah: The Complexities of Black Folk." Interview by George Yancy, *New York Times*: Opinionator: The Stone (April 16, 2015): http://opinionator.blogs.nytimes.com/2015/04/16/kwame-anthony-appiah-the-complexities-of-black-folk

———. "Kwame Anthony Appiah: The Complexities of Black Folk." Interview by George Yancy. *New York Times: Opinionator: The Stone* (16 April, 2015): http://opinionator.blogs.nytimes.com/2015/04/16/kwame-anthony-appiah-the-complexities-of-black-folk

See also Appiah's joint advice column "The Ethicists" in the *New York Times*. www.nytimes.com/column/the-ethicist

Assorted Media and Podcast Pairings

Appiah, Kwame Anthony. "The Case for Cosmopolitanism." Video interview by *Al Jazeera* (18 Feb., 2012): www.aljazeera.com/programmes/talktojazeera/2012/02/2012218133940306474.html

Very Bad Wizards, Episode 4 "Revenge (Part 1)." http://verybadwizards.com/episodes/4

Very Bad Wizards, Episode 13 "Beanballs, Blood Feuds, and Collective Moral Responsibility." http://verybadwizards.com/episodes/13

Very Bad Wizards, Episode 56 "Moral Heroes and Drunk Utilitarians." http://verybadwizards.com/episodes/56

Part III

Metaethics

The Status of Morality

Introduction

Metaethics? What does that mean?

First-order ethics addresses questions like "what is the right thing to do?" or "what are the best ways to live?" Metaethics steps back and tries to figure out what we're doing when we ask these questions. When we say "murdering innocent people is wrong," are we just expressing opinions or attitudes like "Baskin Robbins chocolate chip is delicious"? Or are we stating a fact like "the earth revolves around the sun?" And if we think that moral claims are factual, are we deluding ourselves? Are we like people in Salem debating over whether Elizabeth or Anne is a witch when in fact there are no such things as witches? Finally, if we're not deluded and there are ethical facts, what kind of facts are they? Are they grounded in reason, or intuition, or are they natural facts that we can discover through empirical investigation?

This all sounds pretty abstract. I thought you were against that now.

It is and it isn't. Metaethical issues come up in almost every interview in this book. It's important to understand what we're doing when we reflect on moral questions and engage in moral argument. The three authors in Part III just give a more focused defense of metaethical positions that the authors in the rest of the book either explicitly or implicitly embrace.

Let's go through these positions then.

Michael Ruse in Chapter 8 argues against the view science can determine right and wrong. He discusses both the virtues and pitfalls of taking a Darwinian approach to ethics. And he defends a form of metaethical skepticism or nihilism, claiming that "ethics is an illusion put into place by our genes to keep us social."

Nihilism? Sounds pretty radical!

Don't worry, it's not the kind of nihilism that made Russians decide to blow up train stations in the 1850s. Ruse is pretty optimistic about the implications of his view. The more radical view belongs to Peter Singer and it's the topic of Chapter 9. Singer argues that we can discover true ethical principles about our obligation to others through rational deliberation. And the principles are exceptionally demanding. For one thing, they require us to be completely impartial. We should not give any more weight to our own suffering, or the suffering of family members, than we do to the suffering of strangers. If Singer is right, the vast majority of us are leading deeply immoral lives. And if this sounds counterintuitive, well, Singer (like Greene in Chapter 17) claims that we can debunk intuitions that go against his principles by appealing to evolutionary theory.

Back up a second. Singer believes that we derive these principles through the use of our reason? This sounds exactly like the type of abstract, idealized, hyper-systematic approach to ethics that you were complaining about in Part II.

Singer is a fascinating case, because on the one hand his work is a perfect example of the kind of moral philosophy that I think is misguided and disconnected from the real world. On the other hand, Singer and his ideas have had a tremendous practical impact on the world. More than any living philosopher and it's not close.

Shows how much you know.

I guess so. Now if you're curious about my own metaethical position, just read Chapter 10, my interview with Simon Blackburn. Not only do I agree with Blackburn about almost everything, it was his work that converted me. Blackburn is what we call a metaethical expressivist. Like Ruse, Blackburn denies the existence of free-floating moral facts or moral principles that we can derive from pure reason. But he doesn't think ethics is an illusion. According to Blackburn, when we make ethical judgments, we're not stating facts. We're expressing emotions or attitudes and often trying to convince others to share those attitudes. The attitudes are *based* on facts or beliefs about the world. And the attitudes reflect facts about our individual psychologies. But they are not themselves facts or beliefs. What this means is that depending on their psychologies, certain people can be immoral without being irrational. And that's OK. Like the late great philosopher Bernard Williams, Blackburn thinks that many of the problems in moral philosophy are rooted in this quest to find "the argument that will stop them in their tracks when they come to take you away." I agree with him about that too.

8   Michael Ruse

The Illusion of Objectivity in Ethics

We all have strong moral beliefs and make confident moral judgments. Terrorists are evil; discrimination is wrong. But where do these beliefs come from? One answer is that there are moral facts out there in the world waiting to be discovered, and rational creatures like us are capable of discovering them. Another is that these moral beliefs are part of a specific human psychology that has developed during the course of evolutionary history. According to this view, the urge to help thy neighbor is a result of the same evolutionary process that produced the urge to sleep with thy neighbor's wife. Both urges are adaptations, like the human eye or the opposable thumb, and have evolved because they conferred higher fitness on the organisms that possessed them.

For more than 30 years, the philosopher Michael Ruse has championed this latter view. His 1986 book Taking Darwin Seriously *is a full-length defense of the position that the theory of natural selection has a lot to tell us about our moral lives. Since then, Ruse—the Lucyle T. Werkmeister Professor of Philosophy at Florida State University and an absurdly prolific author—has written numerous books and articles clarifying and expanding his purely naturalistic approach to morality, religion, and epistemology. His most recent book is called* Darwinism and Its Discontents.

Ruse and other like-minded theorists have generated excitement with their views, and a fair amount of controversy as well. Criticism of evolutionary ethics is a bipartisan affair. From the left come attacks from a large and vocal contingent of academics, who range from being baffled to being appalled by the claim that human nature is not entirely a social construction. (The great evolutionary biologist and entomologist E. O. Wilson—coauthor of a number of articles with Ruse—was known to certain university activists as "the prophet of the right-wing patriarchy." During the course of one of Wilson's lectures, a group that called itself Science for the People dumped a bucket of ice water on his head and then chanted "You're all wet.") On the right, there are the hardline moral realists engaged in their search for "moral clarity." To them, Darwinism introduces an element of subjectivity that threatens to undermine the certainty they bring to ethical affairs. And of course there are the religious fundamentalists, who object not only to a Darwinian approach to ethics but to the truth of evolutionary theory itself. Ruse got a taste of this brand of anti-Darwinian sentiment during his involvement in the infamous Arkansas creation trial of 1981. I began our interview—which took place over email and on the phone—by asking about this experience.

June 2003

1   Open Bar at the ACLU

TAMLER SOMMERS: In 1981, the state of Arkansas passed a law requiring science teachers who taught evolution to give equal time to something called "creation science." The ACLU [American Civil Liberties Union] sued the state, and you served as one of their expert witnesses. First of all, what exactly is creation science?

MICHAEL RUSE: Well, it's a form of American fundamentalism and biblical literalism. It's the belief that the Bible, particularly the early chapters of Genesis, are a reliable guide to history, including life history. Creationism itself is not a new phenomenon—it goes back certainly to the nineteenth century. The basic tenets are: the world is 6,000 years old, there was a miraculous creation, a universal flood, that sort of thing. Creation science as such is a phenomenon of the 1960s and 1970s; it was polished up in order to get around the US Constitution's separation of church and state. And that's why they call it creation *science*. Because they want to claim scientifically that Genesis can be proven.

TS: What role did the ACLU want you to play in overturning the law?

MR: I was one of the expert witnesses called to testify against the law. Technically speaking, they were just trying to show that creation science is not science. So my job as a philosopher was to testify as to the nature of science and the nature of religion, and show that evolution is science, and creation science is religion.

TS: And so because of that, it did not deserve equal time in the classroom.

MR: It was not a question of what it deserves. The Constitution forbids the teaching of religion in publicly funded schools in America.

TS: In your book *But Is It Science?* you describe the trial, and you talk about the deposition you gave to the assistant attorney general of Arkansas, David Williams—it sounded like quite a grilling. At one point he asks you how you regard morality. You respond, "I intuit moral values as objective realities." Fortunately, you say, Williams didn't ask what you meant by that. But since it's relevant to the topic of this interview, what did you mean exactly?

MR: I'm not sure, really. I don't think of that as accurate, exactly, as to what my position really is. I think if you look at books that I wrote, like *Sociobiology: Sense or Nonsense?,* I certainly didn't think that morality could be reduced to evolutionary biology, in those days. I'm not sure if I've changed my mind, or come to a fuller understanding of the issue. I think I would still say that part of my position on morality is very much that we regard morality in some sense as being objective, even if it isn't. So the claim that we intuit morality as objective reality—I would still say that. Of course, what I would want to add is that from the fact that we do this, it doesn't follow that morality really is objective.

TS: I like your account of the "hospitality room" the afternoon before the trial. It was you, a bunch of religion witnesses, and an open bar. But they were witnesses for the ACLU, right?

MR: Yes, they were there to testify that it certainly isn't traditional religion to be forced to accept a literal reading of the Bible. Bruce Vawter, a Catholic priest, pointed out that if you go back to St. Augustine and earlier, they've all argued that one should be able to interpret the Bible metaphorically if science and the facts dictate otherwise, and so it follows that the Bible taken literally isn't necessarily true. The theologian Langdon Gilkey was arguing this, too, but from a contemporary theological perspective. Most theologians today, he said, do not believe in an absolutely literal interpretation of the Bible. And there was also George Marsden, an eminent historian who talked about the development of the fundamentalist movement and how it came into being. And again, trying to show very much that this is not traditional Christianity, but rather an indigenous form of American Protestant Christianity.

TS: But you say that the lawyers for the ACLU may have made a mistake in having an open bar right before the rehearsal.

MR: Well, I think they were worried that we'd all be sloshed or hungover before the actual trial. I mean, open bar ... Well, we may have had a few gins, but it wasn't like a ...

TS: Fraternity party?

MR: Or even a meeting of the APA.[1]

TS: So the rehearsal suffered a little, but then in court the testimony went quite smoothly.

MR: It did.

TS: And the judge used a couple of your points in his decision against the state of Arkansas.

MR: Not just a couple of my points. If you look at the judge's decision in *But Is It Science?*, his five or six criteria for what counts as science are taken precisely from my testimony. And you know, I'm not showing off—but that's what he did. And in fact, this is what got people like Larry Laudan[2] hot under the collar.

TS: There were some other well-known expert witnesses, too. Francisco Ayala, Stephen Jay Gould. In your book, you write a nice passage about them. You say, "To hear Ayala talking lovingly of his fruit flies and Gould of his fossils was to realize so vividly that it is those who deny evolution who are anti-God, not those who affirm it." What exactly are you saying here?

MR: I'm saying that if in fact you're Christian, then you believe you were made in the image of God. And that means—and this is traditional Christian theology—that you have intelligence and self-awareness and moral ability. So what I would say then, that not to use one's intelligence, or to deny it or not to follow it, is at one level a heretical denial of one's God-given nature. And so this is the point I made—that in being a scientist, far from being anti-Christian or anti-God, you are utilizing the very things that make one God-like, in the Christian perspective. Of course, on the other hand, Christians are always caught up in this business of faith versus reason. And they love to argue that the most childlike among us can achieve understanding of God, true faith. So faith is very important for Christians. Nevertheless, it's a very important part of Christianity that our intelligence is not just a contingent thing, but is in fact that which makes us in the image of God.

2   "Ethics Is an Illusion Put into Place by Our Genes to Keep Us Social"

TS: Okay, let's talk about Darwinism and morality. Because on this topic, it's not just religious fundamentalists who object to an evolutionary approach. A wide range of people are disturbed by the idea that there could be any connection between Darwinian theory and ethics. Should they be?

MR: Yes, I certainly think they should be. In the past, evolution—Darwinian selection—has been used to legitimize some dreadful political and moral (for want of a better word) views. Hitler is open about his social Darwinism in *Mein Kampf.* Others have done the same. However, being disturbed is not to say that one should not take seriously the possible connection, because people have done bad things in its name. I would not reject the teaching of the Sermon on the Mount because priests have put their hands on little boys' willies.

TS: Do you think the connection has had some positive effects as well?

MR: Yes. In fact, historically one can make the case that social Darwinism has been a force for good as much as for bad. Alfred Russel Wallace used his evolutionism (and he was a co-discoverer of the theory of natural selection) to argue for socialism and feminism. People today also argue for things I find attractive. Sarah Hrdy argues that females are at least as successful as males and as dominant in their way, even though they use strategies that do not involve brute force. Ed Wilson argues for biodiversity in the name of evolution—he thinks if we destroy the rain forests, then we destroy humankind, and this is a bad thing. Of course what I would argue is that the connection between Darwinism and ethics is not what the traditional social Darwinian argues. He or she argues that evolution is progressive, that humans came out on top and therefore are a good thing, hence we should promote evolution to keep humans up there and to prevent decline. I think that is a straight violation of the is–ought dichotomy.[3]

TS: In your books you refer to this as a violation of Hume's law. Can you explain exactly what Hume's law is?

MR: I take Hume's law to be the claim that you cannot go from statements of fact—"Duke University is the school attended by Eddy Nahmias"—to statements of value—"Duke University is an excellent school." Some say Hume was simply pointing to the fact that people do go from fact to obligation and was himself endorsing this move—but I think this is a misreading of Hume and certainly goes against his own philosophy.

TS: So then it seems that Ed Wilson, much as we support his cause, is guilty of violating Hume's law, too. He's getting a normative conclusion—we *should* promote biodiversity—from facts about the way the world is. I know you two are friends—how does he respond to that charge?

MR: Ed does violate Hume's law, and no matter what I say he cannot see that there is anything wrong in doing this. It comes from his commitment to the progressive nature of evolution. No doubt he would normally say that one should not go from *is* to *ought*—for example, from "I like that student" to "It is okay to have sex with her, even though I am married." But in the case of *evolution* he allows it. If you say to him, "But *ought* statements are not like *is* statements," he replies that in science, when we have reduction, we do this all the time: going from one kind of statement to another kind of statement. We start talking about little balls buzzing in a container and end up talking about temperature and pressure. No less a jump than going from *is* to *ought*.

TS: But you agree with Hume that the jump can't be made. Still, you want to say that there is some relationship between ethics and Darwinism, right?

MR: My position is that the ethical sense can be explained by Darwinian evolution—the ethical sense is an adaptation to keep us social. More than this, I argue that sometimes (and this is one of those times), when you give an account of the way something occurs and is as it is, this is also to give an explanation of its status. I think that once you see that ethics is simply an adaptation, you see that it has no justification. It just is. So in metaethics[4] I am a nonrealist. I think ethics is an illusion put into place by our genes to keep us social.

TS: An illusion—so then are you saying that the only true connection is that Darwinism can account for why we (falsely) believe that ethics is real?

MR: No, I distinguish normative ethics from metaethics. In normative ethics I think evolution can go a long way to explain our feelings of obligation: be just, be fair, treat others like yourself. We humans are social animals and we need these sentiments to get on. I like John Rawls's[5] thinking on this. On about page 500 of his *Theory of Justice*, Rawls says he thinks the social contract was put in place by evolution rather than by a group of old men many years ago. Then, in metaethics, I think we see that morality is an adaptation merely and hence has no justification. Having said this, I agree with the philosopher J. L. Mackie[6] (who influenced me a lot) that we feel the need to "objectify" ethics. If we did not think ethics was objective, it would collapse under cheating.

3   Does Morality *Need* to Be Objective?[7]

TS: What do you mean by that? The moral system *needs* us to think that ethics is objective?

MR: If we knew that it was all just subjective, and we felt that, then of course we'd start to cheat. If I thought there was no real reason not to sleep with someone else's wife and that it was just a belief system put in place to keep me from doing it, then I think the system would start to break down. And if I didn't share these beliefs, I'd say to hell with it, I'm going to do it. So I think at some level, morality has to have some sort of, what should I say, some sort of force. Put it this way: I shouldn't cheat, not because I can't get away with it, or maybe I *can* get away with it, but because it is fundamentally wrong.

TS: But what about chimpanzees and other species that engage in altruistic, and some would even say moral, behavior?[8] They probably don't have any notions of objectivity and yet they still do it.

MR: I don't know that they don't. I would say that as soon as one starts to have some sort of awareness, then I would be prepared to say that there is some sense of objective morality—obviously much less than ours. When I come in and my dog looks guilty and I find it's because he peed on the carpet … I mean, sure, part of it is that he's afraid I'll beat the hell out of him, but by and large I don't beat the hell out of my dog any more than I do my kids. So I'd be prepared to say that the dog knows he's done wrong. Now, on the other hand, my ferrets—you know, they'll shit anywhere. I mean, I like ferrets, I love ferrets, but I don't think they have any awareness of right and wrong when it comes to these things. Whereas I really think that dogs and cats do, particularly dogs.

TS: I would definitely say dogs more than cats. Cats don't ever seem to think they're in the wrong.

MR: Right. And you know, I've talked to ethologists about this. Dogs are very social animals. And morality is a social phenomenon. And so in certain respects, dogs might be closer to humans even than, say, gorillas. And certainly orangutans. Orangutans are not particularly social beings at all. And so even though we're much closer phylogenetically to orangutans than we are to dogs, dogs have gone the route of sociality in a way that we have. So you might well find that something like a moral sense appears in dogs more than orangutans. I mean, that all sounds terribly anthropomorphic but it's not entirely stupid. Dogs work in groups, and that is what has made them the successful species that they are. They hunt together, share food. I mean, I'm not a dogologist. But I think it would be interesting to note, do you find cheating behavior? Are certain dogs excluded at some level because they don't play the game? I wouldn't be surprised if something like that happens. And you know, particularly at the chimpanzee level, there seems to be an awful lot of sophistication on who can be trusted and who can't be trusted, and who's cheating, and so forth.

TS: And you would regard that as a belief in objectivity?

MR: Yes, I would. I don't feel the need to insist that they have a full awareness of objectivity, but it certainly seems to me that my dog shows a level of guilt and it's not just a matter of fear.

TS: It's true—I've never hit my dog in my life, but if she's ever done anything wrong, she looks guilty.

MR: Right, and you know exactly what she's done. But believe me, with ferrets, *guilt* is not a word in their vocabulary. We're like dogs, social animals, and so we have morality and this part of the phenomenology of morality—how it appears to us, that it is not subjective, that we think it *is* objective.

TS: But you've said that you think that at bottom there is no objective morality.

MR: The fact that you have a theory about something doesn't follow that you can do it. I mean, you can lie on the couch for years and the therapist can point out that your mother doesn't really hate you, but then you go out into the light of day and know that your mother hates you. What I'm saying is that human nature can't be turned over because of what a couple of philosophers are doing. I mean, David Hume makes this point. If you do philosophy, it all leads to skepticism. You can't prove a damn thing. But does it matter? No! We go on. I take Hume very seriously on this point. Our psychology prevents our philosophy from getting us down. We go on. We play a game of backgammon, we have a meal. And then when we come back to think about philosophy it seems cold and strange. So I think ethics is essentially subjective but it appears to us as objective, and this appearance, too, is an adaptation. It is not just that I dislike rape. I think it is *really and truly* wrong. Rawls of course denies that ethics is subjective, and as a Kantian thinks the answer is that the social contract is a condition of rational people living and working together. But I am inclined to think that rational people might have another social system different from ours. So, in a way, I am a Humean seeing morality as a matter of psychology.

TS: So it's not morality itself, but this feeling of *objectivity* in morality that is the illusion—right? But doesn't that mean that as clearheaded Darwinians, we have to say that there are no objective moral facts? And therefore that it is not an objective fact that rape is wrong?

MR: Within the system, of course, rape is objectively wrong—just like three strikes and you're out in baseball. But I'm a nonrealist, so ultimately there is no objective right and wrong for me. Having said that, I *am* part of the system and cannot escape. The truth does not necessarily make you free.

TS: The truth here being that there is no real right and wrong.

MR: Yes, but knowing that it is all subjective doesn't necessarily mean that I can become a Nietzschean superman and ignore it. I take very seriously Raskolnikov in *Crime and Punishment.* Dostoyevsky points out that even if we have these beliefs that there is no right and wrong, we can't necessarily act on them. And, you know, I see no real reason to get out of the system, either. If I rape, I am going to feel badly, apart from the consequences if I am caught. And the reciprocation—I don't want my wife and daughters raped. But even rape is relative in a sense to our biology. If women went into heat, would rape be a crime/sin? I wrote about this once in the context of extraterrestrials—is rape wrong on Andromeda?

TS: I'm not sure what you mean by "within the system it is objectively wrong." Do you mean that because we have laws and norms against rape, then rape is wrong? Or do you mean that for our species, given our biology, rape is objectively wrong? If it's the latter, aren't you violating Hume's law, too?

MR: I would say that within the baseball system, it is objectively true that three strikes means you're out. It is true, but I would not say it's objectively true that George Steinbrenner should keep faith with Joe Torre. This latter is a Michael Ruse judgment call. There is no ultimate, God-given objective truth about baseball. It is an invention. There is no ultimate truth about morality. It is an invention—an invention of the genes rather than of humans, and we cannot change games at will, as one might change from baseball if one went to England and played cricket. Within the system, the human moral system, it is objectively true that rape is wrong. That follows from the principles of morality and from human nature. If human females went into heat, it would not necessarily be objectively wrong to rape—in fact, I doubt we would have the concept of rape at all. So, within the system, I could justify it. But I deny that human morality at the highest level—love your neighbor as yourself, etc.—is justifiable. That is why I am not deriving *is* from *ought*, in the illicit sense of justification. I am deriving it in the sense of explaining *why we have* moral sentiments, but that is a different matter. As an analyst I can explain why you hate your father, but that doesn't mean your hatred is justified.

TS: So then by analogy, Darwinian theory can explain why we have moral sentiments and beliefs, right? So let's get into the details. Why was it adaptive to have this moral sense? Why did our genes invent morality?

MR: I am an individual selectionist all the way. Natural selection has given us selfish/self-centered thoughts. It had to. If I meet a pretty girl and at once say to Bob Brandon,[9] "You go first," I am going to lose in the struggle for existence. But at the same time we are social animals. It's a good thing to be, we can work together. But being social demands special adaptations, like being able to fight off disease and to communicate. We need adaptations to get on, and this I think is where morality comes in—or the moral sense—and other things like human females not going into heat.

4   "You Don't Make Progress by Sitting on Your Bum Farting on about Spandrels"

TS: I wanted to ask this before—what is it about human females not going into heat that leads to us to be moral?

MR: Human females not going into heat does not make us moral or immoral—but it is an important fact of our sociality and it is an important fact when we are making moral judgments (which are always matters of fact *plus* moral principles). I am simply saying that if women did go into heat, then even if we had the same moral principles—treat others fairly, etc.—it would simply not make sense to condemn someone for fucking the female if he got the chance. Having to take a shit is a physical adaptation, and it makes silly the moral claim that you ought never shit—although it does not affect the claim that it is wrong to go to your supervisor's home for supper and end the evening by crapping on his Persian rug.

TS: That's what I meant—why would it not make sense to condemn someone for raping a human female, if human females went into heat?

MR: Look, in my view, as a naturalist, I think epistemology and ethics are dependent on the best modern science. Look at Descartes and Locke and Hume and Kant. The point is that if women went into heat, then biology really would take over and we would lose our freedom. Have you ever been in a situation where you were sexually frustrated and didn't particularly want to jerk off but ended by doing so? Were you really a free agent? Or what if you are really hungry and there is a plate of french fries in front of you? Does one blame the alcoholic for drinking? I used to smoke and I would not say that I was free. The point is that *ought* implies a choice, and if women went into heat then there would be no choice. I wouldn't have a hell of a lot of choice even though they also wouldn't. So it's not that we are always moral—we certainly aren't—but we have the urge to be moral as one of the package of human adaptations.

TS: Okay, I can see why selection has given us selfish thoughts. A trait that leads you to give up the girl to Brandon every time is not going to get passed on to the next generation. Because you need a woman to pass on traits of any kind. At least for now, with the cloning ban. But adaptations that lead us to be moral seem trickier—especially those that on the surface would seem to decrease chances for survival and reproduction. Take for example the sense of guilt that we might feel when cheating on a spouse. Why would selection encourage a trait like that?

MR: I would be inclined to see guilt as part of the package of emotions that enforce morality. But I would never say that morality stops actions that are bad. Sometimes the guilt does stop adultery, but I suspect more often it is the fear of being caught.

TS: So then is the gist of this that morality has developed as a way of curbing some of our most antisocial or destructive tendencies? And that we have enough natural autonomy so that, sometimes at least, our moral sense wins out?

MR: That is right. We are a balance, or, if you like, a conflict, between selfishness and altruism. This is something that Saint Paul said a long time ago—but not everything that Saint Paul said is wrong. That is, whether the autonomy comes in. I think we are causally determined, but rather like sophisticated rockets that have the ability to redefine their targets in midflight as the new information comes in.

TS: This idea that ethics depends on the best modern science is still fairly unpopular among philosophers, isn't it? I was just at a weekend colloquium on "intrinsic value" and all the talk was about rights, human dignity, and rational agents—concepts that don't have much to do with science. Do you agree with your friend Ed Wilson's remark that the time has come for ethics to be removed from the hands of philosophers, and biologicized?

MR: Ed Wilson is given to too much rhetoric, but essentially I agree. Although there is a lot more interest in evolution and ethics than there was 20 years ago, and respectable people like Brian Skyrms and Elliott Sober have written on the topic.

TS: Both of these authors have developed naturalistic and Darwinian explanations for the evolution of altruism, or of the social contract. And both rely (in Skyrms' case, heavily) on game theory to support their claims. But game theory makes a lot of assumptions, some say unjustified assumptions, about inheritance mechanisms. How do you respond to the charge raised by Stephen Jay Gould and others that theories like theirs, and yours, are really "just-so" stories? That there is too little attention paid to the mechanisms through which complex behaviors, and something like a moral sense, could be passed along?

MR: I am sick of the criticism of "just-so" stories. Look at the volume on commitment just edited by Randy Nesse. There are lots of references to psychologists and others who are working on these issues empirically. Of *course* the game theory people make assumptions. That's how you do science. Get an idea, build a model, check it out, revise and redraw, etc. You don't make progress by sitting on your bum farting on about spandrels.[10] And you can quote me on that.

TS: Done. Another objection I hear often is that if evolution can entirely explain morality, then moral nihilism is a consequence. Life has no meaning. We should all become like raving Dostoyevsky characters, or kill ourselves, or at least train ourselves out of any altruistic tendencies we might have and take advantage of everyone else. Now I can't see any reason why we should train ourselves out of anything, even if moral nihilism is true. Actually, the whole idea seems to violate Hume's law. But it's undeniable that many people find the Darwinian worldview almost unbearably bleak. What would you say to some of these people?

MR: I think ultimately there is nothing—moral nihilism, if you wish. But I think Dostoyevsky was spot-on in *Crime and Punishment* to see that even if we see the full story, it does not mean that we can act on it, given our natures. Raskolnikov confesses of his own will, remember. But generally why should we try to go against our nature? It only makes us miserable. The only time I think it might make sense to try to step out of the moral game is if we saw that it was leading to worse things down the road. Again, Hume as always had the best response—backgammon and a good meal with your friends. Philosophy leads to skepticism, psychology lifts you out of it.

TS: So you wouldn't worry like some do about the cat being let out of the bag—about society at large coming to believe that morality was nonobjective?

MR: I certainly don't worry. I am far, far more concerned about the irrationality of the average American politician, especially Bush—stuff right out of fundamentalist religion about millennia and dispensations and raptures and that sort of thing.

TS: And to those who say something like, "If I thought that all there was at bottom were genes trying to replicate themselves, I'd kill myself," we can say, "No, you won't. You may think you would kill yourself, but you won't. Because you're a human being, and human beings like to have fun, play games, and drink with friends."

MR: Yes, but there's more than just that. I would also say that having Christian beliefs produces a fair number of heavy-duty psychological stresses and strains. I mean, I'm not quite sure that … Christ, the little fuckers, have they—no, I'm sorry, I thought they'd pissed on the carpet.

TS: Was that the dog or the ferret?

MR: The ferret. But they didn't. I mean, frankly, I find it a great relief to no longer believe in God. I don't know why it is but my God was always a bit of a Presbyterian. After creating heaven and hell and then humans, he spends the rest of creation, you know, hating them and making life miserable for them. I find it a great relief not to have that kind of God hovering over me.

TS: Is this a new development?

MR: To a certain extent. My father, who went from one religion to another, finally found peace of mind by arriving at a kind of Voltaire situation. You know, the best we can do is dig our garden, so let's get on with it. And so to a certain extent I find that very consoling.

TS: Overall, then, do you find the Darwinian view of the world to be an optimistic one?

MR: I don't find Darwinism optimistic or pessimistic—that is getting close to reading values out of a scientific theory—but I can live with it OK, and I find it exciting that we have the theory and can explore its full implications, scientific and philosophical, which for me are more or less continuous.

Notes

1 American Philosophical Association, which meets three times a year.

2 Laudan is a philosopher of science who retired early (saying he was sick of the postmodernism that was taking over the university system) and now lives in a small Mexican town with his wife. Laudan was a critic of scientific realism and of claims that a clear line can be drawn between science and nonscience.

3 Ruse is referring to one of the most talked-about problems in ethics—the move from *is* to *ought*. The eighteenth-century Scottish philosopher David Hume was the first to point out that moralists tended to derive statements about what we *ought* to do from statements about the way the world *is*. But according to Hume, no one had ever

provided the justification for such a move. Hume's work is extremely influential for many of the authors in this book because of his focus on the importance of emotions in moral decision-making.

4 Metaethics is the business of trying to justify our ordinary ethical beliefs or systems. Normative ethics involves making judgments about how to behave (e.g., "It is wrong to put your hand on little boys' willies"). Metaethics examines the status of these judgments. Are they objectively true or false? Are they relative to specific cultures or species? These are meta-ethical questions.

5 The Harvard philosopher, probably the most influential moral philosopher of the twentieth century. Rawls passed away in late 2002.

6 The British philosopher, most famous for his book *Ethics: Inventing Right and Wrong*.

7 In Chapter 16, Stephen Stich provides an in-depth discussion about whether we believe ethics to be objective and whether we need to believe that in order for ethics to function. Stich does not agree with Ruse on either of these questions.

8 In Chapter 11, Frans de Waal discusses his views on primate and nonhuman morality as well.

9 The philosopher of biology at Duke University.

10 Ruse is referring to a famous paper by Stephen Jay Gould and the Harvard biologist Richard Lewontin called "The Spandrels of San Marcos and the Panglossian Paradigm: A Critique of the Adaptationist Program." The authors criticize what they believe to be the overly simplistic approach of many Darwinian theorists.

Questions for Discussion

1   Why, according to Ruse, do people worry about taking an evolutionary approach to morality?

2   Despite its disturbing implications, why does Ruse think we should take seriously the connection between evolution and morality?

3   What is Hume's law? How do social Darwinists and some scientists violate it?

4   Why does Ruse think social animals like chimpanzees and dogs have a sense of objective morality? What about orangutans or ferrets?

5   What is the analogy between baseball and morality meant to illustrate? Is it successful?

6   What is the connection between freedom and morality that Ruse illustrates with the examples of sexual frustration, extreme hunger, and addiction to substances?

Suggest Readings

Pennock, Robert T. and Michael Ruse. *But Is It Science? The Philosophical Question in the Creation/Evolution Controversy*. New York: Prometheus Books, 2009. Updated edition.

Ruse, Michael. "Is Rape Wrong on Andromeda? An Introduction to Extraterrestrial Evolution, Science, and Morality." In Edward Regis, Jr. (ed.), *Extraterrestrials: Science and Alien Intelligence*. New York: Cambridge University Press, 1985, pp. 43–78.

——. *Taking Darwin Seriously*. New York: Prometheus Books, 1998.

——. *Darwinism and Its Discontents*. New York: Cambridge University Press, 2008.

——. "Michael Ruse on Evolution, Creationism, and Religion." Interviewed by Daniel Ansted, *Patheos*, Jan. 4, 2013. www.patheos.com

——. "Does Evolution Explain Religious Beliefs?" Interviewed by Gary Gutting. *New York Times*, July 8, 2014. opinionator.blogs.nytimes.com.

Podcast Pairings

Very Bad Wizards, Episode 3 "We Believe in Nothing!" (Cultural Diversity, Relativism, and Moral Truth). http://verybadwizards.com/episodes/3

Very Bad Wizards, Episode 53 "The Psychology People Love to Hate (Evolutionary Psychology Pt. 1)." http://verybadwizards.com/episodes/53

Very Bad Wizards, Episode 69 "CHiPs on Our Shoulders (Lessons in Objectivity)." http://verybadwizards.com/episodes/69

9 Peter Singer

A Gadfly for the Greater Good

gadfly (ˈgadˌflī/)
noun
1. a fly that bites livestock, especially a horsefly, warble fly, or botfly.
2. a person who persistently annoys or provokes others into action by criticism.

—*Merriam Webster's Dictionary*

Two gadflies bookend the almost 3,000-year history of philosophy. The first is Socrates in late 5th-century BC Athens. The second is Peter Singer in our own time. Of course, Singer is far from the only philosopher who aims to provoke us, to question our common beliefs and subject them to scrutiny. But a true philosophical gadfly gets under our skin. They challenge our behavior, make us question our whole way of life. They make us feel inadequate, like we're not living as we ought to be living. Beginning with his famous 1971 article "Famine, Affluence, and Morality" and continuing throughout his career, Peter Singer has offered simple, easy-to-understand arguments with conclusions that, if true, would radically alter our understanding of what it means to live morally.

If you've taken an introduction-to-ethics course, you already know what I'm talking about—the article is in virtually every introductory anthology. It begins with several facts about the vast amount of preventable suffering, disease, and death in the world and it concludes that the vast majority of individuals who live in affluent nations are not doing anything close to what they ought to be doing to prevent this suffering.

The paper and the argument are models of clarity; there are a handful of plausible premises leading to this unsettling conclusion. And the argument is valid, so if you don't like the conclusion, you have to identify the false or implausible premise. This is much harder than it first appears. "Famine" is a fun article for professors to teach, in spite of its sobering topic. Your previously quiet class won't just participate. They'll get mad. They'll offer objections, usually ones that Singer has already anticipated "The charities are corrupt!" (there are many easily accessible watchdog organizations); "Throwing money at them won't solve the problem—you have to teach a man to fish!" (so give money to education programs or political reform). After objections comes

righteous indignation. "I earned my money! Why should I give it away?"
(Aren't your parents paying a lot of your tuition?) "What if every member of my
family gets cancer—I need to put my money away in case that happens!" (So
why did you buy that X-Box?) Then comes the ad hominem attacks on Singer's
other ethical views, usually inaccurate ("He thinks animals are more important
than humans! He wants to kill disabled infants!") Finally, there's grudging
acceptance, and sometimes a calmer, fairer attempt to challenge the argument.

Don't get me wrong, there are reasonable challenges out there. It's just that
Singer's arguments often bring out the worst in students of philosophy—at least
at first. (Nobody likes to be told they're a bad person.) We discuss several of the
best challenges to his view in our interview. One of them concerns the
importance of Singer's famous "drowning child" case for establishing his
conclusion about our obligations to the poor. The case is simple. You're
walking by a pond and you see a child gasping for breath, about to drown. If
you jump in immediately, you can probably save him. But you're wearing some
fancy clothes and a nice watch. What should you do? The answer is obvious. Of
course, you should save him—who cares about the clothes, we're talking about
a kid's life! Only a monster or a psychopath would keep walking while the child
drowns. But wait, how different is that from ... You can see where this is headed.

In books such as Practical Ethics, The Life You Can Save, *and* The Most
Good You Can Do *Singer has used this case as an analogy for our own*
situation. We spend money on cars, televisions, restaurants, NFL Sunday
Ticket, and so forth. If it's so obvious that we should save the drowning child,
then why is it OK to spend money on luxuries rather than donating to save
children and adults from preventable diseases all across the world? A good
question, and one we all have to wrestle with every day.

Peter Singer is Ira W. DeCamp Professor of Bioethics at Princeton
University. He also has a regular visiting position at the University of
Melbourne. He is the author of too many books and articles to list here. Even
more impressive is the practical impact he has had on the world. No living
philosopher comes close. With his book Animal Liberation, *Singer almost*
single-handedly created the modern animal welfare movement. And for over 40
years, Singer has inspired people to increase their charitable giving, often
significantly. We began the interview by discussing the case of the drowning
child and its role in the "Famine, Affluence, and Morality" argument. Singer
was in Australia so I interviewed him over Skype.

August 2015

1   A Sea of Drowning Children

TAMLER SOMMERS: Like everybody who teaches intro to ethics, I assign the
famine paper where you introduce the case of the drowning child. And I'm
always surprised when I reread it. These days, the case is discussed as an
analogy for our everyday situation—millions of children die every day of
preventable diseases, what are we going to do about it? But you don't

really press that analogy in the original paper. Instead you use the case to establish a more general normative principle about our obligation to prevent suffering.[1]

PETER SINGER: Well, I do consider whether it makes a moral difference that the child is only a few yards away rather than across the globe.

TS: Right, you note that the general principles take no account of distance. But how important is the aptness of the analogy for establishing the conclusion of that article?

PS: I'm saying, look, if you feel you ought to save the child in the pond then it's implausible to think that just because somebody is further away, you don't have a responsibility to save him. So that gets people started on a train of thought about what exactly makes a morally relevant difference in terms of our obligations. In later work I've been more explicit in developing the analogy that way, particularly in *The Life You Can Save*. I look at a range of attempts to explain why our situation—the situation of affluent people and children dying of preventable diseases—is not analogous to the drowning-child case. And I argue that those attempts don't work.

But yes, you're right about the article. And actually, I don't think an argument from an analogy is enough to carry the weight of what I'm trying to establish. The analogy is helpful in eliciting our intuitions about the responsibility to help people in need. So I use it to establish some broader principles and then argue on the basis of those principles.

TS: Even as a means of establishing the principles, there's the question of how well the analogy captures our everyday situation. You noted that distance is not a morally relevant factor and I'd certainly grant you that. But there may be at least one morally relevant difference, which is the following. The drowning-child scenario is a singular event in your day-to-day life. Most people never pass a drowning child that they could save. But that's obviously not the case when it comes to helping children all across the globe. A more apt analogy might be one where the moment you step out of your house there are thousands of drowning children in ponds everywhere. And as soon you jump in to save one, there are already two more children in her place.

This has been raised as an objection to the argument. Because in my version of the case, it's not as intuitively obvious what obligations we have to all the children. Yes, you ought to save a bunch of them. But at some point it might be morally acceptable to go about your business, or even do something with no moral significance like eat at a nice restaurant. And, if that's true, the case would no longer support your general principle—at least in their absolute forms.

PS: Obviously it's hard to really imagine what we would do in your version of the case or how we would live with it. But I think I'd be very uncomfortable if I went to a nice restaurant and I knew that there were children drowning outside that I could help. Obviously there would be some things that I would still have to do. I'd have to go to work, to earn some money. I have to keep myself and my family from starving, those sorts of things yes. But the luxuries? I don't know.

I suppose there are places in the world that are closer to this reality. If you look at highly inegalitarian societies, you'll see wealthy people going to the opera and perhaps there are really poor people, beggars, dying outside. But it's not exactly parallel to the drowning child because the opera-goers may not know if the beggars' lives really are in imminent danger.

TS: But if this case better captures our everyday situation, and we're less confident about our intuitions there, doesn't it undermine its effectiveness for your argument?

PS: No, it raises a question about how we *would* behave. How we *ought* to behave in these situations is a different question. I suppose what it does suggest is that the intuitive response that we have in the single-child-in-the-pond situation is distinct from the intuitive response we have in the many-children-drowning-all-the-time situation you just described.

So complicating the case like that does show that intuitions alone are not really enough to determine our obligations. For this, you need to get back to some basic principles. But, in a way, as you mentioned, I said that in the original article.

2   Our Obligations to the Needy

TS: So let's look at those principles. You give two versions of it in the original paper, strong and weak. Can you explain what those are?

PS: Sure, the moderate version holds that if you can prevent something bad from happening without making a morally significant sacrifice, you ought to do it.

TS: What counts as morally significant?

PS: Well, if you're buying fancy clothes, or expensive dinners, you can't claim that these items have moral significance. And if you could use the money you spend on those clothes to prevent something bad from happening, you ought to do it. I added the moderate version because I realized many people would find the stronger version of the principle impossibly demanding. The strong version says that you ought to prevent bad things from happening until you get to the point where your sacrifice is of *comparable* moral importance. In other words, you're obligated to help until you get to the point where you've reduced your own assets so much that further transfers aren't really going to make a significant difference in suffering—

TS: —Because they're going to hurt me as much as they're going to help the other person.

PS: Yeah, roughly that's right, allowing for transfer costs and so on.

TS: And of course, you'd have to take that same attitude toward your children's suffering as well, right? The strong version doesn't allow you to be partial to your family.

PS: That's right.

TS: You say in the original article that you think the strong version is true. Do you still believe that?

PS: I do still think the strong version is true in one sense. But I also think we ought to be aware of what will actually motivate people. So I've become more reticent about discussing the truth of the strong version because I think it may be counterproductive. In the end, my goal is to get people to alleviate suffering and prevent diseases that kill kids in developing countries. In *The Life You Can Save*, for example, I have a much more modest scale of suggested giving. In *Practical Ethics*, I talk about tithing, giving 10 percent of your income. Tithers still shouldn't feel like they're doing *everything* they ought to be doing. But they can feel reasonably comfortable that they're doing a lot more than most people.

It is important to try to think how to motivate people. It depends on what hat I'm wearing. As a philosopher, I try to clarify what I think is the true position about what we ought to do. As a public advocate, I'm trying to make the world a better place.

3   The Point of View of the Universe

TS: Let's talk about these principles with your philosopher hat on. I wanted to ask you about the justification for the stronger moral principle—why you believe the principle is true. In *Practical Ethics* (your book from 1979), you concede that it can't be derived from pure reason. So you took a more subjectivist or Humean approach that ultimately grounded the principle in our emotions, desires, or subjective capacities. But in recent work your view has shifted. Can you explain how?

PS: It's shifted in that I no longer accept Hume's view that reason must always start from a desire. I now think some things are irrational no matter what your desires are. An example would be something like Parfit's case of future Tuesday indifference.[2] I came to think that Hume was wrong about this kind of case. From an egoistic perspective, it's irrational to be partial over time. And I thought this idea could be extended to partiality over a range of moral questions.

TS: And that's what's so controversial about the principle—the impartiality, the idea that when we think about our moral obligations, we should adopt "the point of view of the universe."[3] We should regard all suffering as morally equal and act accordingly. The implications of this can be pretty tough to swallow. Because let's say that my daughter suffers from a serious but nonfatal health problem that makes her life much harder than it could be. There's an operation to cure it, but it's very expensive. According to the strong principle, I ought to donate the money for the operation to prevent greater suffering; it would be morally wrong for me to get the operation for my daughter. It's impossible for me to accept that conclusion, it's too counterintuitive. Can you demonstrate that I'm being irrational?

PS: The future Tuesday case demonstrates the irrationality of partiality over time. Katarzyna de Lazari-Radek and I then argue that we can debunk this intuition that it's rational to give more weight to my own interests or the interests of those close to me. And if we can debunk it, we can get to impartiality across persons as well as over time.

TS: Right, that's the crucial move: this idea of how we can debunk intuitions that go against the impartiality principle. Like Josh Greene [see Chapter 17], you've appealed to evolutionary theory and neuroscience as a way of doing this. Can you explain how that strategy works?[4]

PS: Yes, so through the work of Josh and others we know more about how moral intuitions are formed. And it's reasonable to say that they were formed as a result of evolutionary selection. We were living in small face-to-face societies, and we developed the intuitive responses that were best fitted for survival and the survival of our offspring in those situations. Given that, you can argue that there's no particular reason why these intuitions actually track the truth of our moral judgments. This is something that Sharon Street has argued as well.[5]

TS: Right, although she uses the strategy to debunk moral realism entirely.

PS: Exactly. But we argue that this is too swift. You can distinguish between intuitions that have evolved in the manner I just suggested and intuitions that haven't. The former are not likely to be truth-tracking. But consider the intuition supporting Sidgwick's axiom of rational benevolence that requires us to be impartial across different people.[6] It's very hard to see how that intuition could have conferred any evolutionary advantage. That intuition is therefore likely to be a rational insight into moral truth.

TS: This is the part of the strategy that I've struggled with. Josh and Liane Young, we debated this very point. Because when considering the benevolence axiom requiring impartiality, that seems like precisely the intuition that people *don't* have. People do think it's permissible or even obligatory to favor the interests of family members, friends, and so forth. In many cultures, people think it's deeply immoral to value the welfare of strangers over the welfare of their group. So, given that most people don't have this intuition, what's the basis for calling it rational?

PS: I agree with you that ordinary people believe they have obligations to their kin that they don't have to strangers. Of course, that is exactly what you would expect in terms of the evolutionary story. But at the same time, if you look at people who have reflected and thought about ethics a lot more, not just in our culture but in a wide range of cultures and a wide range of historical periods, you get a large number of thinkers talking about this idea of the universal point of view, of universalizability, the golden rule, and so forth. This is consistent with what we're trying to argue. You only reach the conclusion when you manage to reason clearly and put aside the evolved intuitive responses. And there's not a lot of people who do get to the point of reasoning clearly and who put aside those evolved responses.

TS: So the fact that you see some version of the axiom in a small number of moral and religious traditions—that's the whole justification for calling it rational?

PS: There has to be a sense in which we find the principle to be self-evident. Because Sidgwick says it's a self-evident axiom. If it's a self-evident axiom, you have to distinguish it from other intuitions we have. How would I distinguish it from the other intuitions? By the evolutionary debunking account of those intuitions.

TS: But I'm still not clear on the basis for calling it self-evident. Is it just that a few different traditions have theorized their way toward it? That doesn't seem like enough.

PS: No, no, that's not the justification. It's not just some quote that I've come up with, or that my particular culture or group of people have come up with. It's a kind of truth that people who think carefully can reach.

TS: But why should I believe you that it's a "truth," given the miniscule proportion of people who accept it?

PS: Well, I think there are mathematical intuitions that a lot of people don't have as well that we know to be true.

TS: Is that true? Most mathematical axioms have near universal assent because of their simplicity, right? Think of Euclid. The more complicated theorems are counterintuitive but they're derived from simple axioms that we all agree about. Or maybe if it's something like a counterintuitive relativity principle, we accept it because of its great predictive and explanatory power. Either way, we have clearer grounds for calling them true. You see what I'm saying?

PS: There are some people that can actually see mathematical truth— Ramanujan[7] or someone like that—they actually see that some things are true that other people don't see. And then they have to prove them. And then other people say "oh really? I don't see that." And then you work it out and say "right, OK, that is a theorem, you're right." So I think there is something going on there which I think we don't really fully understand.

TS: But the benevolence principle is an axiom, right? So how do we know who is the Ramanujan of morality? We're open to the axiom being true but we don't see its truth, and we've never seen a proof that demonstrates this. Why should we accept it?

PS: Well, you'd need to sit down with these people and ask them to reflect on it. You can say to them: "Look, I understand that you may care more about your daughter rather than a stranger and I would too. But do you really think that your daughter's welfare is more important? Putting aside your own concerns, do you really think that her welfare is independently more important than the welfare of someone else's child?" I think people will come around.

4 Runaway Debunking

TS: Another problem with evolutionary debunking strategies is that they might go farther than you want them to. You might end up debunking *all* of our moral intuitions which would leave us with moral skepticism. (And I know you're not a moral skeptic.) Take, for example, the intuition that suffering is bad. Or the intuition that we have an obligation to prevent any suffering at all. These judgments also seem to be the product of evolutionary forces—an aversion to pain, an evolved sense of empathy, processes like kin selection, reciprocal altruism, gene-culture co-evolution, choose your favorite story. So if we're going to distrust intuitions that are the product of evolutionary processes, doesn't the benevolence baby go out with the partiality bathwater? Or do you disagree that we can give evolutionary accounts for the intuitions I just mentioned?

PS: You certainly can. It's clearly true that our sense of pain and suffering evolved because it helps us to avoid various dangers. But—and this is an argument that I suppose is still going on and getting sorted out—I think you can say that here we have direct acquaintance with suffering. And this direct experience is what causes the judgment that suffering is bad and that we should avoid it. It also causes the judgment that it's a bad thing not just for me but for anyone. The direct experience makes it a judgment that, in a way, we can't resist making. It's not just an empirical fact that we can't resist it. We actually have direct knowledge of what it's like, and direct knowledge that it's bad.

TS: But what about the judgment that it's OK to favor my daughter's welfare? There's a way in which I can't resist making that judgment either.

PS: I don't agree with that. I can say that I can't resist preferring my daughter's welfare over that of a stranger. That's true. But I can also think that maybe it's not the right thing to do. I can raise that question. And I think we do raise it all the time. We raise it about not only our kin but our own interests as well. There are things we want, but we can question whether it's right to want them.

In the case of the badness of suffering I think it is different. We can't really pretend to ourselves that it's not a bad thing when we suffer. And if we then come back to the first principle that we were talking about, the impartiality principle, we have to accept that it's a bad thing when anyone suffers, you know, other things being equal.

TS: But that's what we're debating, the impartiality principle. So I grant you that we can't resist saying that our own suffering is bad because we have direct experience with it. But I also have direct experience of my daughter suffering (fortunately nothing serious). And in that particular context, it seems a little arbitrary to say that I *can* resist thinking I should do my best to alleviate it.

PS: I think the two things that you talked about are different stages of the argument. We talk about it in *The Point of View of the Universe*. We accept that suffering is bad. And we also accept the universal benevolence axiom: I have to be equally concerned about that whatever is good or bad for everyone else as I do about whatever is good or bad for me. You conceded that I can't deny my own suffering is bad. And of course I agree that your daughter's suffering is bad. If we then add the universal benevolence axiom, which is a form of the impartiality claim, then I think we get to where we want to get to.

5   Complexity and Indeterminacy in Moral Life

TS: Now I'm wondering as we're talking about this, whether the plausibility of your argument depends, in part, on this stark contrast between a purely egoistic perspective and the universally benevolent perspective. And this is how Sidgwick frames it so it's not surprising. But of course those aren't the only two perspectives. They're just extreme ends of a whole spectrum of ethical positions. The perspective of universal benevolence can sound a lot more plausible if the only alternative is pure egoism. But what if you toss in another perspective—a W. D. Ross[8]-style blend that combines elements of egoism, universal benevolence, and special obligations to particular people? Then it starts to seem a little like special pleading for the evolutionary debunker to pick and choose what they can call rational and what they call irrational.

PS: It is true that when we're talking about what's rationally required we're making an extreme claim. Because we are talking about what would we do if we were fully rational beings. And we know that we're not fully rational beings. So there is a sense in which a morality for fully rational beings is not going to suit us as we are. And that's part of the Humean story that you have to take humans as they are, with their variety of feelings and derive something out of that. I think to some extent these are different projects.

TS: OK, but that's not what I mean exactly. This is not another version of the "it's too demanding" or "we're not fully rational creatures" objection. It's an objection that concerns what full rationality requires. When we ask what rationality requires, our options shouldn't be limited to impartial benevolence or pure egoism. We should include these intermediate positions. And these positions have a bunch of principles that combine partiality, impartiality, and special obligations. Moreover, just like with universal benevolence, many of these intermediate positions would not have obvious evolutionary explanations.

PS: Perhaps. But they would also be indeterminate, right? At various points, it would be indeterminate how much we ought to give to strangers and how much do you give to yourself? And there would be a whole range of questions involving your family too. If your daughter has an ingrown toenail, and you could save a child's life with the money for treating your daughter's ingrown toenail—then probably you'd think you ought to save the life. If your daughter's going to lose a foot, then you might say well, no, I'm going with my daughter. So it needs more specification, more specification about where I draw the line and also why this is where I draw the line.

TS: But you could view the indeterminacy as a benefit rather than a deficiency. Because it accurately reflects the complexity of our moral lives. In many domains of judgment, there are clear cases on both sides and a vague middle where it's impossible to draw a line. There is no line. If she wants a $10,000 operation to remove a harmless blemish on her wrist, then I should probably spend that money (if I have it) to save as many lives as possible. But if she would lose her foot, then I'm not just permitted but obligated to pay for that surgery. And then there are all these cases in the middle that are indeterminate. They're indeterminate because moral life is like that.

PS: I'd still like to know more about why it is like that. You're saying there's a lot of complexity in our moral lives and that's the way it is. But why is it that you're obligated to save your daughter's foot rather than save the lives of three strangers? That's too much a matter of saying: "those two cases are clearly one on each side of the line because that's my intuition." I want to know more. I want to know why.

TS: Right and here I would appeal to reflective equilibrium, which I know you've criticized in your work. But just to borrow something from it, I would say this. They're not just intuitions, they're considered intuitions. I endorse them after a great deal of reflection about their nature and their origins. As I said to Josh Greene, I've read about kin selection—I'm fully aware of the history behind my intuition that I have special obligations to my child. Nevertheless, I endorse the intuitions upon reflection. Why? Because even with full knowledge about its origins, it still seems more plausible than an intuition that I ought to be impartial. In the end, considered intuitions with full information about the relevant empirical facts—that's all we have to go on when we evaluate moral principles. I guess it's that last part you would disagree with.

PS: Yes, exactly, that last part. Obviously different societies and different cultures have different sets of intuitions that they feel very strongly about. But we don't think it's sufficient if, for example, someone says "I have this very strong intuition that homosexuality is wrong." We reject that now. Yet there are plenty of cultures where that's a very strong intuition. I think we need to get beyond that. If you really take the reflective equilibrium model seriously, you end up with a kind of social relativism that I find very disturbing.

6   Empathy and Animal Welfare

TS: Are you familiar with Paul Bloom's recent attacks on empathy?

PS: I am, yes.

TS: Paul and I had a spirited debate about them in this book [see Chapter 13]. I imagine that you'd have a lot of sympathy with Paul on this. Do you agree with him that we should be wary of empathy as a guide to moral judgment and behavior?

PS: I do, but we need to be careful what kind of empathy we're talking about. My understanding is that Paul is talking about the form of empathy in which people identify with particular other individuals.

TS: Mostly, yes …

PS: So this is the baby-in-the-well case, where people know about this particular child, she's down in the well, and so they send in millions of dollars to save this child. But they don't have that sort of empathy with the children who are dying from malaria in distant countries because they don't know who they are, they can't put a face to them. And then there's another study in which you have people on a waiting list for surgery, and you tell the participants particular things about one of them. And then the participants are allowed to reorder the waiting list, and they bring the person they know about to the top—because now they empathize with her. And they do this even though this person's medical need is less urgent than people they are jumping her over.

TS: So this is the kind of empathy that results in judgments that go against the impartiality principle. That's your concern.

PS: That's right, that's right. But if you're talking about empathy in a different sense, if you're thinking "look, all these kids dying from malaria, think about what they're suffering, think about how terrible it is for the parent to lose their child from malaria," that's a different story. That's an attempt just to get people to understand that the lives of others are essentially similar to their own or to those of their own kids. And that's something different.

TS: I wanted to briefly apply these questions to another aspect of your work that I'm a huge fan of—your work with animal welfare. To my mind, *Animal Liberation* has had a more positive practical impact on the world than any work of philosophy in the last 100 years. I wanted to ask you about two stories from it that relate to empathy. The first is one that you tell in the 1975 preface. You were in England, you went over to a woman's house for tea. She started telling you how much she loved her dogs and cats, and asked if you had pets. You replied that you didn't. She was surprised and said she thought you were "interested in animals." You replied that you weren't particularly interested in animals and you had never been an animal lover in the traditional sense. What you were "interested" in was preventing the suffering and misery of sentient beings. You believed that animals were sentient beings that were being cruelly exploited for human ends and you wanted to put a stop to it.

PS: And then they served me a ham sandwich.

TS: [laughs] Right, I forgot, that's the punchline. I always thought that story was interesting because unlike many animal welfare advocates, you're not motivated by a sense of empathy with particular animals. It's this general principle about sentient beings that moves you to want to end their suffering. I take it that was the point of the anecdote, right?

PS: Yes absolutely. You don't have to be an animal lover to want to end their suffering. What I saw myself trying to do in that book was to move concern for the way we treat animals beyond the community of people who self-identify as animal lovers. They love being around cats and dogs, or horses or whatever, and basically think "I'm an animal lover so I should be opposed to cruelty to animals."

Of course my view is that this is another major issue of mistreating a particular group. And just as you're against racism even if you don't have any particularly strong feelings for people of an oppressed racial minority, you ought to be against speciesism and the way we treat animals—whether or not you happen to enjoy the company of cats and dogs and horses.

TS: Right, that makes sense. It does seem irrational to get outraged over puppy mills, or leaving a dog in a hot car, while being indifferent when it comes to factory farms for pigs. Because pigs are just as intelligent and capable of suffering than dogs, if not more so.

PS: Right.

TS: There's another story about that book that's not documented, or at least I can't remember where I heard it. But the story is that at some point you agreed that the most effective part of the book for causing reform was not the theoretical arguments that you gave against speciesism, but rather the photographs of painful animal experiments, of factory farms, and—

PS: —No, I never agreed with that. That's wrong. Richard Posner claimed that the pictures were doing most of the work persuading people.[9] In fact, I rejected that claim.

TS: Oh you did? OK.

PS: I mean, obviously I haven't done the research, so I don't really know. But that's certainly not my impression. And there were plenty of horrible pictures around before the book came out.

TS: As a matter of personal history, though, I will say that the photographs in your book and the videos that animal welfare activists can sometimes smuggle out of factory farms—those images played a big role in changing my way of thinking. There's a difference between thinking about factory farms in abstract terms and then seeing what actually goes on there. That's why their lobbyists spend so much time and money to prevent visual information from reaching the general public.

PS: Yes, they're trying to pass legislation even now—these 'Ag-gag' laws. Some of these states have made it a criminal offense to get into a factory farm and take video. That's pretty extraordinary, you're right about that.

TS: It's appalling. And what they want to prevent is precisely the triggering of empathy in people, right? It's true that these videos will trigger more empathy in some people than others. And the cuter animals and the ones who look like us will benefit more. It will probably work better for dogs than pigs, better for pigs than for chickens, and it may not work well at all for certain marine life like lobsters or octopi. But still, the triggering of empathy does pose the greatest threat to their whole institution. I wonder then if you think it might be counterproductive to take Paul's line on empathy too strongly when it comes to ending something like animal cruelty.

PS: I see, I see where you're coming from. Yes, again, I think this example is an interesting one because it shows where empathy is desirable and where it leads you in the wrong direction. The example that you just gave: how irrational it is for people to be very concerned about dogs but not concerned about pigs. The reason for that is that people have more empathy for dogs than pigs, probably because people have dogs as companions so they get to read their emotions a lot better or relate to them better. Or maybe in some way dogs are just more attractive to us because of some physical features about them.

TS: But we're also around dogs all the time, and we're not around pigs. A pig is an abstract entity to many people.

PS: That's true, that's right. These pigs in factory farms are hidden away unless the video gets out. So that kind of empathy can actually be harmful. It's good for dogs I suppose but on balance I'd say it makes it more difficult to get people to do the right thing as far as pigs are concerned. On the other hand, it's true that people may respond to a video showing animal suffering and mistreatment, including pigs and cows and chickens and whatever else it might be. That's important, I agree. If there were no such feelings, then who knows how much harder it would be for the animal movement to make progress?

So, I think that we don't want to cut out those sorts of feelings. We certainly want to retain this broad empathy with suffering beings. And we need to be able to see and understand the suffering that's inflicted on these beings, to understand what it's like and to say it's something that we don't want. So I'm not trying to get rid of all empathy. It's really important for a lot of our social causes.

TS: So the crucial thing, then, would be to flesh out a principled distinction between the right kinds and wrong kinds of empathy.

PS: Yeah. That's right. And I guess emotional empathy is motivationally important for most people. But it can also be misleading. But even there, if we want to change people's attitudes and behavior in regard to an area, you have to work with them as they are. So yes, we have to draw on the kinds of things that they will respond to. And we can try to do that without reinforcing the tendencies that you don't want, for example to focus all our resources on helping one particular individual whose picture we have seen, or about whom we know some salient facts, when we could do more good by spreading these resources over others with whom we lack empathy because we cannot identify with them as individuals.

Notes

1   Singer actually gives two versions of this principle. The stronger version is "If it is in our power to prevent something bad from happening without thereby sacrificing

anything of comparable moral importance, we ought, morally, to do it." The moderate version is "If it is in our power to prevent something bad from happening without thereby sacrificing anything of moral significance, we ought, morally, to do it." We talk in more detail about those principles below.

2   Singer is referring to Derek Parfit's example of a person with ordinary desires except that he doesn't care about his pains and pleasures on future Tuesdays. Parfit writes: "This indifference is a bare fact. When he is planning his future, it is simply true that he always prefers the prospect of great suffering on a Tuesday to the mildest pain on any other day." According to Parfit, this shows that certain preferences can be irrational, no matter what the person's core desires are. Simon Blackburn briefly discusses this case in Chapter 10.

3   This phrase comes from the philosopher Henry Sidgwick. It's also the title of Singer's 2014 book on Sidgwick co-authored with Katarzyna de Lazari-Radek.

4   In Chapter 17, Liane Young and I raise further challenges to the strategy Singer outlines in this section and the next. It might help to read these two interviews in tandem.

5   See her 2006 article "A Darwinian Dilemma for Realist Theories of Value." *Philosophical Studies* 127 (1):109–66.

6   Sidgwick describes this axiom in his book *The Method of Ethics* (London: Macmillan, 1874): "[E]ach one is morally bound to regard the good of any other individual as much as his own, except in so far as he judges it to be less, when impartially viewed, or less certainly knowable or attainable by him"

7   Srinivasa Ramanujan was a mathematical prodigy and genius, who made exceptional contribution to number theory without any formal training. On numerous occasions he was able to intuit the truth of (non-obvious) mathematical propositions long before their truth was established with formal proofs.

8   W. D. Ross defended a form of moral realism called "intuitionism." Like Singer, Ross believed that we could intuit certain ethical truths. But Ross was a critic of consequentialism, arguing instead that we have a variety of moral duties and special obligations and no systematic way of prioritizing them.

9   See www.utilitarian.net/singer/interviews-debates/200106--.htm; it's an exceptionally interesting and revealing debate.

Questions for Discussion

1   What is the role of the drowning-child case in Singer's original article "Famine, Affluence, and Morality"? How has the function of the analogy changed in more recent work?

2   Why might the "many children in many ponds" variation serve as a challenge to Singer's use of the case as an analogy for our own everyday situation?

3   Singer offers two versions of the principle concerning our obligations to prevent suffering: a strong version and a qualified one. What are those principles? Give an example where the strong principle would oblige you to perform an action, but the weak principle would not.

4   Singer believes that the strong version is true, but he believes that defending it may be "counterproductive." Why?

5   Why does Singer no longer accept Hume's view about the connection between reason and desire?

6 What is Sidgwick's axiom of rational benevolence? How does Singer defend it? What are the two challenges that I raise against the axiom and how does Singer respond?

7 Why is Singer ambivalent about empathy as a guide to moral judgment and behavior?

Suggested Readings

Singer, Peter. "Famine, Affluence, and Morality." *Philosophy & Public Affairs* 1(3) (1972): 229–43.

——. *Animal Liberation: A New Ethics for our Treatment of Animals*, New York: New York Review/Random House, 1975.

——. *Practical Ethics*. Cambridge: Cambridge University Press, 1980 (2nd edn, 1993; 3rd edn, 2011).

——. "Ethics and Intuitions." *Journal of Ethics* 9(3/4) (2005): 332–52.

——. "The Singer Solution to World Poverty." *New York Times Magazine*. September 5, 1999. www.nytimes.com/1999/09/05/magazine/the-singer-solution-to-world-poverty.html

——. "The Life You Can Save" (first chapter in the *New York Times*, March 10, 2009). www.nytimes.com/2009/03/11/books/chapters/chapter-life-you-could-save.html

——. *The Life You Can Save: Acting Now to End World Poverty*. New York: Random House 2009.

——. *The Point of View of the Universe: Sidgwick and Contemporary Ethics* (with Katarzyna de Lazari-Radek), New York: Oxford University Press, 2014.

——. *The Most Good You Can Do: How Effective Altruism Is Changing Ideas about Living Ethically*. New Haven, CT: Yale University Press, 2015.

Assorted Media and Podcast Pairings

Singer, Peter. "The Why and How of Effective Altruism" TED talk. March 2013. www.ted.com/talks/peter_singer_the_why_and_how_of_effective_altruism?language=en

Very Bad Wizards, Episode 28 "Moral Persuasion." http://verybadwizards.com/episodes/28

10 Simon Blackburn
Beyond the Knave

Imagine a man named Jack who follows the rules of morality only when it's in his interest to do so. He's smart, perceptive, and a good judge of how people will perceive behavior. He knows the damage of a bad reputation to his long-term self-interest, and so he takes great care to avoid acquiring one. The world perceives him as honest, fair, and compassionate, an all-around good person. What they don't realize is that Jack is utterly indifferent to the suffering of others. He performs the most flagrantly immoral actions whenever he can get away with them. David Hume coined a term for people like Jack—the 'sensible knave'—and no figure has loomed larger over the history of moral philosophy.

Ever since Plato (first in his dialogue the Gorgias *and then the* Republic*), philosophers have tried to show that sensible knaves are not just immoral but irrational. This is no easy task. The knave simply does not care about other people—what rational argument could convince him to take their interests into account? Hume himself believed this project was futile: "if [the knave] feel no reluctance to the thoughts of villainy or baseness," he wrote, "he has indeed lost a considerable motive to virtue." We can do our best to prevent people like Jack from harming us, but we can't demonstrate their irrationality.*

That certainly does not stop philosophers from trying. To this day, they fill the ethics journals with new attempts to refute the sensible knave. They worry that without this refutation, morality would be too subjective, too dependent on the contingent features of a person's psychology. And that would lead to moral relativism or nihilism—a frightening, anarchic state of affairs.

Or would it? Not according to Simon Blackburn. Blackburn is a Humean, the foremost philosopher of our time working in that tradition. Like Hume, Blackburn believes that refuting the knave is hopeless because moral behavior and judgment is ultimately grounded in our attitudes and sentiments. Since the knave, by definition, lacks the relevant moral emotions—he cannot be reasoned into behaving morally. Yet Blackburn is not a relativist or nihilist. Blackburn has devoted much of his career to developing an account of moral discourse called "quasi-realism" (a label he now regrets) that allows us to assert the truth of moral claims while at the same time recognizing the sentimental basis of morality. It's a delicate balancing act, one that I used to dismiss out of hand,[1] but have since come to accept.

In recent years, Blackburn has also become an ambassador for the field of philosophy writing accessible books, articles, and reviews for wider audiences. Although Blackburn can play technical analytic philosophy games with the best of them, he has become increasingly skeptical about the value of these games. Since I share this skepticism, I began our interview with a question on this topic.

Blackburn is a Fellow of Trinity College, Cambridge and has an appointment as Research Professor at UNC Chapel Hill as well. He is the author of too many books to list here, most recently of Mirror Mirror, *a meditation on the self-directed emotions. I interviewed him in his office in Chapel Hill.*

December 2014

1   The Same Basic Questions

TAMLER SOMMERS: In your recent writings you sound like someone who's deeply concerned with the state of analytic philosophy, at least in some areas—is that fair to say?

SIMON BLACKBURN: Yes, I think it is. I'm out of sympathy with some strands of analytical philosophy. Analytical philosophy can rapidly get quite technical and I don't like being made to work harder than I need to do. If we can avoid technicalities I think that's good. Of course there may be places in philosophy, such as logic, where you can't avoid technicalities. That's fine too. But it's got to be kept in its place.

I also think that analytical philosophy concentrates quite rightly in some respects, on the meaning of remarks, on what's said, and on the truth conditions of certain claims—what makes them true. And that's fine but it can't come at the expense of forgetting that it's *people* who use language. Real people use concepts like 'good' or 'knowledge' or 'truth' and I think you've got to keep a very strict sort of human angle on all these concepts. Otherwise, they float off to heaven. They float off to Plato's place outside the cave, where the sun shines.

TS: Or to trolleys.[2]

SB: Or to trolleys, yes. And you get a proliferation of 'isms' and questions about these 'isms' which are untethered from anything much in human life.

TS: By 'isms' you mean the theories?

SB: Theories, exactly. I sympathize with the ordinary reader (if there is such a person) who opens a contemporary philosophy journal and can't make heads or tails of what's going on. And I think that's a terrible shame. Any educated individual who picks up Hume, or Locke, or Berkeley can have a good sense of what's going on. That's been lost, and I think that's a pity.

TS: I couldn't agree with you more, but let me raise the common objection to this sort of complaint. Nobody expects journals of biology or journals of physics to be accessible, right? What makes philosophy different from some of these other fields where we accept their technical terminology and inaccessibility?

SB: Right, good. Well, if philosophy had a string of cumulative results to its name, as physics does and biology does, it would be different. We unmistakably know more in those fields than we did a couple of centuries ago. We've got technology riding on the back of physical theory and so on. If philosophy was like that, I'd accept the parallel. But there's no evidence at all that it is like that. The same basic questions keep recurring and being handled again and again in different ways.

So the more apt comparison I see would be with humane studies like history or literature, perhaps art itself, and drama itself. And there, nobody says 'Oh, it's terribly shocking that we can't write plays any better than Aeschylus or Shakespeare.' You don't expect progress in those fields because the same old problems are human problems. And they're going to revolve and come back in different guises, in different places and times. So here's a constant industry of revisiting, imaginatively, aspects of the human condition. And I think that's what philosophy does.

TS: What is it about fields that lack notable progress that makes them less amenable to technical study?

SB: Well, I think that if we could be sure that the technology was taking us somewhere, I'd be much happier. But very often, technical work seems to elaborate views that may themselves be very controversial, very dodgy. To give an example, David Lewis, a philosopher for whom I have the greatest respect, dominated large tracts of philosophy in the late twentieth century. He made it possible to talk about possible worlds. Possible worlds became a sort of playground for logicians, and there's been lots and lots of studies of whether when I say "If the Twin Towers hadn't fallen down the world would be a much better place than it is" am I talking about nearby possible worlds in which the Twin Towers don't fall down, and so on and so on.

And you can get results. You can get technical results in modal logic and they're quite fun if you like that sort of thing. But as far as our understanding of possibilities and counterfactuals go, I'm not convinced that the technology has helped at all. I think modals have their own problems, they're difficult to understand. But I don't know that we need a metaphysics of possible worlds to help us understand them. So I see a split between the kind of questions I'm interested in and the kind of questions that technology helps with.

2   The Slave of the Passions

TS: OK, well let's get to some of those questions then. A good place to start is with Hume's famous remark that reason is, and ought to be, the slave of the passions. What does Hume mean by that remark, and why has it been the cause of so much controversy and resistance?

SB: Well, of course, it's a remark that comes from *A Treatise of Human Nature* which he wrote when he was a young firebrand.

TS: A firebrand—that's hard to imagine from his portraits.

SB: I know, but I think he was! And the "slave of the passions" quote never comes back in that unqualified, punch-in-your-face form in his *Enquiries*[3] and his *Essays* which he also wrote throughout his life. So, it was a young man's sort of war cry. And of course it's a very resonant war cry. The obvious thing to think of is Plato's myth of the charioteer in the *Phaedrus*.[4] For the Greeks, or at least for Plato, the human soul can be compared to the chariot. The chariot is pulled—it needs horses. Appetite is one of the horses and the other is more akin to shame or spirit.

TS: A kind of honor, right?

SB: Something like that, a sense of honor. That's another of the horses. And both of these horses are unruly. They will dash off in all directions and capsize the whole thing unless they are guided by reason, who is the charioteer and is to be in control. That's a very famous image, and of course Hume is reversing it completely.

But it's important to understand what he meant by 'reason,' and it's not entirely easy. I think he sees reason as giving us three things. It gives us knowledge of the situations we're facing through our senses. It gives us inferential powers, and powers of theorizing to some extent, certainly about cause and effect. And it gives us our logical and mathematical capacities.

Hume's point, then, is that all of that gives us guidance, but not more, about what to do. Should I go to the cinema or stay at home and read a book? Should I just go outside and count the blades of grass on my lawn? Well, I can reason as much as I like but unless my reason touches something which in turn touches a desire or a concern or a passion which excites me it's a pointless exercise.

TS: So we have to start out with a desire or passion—counting grass is boring, I love my book—in order for our reason to be useful.

SB: You could go so far as to say that our reasoning capacities are just at the service of our desires, needs, concerns, projects, things that cause us pain and pleasure. And in the *Treatise* especially, Hume thinks we're under the domination of two masters—pain and pleasure. Avoid one, go for the other. However, we do not *just* have private, egoistic concern, but also sympathetic concerns for others. So I can be very bothered about your pains or pleasures and eventually we get a richer psychology of desire and concern on this basis.

TS: I've never fully understood the problem with this. There's a clear sense in which our desires and attitudes—including guilt, shame, pride, anger, gratitude, empathy—are prior to reasoning. Reason can't do anything until it gets that little jumpstart that lets us know what to aim for.

SB: That's right. Reason needs to get its hooks into something that concerns us.

TS: What do you think is at the root of resistance to that idea?

SB: Well, I think resistance begins to flourish when people see Hume putting our *moral* convictions and capacities on the desire side, or the sentiment side, and not on the reason side. People want bad guys to be shown to be unreasonable. They want to show that the bad guys are misusing their practical reason.

TS: By 'people' do you mean people, or philosophers?

SB: I mean philosophers, yes. It'd be really nice to show the bad guys, the guys who aren't sympathetic, who aren't prudent, who aren't concerned for others, who are unprincipled, who tell lies, cheat, steal—the hope is that we can tell those guys not only that they're bad, but that they're *irrational*, that they are somehow failing to see something analogous to someone not seeing that $2 + 2 = 4$. Or failing to draw an elementary logical inference.

TS: Can you relate to that at all? Because I've never thought it was important to show that even the worst criminals or tyrants are irrational.

SB: Yeah, I agree. I have very little sympathy with it, which is why I'm comfortable with Hume in this area. But over the years I've learned that my colleagues don't think like that. The wicked part of me suggests that this is because they value their role as guardians of reason. We are the guys who can tell you what to do, because we philosophers have the authority of reason behind us. And nobody likes supposing that if they stand on a podium and tell people what to do they're merely, as these people would say, expressing their own attitudes, desires, wishes for how things go.

TS: So it's our way of trying to hold on to our status as philosopher kings.

SB: That's right. The authority. But I think Hume actually can make a role for authority because he knows that some people are better at living their lives than others. He's got his own standards and there's no reason why we shouldn't advise others or listen to the guys who seem to be able to do it well, as we do in any other craft.

TS: Like film criticism for example.

SB: Yeah, exactly. Art criticism. People who make you notice more, to think of aspects you wouldn't have thought of by yourself. All of that is fine by Hume.

3 What Is Quasi-Realism?

TS: So let's move on to your own views in metaethics, which is an inquiry about the status and meaning of moral claims. Here's how the topic goes in an intro class. The first position is a realist one. In one form of moral realism you assert that there are moral properties out there in the world. Many moral realists see moral facts and moral properties as part of "the furniture of the universe," as J. L. Mackie says, the fabric of the universe.[5] There's also a more rationalist form of realism, people like Kant who try to derive moral laws out of pure reason.[6]

On the other side, you have the moral skeptics or error theorists. They agree with the realists that people *believe* that there are moral properties or moral facts of some kind floating around in the world. But for various reasons they think that's untenable. So skeptics believe that widespread error pervades moral discourse. They see debates about right and wrong as in one sense analogous to the old debates over which people in the village were witches. The whole debate is misguided because there's no such thing as witches.[7] Similarly, there are no facts about right and wrong.

And then finally there's a metaethical position that began with the terrible label 'non-cognitivism.' But we can also call them expressivists, as you do. They agree with the skeptic that there are no moral properties in the universe nor are there truths of pure reason. But they also think that nobody presumes that there are any such things in the first place. One of the first philosophers to put it like this was A. J. Ayer. According to Ayer, when we say "stealing is wrong," we're really just expressing our disapproval of stealing. And then C. L. Stevenson added that we might also be expressing a desire that other people share our attitudes. "I disapprove of stealing, and I want you to disapprove of it too!" So according to the expressivist, when I say 'stealing is wrong' I'm not making a mistake any more than I am when I say 'eggplant is disgusting' or 'blueberries are delicious.' I'm just expressing an attitude, not trying to describe something that is true about the world.

You plant yourself in the last camp, right? Explain what the position is in more detail and then how you have contributed to developing it.

SB: Well you've put it very nicely and you've shown where the battle lines were drawn. Well-known philosophers including Ayer, Stevenson, Hare, and even Wittgenstein defended the view. The position was quite respectable until the 1960s and then for some reason a kind of backlash started. Partly, it grew out of a kind of anti-existentialist feeling. There was a feeling that you can't just choose in a vacuum. You can't let your sentiments swamp you, you need to pay attention to people who thought hard about how life goes well and how it goes badly.

The other thing is that morality doesn't appear linguistically to be just an expression of feeling.

TS: You mean its grammatical structure?

SB: Yes and that has quite a lot of ramifications. So, we can put their point like this: If the expressivists were right, we could get by going around saying "boo" to this or "hooray" for that, just expressing an attitude. So you say "I'd like to go and throw stones at a cat." And I say "Boo to that!" Or, "you mustn't!" I can prescribe that you don't do it. And a lot of ethics does go on like that, in the manner of the Old Testament: thou shalt, thou shalt not, is just rules and prohibitions. But we also announce things in the assertive propositional form. And we say "That's good, you better believe it" or "That's wrong" as if we're expressing facts. And it comes across as rather like "That's square" or "That's cubic." The pushback against the expressivists largely consists in saying that they can't account for that propositional or assertive sort of appearance. And there are a number of technical arguments …

TS: Maybe you could give the simplest version of the Frege–Geach problem.

SB: Yes, sure. It's called the Frege–Geach problem because the basic form of argument was there in the writings of the great German founder of analytical philosophy, Gottlob Frege. It was resurrected by Peter Geach with famous articles in the early 1960s. It went something like this.[8]

One of the things about the propositional or assertive form of ethics is that you can conditionalize. So suppose you say "Mary is behaving badly." and I say, "Well maybe, but if Mary is behaving badly, Peter is behaving much worse." Now, while I've said "If Mary's behaving badly then Peter's behaving much worse," you couldn't fit a "hooray" or a "boo" or a command after that "if." I can't say, "If boo to Mary, then boo boo to Peter," because it just doesn't fit the frame, as the linguists would call it. In the same way that I can't say "If is Peter coming to lunch?" The question won't fit into an "if." And Geach pointed out that prescriptions ("do this") and expressions of delight, like "Hooray for this" don't fit into these "if" contexts.

TS: But how is this a special problem for ethical discourse? Couldn't you run the same argument for aesthetic or taste discourse? If *The Godfather* is great and *Twilight* is terrible, then this movie, which is better than *The Godfather*, is better than *Twilight*. It's the same thing. But nobody thinks this shows that our taste and aesthetic discourse must be cognitivist or objective, right?

SB: Good. I think your reaction is eventually the right one. I well remember I first learned of the Frege–Geach problem in a pub from a friend. My initial reaction was 'well that's not much of a problem' because it seemed as though, well, it's up to us to choose our linguistic forms. I think I used an example very like yours. I mean, if I can go to English football teams, if I'm on the terraces I say "Boo, Arsenal!" It doesn't seem to matter whether I transfer to saying "Arsenal sucks!" which is the sort of thing that sports fans say. But if "Arsenal sucks!" is a way of expressing my contempt for Arsenal, I can then say "Mind you, if Arsenal sucks Tottenham sucks worse," or, "If Arsenal sucks, then we shouldn't go to the game next Saturday." So it looks as though we've just got a useful extension of our linguistic repertoire enabling us to put what is fundamentally an expression of attitude into this proposition-sounding form. And that enables us to say various things we want to say. And I still think that's fundamentally the right reply.

TS: And yet ...

SB: And yet. The mood at the time was that these sort of details matter. The mood was that we have to get them right, and it's certainly tricky to get them right. Geach had one very powerful point, which I'll just mention. He said, "Ok so you're expressing your attitude, your contempt for Arsenal by saying 'Boo to Arsenal!' or 'Arsenal sucks!'" But when you say "If Arsenal sucks, then something or other," you're changing the meaning of the sentence. It's now doing something a bit different. Geach pointed out that that by itself won't do, because in ethics when you've got the simple sentence and the conditional sentence, they together make a logical match. They mate together logically in the logical form of modus ponens. If you have both premises, 'Arsenal sucks' and 'if Arsenal sucks then we need to avoid the match' you can conclude 'we need to avoid the match.' The thought was that expressivism is somehow not getting ethics inside that structure.

TS: But there has to be something special about ethics for this to be a problem, right? If the same problem applies to taste judgments and aesthetic judgments—which very few people think of in objective or factual terms— then it seems like more of a weird semantic puzzle rather than a reason to reject ethical expressivism.

SB: Well, yes, I don't remember Geach talking about aesthetics but in fact his argument would work as well or as badly against the view that when I say "This is a beautiful vase" I am expressing appreciation or pleasure at the visual appearance of the vase. Now it seems obviously right to almost everybody. What else am I doing? Beauty lies in the eye of the beholder is an old proverb. And we can say a lot about what aesthetic pleasure is and so on, but if you leave that aside, the expressivist account looks dead right. And yet Geach could come along and say, "Suppose you say it's a beautiful vase. If it's a beautiful vase, then we ought to buy it. So we ought to buy it." It's valid. You've got the same problem. It's valid. But that was the argument. It puzzled people. So I tried to explain the phenomenon on behalf of expressivism. Allan Gibbard approached the same problem at the same time.

TS: I was going to ask you how your expressivist view—which you called "quasi-realism"—contributed to the earlier versions. Is this one of the things—that it can address problems like this?

SB: Yes. That's almost exactly right. I'm not original in being an expressivist. Ayer, Stevenson, and (I would argue) Hume, and Adam Smith, were there before. So expressivism is an established tradition. Then in the 1970s, John Mackie wrote a book, *Ethics: Inventing Right and Wrong*, which defended the error theory that you mentioned before. Mackie claimed that there was just an error in our ordinary thought about ethics because it was infused with dubious metaphysical assumptions. And it had to be really modified beyond recognition or abandoned or something. It's not quite clear what he actually counseled in practice, but anyhow it was an error.

The options, he thought, were that you're either a kind of rampant Platonist, you believe in a third world of norms and duties and obligations and reasons and values. Or you just abandon the whole thing, and there's no expressive account of it that keeps it afloat.

TS: And he didn't rely, to his credit, on any kind of logical trick.

SB: No, I think what bothered Mackie was authority. He was an Australian. Australians hate authority.

TS: The bindingness, right? He thought that it was essential to our concept of moral values that they exert some mysterious motivational force on us to act in accordance with them.[9]

SB: Yes, ethics has a 'to-be-done-ness,' as he labeled it. And Mackie wrote that expressivism formed no way out because it couldn't capture that. It had gone into the shadows.

TS: Yeah, that resonates with me more than the logic issue, and always did.

SB: Well, I came along and I guess my contribution was to say that I'm not having expressivism pushed out of doors. It seems to me right, and seems to me Hume does it marvelously, Adam Smith does it just as marvelously. Something's gone wrong with the way these debates are being conducted. So I invented 'quasi-realism,' which is a term I now regret, but I'm saddled with it.

TS: Why do you regret it? Just because it has a technical sounding feel to it?

SB: Yeah, exactly, exactly. It sounds more frightening than it should be. And all I wanted to say was that you can be an expressivist and do justice to both the Frege–Geach phenomenon and the Mackie phenomenon. You end up sounding a bit like G. E. Moore or Plato, but you've saved your soul in the process. You haven't gone into metaphysical heaven.

TS: So how does your view allow you to do that in a way that Ayer and Stevenson, that sort of combined view, doesn't?

SB: Well, Stevenson was a fair amount of the way there because he saw that one of the functions of moral language is expression. But a large part of what we're trying to do is coordinate with other people. Moral dissent in a community is unpleasant, dangerous, and it's something we need to negotiate. If you think fox hunting should be banned, I think fox hunting is fine, we've got a problem. Because you're trying to stop me from doing something maybe I want to do, and we need to talk it through if we can, we have to find a compromise, maybe, to satisfy each other's deepest concerns with this issue.

So, moral language is not simply sounding off: 'Here I stand, that's the end of it.' It also has a pragmatic function, a use. There's a utility to moral language with all of its ins and outs that I wanted to preserve. Furthermore, it's not because we're describing a mysterious part of the universe. It's because we care about things and we want to express these ordinary cares and concerns to each other and negotiate disagreement. So we've got to coordinate and cooperate. If we can't do that we risk war, literally, sometimes.

So I was not having an error theory. I said, no, this activity of evaluating things, comparing them, insisting on them, giving permission, withdrawing permission. These activities are too central to human life for the philosopher to come out of his study and say, oh, they're all mistaken or based on a mistake. That can't be true.

TS: Why can't it be true? It's true in certain areas, right? Like the example I mentioned earlier, witch discourse. We used to talk about witches, we called people witches, we argued about who was a witch and who wasn't a witch, and the whole debate was based on a mistake. So why can't ethics be like that?

SB: The problem with witchcraft is that at its heart there is a simple empirical falsity: that old women can make nasty things happen by magical means. They can't. Old women can make nasty things happen, but they do it by perfectly ordinary means. There's no empirical theory, no bad causal theory attached to good, bad, right, wrong, just because they're expressions of attitude. Of course, people can make mistakes in their value judgments because they make mistakes in causal judgments, that's for sure. I might say that you broke my vase and that's a bad thing, so you owe me reparation. But if you didn't break the vase, then my moral account of the situation is bad because my empirical understanding is bad.

TS: Which was Ayer's big point I take it, right? That so much of moral disagreement is actually disagreement about the relevant empirical facts.

SB: Yes, much of it is about the empirical facts.

TS: So, let's say I'm arguing with Descartes about whether it's OK to dissect animals while they're alive, that argument could just be over the question of whether animals can feel pain. And that's an empirical question. If I could convince him that they do feel pain, he might be horrified. And then we'd probably agree that it is wrong to dissect them.

SB: Exactly. Exactly.

TS: But you concede to Mackie and Geach that there is something about our ethical discourse that the Stevenson–Ayer view fails to capture.

SB: Ayer, for example, thought that moral discourse, because it was expressivist, didn't admit of any notion of truth. But out in the street people will say things like "it's *true* that Johnny ought to offer reparation." And others will disagree and say it's not true because he didn't break the vase. So we now need to marry expressivism with this sort of reasonable understanding of how we can use notions like truth.

I don't like the label non-cognitivist, because look, I know, and so do you, that it's wrong to stomp on blind babies for fun. Now, that's not a very pretentious piece of moral knowledge, it's fairly near the bottom. But it's a piece of moral knowledge. Now, what do I know? What does that mean? Well I've got an expressive account of knowledge. I think to make a claim about knowing that something is wrong is to enter a claim to status—a status to call a question done and dusted and finished. And I claim that status for it's wrong to jump up and down on blind babies for fun.

TS: So you're expressing a near-certainty that you could never be persuaded otherwise.

SB: That's right. Never properly persuaded otherwise. Somebody might hit me on the head or something but that would mark a decline, it wouldn't mark an improvement in my understanding.

TS: So you've incorporated an idea of mind independence to the expressivist account of ethics.

SB: Oh yes.

4 Mind Independence and Moral Disagreement

TS: OK, so here's my challenge then, and it might come from a different side than you normally get. Why do you feel you need to preserve that idea of mind independence? Is this conceding too much?

SB: Well, we've got to be careful here. There's a sense in which I'm absolutely cool about mind dependence. That is, if we did not have these attitudes, these plans and policies and social needs to coordinate with each other, we wouldn't be moralizing. We wouldn't be evaluating in the way we do. So in that sense, all the practices are mind dependent.

However, when it comes to describing and deploying our standards, our own attitudes drop out of view. It's as though they provide a lens through which we see things. But what we talk about, and what sways us, are not facts about ourselves. It's quite hard to understand this, but there's a lovely phrase of St. Augustine which I'm very fond of. Augustine says, "In the pull of the will and of love lies the worth of everything to be sought or avoided, or to be thought of as greater or lesser value."

TS: I like that but what does it mean exactly?

SB: If we weren't passionate creatures we wouldn't be pulled, we wouldn't be loving, and we wouldn't be valuing things. However, the passions give us a kind of lens, a perspective, through which we see things and evaluate them. But then when we're actually moralizing or evaluating conduct, what makes it good or bad is very often something very separate from us. So, take your case of Descartes. Descartes is doing vivisection ... I know he did dissections but I'm not sure he did vivisections, did he?

TS: I'm not sure.[10]

SB: I don't know. Well let's suppose he is, he's vivisecting some poor dog or something. And I look at that and I'm absolutely revolted by it. I think it's absolutely terrible and he shouldn't be doing what he's doing. But what if he's a callous medic and he thinks it's OK because he's gaining knowledge. Then we've got a moral disagreement. If you ask me what's so bad about it, I don't talk about myself, I talk about the dog. It's causing the poor dog intense pain, that's what's bad about it. And the fact that it's causing the dog intense pain is not dependent on me. What's dependent on me is that I deploy that fact to moralize against Descartes.

TS: That makes sense. And of course that's true of all these other areas. If I say *Taxi Driver* is a great film and you ask me what's great about it, I'm not going to describe anything about myself. I'll talk about the performances, the screenplay, the cinematography, and so forth.

SB: That's right, it's exactly right. And I accept that parallel. I think aesthetics and ethics are on all fours here. This means that when you say something like 'beauty lies in the eye of the beholder' you've got to be a bit careful

TS: Right, right. It's a misleading phrase.

SB: Yes, it's a misleading phrase because no, her beauty lies in her cheek and jawbones and the flashing green eyes or whatever it is. But of course, the fact that I find those beautiful, that's certainly a fact about me. And if we find them beautiful, it's a fact about us. But if we're asked what makes her beautiful we have to go back to the thing.

TS: So that's the mind independence—

SB: —That's the bit of mind independence, exactly.

TS: What do you take to be the toughest objection to that view? Or the most common challenge?

SB: Well, if we get away from the technology that followed on the Frege–Geach thing, I guess with old age coming on I think the toughest challenge is psychological rather than philosophical. I think the toughest challenge is that people are afraid of standing on their own feet. Kant said that the motto of the Enlightenment was "Dare to Know"—*sapere aude*. And I think that was very profound. I'm not sure he actually followed it through, but when we talk about Mackie we said that it's the authoritative nature of ethics that bugged him. People fear that expressivism, even with all the trappings I gave it, takes away authority. They worry that it takes away the sanctions of morality or its binding power.

TS: Ultimately it will be a matter of taste.

SB: That's what they fear, I think. And I think there's no reason for that fear. Now, one's got to be careful. Human beings can be pretty nasty. But, at our best, we can cooperate, we can be kind to each other, we can be charitable, we can take each other's pains and pleasures as our own.

TS: Ok, so let me press this challenge with the vivisection example. Say you're Descartes and you ask me to give reasons for why it's wrong. And I give you the relevant empirical facts, the pain and the suffering of the animal. And now you come back to me and say "What's your point? I know the animal is suffering, but so what?" So now I say: "It's just wrong to cause another creature pain to satisfy your curiosity." And you reply: "No it's not—it's just an animal, you weirdo."

And we get to this point where we're not disagreeing over empirical matters, we're just disagreeing on whether it's OK to cause an animal suffering. Now on your view, there's not much else we can do—we're just expressing two very different attitudes about the value of the dog's pain. I can't point to this real property of wrongness. I can say that I care about the animal. But I don't have anything that makes me right and the other person wrong.

SB: Yeah, I think that's true, and at the end of the day we have to all confess to that. But here I don't think the expressivist is in any worse boat than anyone else. For all the metaphysical accretions and additions, the realist can't do any better. He can just say, look, I intuit that it is wrong. Or, I look to the Platonic heavens and I've discovered that it's wrong. Well that's just whistling.

TS: So then it's the same problem but in epistemological terms.

SB: Yes, that's right.

TS: Here's the thing that converted me. I was on Mackie's side until I read and then taught your article "Error and the Phenomenology of Value." In that paper you pointed to the difference between Mackie's famous first chapter where he provides the error theory, and then the rest of the book (which nobody ever reads) that addresses the question: "OK, there are no moral facts—what do we do now?" The deep point in your paper is what we end up doing turns out to be exactly like what we would do if there really were these moral facts or properties.

SB: Yeah, that's right. That was, I think, the real Achilles heel of Mackie's. Having banged the drum for error and then asked "what now", the answer is that we discuss things like whether suicide is permissible, all the rest of it. If somebody says bravely that we must stop evaluating things, we must stop moralizing, and I say OK. Now what? Well, we evaluate things.

I've never written a paper with this as its main theme but I've often thought of it. Suppose I became convinced that Geach was right and I think "Oh my God this is awful." Everyday moral thinking and ways of expressing ourselves are deeply confused. We have to go back to boo-hooray language, thou shalt, thou shalt not. I foresee that in five minutes we would start talking like we used to talk. The pressures to have good inferential roots we can all follow, the ordinary everyday if–then logic just make it inevitable. Just as if we said: "I'm going to be a puritan, I'm only going to say 'boo to Arsenal' and I'm never going to say 'Arsenal sucks.'" In ten minutes you're going to find that you need to say it.

TS: Like an error theorist who says "I'm never going to say 'factory farming is wrong,'" I'm just going to say "I strongly disapprove of factory farming," or "boo factory farming." But then you're still going to want to convince somebody to share your disapproval. And then you'll be back in the propositional language of morality. Maybe that's what separates ethics from something like taste. With taste, we're willing to stop trying to persuade other people much earlier than we are with ethics.[11]

SB: That's right. I think often when people are going around an art gallery, they're much more content with a conversation which consists in swapping responses or pointing out things they enjoy. They're not so set on achieving coordination. It's not always true, because it can be disturbing and might unsettle your friendship if you're really out of kilter.

TS: Yeah. And specifically people you care about. I'm concerned about my daughter Eliza becoming a real movie/film fan and connoisseur—probably as much or more than I am her moral education. And when I get in that mode I'll be as assertive and use all sorts of propositional language. I'll say *Modern Times* is brilliant, *The Goonies*[12] is overrated and so forth. But with other people it just doesn't bother me as much. I guess the sphere of who we care about is wider in ethics too.

SB: The realms over which disagreement becomes important seem much greater and much more common. Yeah, it's an interesting question. You know, if we take a comparison, my wife and I go to the art gallery, we've got a spare couple of hundred dollars and we'd like to buy a little print or something and we disagree about which art to buy. Well, OK. But now suppose we disagree about whether guests in the house should be allowed to smoke or something. Then it's harder to just forget it or live and let live.

TS: It affects you more.

SB: It affects you more, whichever side loses is going to be resentful and annoyed and it's potentially a cause of divorce.

TS: Even though it's not really a moral question in the end.

SB: No it's not but it's got that sort of practical need to coordinate.

5   Reasons, Reasons Everywhere

TS: Recently, there's been a renewed focus on reasons that has invaded normative ethics and metaethics. There's so much attention and effort trying to make sense of sentences like 'he has normative reason to X' or 'there is a normative reason for her to Y.'

SB: Oh yes.

TS: Let's take an example you talk about: Bernard Williams' abusive husband. People want to say that he has reason to treat his wife better.

SB: Right.

TS: But Derek Parfit[13] believes as an expressivist, you can't say this. Or that you can't say: "he has decisive reason to treat his wife better whether he wants to or not." So I'll put on Parfit's hat, although it won't fit very well. You do think that he should treat his wife better. And you think that's a fact—well, I don't know if you think it's a fact but you think it's true. Why don't you have to withdraw any of your expressivist bona fides?

SB: Even old-fashioned Freddy Ayer, without any bells and whistles, was allowed to say he should treat his wife better. That's an elementary sort of judgment which any decent person would make. Putting it in the vocabulary of reasons, for me, is optional. It doesn't add or subtract anything. But if I want to talk about reasons in connection with the wife-beater, just as I say you ought to stop, you ought to reform, I'm just as happy saying 'your wife's distress is a reason for you to reform.' It's a fact about the situation that makes it so appalling.

TS: I guess what Parfit wants to preserve is the idea that the husband has a decisive reason.

SB: The language is unfortunately floppy here. If we tighten it a bit we can draw a distinction. I'm very comfortable saying 'there is a reason' because that's me in my own mouth expressing what I think about this situation. As for 'he has a reason,' I think we should reserve that for descriptions of the wife-beater's psychology, what he gets moved by.

TS: Whether or not he has a reason to do anything depends on his psychology.

SB: Absolutely. He's a ... he's a confirmed wife-beater. Let's suppose he comes from a culture that doesn't value women, that gives the husband some kind of religious authority over his wife, or maybe like Descartes and the animals he doesn't really believe that women feel pain or something.

TS: He has a deficit of empathy.

SB: He has a deficit of empathy … he's really a very nasty piece of work when it comes to his relations with women. Well, he has no reason to reform. I can't get a grip on his motivational states and show him that he's got a reason to reform.

TS: But isn't this what bugs people like Parfit so much, the idea that you can't say that he has reason to do something, right?

SB: I can say there is reason for him to act very differently. It just seems more useful to keep the 'he has reason' … for a description of his psychology. As I say in "All Souls Night," anybody who's sane has the Augustinian view that it's features of the object that we look to, the animal's pain, his wife's distress, but when we look to them we do so with our own sentimental dispositions and attitudes.

TS: Right, I think you use an example of crossing a street. And, yes, the reason you shouldn't cross the street is that a bus is coming. There's a reason out there in the world for you not to cross the street. You also have reason not to cross the street, but that depends on your desires and senses.

SB: If I was trying to commit suicide, it would be a quite different thing. And yes, the reasons are out in the street. The bus is the reason.

6 "Vagabond Thoughts That Roam the Public Highway"

TS: I wonder if the whole obsession and concern about reasons—what are they? Do they exist?—is part of a more general phenomenon in philosophy. You take a concept, knowledge for example, and then you find some problem with it. Usually the problem takes the form of not being able to come up with a theory of necessary and sufficient conditions that capture it. There's always some counterexample. That's what happening now with "reason."

SB: That's right.

TS: And if you think there always will be a counterexample, you become a so-called "skeptic" about knowledge. You say we can't truly know anything. And yet, people talk about knowing things all the time. And sometimes their claims about knowing seem false—because we're pretty sure they're misinformed. And other times it seems right. It's funny because when I read this new literature on knowledge skepticism I was taken aback. I originally associated skepticism about knowledge with Pyrrho, the ancient philosopher who had to be led around by his students because he didn't think he had any reason whatsoever to trust his senses. So if there was a ditch in front of him, he'd fall into it without his students guiding him. That seemed like *real* skepticism.

SB: That's real skepticism!

TS: It seems like you can take any branch of philosophy and someone will stake out a skeptical position, often based on their ability to come up with counterexamples to every theory on offer.

SB: Yeah, I'm more apt to start somewhere else and ask what are people achieving in these conversations. What's the good in them? So, I think this was the beginning of what I now see as a sympathy with pragmatism.[14] And I should have been quicker on this. There's a wonderful quotation from C. S. Peirce who says "we must not start with the pure idea, vagabond thoughts that roam the public highway with no human habitation, we must start with men and their conversation." And I think that's a fabulous motto, and I should have it chipped to my gravestone. I'm very keen on people and their conversation and what they're doing when they're conversing.

TS: This is P. F. Strawson's point too in "Freedom and Resentment." Look to the actual practices and attitudes. You build your conception from the ground up instead of from the pure thought down.

SB: That's right. And so my quarrel with Parfit is that he is diametrically opposite. He starts with the truth, the good, the norms. And tries to give a story about how we get their distribution in logical space right. That just strikes me as wrong.

TS: OK, since we're talking about Parfit, I want to read a quote to you from your review of his celebrated new book *On What Matters*. It's not from the review that actually appeared, however. It's the review that originally was going to appear before the *Financial Times* asked you to revise it.[15] Do you know why they did?

SB: I don't actually.

TS: I actually think that the original version contains a deep philosophical point that gets lost in the final version. In the original, you write "It would be a tragedy, [Parfit] tells us on page 2, if there's 'no single true morality.'" And this is the part that was taken out:

> Well, outside the charmed walls of All Soul's College there actually are tragedies. Often the messy pluralities of conflicting moral demands, one might have said, the conflicting demands on human life itself are part of the cause of these tragedies. Inside the charmed walls, I fear, the tragedy is more like that of Ajax slaying the sheep, or perhaps it is the comedy of Don Quixote tilting at windmills.
>
> If I had to guess, I'd say the *Financial Times* thought there might be too much snark in that passage, even by British standards. But when you say that "outside Oxford's walls there are real tragedies," I see a substantive ethical point there. What people like Parfit are doing (and this goes for a lot of contemporary ethicists) is a genuine *moral* failing. In the sense that there's this world of actual moral problems, that they're ignoring them by creating logic puzzles and fantastical thought experiments to solve them.

SB: Well I think this is something any decent philosopher needs to remind himself of occasionally, that we do get very self-indulgent. I blame myself as much as anyone. It's easy to become obsessed by whatever the latest paper in *Analysis* has produced as a counterexample to your pet theory, and then go away and devote six weeks in the summer to it. All the time you're not helping with Oxfam or—

TS: —That's not what I mean though. Let's set aside what we could be doing for Oxfam. The deep point I thought you were making is that as ethicists we need to produce work that addresses real-life moral questions. Because the tragedies are real. But instead they're playing logic games.

SB: Well, yes. This is the problem with trolleyology[16] and a lot of what Roger Scruton nicely described as 'spectral mathematics.' We've got these bloodless scenarios in which there are 11 people on one rock and three people on the other, but the three people are younger than the 11, and where do you send the lifeboat, and you can sit there and ponder and think up reasons.

TS: You were on to this early in *Ruling Passions*. You wrote then that when you abstract the situation from all the real human concerns and circumstances, you won't learn anything important.

SB: Yes, you won't learn about the real mess in a situation where a question comes up about "who we should save?" In fact, in nearly all such situations, it becomes salient somehow what we should do and it resolves itself. The circumstances dictate our actions. Philosophers do spend an inordinate amount of time on these constructed, artificial, abstracted cases. That makes me deeply uncomfortable. I think it contributes to a slightly ridiculous kind of face the profession sometimes puts forward.

TS: I wonder how reliable our intuitions in these cases are even as a reflection of our own values. Does my intuition about trolley cases reveal anything about how utilitarian I am?

SB: I have very little confidence in those diagnostics. I suppose it might reveal some respect that we have for the doctrine of double effect—that there's a difference between performing an action intending a bad consequences, and performing one with an unfortunate side effect, but that you didn't intend to happen. Now, I think that's true, and perhaps it got lost in some utilitarian thinking.

TS: I guess so. Still, when you're doing ethics and you detach yourself from real life, not only are you not devoting that time to work in the Peace Corps, you're actually not even—

SB: —doing ethics.

TS: You're not even doing ethics, exactly. And I thought that was your point in the Parfit review.

SB: Well, yes, that was circling my mind as I wrote that rather rude stuff about Don Quixote and Ajax.

TS: Right.

SB: Another example Parfit has—he's got this character who is indifferent to pain on Tuesdays or something. Tuesday indifference. And he can't give a reason for it, it's not connected to a religious prohibition or anything like that. And Parfit's very anxious that we call him irrational.[17] Well, I'm not anxious about what to call him at all because I've never met him. I don't know what I'm going to call him. It's a very odd preference, it's completely off the dial in fact, so I wouldn't be able to get on all fours with him. I don't know or care what I might end up saying about him.

TS: It's just not a priority to figure out what you think about his status.

SB: It's not a priority at all. I mean, eventually you shrug your shoulders and say I don't know what's wrong with him.

7 Singer's Way of Making a Difference

TS: OK, let me fight back on behalf of this artificial style of ethical theorizing. Take Peter Singer's drowning-child case, another idealization.[18] Now Singer shares Parfit's metaethics, but set that aside. Singer uses cases like the drowning child effectively, more effectively than almost anyone, to connect ethics with real life and real problems. And he's done some great things.

SB: Amazing things, yes. With Peter, I, too, regret his metaethics but it's not very important. And the work he's done … I mean, he's made two big differences to the world. One is for animal rights or animal liberation, animal welfare, you know he pushed it way up the agenda. And secondly he's made a lot of people uncomfortable about the stringency of the duty to help. Now, it's not as if people were unaware of the duty to help. Kant has the duty to help, just about anybody who's put benevolence or fellow feeling or sympathy in their philosophy is going to look kindly on helping, and maybe have a duty to help. But he's made that very effective and he's made people very uncomfortable about one of the shelters we hide behind, which is that the suffering is a long way away. In the modern world you can help the guy in Africa. It's no good saying it's a long way away. And that is very uncomfortable and I'm glad that people are uncomfortable about it.

TS: What makes the drowning child in a pond an effective case in a way that the trolley case is not?

SB: It's interesting, the trolley problem does depend on idealizations like you *know* the guys can't get off the track. You *know* it's going to kill them, there's no emergency brake on this trolley. So it's presented from a state of knowledge that you never actually have in real life. It's highly artificial in that way. This contrasts with cases where you see a drowning child and there's nobody else about. In that version, it's not straining your cognitive resources very much because it can be pretty obvious when someone is in distress in the water.

TS: And for the case to work, you don't have to be 100 percent confident that you'll be able to save the child.

SB: No, you don't have to. You don't actually have to in the trolley case but it becomes computationally heavy … With the drowning-child case, it's much easier to imagine ourselves actually in that situation. You could walk out here tonight and see a situation like that. So I suppose that's what really tugs us. It would be inconceivable to just walk by. Even if you're ineffective and just flap, you're going to flap.

TS: Maybe another difference is that trolley cases, especially now, are meant to show that people subscribe to some kind of principle or some kind of ethical theory. Whereas Singer is just asking how we can reconcile our clear intuition about saving the child with our everyday practices.

SB: Good, yeah, that's good. It doesn't require you to come up with a theory that you can defend against all comers—

TS: —or even have any allegiance to a theory period. That's what is so interesting about the famine relief paper. Even though he's the paradigmatic consequentialist, the argument in that paper doesn't require us to hold any particular theory.

SB: Yeah, that's right. It's very powerful, and I'm not by nature a first-order ethicist. I don't like telling people what to do, as I said I'm fairly liberal. But I think it is awkward, and it's right that it's awkward, that we go to fancy restaurants when there are people who are dying.

TS: And we should know that it's awkward.

SB: And we should feel awkward about it. Yes, I admire that side of Singer enormously.

Notes

1 See Chapter 8, my interview with Michael Ruse.

2 We're referring to "trolley problems" here in the ethics and moral psychology literature (see Chapters 4 and 17 for more discussion).

3 Hume published *An Enquiry Concerning Human Understanding* and *An Enquiry Concerning the Principle of Morals* roughly 10 years after he published the *Treatise.*

4 See also Chapter 3 (Valerie Tiberius) for a discussion of Plato's image of the chariot.

5 See Mackie's *Ethics: Inventing Right and Wrong* (New York: Penguin, 1977).

6 See Chapter 9 (Peter Singer) for a defense of this rationalist variety of moral realism.

7 See Chapter 8 (Michael Ruse) for a defense of moral skepticism.

8 See the *Internet Encyclopedia of Philosophy*'s entry on "Non-Cognitivism" for an accessible description of this problem and responses by Blackburn and Alan Gibbard. www.iep.utm.edu/non-cogn/#H4

9 See *The Stanford Encyclopedia of Philosophy*'s entry on "Moral Anti-Realism" for a description of a wide range of anti-realist views, including Mackie's two arguments for error theory. http://plato.stanford.edu/entries/moral-anti-realism/index.html

10 I'm pretty sure at the time I didn't know the difference. But vivisection is performing operations on live animals for experimental purposes.

11 See Haidt interview for a similar sentiment (Chapter 12).

12 If you're angry and loved *The Goonies* as a kid, go watch it again. It does not hold up.
13 Derek Parfit is an Oxford philosopher, a moral rationalist, and frequent opponent of Blackburn (who is at Cambridge). See this piece in the *New Yorker* for an accessible introduction to his work. www.newyorker.com/magazine/2011/09/05/how-to-be-good
14 See the *Internet Encyclopedia of Philosophy*'s entry on "Pragmatism" for a description of this position. www.iep.utm.edu/pragmati
15 Blackburn's version can be accessed here: www2.phil.cam.ac.uk/~swb24/reviews/Parfitfinal.htm. The version that appeared in the *Financial Times* can be found here: www.ft.com/intl/cms/s/2/2bf7cf30-b9e1-11e0-8171-00144feabdc0.html
16 See Chapter 17 (interview with Josh Greene and Liane Young) for more discussion about "trolleyology."
17 Peter Singer (see Chapter 9) says that the Tuesday indifference case was in large part what inspired him to give up his Humeanism and become a rationalist.
18 See my interview with Singer in Chapter 9 for a long discussion on the role of the drowning-child analogy.

Questions for Discussion

1   Why does Blackburn think philosophy is more like humanities disciplines (like history or literature) than scientific disciplines? What is the problem with comparing it to the latter?
2   How does Blackburn interpret Hume's famous dictum that reason is "the slave of the passions." Why are many philosophers uncomfortable with this idea?
3   How does Blackburn's "quasi-realist" view differ from other metaethical views like moral skepticism and moral realism?
4   Why does Blackburn still see morality as "mind independent"? In what sense can we still say that moral judgments are true or false?
5   How does the moral expressivist or non-cognitivist make sense of moral disagreement? Why, according to Blackburn, are realists in no better position to resolve these disagreements?
6   Why does Blackburn reject moral skepticism or "error theory," the view defended by J. L. Mackie?
7   How does Blackburn incorporate moral reasons into his position? In what sense are reasons "out there in the world" and in what sense are they not?

Suggested Readings

Blackburn, Simon. "Error and the Phenomenology of Value". In Ted Honderich (ed.), *Morality and Objectivity*. London: Routledge & Kegan Paul, 1985.
——. "How to be an Ethical Anti-Realist," *Midwest Studies in Philosophy* 12(1) (1988): 361–75.
——. *Ruling Passions*. New York: Oxford University Press, 1998.
——. *Essays in Quasi-Realism*. New York: Oxford University Press, 1993.
——. "Reason and Passion." In Hugh LaFollette (ed.), *The International Encyclopedia of Ethics*.

Oxford: Wiley-Blackwell, 2013.

——. "All Souls Night," [n.d.] www2.phil.cam.ac.uk/~swb24/PAPERS/Allsoulsnight.htm

Assorted Media and Podcast Pairings

Sam Harris, Lawrence Krauss, Simon Blackburn, and Steven Pinker on Science and Morality. (youtube.com) www.youtube.com/watch?v=Yuo8nvBaGUY

"Truth and Relativism" (youtube.com) www.youtube.com/watch?v=ef9xi-a1KPM

Very Bad Wizards, Episode 65, "Philocalypse Now." http://verybadwizards.com/episodes/65

Very Bad Wizards, Episode 69, "CHiPs on Our Shoulders (Lessons in Objectivity)." http://verybadwizards.com/episodes/65

Part IV

Morality Behind the Curtain

Introduction

This is the longest part of the book—what's the common theme of these interviews?

The earlier parts approached ethics from a philosophical perspective. The interviews in Part IV pull back the curtain to reveal the origins of morality and the psychology behind our moral beliefs and behavior.

What are some of the questions you address in this part?

Why are we moral anyway? Why do we give anonymously to charity, and get a nice warm fuzzy feeling when we do it? Why do we feel guilty when we break promises or cheat friends and even strangers? Why do we think it's morally appalling to walk by a drowning child in a pond, but perfectly okay to buy big-screen TVs and expensive NFL packages (when that money could save the lives of African children)? Why do different cultures have such different moral beliefs and practices? What's the nature of these moral disagreements? Can they be resolved?

So these researchers are dealing with the more descriptive side of ethics. They're explaining how it works rather than defending particular moral beliefs or positions.

Yes, although there's still plenty of debate about ethical questions for all you philosophy junkies out there.

So tell me about the line-up.

In Chapter 11, the primatologist Frans de Waal discusses the evolutionary roots of moral feelings like empathy, how they trace back to before our split with other primates like chimpanzees and bonobos. The evolutionary history of morality, according to de Waal, undermines the idea—all too common in economics—that human beings are purely self-interested creatures. Next up the psychologist Jonathan Haidt argues against the view that we reach most of our moral judgments through reason and rational reflection. According to Haidt, our emotions drive our judgments and reasoning is more often post hoc, justifying (or rationalizing) conclusions we've already reached via our emotional responses.

As a philosopher, you can't be too happy about that view.

I'm fine with emotion-driven theories actually. But the psychologist Paul Bloom pushes back against them in Chapter 13. Bloom recognizes the non-rational factors influencing our judgments but argues that they do not undermine the notion of a responsible agent, capable of rational reflection and deliberation. And delving into the philosophy side of things, Bloom challenges the view that our emotions (even the "nice" ones like empathy) provide us with a good or proper guide for moral and policy decision-making.

Sounds like a lively debate. What comes next?

The anthropologists. In Chapter 14, Joe Henrich discusses his work in Fiji and the Peruvian Amazon that shed important light on the cross-cultural differences in beliefs about justice. And in Chapter 15, Alan Fiske and Tage Rai offer a theory that explains moral disagreement by analyzing the different ways that people from all cultures relate to one another.

I could use a philosopher to help put all this in perspective.

You're in luck. In Chapter 16 Stephen Stich examines the philosophical implications of this research in psychology and anthropology. Stich argues that most ethical theories (as well as theories in other areas of philosophy) rest on a "problematic bet" that there isn't substantial variation in philosophically important intuitions. According to Stich, the evidence from these fields suggests that the bet is all but lost. And finally, in Chapter 17, neuroscientists Joshua Greene and Liane Young discuss their groundbreaking research using functional MRI machines to investigate the neuroscience behind moral judgment. Greene uses this research to argue for a similar position to Singer's, but Young and I are not entirely convinced.

I imagine that some people will find this research and its conclusions unsettling. We're only moral because it helped our hominid ancestors leave more offspring? Right and wrong can depend on where you live? That's not morality! Maybe this curtain should stay closed.

I think the story of how and why we are moral is too fascinating and complex for that kind of pessimism to be sustained. And besides, getting a better understanding of how morality works in no way diminishes the central role that it plays in our lives!

11 Frans de Waal

Lessons from Our Primate Relatives

Two elephants walk together at night. (No, this isn't a joke—it's a scene from a wildlife reserve in Thailand.) There is heavy rain, and the older elephant slips and falls in the mud. She's unable to get up. The younger elephant, unrelated to her companion, stays beside her for most of the night. The next day a group of mahouts, elephant caretakers from the wildlife reserve, try to hoist the elephant up to her feet with braces and ropes. In all the commotion—a crowd has gathered to watch the rescue—the younger elephant remains by the side of her fallen friend. The mahouts and the crowd shout for her to move out of the way, so they can get better leverage. But she won't budge. Instead, she burrows her head under the body of the other elephant and tries to lift her up. She does this several times, risking injury in the attempts. Incredibly, the younger elephant appears to recognize that the mahouts want to help rather than hurt her friend. She times her pushes, or so it seemed to me, with the hoisting of the mahouts.

Until recently, biologists thought such complex behavior—behavior with an undeniable moral dimension—was exclusive to human beings. As much as anyone in the world, Frans de Waal, the C. H. Candler Professor of Primate Behavior at Emory University, is responsible for changing this perception. Starting with Chimpanzee Politics—*his fascinating account of the intrigues and machinations of a chimpanzee troupe in the Arnhem Zoo[1]—and continuing through more recent books like* Good Natured *and* Our Inner Ape, *de Waal has illustrated the uncanny similarities between human beings and our primate relatives. De Waal has not restricted himself to descriptions of behavior, however. He is famous for his willingness to enter into the largely taboo world of animal emotions, where research is routinely dismissed as "anthropomorphizing." The result is an impressive array of evidence suggesting that we are not the only species to have moral feelings.*

De Waal's research is no friend to human vanity. In the grand tradition of Galileo and Darwin, de Waal provokes those who seek to draw a clear line between human beings and everything else. But his message is an optimistic one. If human morality has deep roots in our evolutionary past, then we can expect it to be more resilient, less susceptible to the contingencies of history. Seeing morality in this light also undermines the view of human beings as inherently selfish—a view that de Waal terms "veneer theory." Morality, according to veneer theory, is merely a recent cultural invention, a thin veneer that masks our "true" selfish animal nature. De Waal's criticisms of this theory (which we discuss at some length below) are the topic of his most recent book at the time of the interview, Primates and Philosophers. *The book is based on lectures de Waal presented at Princeton University, and features responses to his work from four renowned philosophers and authors.*

De Waal is also a remarkably hospitable interview subject. When I arrived in the morning, I was treated to a tour of the primate center and a bucket of apples to throw to the chimps in their enclosures. (There are very few things I'd rather do than toss apples to chimpanzees.) After the interview, Josh Plotkin,[2] one of de Waal's graduate students, showed me videos of his work in Thailand— including the video depicting the elephant rescue attempt described above. That evening, I was invited to de Waal's house for a dinner highlighted by hitchhiking stories from his wife, Catherine, and capped with a shot of "the cognac of tequilas." The interview itself took place at the Yerkes National Primate Research Center, about 40 minutes north of Atlanta.

January 2007

1   Bonobos Gone Wild

TAMLER SOMMERS: I want to discuss your work with chimpanzees especially, but let's start by talking about the bonobos, the closest primate relative of the chimpanzee. Your accounts of bonobos have always been great reading. You call them the "hippie ape," you describe some of their interactions as "orgies"—the reader gets a general sense of them as a sort of nonviolent free-love egalitarian noble-savage kind of animal. You'd think they'd be the celebrities of the animal kingdom. Instead, they are, in your words, "the forgotten ape." Why have they been forgotten?

FRANS DE WAAL: Well, first of all, we've only recently learned about the bonobos. The first discovery of these types of apes was the chimpanzee, whom Europeans have known since the seventeenth century. And even the few bonobos we did know then were called chimpanzees—everything was a chimpanzee at the time. So that's one reason they were discovered much later. The fieldwork was done much later. There were very few captive studies. The other reason is that the story of the bonobo didn't fit the thinking.

TS: Which thinking is that?

FDW: The postwar thinking was that we're an aggressive species. Which is pretty logical after World War II. But it became a kind of obsession to ask: Why are we so aggressive? Is it an instinct or is it not an instinct? Is it ingrained in our natures or not? That was the issue. One camp, mostly biologists, claimed that we were by nature aggressive. And a group of anthropologists used the chimpanzee initially as a counterexample. These anthropologists said, "Look at the ape. Our close relatives just travel through the trees and eat fruit and are peaceful. So that means that our ancestors were probably peaceful and aggression is a cultural product."

TS: Probably a comforting thought.

FDW: Yes, but in the 1970s, when the first reports came out about chimpanzees killing each other and killing monkeys, all of a sudden the counterarguments to the biologists were wiped off the table. And people saw this as the ultimate proof that human beings are an aggressive, nasty, and selfish species. The chimpanzee became the primary model for the human species and everything just clicked into place. That was the new model: "We are aggressive, they are aggressive, we must have been aggressive for six million years. Look at the ape."

TS: And then came the bonobos.

FDW: Yes, then along came the behavioral data on bonobos in the 1980s. And they didn't fit into the *new* picture. And they still don't fit into that picture. And so there are still people who will argue that the last common ancestor for humans was more chimplike. But there's no good argument for that. Genetically, they are exactly equidistant to us as they are to the chimpanzee. There's no good reason except for an ideological reason. They don't fit the new thinking about the inherent aggressiveness of human beings.

TS: They fit the previous thinking.

FDW: Yes. Basically, if your view is that human beings are an inherently aggressive species, then the bonobo is problematic. If your view is that humans have all sorts of characteristics including being highly cooperative, then the bonobos are a very interesting example to look at. I take the position that I don't know which one better reflects our own nature. I think we have a lot of both.

TS: Can you describe some of the ways bonobos break out of the warmongering mold?

FDW: First, there is no evidence from the field or from studies in captivity that bonobos kill each other. This has been seen many times in chimpanzees: killing each other, killing infants. For bonobos this has never been seen. They are friendlier, more peaceful. It's not that they are never aggressive; they are. But they don't kill. And they have a very effective way of avoiding aggression, which is their sexual interactions. So that's one issue. And the other is that female bonobos collectively dominate the males, which probably also helps control aggression. So it's a female-dominated species, and a very sexy species, none of which fits the thinking of mostly male theoreticians.

TS: You tell a funny story in *Our Inner Ape* about a lecture in which you described the failure of male bonobos to fight and establish dominance over the females. An audience member raised his hand and asked: "Well, what's *wrong* with them? What's wrong with these male bonobos?"

FDW: Right. Many male scientists react that way. Bonobos are uncomfortable to have around. They're too peaceful, and they're female-dominated. We can't handle that. Now, I personally don't think that our ancestors were female-dominated. That developed for the bonobo. But even if our last common ancestor was female-dominated, that would be very interesting.

We would need a different evolutionary story to explain how we got where we are. I always feel that facts that are inconvenient for certain theories should be faced straight-on rather than be neglected.

TS: I like what you said in one of the books—that the male bonobos have it pretty good. They're sexually liberated, they have a low-stress existence …

FDW: There's objective evidence for that. Most groups of chimpanzees have twice as many adult females as males. Most groups of bonobos have equal numbers of adult males and females. Since the birth ratio is 50–50 for both species, there must be a lot of male chimpanzees who die early. And that probably has to do with all the fighting and tensions and stress levels and so on. So in terms of health and longevity the male bonobo has a better life than the chimpanzee male.

TS: I have to bring up "GG-rubbing." My wife and I have *The Forgotten Ape* on a table in our living room, and any time we have a party, if it's a good party, anyway, someone will start flipping through the book and showing everyone the pictures of the female bonobos GG-rubbing.

FDW: [*laughing*] Is that right? Like having *Playboy* on the coffee table.

TS: Right, *Primate Playboy*. Something about the act, the name—it's a great name, *GG-rubbing*. And the picture. It demands attention. What is GG-rubbing, exactly? And what is its purpose? Why do female bonobos engage in it so often?

FDW: GG-rubbing is when females cling to each other almost like mother and child, and they rub their genitals together—basically a sexual interaction. In the US there's a shyness about sex, as you probably know, so many people who work on bonobos in this country don't want to call it sex. So they would say it's "affiliation" or it's "friendly"—

TS: —It seems extremely friendly—

FDW: —or they'll say it's not sex because it's not reproductive, which excludes, I suppose, all gay sex as sex. In fact, I thought it was amusing when the Paula Jones case came along in the US, that they actually had to find a definition of sex. Because Clinton tried to deny that he had sex with someone, and so the court came up with a definition—and they said sex is all contact involving the genitals. So it's official now: GG-rubbing has officially been declared sex. I use that argument if anyone wants to call it something else. And it clearly is sex. They rub their genitals and their clitorises together. Partly it resolves conflicts between them. Partly it's a conciliatory thing. It's a greeting. Mostly it promotes bonding between them. And the bonding is a very strong political instrument, because female bonobos only dominate the males collectively. A female is not individually capable of dominating a male. So GG-rubbing is basically a political tool.

2　The Real Darwinian Position

TS: Much of your work recently has been aimed at correcting another misconception—that morality is exclusively a human invention, something that evolved long after we split from other apes. Do you think apes and bonobos are moral species? Do they exhibit moral behavior?

FDW: Well, I usually don't call it moral behavior. I tend to call it building blocks or *prerequisites* for morality. I don't think that chimpanzees are moral beings in the human sense. But they do have empathy, sympathy, reciprocity. They share food, resolve conflicts. All of these elements are present in human morality. So what I argue is that the basic psychology of the great apes is an essential *element* of human morality. Humans add things to that, making our morality far more complex. And that's why I don't want to call chimpanzees moral beings, exactly.

TS: Why do you want to hesitate if you believe that chimpanzees have gratitude and empathy, indignation, maybe—what we call the moral emotions?

FDW: They have the moral emotions, yes. You can see gratitude, outrage, a sense of fairness—you can see parallels and equivalences in all the great apes. But to get to morality you need more than just the emotions. So yes, empathy is a good thing to have. And I cannot imagine how humans could have morality without empathy, but what morality adds to that, for example, is what Adam Smith termed the "impartial spectator." You need to be able to look at a situation and make a judgment about that situation even though it doesn't affect you yourself. So I can see an interaction between two humans and say this one is wrong and this one is right. I'm not convinced that chimpanzees have this kind of distance in their judgments. They certainly have judgments about what they do and how they interact with others. And how others treat them. I'm sure they have opinions about specific social interactions and how to react to them, but do they have opinions about more abstract concept about what kind of society they want to live in? Do they have a concept about fairness between others, or do they only care about fairness for themselves? That kind of distance that you see in human moral reasoning. I'm not sure you'll find that in a chimpanzee.

TS: Correct me if I'm wrong, but I thought I read something in *Chimpanzee Politics* and some other work indicating that chimps do react with a kind of indignation when they see one chimp mistreating another chimp. A third party will react, punishing the offender.

FDW: Yes, true. Yes.

TS: Wouldn't that count?

FDW: Yes—I think you can probably find examples of this in chimpanzee life. But in a way, even the interactions around them affect themselves: these are their friends, their relatives, their rivals. They are never impartial spectators. If chimpanzees have a morality, it likely is a self-centered morality.

TS: Can you give some examples of empathy in other species?

FDW: Well, yes. Today, you saw that old [chimpanzee] female Penny, who can barely get up on the climb bars, right?

TS: Yes.

FDW: We often see young females push her up onto the climber. So that's altruistic helping because it's really hard to imagine that they're doing it to get some favor back from this old lady. I give many examples in my books of sophisticated empathetic behavior in chimpanzees, including those that clearly require "theory of mind"—the ability to take the perspective of other chimps.

TS: So you think when a young chimp is helping Penny up the climb bars, she feels her frustration in some way, and she does this by taking her perspective, imagining what it must be like not to be able to climb on her own?

FDW: Well, the young chimp must understand Penny's goal and also the trouble she has trying to reach her goal. That's a very complex action right there. In humans there is a literature that says that perspective-taking requires a strong sense of self. A "self–other" distinction. Which is why in children, perspective-taking comes only at 2 years, when they are able to recognize themselves in the mirror. So we did the mirror-recognition experiments with chimps and also recently with elephants. Because elephants are very well known as highly altruistic animals. And they have large brains. So the thinking was that more complex empathy, based on perspective-taking, must correlate with mirror recognition.

TS: I saw Yale biologist Laurie Santos give a talk on perspective-taking or "theory of mind" capacities in monkeys, and I was amazed by the question–answer period. Hands shot up—everyone tried to come up with alternate explanations for her findings, even ones that were ad hoc to a bizarre degree. There was such deep skepticism, which was surprising from an outsider's perspective. From my point of view, I thought, of *course* other animals can take the perspective of others; of *course* they can imagine what other monkeys or chimps are thinking or feeling. But obviously that's not the common view among biologists.

FDW: It's a recent bias. Previous experiments showed that chimpanzees had this ability, and in that period—this was in the 1970s—the findings didn't get much attention. No one cared. Then a bunch of studies came along in the 1980s that cast doubt on those findings. And then everyone jumped on those studies and said: "There it is! Now we have the big difference between humans and animals—'theory of mind,' taking the perspective of others. That's what distinguishes us." I think that people are extremely eager to find that kind of difference. There's a long history, going all the way back to Darwin, before Darwin, where certain small items were believed to be uniquely human features. At one time there was thought to be a small bone in our jaw that was only human, but then they found it in other species. The ability to use tools was a big one, until Jane Goodall discovered tool-use by chimpanzees in the field. Then language. And recently theory of mind became the big thing. But now, of course, it's crumbling. There are more and more findings coming out that perspective-taking is not even restricted to primates—probably dogs have it, some birds may have it.

TS: Dogs have it? I knew it!

FDW: Yes, there are good findings on dogs, ravens, goats. At some level or other, perspective-taking is present in many animals. It may reach its highest level in big-brained animals—dolphins, elephants, chimpanzees, and I'm sure humans go beyond this ... but it's a continuum. We're farther along on the continuum, but it's not completely absent in other animals. And that's upsetting to a lot of people.

TS: Meanwhile, your most recent book, *Primates and Philosophers*, attacks the view that *human beings* aren't really moral, never mind nonhumans. You argue against the view that human morality is a thin veneer, a kind of cultural overlay or hypocritical mask covering our deeply selfish animal nature. You see this as fundamentally misguided because of the connection between our morality and animal emotions.

FDW: The interesting thing about my position is that it's really the old Darwinian position: human morality is an outflow of primate sociality. That's how Darwin saw it—it's an outgrowth of the social instincts. It's also very close to a Humean position and to Adam Smith. It's a moral sentimentalism—the view that emotions drive morality. In the last 30 years, people have abandoned that view. Richard Dawkins; Robert Wright in *The Moral Animal*; Michael Ghiselin; T. H. Huxley, a contemporary of Darwin's. They all take this position that evolution could never have produced morality, because evolution produces only selfish, nasty, aggressive individuals. And obviously human morality is a way of going beyond that. So evolution could not have produced human morality—it is something *we* came up with. What annoys me is that this is being sold as a *Darwinian* position. As if the true Darwinian paradigm dictates that evolution cannot have produced morality. But if you read Darwin's book *The Descent of Man*, it's very obvious that Darwin himself did not agree with this view at all.

So we've been fed a bogus "Darwinian" position for 30 years, one that confuses the way evolution works with the things that evolution produces. Because the way evolution works, yes—it's a nasty process. Evolution works by eliminating those who are not successful. Natural selection is a process that cares only about your own reproduction, or gene replication, and everything else is irrelevant. But then what natural selection *produces* is extremely variable. Natural selection can produce the social indifference you find in many solitary animals. But it can also produce extremely cooperative, friendly, and empathic characteristics. But this product of natural selection is ignored. And so, for example, human empathy is often presented as some sort of afterthought of evolution or something contrived— some people have argued that we are never *truly* empathic and kind. But if you look at the neuroscience literature on human empathy, it's obvious that it's an automated reaction. That's a strong counterargument to the claim that empathy is a contrived, culturally influenced trait. Because people cannot even suppress empathy. So take, for example, people in a movie theater where something terrible is about to happen. What do people do?

TS: They slam their hands over their eyes.

FDW: Yes. The reason we do that is that empathy is such a strong reaction, we have no control over it, and the only way to get control over it is to block the images. So I think empathy is a deeply seated characteristic of the human species. And it's by no means limited to the human species; it's a very old mammalian characteristic. Recently a paper came up on mice empathy. So it's a very ancient characteristic which fits with Darwin's position and my position on empathy and its origin. In *Good Natured* and *Primates and Philosophers*, I take a stand that this whole line of thinking is confused—the line of thinking that says by nature we're nasty and so we can never *naturally* get to morality. It's not that I don't think culture influences human morality. I do think that. But certainly we didn't start from scratch when we evolved morality.

TS: We started with moral emotions—which are as much a part of our natures as the selfish drives we have.

FDW: Absolutely.

TS: In your book you say that the "veneer theory" is a result of something you call "Beethoven's error." Can you explain what that is?

FDW: Beethoven's error is the confusion I alluded to between process and outcome. The focus on the process of natural selection started in the 1970s with Dawkins, who popularized the view that selection occurred at the level of the gene. This took us to the bare minimum and everyone focused all the attention on the selection process. But if you do that, you forget about the beautiful things that the process can produce. People like Dawkins focused their whole mind on the *nastiness* of the selection process. And they were intent on providing a sort of shock therapy to people in the social sciences and philosophy. And when the social scientists would say, "But sometimes people are kind to each other," they would reply, "No, no, that's all made up, they're faking that. There has to be some sort of selfish ulterior motive behind it." And so I called this type of error the "Beethoven error" because Beethoven produced his most beautiful music under the most atrocious circumstances (his Vienna apartment was described as disorganized and incredibly dirty). And that's true for a lot of process–outcome errors. Take cooking. The process of cooking is by no means clean and attractive. If you go into a Chinese restaurant's kitchen, you probably don't want to eat Chinese for a while. But you *do* eat it because we make that distinction. We forget about the process and enjoy the product. Natural selection produces some beautiful things—like genuine empathy.

3 "Human Caring Is Predicated on Affordability"

TS: On to a more philosophical topic. You seem to believe we can learn some moral lessons from the behavior of other nonhuman primates today. How does that work? What can the behavior of chimpanzees and other primates teach us about our own behavior? How can we derive claims about how we ought to act?

FDW: I'm not sure we can directly derive it.

TS: Well, okay—how can primate research *influence* the way we want to guide our behavior or design our institutions?

FDW: If you start from the assumption that humans are entirely competitive and that everything is regulated by selfish motives—and Americans do this more than Europeans—you end up with the conservative streak which is largely based on this kind of social Darwinist idea: let people fend for themselves, they will ultimately improve themselves or they'll die off, which is also fine. That sort of very harsh political ideology is often sold as being *congruent* with how nature operates. You look at free-market capitalism as an extension of nature. Wall Street is a Darwinian jungle. But this is not how human nature actually operates. People are not completely guided by selfish motives. A lot of work coming out of behavioral economics challenges this view that humans act selfishly even in *economic* life, never mind social life. Even economic decision-making is not driven exclusively by selfish motives. And social life, social considerations, and behavior are even less purely tied to selfish drives. A full understanding of human nature, helped by an understanding of the nature of our closest primates, will very quickly lead you to the conclusion, as Adam Smith well understood, that free-market capitalism needs to be counterbalanced by social motives. And then you'll get more of a mitigated type of capitalism, a softer capitalism. That doesn't mean you eliminate the free market. But it means that you build a society in which there is care for the poor, where there is reciprocity for others.

TS: But I'm still not clear on how you "get" that mitigated capitalism …

FDW: Take Hurricane Katrina, for example, which in the US exposed the line of thinking that we don't need to care about the poor, that they will fend for themselves. So then the biggest disaster of the century comes and the poor are left behind. All of a sudden, the American people were very embarrassed about what happened. All of a sudden, people were embarrassed by the fact that they didn't really care about the poor—that they had just let them drown. Most people had fled the city, leaving the old, sick, and poor behind. The people who couldn't move into the hospitals were just left behind. This was an interesting moment in American history, because all of a sudden it exposed this line of thinking as not compatible with how we *want* to be. And in fact it's not compatible with how we are as a species.

TS: But when you say that a true understanding of human nature gets us a softer mitigated capitalism, that leads me to believe that if the social Darwinians were right about the inherent selfishness of human beings, they would have been justified in setting up a hard, ruthless capitalism. Do you believe that?

FDW: Imagine that we were exactly as described by social Darwinists or Republicans—selfish, 100 percent incentive-driven, that's all. Then there would really be no reason to change society. We could go full-blown toward capitalism and a free market and see what happens.

TS: You really think there would be no reason to resist this even if we *were* primarily driven by selfish motives? Isn't it possible that we should care for others just because we think it's the right thing to do, even though we may not want to do it?

FDW: You think that people will do things that are right, even if they don't want to?

TS: They might … we don't always do what we want to do.

FDW: I don't think that people will do that. The fact that the American people were embarrassed by Katrina, or that a large proportion of the American people want improved healthcare, or to care for the poor, is I think purely because there is a level of empathy. You need to indoctrinate empathy *out* of people in order to arrive at extreme capitalist positions. And those people who will publicly argue that we don't need to care about the poor, they will care privately, if they have a poor family member, they will take care of that family member. So it's only *other* poor people they don't care about.

TS: Of course; it's still *their* family, right? As you note, the dark side of our nature is that we favor the interests of our "in-group," especially the family, although that can be broadened a little. But the farther that goes, the less we care about others, and the more we're willing to act violently toward them and neglect them.

FDW: I think that human morality evolved as an in-group phenomenon, to strengthen the in-group and increase its cohesiveness. This was partly needed for competition with other groups. So what you did to the other groups didn't matter. You could hack them to pieces, that would be perfectly fine, as long as you didn't hack *each other* to pieces—within the in-group. And that's a really interesting thing. The worst side of human nature, which is really intergroup violence between religions and between ethnic groups or nations, this side is *also* linked to the evolution of morality. And that's also why if people now argue that we need to expand morality and have universal human rights, and that we need to care about people elsewhere in the world, they have a big challenge ahead of them.

TS: Can primate research help them take this into account—help them see that we're not built for caring about people with whom have no connection with at all?

FDW: Of course, I'm not saying we *shouldn't* care. I don't think primate research offers that kind of moral guideline. All I'm saying is that it will be a challenge. I think as soon as we lose our wealth, the caring we do have for distant out-groups will disappear. Given that we are wealthy as a nation, in that sense, we ought to care about others. But as soon as there's a crash in our economy, like in the 1920s, say, something really serious,[3] will we still care about distant people? Human caring is predicated on affordability. Moral obligations to the out-group are not—however much philosophers might wish them to be so[4]—independent of moral obligations to the in-group. Our first priority is the survival of ourselves and our close kin. I call this the role of loyalty: we have varying degrees of loyalty, and they are just not equal for distant and close people, or for humans and animals, for that matter.

TS: You also say that we have a mental switch that when triggered can turn friend into foe. An attack of some kind can trigger this. You said that our reaction to Iraq is perhaps an example of this kind of primitive impulse that you see even in chimpanzees.

FDW: If you hit yourself with a hammer, you're going to blame someone—anyone. Frustration leads to angry reactions. This is known as the scapegoat effect, which occurs even in rats. You place two rats on an electric grid and shock them: they will attack each other as if the other is to blame for the pain. In primates, we often see that if there are tensions among higher-ups, they pick on a low-ranking individual to attack it. I felt the same happened in the United States after 9/11. A big and mighty country got attacked on its own soil—something it's not used to—and so someone had to be blamed, someone had to be attacked to let off steam. The target's actual guilt was a secondary concern. Afghanistan was not big enough for the angry reaction the US wanted to show. What struck me most was the cheerleading in the media. At the moment, everyone is backtracking and questioning the wisdom of the attack, but at the time it happened, all I saw was great enthusiasm. As a result, what is it, 500,000 Iraqis are gone? It's a disaster.

4 "Good Old Primate Diplomacy"

TS: Why do you think chimpanzees and bonobos have such different types of existences? They're such close relatives, genetically speaking, and yet violence and aggression are so common in one species, and harmony and GG-rubbing are so common in the other. What accounts for that difference?

FDW: Well, the leading theory is that bonobos live in a richer environment. They have the whole forest for themselves; they don't share it with gorillas. (Whereas chimpanzees are in competition with gorillas.) And this permits female bonobos to travel together. Chimpanzee females do not have that same opportunity because in order to gather food they have to travel separately. Oddly enough, that could be the reason for everything. Because if the females can travel together, they can form bonds and coalitions, and a lot of things like female dominance can follow from there.

TS: Is there a lesson we can draw from their environmental differences? Should we encourage a kind of society where women can travel together, and with their children—which might lead to a less-aggressive dynamic? Or are other social, environmental, behavioral differences too great for this to work ...

FDW: That's the problem. We have such a different past in terms of family building. We are in a situation where the nuclear family is so important, which bonobos don't have. So I'm not sure how from there you get to some kind of bonobo society where everybody mates with everybody. We have been subject to different evolutionary pressures, which is very difficult to return from.

TS: Would it be a fool's errand to try?

FDW: I think so. We have a social system where there is male investment in offspring. That always means that you get a protection of the investment. So males have reasons to develop social systems and moral systems that protect the family—emphasizing virginity, emphasizing fidelity, at least for the women, not necessarily for the men, but certainly for the women. Our society is designed around that system. So if we were to move in the direction of the bonobos, we would destroy that system. And that would create other serious problems. The funny thing is that many people look at bonobos as a kind of paragon, the type of situation we want to have— egalitarian relationships, free sex, peaceful. It all sounds very wonderful, but I don't think it's an option given where we are now.

TS: But on the other hand, you do seem to think there's a lot of cultural variability within our own species. Yes, the genes "hold culture on a leash," as E. O. Wilson said, but how long is the leash? And how much control do we have over where we go when attached to it?

FDW: There are certain cultures that emphasize harmony. For example, the Japanese culture emphasizes getting along in a way that American culture does not. The emphasis here is more that you have to stick up for yourself— don't get beaten up by anyone. Beat them up. It's a very different attitude. I don't know what triggers a society to move in one direction rather than another direction. But I'm a primatologist, not a sociologist.

TS: But you haven't been shy, though, about imagining ways in which the theories and themes from your work might affect social policy for human beings.

FDW: Well, the only thing I can say is that you will find people (or animals) being more cooperative with each other if you emphasize shared interest. And that's what, for example, Japanese society does. In this society, you could emphasize shared interest or group interest more, that would be the way to do it. Instead of saying something like "You shouldn't fight!"

TS: So do you think that you've learned things as a primatologist that can be applied to human problems? Or is that not something that really interests you?

FDW: No, it is of interest. Because, for example, in the US there are many conflict-resolution programs at schools. They basically tell kids to shake hands after fights and say, "I'm sorry." That's not going to do *anything* to resolve the real conflict. Of course kids are smart enough to learn that

that's what the teacher wants, so that's what they're going to do. But you're not changing the *attitudes*. What you need to do is teach them that there is value in relationships or value to the group and then the rest will follow. There will be fewer fights, less conflict. And there are great social psychology experiments to back this up. If you create competition between groups, you'll find higher social cohesiveness within the groups. The same thing happens to nations. A nation at war, like the US was a couple of years ago, is a more cohesive nation. So those kinds of lessons to me are pretty obvious.

TS: This reminds me of your discussion of sex differences too. One of the things you talk about is how males—and you see this in humans and chimpanzees—will fight more often, but they are much better at conflict resolution. Whereas females don't fight as often, but when they do, it's for keeps. There's no resolution.

FDW: That's sometimes controversial, because people always assume women are more peaceful than men. Which in many senses is true. Look at the murder rate. But I do believe that women are not nearly as good at conflict resolution, and that's why they try much harder to avoid conflict. And they're often successful. But when the conflict surfaces ...

TS: Women hold grudges.

FDW: Yes, often there is no resolution. A lot of women, especially intellectual women, can't stand that idea. They've grown up on the view that women are good and men are bad. What men do is compete and fight—and that's all they can do. But it's actually, who was it, Golda Meir, I don't know, a female politician said something to the effect that "It's good that men wage war, because it's only men who can make peace."

TS: In other words, Obama 2008?

FDW: Remember, I'm not voting.[5] But if you want my opinion, what the US needs most at this point is a leader who understands that this country, however important, has only 5 percent of the world population. You're as much caught in the web of international affairs and global economy as anyone else, so instead of trying to play the bully—without much success, I might add—you'd be better off with good old primate diplomacy. What you need is a groomer-in-chief.

Notes

1 De Waal was approached by television producers about making a reality TV show based on this book. The show would document the behavior and strategies of two groups under similar conditions—one made up of chimpanzees, the other made up of humans. De Waal declined after learning that the producers wanted him to stage some of the behavior of the chimpanzees.

2 Josh has recently become well known in the popular press for leading the first study (with de Waal) to demonstrate that elephants can recognize themselves in mirrors.

3 This interview, of course, took place in early 2007.

4 De Waal is almost certainly referring to Peter Singer here. See Singer's interview with Sahar Akhtar in the February 2006 issue of the *Believer*. Singer is one of the authors that responds to de Waal in *Primates and Philosophers*.
5 De Waal is a Dutch citizen.

Questions for Discussion

1 Describe the initial disagreement in the 1970s among biologists and anthropologists about chimpanzees and what they can tell us about human nature.
2 What about discovering bonobos and their 'culture' threatened to undermine the older view of human evolution?
3 Why is de Waal hesitant to say that chimpanzees are moral beings?
4 What are the "building blocks" of morality, according to de Waal? What role do emotions and feelings play in moral behavior?
5 Why might it seem like the truth of Darwinism is incompatible with genuine human morality?
6 What is "Beethoven's error" and why does it lead people to misunderstand the connection between morality and the theory of natural selection?
7 What is "veneer theory" and why doesn't it reflect "the real Darwinian position"?

Suggested Readings

De Waal, Frans. *Chimpanzee Politics*, rev. edn. Baltimore, MD: Johns Hopkins University Press, 1998 (first published 1982).
——. *Good Natured: The Origins of Right and Wrong in Humans and Other Animals.* Cambridge, MA: Harvard University Press, 1996.
——. *Our Inner Ape: A Leading Primatologist Explains Why We Are Who We Are.* New York: Riverhead, 2005.
——. Primates and Philosophers: How Morality Evolved. Princeton, NJ: Princeton University Press, 2006.
——. *The Age of Empathy: Nature's Lessons for a Kinder Society.* New York: Broadway Books, 2010.
De Waal, Frans and Frans Lanting. *Bonobo: The Forgotten Ape.* Berkeley, CA: University of California Press, 1997.
Kitcher, Phillip. "Ethics and Evolution: How to Get Here from There." In Stephen Macedo and Josiah Ober (eds.), *Primates and Philosophers: How Morality Evolved.* Princeton, NJ: Princeton University Press, 2006, pp. 120–39.
Plotnik, Joshua M., Frans de Waal, Donald Moore, and Diana Reiss. "Self-recognition in the Asian Elephant and Future Directions for Cognitive Research with Elephants in Zoological Settings." *Zoo Biology* 29(2) (2010): 179–91.
Wright, Robert. "The Uses of Anthropomorphism." In Stephen Macedo and Josiah Ober (eds.), *Primates and Philosophers: How Morality Evolved.* Princeton, NJ: Princeton University Press, 2006, pp. 83–97.

Assorted Media and Podcast Pairings

Frans de Waal TED Talk: "Moral Behavior in Animals." www.ted.com/talks/
frans_de_waal_do_animals_have_morals

Very Bad Wizards, Episode 33 "Monkeys, Smurfs, and Human Conformity (With
Laurie Santos)." http://verybadwizards.com/episodes/33

12 Jonathan Haidt

Comfortably Dumbfounded

These are indignant times. Reading newspapers, talking to friends or coworkers, we often seem to live in a state of perpetual moral outrage. The targets of our indignation depend on the particular group, religion, and political party we are associated with. If the Terri Schiavo case does not convince you of this, take the issue of same-sex marriage. Conservatives are furious over the prospect of gays and lesbians marrying, and liberals are furious that conservatives are furious. But has anyone on either side subjected their views to serious scrutiny? What's the response, for example, when conservatives are asked exactly why gays and lesbians shouldn't be allowed to marry? "It threatens the institution of marriage." OK. How? "Marriage is between a man and a woman." (Some liberals give this answer as well.) Right, but why? "It's unnatural." Isn't that true of marriage in general? "Well ... look ... I mean ... it's just wrong!"¹

If you're familiar with the work of Jonathan Haidt, it will come as no surprise that resentment, disgust, and outrage are rarely supported by fully developed arguments and deliberation. A psychologist and Professor of Ethical Leadership at New York University's Stern School of Business, Haidt has devoted his career to the study of moral judgment and decision-making. His results are revealing and perhaps a bit unflattering. We tend to think of ourselves as having arrived at our moral judgments after painstaking rational deliberation, or at least some kind of deliberation, anyhow. According to Haidt's model—which he calls "the social intuitionist model"—the process is just the reverse. We judge and then we reason. What, then, is the point of reasoning, if the judgment has already been made? To convince other people (and also ourselves) that we're right.

To support his model, Haidt has devised a number of ingenious experiments. He presents scenarios designed to evoke strong moral responses ("It's wrong!"), but ones that are hard to justify rationally. (Examples include: having sex with a chicken carcass you're about to eat, wiping your toilet with a national flag, and, as we'll see, brother–sister incest.) Although the goals of these experiments vary, the results all point to the causal importance of emotions and intuitions in our moral life, and to different roles for reason from the ones we might expect or hope for. Haidt's model goes against some dominant trends in moral and social psychology, in particular the theories of well-known psychologists Jean Piaget and Lawrence Kohlberg, whose work appeared to support rationalist models of moral judgment (where reason plays the primary causal role in moral decision-making). But as Haidt himself notes, his own work can be placed within a grand tradition of psychology and philosophy—a return to an emphasis on the emotions which began in full force with the theories of the Scottish philosopher David Hume.

One last thing to say about Jon Haidt: he gives the best conference talk in the business. There are slides, great visuals, videos of fraternity guys trying to explain why sleeping with one's sister is wrong, images of a toddler perturbed about not getting the same number of stickers as the child beside her (or, in one hilarious case, a 3-year-old who isn't perturbed at all), and plenty of sharp insights and jokes. The research Haidt presents has implications for philosophy, anthropology, psychology, and even the culture wars in America; not surprisingly, it provokes controversy and lively debate. I interviewed Haidt after a conference at Dartmouth College.[2]

May 2005

1   Reason Is the Press Secretary of the Emotions

TAMLER SOMMERS: I want to start out talking about the phenomenon you call "moral dumbfounding." You do an experiment where you present five scenarios to a subject and get their reaction. One of these scenarios describes a brother and sister—Julie and Mark—vacationing in the south of France. They have some wine, one thing leads to another, and they decide they want to have sex. They use two different kinds of contraception and enjoy it, but they decide not to do it again. How do people react to this, and what conclusions do you draw from their reactions?

JONATHAN HAIDT: People almost always start out by saying it's wrong. Then they start to give reasons. The most common reasons involve genetic abnormalities or that it will somehow damage their relationship. But we say in the story that they use two forms of birth control, and we say in the story that they keep that night as a special secret and that it makes them even closer. So people seem to want to disregard certain facts about the story. When the experimenter points out these facts and says, "Oh, well, sure, if they were going to have kids, that would cause problems, but they're using birth control. So would you say that it's OK?" And people never say, "Ooh, right, I forgot about the birth control. So then it *is* OK." Instead, they say, "Oh, yeah. Huh. Well, OK, let me think."

So what's really clear, and you can see it in the videotapes of the experiment, is: people give a reason. When that reason is stripped from them, they give another reason. When the new reason is stripped from them, they reach for *another* reason. And it's only when they reach deep into their pockets for another reason, and come up empty-handed, that they enter the state we call "moral dumbfounding." Because they fully expect to find reasons. They're *surprised* when they don't find reasons. And so in some of the video tapes you can see, they start laughing. But it's not an "it's so funny" laugh. It's more of a nervous-embarrassment, puzzled laugh. So it's a cognitive state where you "know" that something is morally wrong, but you can't find reasons to justify your belief. Instead of changing your mind about what's wrong, you just say: "I don't know, I can't explain it. I just know it's wrong." So the fact that this state *exists* indicates that people hold beliefs separate from, or with no need of support from, the justifications that they give. Or another way of saying it is that the *knowing* that something is wrong and the *explaining* why are completely separate processes.

TS: Are the subjects satisfied when they reach this state of moral dumbfounding? Or do they find something deeply problematic about it?

JH: For some people it's problematic. They're clearly puzzled, they're clearly reaching, and they seem a little bit flustered. But other people are in a state that Scott Murphy, the honors student who conducted the experiment, calls "comfortably dumbfounded." They say with full poise: "I don't know; I can't explain it; it's just wrong." Period. So we do know that there are big differences in people on a variable called "need for cognition." Some people need to think about things, need to understand things, need to reason about things. Many of these people go to graduate school in philosophy. But most people, if they don't have a reason for their moral judgments, they're not particularly bothered.

TS: So your conclusion is that while we might *think* that reason or reasons are playing a big causal role in how we arrive at moral judgments, it's actually our intuitions—fueled by our emotions—that are doing most of the work. You say in your paper that reason is the press secretary of the emotions, the ex post facto spin doctor.

JH: Yes, that's right.

TS: What do you mean by that, exactly?

JH: Reason is still a part of the process. It just doesn't play the role that we think it does. We use reason, for example, to persuade someone to share our beliefs. There are different questions: there's the psychological question of how you came by your beliefs. And then there's the practical question of how you're going to convince others to agree with you. Functionally, these two may have nothing to do with one another. If I believe that abortion is wrong, and I want to convince you that it's wrong, there's no reason I should recount to you my personal narrative of how I came to believe this. Rather, I should think up the best arguments I can come up with and give them to you. So I think the process is very much the same as what a press secretary does at a press conference. The press secretary might say that we need tax cuts because of the recession. Then, if a reporter points out to him that six months ago he said we needed tax cuts because of the surplus, can you imagine the press secretary saying: "Ohhhh, yeah, you're *right*. Gosh, I guess that *is* contradictory." And then can you imagine that contradiction changing the policy?

TS: I'm having a hard time doing that.

JH: Right. The president dispatches the press secretary, and the secretary's job is basically to lie—to just make up a story. Should I take that back? No, I won't take that back. The press secretary's job is to be a *lawyer*. To argue for a position. And he doesn't need to consult with the president about what the real reasons were for instituting the policy. Those are irrelevant. He just needs to build the best case he can.

TS: You brought this up in your talk at Dartmouth, and I like the analogy. You said that when it comes to moral judgments, we think we're scientists discovering the truth. But actually we're lawyers arguing for positions we arrived at by other means. So, setting aside a few philosophy graduate students, do you think this is how our moral life works?

JH: For most people, most of the time, yes. There's a question of what you could call the ecological distribution of moral judgments. Now, by moral judgment I mean any time you have a sense that someone has done something good or bad. Think of how often you have that sense. If you live in a city and you drive, you probably have that sense many times a day. When I read the newspaper, I think unprintable thoughts, thoughts of anger. So I think moral judgment is ubiquitous. Not as ubiquitous as aesthetic judgments. As we walk around the world we see many beautiful and ugly things. But we don't deliberate about them. We just see things as beautiful or ugly. My claim is that moral judgment is very much like aesthetic judgment. In fact, whenever I'm talking with philosophers who are trying to get me to clarify what I'm saying, if I ever feel confused, I just return to aesthetic judgment, and that saves me. I think whatever is true of aesthetic judgment is true of moral judgment, except that in our moral lives we do need to justify, whereas we don't generally ask others for justifications of aesthetic judgments.

TS: So now where do these moral intuitions come from? I guess I'm looking to see if you think they're a product of evolution.

JH: Yes, I do. We're born into this world with a lot of guidance as to how to make our way. Our tongues come with various receptors that make us respond well to fruit and meat. Our bodies are designed to give us pleasure when we encounter fruit and meat. And to get displeasure from bitter sensations. So our bodies are designed to mesh with properties of the real world, the real *physical* world—to track nutrients and poisons.

Similarly, our minds come equipped to feel pleasure and displeasure at patterns in the social world. When we see someone cheat someone else, we feel displeasure, dislike. And this dislike is a signal to us to avoid that person, to avoid trusting that person or cooperating with him. When we see a heroic act, or an act of self-sacrifice, or charity, we feel an emotion that I call moral elevation. We feel a warm, very pleasurable feeling that includes elements of love. We're much more likely to help such people, to trust them, and to want relationships with them. So just as our tongues guide us to good foods and away from bad foods, our minds guide us to good people, away from bad people.

TS: And having these feelings was adaptive—they contributed to greater individual fitness—in the time we did most of our evolving?

JH: Yes. There are a couple of watersheds in human evolution. Most people are comfortable thinking about tool use and language use as watersheds. But the ability to play non-zero-sum games was another watershed. What set us apart from most or all of the other hominid species was our ultrasociality, our ability to be highly cooperative, even with strangers—people who aren't at all related to us. Something about our minds enabled us to play this game. Individuals who could play it well succeeded and left more offspring. Individuals who couldn't form cooperative alliances, on average, died sooner and left fewer children. And so we're the descendants of the successful cooperators.

2   Drew Barrymore: Hot or Not?

TS: I want to talk about the philosophical implications of your model for a moment. When I came across your work, I thought it provided a good deal of support for a position we can describe as moral skepticism. In particular, I thought the social intuitionist model makes plausible the claim that there is no such thing as objective moral truth, even though human beings *believe* that some of their moral judgments are objectively true.[3] But you don't draw skeptical conclusions from your findings, do you?

JH: For me it all hinges on the distinction made by David Wiggins between anthropocentric truths and non-anthropocentric truths. If anybody thinks that moral truths are going to be facts about the universe, that any rational creature on any planet would be bound by, then no such facts exist. I think that moral truths are like truths about beauty, truths about comedy. Some comedians really are funnier than others. Some people really are more beautiful than others. But these are true only because of the kinds of creatures we happen to be; the perceptual apparatus—apparati—that we happen to have. So moral facts emerge out of who we are in interaction with the people in our culture.

TS: So you would call those *truths*? Take someone like Drew Barrymore— some people find her fairly hot while other people don't see what the big deal is. You would say that there is some *truth* concerning what her aesthetic appeal really is?

JH: Well, apparently, if there's that much disagreement about her, she must be somewhere in the middle. There's much less disagreement about Catherine Zeta-Jones and George Clooney. So they are more attractive than Drew Barrymore.

TS: So in other words, the way you determine the truth is by how much agreement there is?

JH: It's not that simple. But these are truths in which how people respond is the most important piece of evidence. You could never say that person X is really hot even though nobody thinks so. I think about it this way. One of my favorite quotes is from Max Weber: "Man is an animal suspended in webs of significance that he himself has spun." So I think that with morality, we build a castle in the air and then we live in it, but it is a real castle. It has no objective foundation, a foundation outside of our fantasy—but that's true about money, that's true about music, that's true about most of the things that we care about.

TS: So give me an example of some ethical truths in the limited sense that you're talking about.

JH: Let's see ... you should value and repay those who are good to you. You should protect and care for those who you are superior to, in a dominant position to. You should not hurt people unless there's a very good reason to do so—where good reason means a moral reason, not just a reason advantageous to yourself.

TS: So let's take one of those: you should take care of those people who are in an inferior position to you—

JH: —You have a position of authority over them ... so you should take care of them.

TS: What makes that true?

JH: What makes that true ... what makes that true ... now I feel like I'm the subject of one of my own dumbfounding experiments.

TS: Well, that's what I'm wondering. Why isn't this one of those cases?

JH: Nothing *makes* it true—it's a truth that grows out of who we are ... what makes that true ... See, I guess that's the wrong question. This is—I know that philosophers are very into justifications but ... nothing makes it true.

TS: OK, but then how—

JH: —Well, OK, let's see. Catherine Zeta-Jones is beautiful—what makes *that* true? Um, her ... shape, I suppose.

TS: But don't people think that there's a difference between moral truths and aesthetic truths? If someone doesn't find Catherine Zeta-Jones beautiful, for whatever reason, you don't necessarily think that he's *wrong*, do you?

JH: I might, actually.

TS: Most would think that maybe he just has different tastes. Maybe he likes blondes, he likes men, he hates the Welsh, or whatever. But now take a moral judgment, like "It's wrong to torture people." If someone says, "No, it's not wrong at all ... it's fun, actually, you should try it," you don't just think: To each his own. You think he's *wrong*, that he's made a mistake. And that's where you want justifications—you want to be able to convince people that they're wrong in a way that has nothing to do with their individual preferences on the matter.

JH: That's right. So we need justifications for our moral beliefs; we don't need them for our aesthetic beliefs. We can tolerate great diversity in our aesthetic beliefs, but we can't tolerate much diversity in our moral beliefs.

We tend to split and dislike each other. I recently wrote a paper on moral diversity, addressing the fact that many people, especially in academic settings, think that diversity is a virtue in itself. Diversity is not a virtue. Diversity is a good only to the extent that it advances other virtues, like justice or inclusiveness of others who have previously been excluded. But people are wrong when they say that everything should be more diverse— even, say, rock bands. It's an error, an overgeneralization. I'm sorry—back to your question. And this relates to the distinction between moral pluralism and moral relativism. I subscribe to the former, not the latter.

TS: What's the difference?

JH: What I want to say is that there are at least four foundations of our moral sense, but there are many coherent moral systems that can be built on these four foundations. But not just *anything* can be built on these four foundations. So I believe that an evolutionary approach specifying the foundation of our moral sense can allow us to appreciate Hindu and Muslim cultures in which women are veiled and seem to us to lead restricted lives. These are not necessarily oppressive and immoral cultures. Given that most of the world believes that gender-role differences are good and right and proper, these cultures are unlikely to be wrong—by which I mean, they are unlikely to be incoherent or ungrammatical moralities. We in America, especially liberals, use only two of these four bases. Liberals use intuitions about suffering (aversion to) and intuitions about reciprocity, fairness, and equality.

But there are two other foundations—there are intuitions about hierarchy, respect, duty ... that's one cluster. And intuitions about purity and pollution, which generate further intuitions about chastity and modesty. Most human cultures use all four of these bases to ground their moral worldviews. We in the West, in modern times especially, have to some extent discarded the last two. We have built our morality entirely on issues about harm (the first pillar), and rights and justice (the second). Our morality is coherent. We can critique people who do things that violate it within our group. We can't critique cultures that use all four moralities. But we *can* critique cultures whose practices are simple exploitation and brutality, such as apartheid South Africa or the American slave-owning South.

TS: OK, but *why* is it that we can critique apartheid South Africa whereas we can't critique a culture that uses genital mutilation where chastity and fidelity of females is considered a high virtue? What makes us able to do one and not the other?

JH: You have to look at any cultural practice in terms of what goods it is aiming for. Veiling, or keeping women in the home, is usually aimed at goods of chastity and modesty. Not all human practices are aimed at moral goods. Sweatshops, child pornography, child slavery, the slavery of Africans in the American South—none of these is aimed at goods provided by any of the four foundations. These are just people hurting and exploiting others for their personal monetary benefit.

TS: Do you ever worry that you're doing what the subjects in your experiments do? That is, that you're attempting to justify a strong intuition against exploiting people, and then trying to come up with a reason why *that's* wrong—whereas maybe your intuition doesn't flash as powerfully against the veiling of women? I would think in your work that that's something you might be extremely sensitive to. How would you answer the charge that you're merely trying to come up with a reason why exploitation of different races is wrong, and veiling of women is not, without providing a sufficient basis for this judgment?

JH: That's an excellent question. Consistent with my theory, I must say that I never looked at the other side and considered whether I might be wrong in that way. We tend to think that we're right, and we're not good at coming up with reasons why we might be wrong. So that's a great question to think about, whether I am motivated to apologize for or justify some practices and not others. That said, I certainly don't think I'm motivated in that way … my first experiences in Muslim or Hindu cultures were emotionally negative, in seeing the treatment of women and the hierarchy. It took me a while to get over that. And to see that these practices offended my American sensibilities, but that I was being ethnocentric in that respect.

The women that I spoke to in India—while there was a diversity of opinion, most of them did not see it as American feminists see it; they did not see veiling as something imposed upon them, to oppress them, to deny them freedom. In contrast, most black slaves in the American South were not happy about their position. And many slave owners knew that what they were doing was wrong, or at least they were ambivalent about it. Now, you might say: Well, maybe the women have been brainwashed? So there are two tests you can do. The first is to ask: do the people who appear from the outside to be victims endorse the moral goals of the practice? The second test is: how robust is this endorsement? Even when they learn about alternative ways in other cultures, do they still endorse it? So while you might have found black slaves in the South who were so brainwashed that they accepted their status, I believe that if they heard about other countries where blacks were not enslaved, they would not insist that blacks ought to be enslaved.

TS: OK, so then tracing it back to these four modules or bases on which moral systems are based. Because that's where you're going to provide your justification for whether we condemn other cultures or whether we can't …

JH: That's right, those are the four pillars in the air upon which we'll build our culture-specific moralities.

TS: These four pillars are a product of evolution. How do you respond to the age-old philosophical question that you can't derive an *ought* from an *is*? Darwinism gives us a *descriptive* story of why we might endorse things that come out of them. How do you get the claim "one *ought* to treat people below you kindly" out of this "don't harm people" module that's in place because of its contributions to biological fitness? That's the puzzle. Because when you do put your foot down and say that a culture ought not to act in a certain way, how are you getting that *ought* from a purely descriptive story about pillars of morality that evolved for non-moral reasons?

JH: You keep asking me to provide some kind of external justification, to go outside the system. But when I'm within the game—

TS: —Not external justification ... even internal, I'm just looking for any kind of justification.

JH: Well, from within the game, within our web of significance, it's wrong to hurt people.

3   Do Liberals Have an Impoverished Moral Worldview?

TS: Let's take a more concrete question: gay marriage. You brought this up in your talk at Dartmouth and the one I saw at Duke. You say that conservatives in America employ all four of the modules, whereas liberals only employ two. You said that liberals have an *impoverished* moral worldview, and that conservatives somehow have a richer moral life. Now, I don't know if that's just a way to shock the liberal intelligentsia ...

JH: No, I meant it, although I don't mind doing a bit of shocking.

TS: You said that we as liberals have pared down our moral foundations to two modules, fairness and do-no-harm—whereas perfectly intelligent conservatives have all four modules.

JH: Exactly.

TS: So if you take gay marriage, and let's say we're not in Massachusetts— we're in Mississippi, and you have people who have the *intuition* that gay marriage is really wrong, that it's *impure*. Because they have that purity module that liberals lack. Do you want to say that in that culture that gay marriage is really *wrong*?

JH: I think it depends on the kind of society you have. I'm glad that we have a diversity of societies in this world. And some societies become experts in lives of piety and sanctity and divinity. The four modules are not virtues themselves. Virtues come out of them. America is very much about individual happiness, the right to expression, self-determination. In America you do need to point to harm that befalls victims before you can limit someone else's rights. While there's not necessarily an objective truth about whether gay marriage is right or wrong, when you look at the values and virtues that we hold dear in America, and you look at who is helped and harmed by legalizing gay marriage, if you start with a utilitarian analysis, so many people benefit from gay marriage and no one is directly harmed by gay marriage. So that in itself argues in favor of gay marriage.

On the other hand, conservative morality looks not just at effects on individuals, but at the state of the social order. The fact that acts that violate certain parts of the Bible are tolerated is disturbing to conservatives, even though they can't point to any direct harm. So I do understand the source of their opposition to it. And this is a difficult case, where it can't work out well for everyone. Somebody has to give. If we were in a Muslim country, or a Catholic country where much of social and moral life was regulated in accordance with purity and hierarchy codes, then it would be very reasonable to ban gay marriage. But we are not in such a country. We are in a country where the consensus is that we grant rights to self-determination unless a limiting reason can be found. So in this case, I think conservatives have to give. It is *right* to legalize gay marriage.

TS: I want to make sure I understood that. If we were in the 1930s—I don't want to stereotype—but 1930s Alabama, there's a pretty safe one, maybe the modules of purity and tradition played more of a role than they do now. Let's say you're the father of a man who wants to marry another man. You would feel comfortable saying to your son that it's wrong to marry—it's *wrong* for you do that.

JH: I do think that facts about the prevalence of homosexuality and the degree of repugnance to it are relevant. In the present case, 5 percent of people are gay. That's a lot of people. And in the present case, repugnance against homosexuality is not nearly as strong as it used to be. I think we are now at the point where we *ought* to legalize gay marriage, and some people just won't be happy about it. But now look at Justice Scalia's argument in opposing *Lawrence* v. *Texas*. Scalia's argument is very interesting. I think it's ultimately wrong, but wrong for an empirical reason. I'm paraphrasing: he said, "If we have to legalize sodomy, the next step will be incest and sex with animals." But I don't think that would be the next step. Five percent of people cannot live full happy lives if homosexuality is outlawed. If 5 percent of people could not live full happy lives without having sex with their siblings, or with sheep, then we'd have a difficult moral problem on our hands. But we don't. Very few people fall into either category. So legalizing homosexuality is not the first step on a slippery slope to legalizing everything.

TS: OK, but getting back to my question, we're in 1930s Alabama. Five percent of the people are still gay, I imagine, but repugnance is *much* higher. Is it wrong then? Or maybe you think it's not a proper question.

JH: No, I think it's a very good question. The amount of shock and outrage would have been much greater then than it is now. Plus, back then they didn't know the facts about homosexuality; they didn't know that it's caused by hormonal conditions in utero, it's not a choice. Now that we know these facts we're in a much better position than they were then. I don't know if that answers your question.

TS: Well, maybe it does. Correct me if I'm wrong: maybe you want to say yes, in that case it probably would have been wrong. Maybe you want to say to your son: No, you ought not marry that man, or even carry on a relationship with him. *But*, given that we're not in that situation now, that's changed. Is that not a fair analysis of what the implications of your theory are?

JH: Yes, I think so. Given that there's not an objective (non-anthropocentric) fact of the matter, and what makes our moral life so interesting is that any particular act can be justified or opposed by reference to a different constellation of these four modules, of these foundational intuitions, it really is a matter of argument, public discussion, triggering people's intuitions, and somehow or other the chips fall in a certain way. Sometimes, with time, they fall in a different way. Ten years ago, or even three years ago, we never thought that we'd be this close to having gay marriage—we have it, actually.

4 "Everyone Is Morally Motivated"

TS: Let's continue with this culture-war discussion. You tend to sound quite pessimistic about the state of affairs in America. What are the prospects of discussion between conservatives and liberals, given that conservatives make use of two modules—purity and hierarchy—that we liberals care little about? Are we speaking different languages? How can we get past this?

JH: First, it would help if liberals understood conservatives better. If I have a mission in life, it is to convince people that *everyone* is morally motivated— everyone except for psychopaths. Everyone else is morally motivated. Liberals need to understand that conservatives are motivated by more than greed and hatred. And Americans and George Bush in particular need to understand that even terrorists are pursuing moral goods. One of the most psychologically stupid things anyone ever said is that the 9/11 terrorists did what they did because they hate our freedom. That's just idiotic. Nobody says: "They're free over there. I hate that. I want to kill them." They did this because they hate us, they're angry at us for *many* reasons, and terrorism and violence are "moral" actions, by which I don't mean morally *right*, I mean morally motivated.

TS: And at the same time you want liberals to understand that we didn't go into Iraq just for oil or Halliburton.

JH: Of course not. Bush is Manichaean. He really believes that we are in a battle of good versus evil. Now I think that *strategically* he led us into disaster. But I never believed for a moment that this was about oil.

TS: As an aside, I completely agree with you on this. Being in an academic environment, I'm very frustrated with how people view conservatives—as moral monsters whose only goal is to pursue evil. It's a little like the pro-choice, pro-life debate, where the pro-choice faction looks at the other side as though all it wants to do is oppress women.

JH: Exactly, exactly. That's the press secretary at work; that's what he does. The press secretary doesn't just explain your actions in the best light. He strips away any *possible* moral motivation for the opponent. It's the same thing. Liberals want to understand conservatives as motivated only by greed and racism. They think that conservatives just want to hurt minorities and get money. And that completely misses the point.

TS: So what would be the consequences of everyone understanding that the other side is morally motivated? I guess we could just get down to the nuts and bolts of the issues at hand.

JH: We would become much more tolerant, and some compromise might be possible, for example, on gay marriage. Even though personally I would like to see it legalized everywhere, I think it would be a nice compromise if each state could decide whether to legalize it, and nobody was forced one way or the other by the Supreme Court. And then gay people who lived in Alabama, if they wanted to get married, could go to Massachusetts.

TS: So there are some nice social implications of your theory—if we can understand and apply it properly. I'm curious how your theory has affected you personally. There's a large element of self-deception that's involved in moral judgment, according to your model.

JH: That's right.

TS: So I'm curious how that's affected *you* in your day-to-day life. Are you more distrustful of moral judgments that you make? Do you find yourself questioning your own motives or beliefs, or do you not take your work home with you?

JH: Well, for one thing, I am more tolerant of others. I was *much* more tolerant of Republicans and conservatives until the last two years. George Bush and his administration have got me so angry that I find my hard-won tolerance fast disappearing. I am now full of anger. And I find my press secretary drawing up the brief against Bush and his administration. So I can say that doing this work, coming up with this theory, has given me insight into what I'm doing. When I fulminate, my press secretary writes a brief against Bush. Once passions come into play, reason follows along. At least now I know that I'm doing it.

TS: Do you say to yourself: Wait a minute, reason is the press secretary of my emotions—I now have reason to distrust this anger?

JH: I don't do that.

TS: Do you think you should?

JH: No. Because I don't think there's an objective truth of the matter.[4] Also, outrage is fun. Outrage is pleasurable. I'm enjoying my outrage.

TS: OK, then let's bring this back full circle. What do you think of Julie and Mark and their consensual sex in the south of France? Is it wrong?

JH: It's fine with me. Doesn't bother me in the least. Remember: I'm a liberal. So if it doesn't involve harm to someone, it's not a big deal to me. Liberals love to find victims, and incest cases are usually ones in which someone is being harmed. But that's the trick of the question. They're both adults, and it's consensual. So liberals have an especially hard time trying to justify why it's wrong. But I wrote the story, so I know the trick.

Notes

1   Remember that I wrote this in 2005, 10 years before the Supreme Court's ruling that same-sex marriage was a right.
2   In the 10 years since this interview took place, Haidt's work has garnered quite a bit of attention in the popular press. His book *The Righteous Mind: Why Good People Are Divided by Politics and Religion* (New York Penguin, 2012) generated a lot of fruitful debate. He has given three TED talks, appeared on the *Colbert Report*, and lately it seems that a month can't go by without op-ed columnists from the *New York Times* and elsewhere referring to his research.
3   For those who are philosophically inclined, my thinking is as follows: We have moral intuitions. These intuitions were not selected for their ability to "track moral truth," nor were they even selected for their contributions to human happiness. They were selected because they enabled individuals and their relatives to leave more offspring. At the same time, though, these intuitions lead us to believe that the truth of our moral judgments is self-evident. (Think of the Declaration of Independence.) So to me it seems that Haidt's model lends some support to what philosophers call an error theory of morality—a theory that attributes widespread error to human beings about the status of moral claims.
4   Upon reflection a few months later, Haidt agreed that he should question his anger, and that his response here was a post hoc justification of his anger.

Questions for Discussion

1   What is the social intuitionist model of moral judgment? How does it differ from the rationalist model? Is Haidt offering a descriptive theory or a normative theory?
2   What does Haidt mean when he says that "reason is the press secretary of the emotions"?
3   How does the case of Julie and Mark support the case for Haidt's model?
4   What, according to Haidt, are the four (or five) pillars or foundations of morality?
5   How does Haidt explain persistent disagreements between liberals and conservatives?
6   How might Haidt's theory help conservatives and liberals understand each other better?
7   What is the difference between moral pluralism and moral relativism? How does it relate to Haidt's theory of moral foundations?
8   What does Haidt mean when he argues that everyone is morally motivated? How can this help liberals understand conservatives and vice versa?

Suggested Reading

Haidt has written a boatload of engaging and accessible articles in recent years. See his webpage at http://people.stern.nyu.edu/jhaidt for links to his interviews, articles, and media appearances on the topics we discuss in this interview.

Podcast Pairings

Very Bad Wizards, Episode 32 "Disagreeing about Disagreement." http://verybadwizards.com/episodes/32

Very Bad Wizards, Episode 39 "How Many Moralities Are There? (Part 1)." http://verybadwizards.com/episodes/39

Very Bad Wizards, Episode 40 "How Many Moralities Are There? (Part 2—with Jesse Graham)." (Note: Jesse Graham is a collaborator of Haidt's and co-authored a now classic paper on moral foundation theory.) http://verybadwizards.com/episodes/40

13 Paul Bloom

Reason Restored

Much of the 2,500-year history of moral psychology has focused on two questions. The first is descriptive: how do we arrive at our moral judgments? The second is normative: how should we arrive at our moral judgments. And for almost all of the years, the dominant answer to both questions was the same: reason. Plato's image of the chariot from the Phaedrus *summed it up best. Our emotions and our sense of honor are the horses, and reason is the charioteer. That's how it is and that's how it should be.*

In the new century, however, the tide began to turn. Jonathan Haidt (see Chapter 12) summarized the shift in his article "The Emotional Dog and His Rational Tail." Evidence in behavioral economics and social psychology suggested that our emotions were the primary factors driving our moral judgments. Reason was relegated to the role of "press secretary" (Haidt's phrase)—offering post hoc justifications for judgments we already reached through our emotional responses. And thanks in part to a renewed interest in virtue ethics,[1] as well as the work of feminist philosophers defending an 'ethics of care,' philosophers began to take emotions seriously again as proper guides for moral judgment. Reason, many argued, focuses too much on abstract idealizations; the emotions are more sensitive to context, to the particulars of real-life moral questions and problems.

Not so fast, says Paul Bloom, the Brooks and Suzanne Ragen Professor of Psychology at Yale University. Bloom's research has covered a wide range of topics, from our intuitive dualism (a belief that world contains both matter and immaterial souls) to the psychology of pleasure to baby morality, and much more. His new project sets its sights on this new paradigm. In two recent articles for the New Yorker *and* The Atlantic, *Bloom argues that the pendulum has swung too far against reason on both the descriptive and normative questions.[2] On the descriptive side, Bloom objects to the new view of human beings as "biochemical puppets," driven by wholly irrational forces over which we have no control. While conceding that these influences exist, Bloom argues that they do not undermine the idea of a responsible agent, capable of rational deliberation. On the normative side, Bloom has taken a hard line stance against the idea of emotions as a guide to good policy. And he does not pick easy targets. Many researchers warn against the effects of emotions like anger, envy, and revenge feelings, but Bloom has taken on the most beloved moral emotion of them all: empathy.*

Bloom is the author of four books, most recently Just Babies: The Origins of Good and Evil. *He is a wonderfully clear and lively writer, appealing both to scholarly and popular audiences, often in the same work. (He is also a favorite guest on the Very Bad Wizards podcast.)[3] And though Bloom may be empathy's arch nemesis, he is also one of the nicest and funniest people I have encountered in this profession. I interviewed him at his beautiful home in New Haven, CT. Observing a Jewish tradition that dates back nearly as far as the history of moral psychology, we argued, debated, and then had take-out Chinese.*

June 2014

1   A Pox on Empathy!

TAMLER SOMMERS: You recently wrote a piece for the *New Yorker* that was critical of one of our more cherished emotions: empathy. First, how do you define empathy and how do you distinguish it from sympathy?

PAUL BLOOM: The terminology here is murder. People use these words in very different ways. For me, empathy is feeling what you think other people feel, putting yourself in their shoes. So, if you bang your knee and I wince, that's empathy. So empathy is feeling someone else's pain or pleasure. Sympathy, or compassion (and I use the terms interchangeably) is caring about other people, caring about their fates.

TS: So the way you define it, empathy is when I feel your pain. But it's a further step for me to care that you're hurt and want to help you.

PB: Exactly. We can best understand the distinction by seeing them at work and seeing how one doesn't entail the other. You can have empathy without sympathy. Suppose you see me on the street and I'm in terrible pain and you feel bad too. Well, that's empathy. It's possible that could lead you to say "I care about that guy" and then move to help me. But it's also possible that you could turn away—my pain is causing your pain, so you turn away and walk away. It's even possible you could give me a kick and get mad at me for causing your pain. That would be empathy without sympathy.

TS: How about sympathy without empathy?

PB: Well, I could really care for somebody and not put myself in their shoes. So, here's an example. This example isn't mine but I forget whose it is. You watch people you love make a fool of themselves and you feel terrible. But they don't know they're making a fool of themselves. They're telling some incredibly offensive joke, and you're feeling mortified for them. This can't be empathy, because they're feeling fine—they're great. But you love them, and you know what they're doing to themselves. You feel compassion, you care about them.

TS: Right, although if someone is making a fool out of themselves, then maybe what I'm feeling is the emotion they *would* have "if they only knew". The big hypothetical: if they knew how they looked or how people were looking at them, they would be so embarrassed. Because otherwise, why would I feel embarrassed? You're right that this doesn't match up very well with empathy, but it also doesn't match up well with a kind of cognitive or rationally motivated judgment.

PB: I think you're right, and the conclusion from that is that sympathy can be a very emotional thing. I was just at this conference this month and I talked to this monk Matthieu Ricard. He was such a cool guy.

TS: I read his book, the one he did with his dad who's a famous atheist French philosopher. It was fantastic, inspiring.[4]

PB: I'm probably the least spiritual person in the world, and I didn't think we'd get along. But, I'm giving my riff against empathy and he agrees with me, which stunned me. He says, "I don't want to nurture empathy. Empathy makes you tired, empathy makes you miserable. I want love." And in fact, he says that to be a good person, and to feel love toward others, don't experience what they're experiencing. Keep your distance, at some level, but feel love and compassion for them. And I find that powerful, and I agree with that. And he's a monk so …

TS: Aside from the fact that he's a monk, why do you agree?

PB: An example I give is actually from an experiment by Dan Batson, psychology's most important altruism researcher. He has this experiment where there's a girl and she's waiting in line for a medical intervention. Batson gets people to take her perspective, triggering empathy, which triggers compassion, which makes them very likely to want to move her up the list. And in fact as we're speaking there's a news story about a little girl who is waiting to get a lung but she can't because of the rules. And people are petitioning. Batson points out correctly that it's a very compassionate response. But it's also not moral.

TS: What do you have to assume about morality to say that?

PB: That morality entails some sort of fairness and impartiality.

TS: You think that's inherent and necessary to morality?

PB: I think it's at the core of morality.

TS: One objection I had to your critique of empathy is that it seemed like you were holding empathy to an impossible standard. It was as if someone wrote an article called "The Case against Blueberries" or "The Case against Kale," and they say: "look, yes, blueberries are nutritious, really delicious, but they can't cure cancer." Not only that, you can eat too many blueberries (or too much kale) and get sick. So, blueberries and kale can't solve all of our health problems.

Well, yeah, but no one ever said they could. With empathy, it seems like we have something that's morally healthy for the most part, and an important foundation for morality. But instead of dwelling on that aspect of empathy you dwelled on its shortcomings. If I'm Empathy responding to you I'd say: "Well hey—I never pretended I was going to solve *all* moral problems and lead to *all* the correct moral judgments."

PB: I'm a fan of empathy for certain things. When it comes to intimate relations, I think it is indispensable. I would not want a child, a parent, or a wife without empathy. Or a friend without empathy who couldn't make an effort to feel what I feel—not just to understand it, but to feel what I feel. You know, if I'm really sad, and I want somebody close to me, I want some of that sadness to move on to them. I think that's part of a relationship. And if I'm happy, I want my happiness to move on to that person. And to find somebody who lacked that would be a strange relationship, even putting aside the cognitive inabilities that would go with not feeling that, there's also just a lack of personal contact.

So, I'm down with empathy for *that*. But I think empathy is horrible when it comes to public policy. The reason why this isn't quite analogous to kale and blueberries is that there are people, including our president, who champion empathy whenever it comes to public policy. There are people like Jeremy Rifkin who say that the solution to all our global problems is an empathetic community. Empathy will solve the world's problems. I think they're just flat-out mistaken, and I think this is a serious mistake because it's not just that empathy is merely only part of the story. Actually it often leads us astray. In that article, I give some examples where empathy causes waste, suffering.

TS: So is it fair to say that you're against the overblown rhetoric about empathy rather than empathy itself?

PB: More than that, I'm against using empathy as a way to make policy decisions. And I think that's done a lot.

TS: But when you're trying to come up with policies about poverty, don't you want to have some sort of empathetic understanding of what it's like to be poor, or to go to an inner-city school? Or think of our drone policies. When we decide about that, don't you want to consider how it feels to have drones circling in the sky, hovering over you round the clock?[5] That's something you would want, not merely a cold-blooded analysis of the extent that drones will accomplish certain goals—

PB: —There's something deep in what you're saying that I haven't emphasized enough, which is that to make any interesting policy decision you want the information about people's experiences. It's incredibly important. So, before launching drones, find out how people respond to drones, how people respond to this and that. And that requires being able to look inside people's heads in a sense, feel what they feel, and there I think understanding is relevant. Some people call this "cognitive empathy" and that's fine. This isn't the sense of empathy that I'm arguing against.

One way to express my beef with empathy is that for any interesting policy decision, there's going to be factors pulling you in both directions. And that's just the way any hard decision goes. And, empathy can be used to tip the balance either way.

TS: You mean that both sides can use it?

PB: Right. You want drones? Tell me a story about the victims of terrorism. You don't want drones? Tell me a story about somebody who had his family blown up by a drone—it could go either way. You want gun control? Focus on the victims of a gun accident, gun crime. You're against gun control? Tell me about a defenseless victim.

TS: So you're against not empathy, but selectively applied empathy or empathy as the *only* guide to policy, right?

PB: No, it's stronger than that. Empathy is by definition selectively applied. Not even randomly. We feel empathy for those who look like us. We feel empathy with those of the same color, same situation. And that has made a huge difference for where the money in charity goes. We're talking billions of dollars here. It makes a huge difference for how wars start. Wars are often triggered by the suffering of people, and our empathy toward people. It has a huge implication on the criminal justice system. There's a disproportionate number of minorities in the criminal justice system. It's not some sort of accident.

Here's a proposal I would make, and this at least expresses my feelings toward empathy. I would like the world to be such that people who use empathy in a political campaign or a social campaign are viewed with the same disgust as those who use racism or xenophobia.

TS: Wow.

PB: If you want a law to pass and you say "We need this law because there's this suffering little girl and her life has been destroyed by government regulation or by Obamacare—or by the Republicans"— well, you can always find these little girls. People should say that's bullshit, it means nothing.

TS: OK, but what if you say "Here's a suffering little girl who got hurt by Obamacare, but there are 15 suffering people that were helped by Obamacare." It seems like empathy is valuable as long as you're not trying to exploit it. Isn't what you're describing the abuse of empathy rather than empathy itself? As long as people are feeling empathetic for everyone who is going to be affected by the policy rather than just one person who is going to be affected by the policy.

PB: Yes. But empathy doesn't work that way, it's not in our nature. I got into a discussion with a philosopher who asked what if you had super empathy that allowed you to feel the feelings of everyone affected by a policy. So, a million people here, a million people there, and also future people. And then use that empathy to guide you in your decision. If that were true, then I'd be fine with it. But that's not how people work.

You know, your example is interesting. A little girl whose life is made worse by Obamacare versus 15 people whose lives were made better. I bet if that experiment was done you'd side with the little girl because empathy is ridiculously innumerate. The way empathy works is that one is more than two. There are plenty of studies that show this. So that's the problem.

Sure, sometimes empathy gets it right. Racism sometimes gets it right; flipping a coin sometimes get it right. But I would say, a pox on it!

2 My Name Is Inigo Montoya. You Killed My Father. Prepare to Hire a Good Lawyer

TS: OK, enough about empathy, let's talk about revenge. You say in your book that our willingness to engage in third-party punishment, even at cost to ourselves, is grounded in our instinct for personal revenge. This leads to the emergence of an impartial third-party justice system, which you say is a good thing. And, once that happens, then the revenge instinct is best transferred to this justice system.

PB: That's right.

TS: You give the example where your car window was smashed. And you had a feeling of outrage but it was better to let the police handle that than for you to go around searching for the guy that did it. You also write: "If Inigo Montoya were around right now, he wouldn't need to storm the castle to bring his father's murderer to justice, the police would do it for him and fewer people would have to die." But would that really be a good thing? For Inigo Montoya not to feel that instinct of personal revenge?

PB: You'd have fewer people dying.

TS: Right, but there's something we lose too when we let an impartial third-party justice system handle all of our business.

PB: Manliness?

TS: Not exactly, and I hate that word—it sounds like the opposite of what it's supposed to mean. But we do lose some virtuous qualities, right? Inigo Montoya was very courageous, loyal to his father and to his honor. None of that can express itself if he just lets an impartial justice system punish the six fingered man. The example I use in this context is *True Grit*. Mattie Ross is awesome. Part of what makes her awesome is that she personally sees to the avenging of her father's death. She'd be a lot less awesome if she had hired some mercenaries to go get her father's killer, while she kicked back in a rocking chair and waited for them to bring him back to Arkansas. By going after the killer herself, she shows how much she loved her father. And that's really the only way she shows it. She's not an emotional or sentimental girl, but she shows the depth of her love through her willingness to risk her life to get the murderer. She displays courage, loyalty, all those things that you can't display if you just call the police.

PB: I think you're right. At the end of Pinker's book *The Better Angels of Our Nature* he talks about the decline of violence. One of the forces of the decline in violence was what he describes as feminization. Which is a decline in the manly virtues that you're talking about. And Pinker argues that, basically, we've shifted from a culture of honor to a "culture of dignity." And that was one factor leading to the decline of violence. And then he addresses the view advanced by his colleague Harvey Mansfield, which is that much is lost when we lose the manly virtues. And this is the point you're making and I think you're right.

But I agree with Pinker's response, which is that more is gained. So, I agree here. In a world where somebody murders your father, you track them down, bring justice yourself, you get to exhibit the virtues of courage, and loyalty and love that maybe you couldn't otherwise by calling the cops. And I think that's what fools us sometimes. Because even when the cops are available if a neighbor molests our kid, we might go over there and blow his brains out.

TS: You think that's wrong? To go and confront the guy that molested your kid?

PB: I think that, as a matter of broad public policy it's wrong.

TS: OK, but what about as a matter of personal morality?

PB: Some philosopher, I forget who, said the best response to a personal insult is to give the person a sound punch in the nose.

TS: I think that was Derk Pereboom.[6]

PB: Maybe. So let's take that as an example. It feels a lot better, punching someone in the nose, rather than saying "Well we must agree to disagree" and walk away. Or to sue the person in civil court. But, from a standpoint of how I want the world to work, I would rather give up certain things and increase the chances of me and those I love living long, happy, unmurdered lives.

TS: Up to what point? I mean, you have two sons, right? Say one of your kids is getting bullied. Not in a way that's life threatening or anything, just getting bullied. Would you want him to be a snitch or a tattletale and just run to the principal? Or would you want him to stand up for himself and try to fight the kid? Again, you're in a nice Connecticut neighborhood. Nobody's going to come to your house and do a drive-by if your son beats the crap out of the bully. The worst that happens is your son gets his butt kicked. But at least he stood up for himself. What would you rather have your kids do in those situations?

PB: I think the answer depends on what society we are in. It's more of a local question. In this school I give this answer, in that school I give that answer. So, if it's a school where the kids in essence are in a culture of honor—and I think many schools are—then I would advise my son to fight back because otherwise he would lose respect, standing, face. But if it's a school like my kids go to where there's a strong culture of dignity, a strong anti-bullying and anti-violence culture, I would actually want him to go to the authorities and get it resolved. Because it wouldn't ruin my kid's standing in that society. Now it's true, my kid then would not get to exercise his manly virtues—but, really, what's he gonna do anyway?

TS: What's the downside of encouraging him to ignore the norm that encourages going to the authorities, and have his own code: "You messed with me, I'm going to stand up for myself. I'm not going to snitch unless I have to."

I mean what's the downside of that aside from maybe him getting suspended for a few days?

PB: So, there are certainly downsides—losing a fight could involve injury, and there's some degree of risk, and being humiliated. Being suspended is not pleasant, so there are downsides. Now what are the upsides? Well, in some societies, the upsides are if you don't do it you can't hold your head up among these people and that's a huge thing. I agree with that.

TS: But even in this culture, there's a virtue upside maybe. A personal code that says: 'I don't care what the surrounding norms are: I stand up for myself.' Not for stupid things like someone cutting you off on the highway. And not when you risk getting killed or seriously injured. But in general, yes, I handle my own business.

PB: Which world would you rather live in? One where people settle disputes with their fists or one where people are looking to the culture, talking it out, seeking mediators, and so on?

TS: I don't want to live in either one of those worlds entirely. I want a world where there are limits. You're not going to risk your life to stand up to the bully, but you will risk getting your butt kicked. By the way, this reminds me of your tattling discussion in the book. You say that there are two reasons kids like to tattle. First, they show the adult how moral they are. And second, they satisfy their own sense of justice. But there's also a huge stigma for kids about being a tattle-tale, right? It's a pejorative word—it's shameful to be a tattle-tale.

PB: You know, you're right and actually it's an interesting question: why is that? One answer might be that we live in a culture of honor where you're encouraged to fight your own battles. But I think the stigma of tattle-taling goes beyond that. Because we have third-party punishment and it's still stigmatized. I think people see tattling as unfair.

TS: Unfair in what sense?

PB: I see you talk disrespectfully toward undergraduates, and so I go to your department chair. You're thinking that I wronged you, right?

TS: I'd want you to talk to me first.

PB: Exactly. That's the first thing you'd say to me, you should have talked to me first.

I think you raise a good point—I will concede that sometimes, personal revenge, personal payback, standing up for yourself in those physical ways, is actually a good thing for a person to do. It is good for your character, it exercises a mental trait that is well worth exercising. And, it's even good when other people witness it, and for the people who the bully tries to intimidate. I will concede all of that and I think some of these intuitions are at play when we agree that tattling is wrong, even in an academic setting.

But I still think on the whole that this culture of honor is something we have to lose, or we're better off losing at least in the physical way. I think it's similar to when people talk about rituals involving male/female differences, and chastity, and respect and all kinds of manners and so on. Some of these things, when viewed in isolation, are beautiful in and of themselves. And they're defensible in that sense, but the cost might be just too high. You can't have a society which has a strong ethos of nonviolence, which I really want, but at the same time allow kids to punch each other in the nose in school fights.

TS: I guess. But even in a non-honor culture, you don't want to encourage a society of tattle-tales either.

PB: You want to return to the time of duels?

TS: [*laughing*] No.

PB: Anthony Appiah in his book *The Honor Code* argues that duels stopped because they started to look ridiculous and people make fun of people doing them.[7]

TS: Right—now when we think of dueling, we think of French guys slapping each other with white gloves.

3   Morality, Math, and Porn

TS: You make two analogies which are really interesting. The first is the analogy of morality and mathematics, and specifically the zero concept. And then of course there's the one between morality and pornography. Can you explain both of those analogies?

PB: Do I make an analogy of morality and pornography? I don't remember that!

TS: Well, the analogy is in response to the idea that morality couldn't have evolved by natural selection.

PB: OK, right. The morality and pornography example is a response to an extremely bad, but extremely popular, argument which goes like this. We are often nice in ways that don't benefit our genes in any imaginable sense. Ergo, morality could not be the product of evolution. And so morality must be a gift from God. This argument ignores the fact that there is a difference between the forces that cause something to evolve and the things that trigger it in its current day. An obvious analogy is pornography. So, pornography causes men to devote time, energy, sperm, and so on yet it has no reproductive benefits. Are we then forced to conclude that pornography is a divine miracle?

TS: Well, people say that this is a golden age for pornography.

PB: [*laughs*] Yes, I've heard that too. Anyhow, the example of zero is, as you point out, more interesting. It's in a discussion of our moral responses to friends and family and strangers. The point of the analogy is that we have these natural moral responses to friends and family, which can be readily explained in evolutionary terms. But we are also nice to strangers. We give money to them, we volunteer to help them, we value their lives. Some of us even care about non-human animals, so much so we refuse to eat meat.

How do we explain this? I think morality toward strangers is like zero. The evolutionary story of how we come to make sense of zero is that there isn't one. We're not wired for it at all. Zero is a discovery smart people have made. It's understood by children with great difficulty. And I think issues involving impartiality, fairness, kindness to strangers are the moral equivalent to zero.

TS: You say that the wrongness of slavery is a discovery in the same way that I guess zero is a discovery, or Newton's laws is a discovery.

PB: To a philosopher like you I guess that sounds like a form of moral realism.

TS: Well, maybe. I would need to know the sense in which it's a discovery. The case of zero seems like a discovery of reason. But with slavery, maybe it's the Humean in me, but that seems like it could be more of an emotional discovery, maybe one involving your arch-nemesis: empathy.

PB: No, I think it is a discovery of reason. I think we've come to these conclusions that say slavery is wrong because we have some sort of antecedent notions of what's moral we can build upon. And another way this is a little like math, to some extent, is that it can bring us to interesting conclusions. And that's what moral philosophers and ethicists tend to do. "If you believe this and this, well it follows that you should also believe that." People say, "You can't argue about morality." But of course we do that all the time. We point out inconsistencies—"You can't say both that X is wrong if but then not complain when your favorite politician does it." We work these things out. That's what moral argument is.

TS: True, but there are often fundamental disagreements, right? You think it's OK to favor your son's welfare over a strange child in a foreign land. Peter Singer would say that's irrational.[8] Your son doesn't feel pain or happiness any more or less than a child in Africa. Then you say "I favor him because he's my son." And he presses you: "Why does that matter?" "Because he's my son. It's a basic intuition." And on it goes. You don't have that with mathematics, or at least you don't have it to anywhere near the same degree. There aren't mathematical disagreements at this fundamental level.

PB: I'm sympathetic to what you're saying. Yes, there are some moral principles that can't be justified. But there are all sorts of moral things you can make sense of. Why would you hold the door open for somebody? Well, duh, because that's nice and helps them get through. Wouldn't you want someone to do that for you? These are the sort of arguments one would be encouraged by. We never talk about them because they're sort of obvious but they're important and they're significant.

Then there are the really hard cases, and I think your first example is the hardest case of all. And it's one that I've personally struggled with. On the one extreme, I'd give everything to my family and nothing to anyone else. That seems wrong. The other extreme is that I'd give perfectly equal, and that seems wrong too. I feel we should live in the middle. I have no idea how to figure out what to do. I have gut feelings but I don't know how reliable they are. Here's an example. If I'm rushing to bring my son a new video game as a present and I rush by and somebody is drowning, I would stop and pull the child out of the lake even at the expense of letting my son wait. That seems obvious, right?

TS: Yes.

PB: Right. But if I was rushing to give my son a new heart, then I might run by the drowning person. And if I hear that you ran past a drowning person I'd say you did the right thing, I can't blame you.

TS: Right and imagine if I dove in with the heart to rescue the stranger, because I was playing the odds. I figured I can definitely save this drowning person, but I'm not sure if the heart will save my daughter—you'd think I did something wrong, right?

PB: Yes. And then it's complicated. What if it wasn't the heart but it was the eyes? These are really hard questions. I think those are the hardest questions. But so much of morality isn't like that. Take a case like animal welfare. People can argue about the treatment of animals, and the case is pretty strong that certain things we do cause the animals great pain in order to give us unnecessary pleasure and that this is a really bad thing. And it's true somebody could say, "I don't give a shit about animals and I don't think they matter morally at all." And someone could reply: "They matter because they suffer—what makes humans so special?" And the argument can go on.

4 What Is the Engine for Moral Change?

TS: OK, but many cases of converging moral agreement aren't the result of rational arguments. Let me take your own example. You say in your book and it's a great line: "It might well be that the greatest force underlying moral change in the last 30 years in the United States was the situation comedy." You credit *The Cosby Show* for undermining racism, and *Will & Grace* for bringing people around to same-sex marriage. I totally agree with you but that seems to be undercutting your point. The same arguments for treating gay people equally were available pre-*Will & Grace*. There haven't been any new decisive arguments that convinced everyone.[9] It was just people saying "Oh, OK, I don't feel that this is disgusting or weird or creepy or unnatural anymore. They're just normal people." That's not a discovery of reason, that's familiarity and empathy.

PB: So here my view is interestingly nuanced! I think reason is a force that drives moral change.

But other factors surely play a role as well, both good and bad, and sometimes people who have arrived at a conclusion often use these other factors to persuade people to join their side.

Exposure to others often has a good effect, and this is a good thing about television. On the other extreme, I think we entirely overrate, in our societies, the importance and value of honor because it is so exhilarating to see it on TV. So, punching somebody in the nose for insulting you is a common TV way to resolve a dispute. And it's always done by a hero and it's always right. Well, you do it in New Haven and you'll get a criminal record, you'll be expelled from school, and people won't like you.

So, sure there's often a trickle-down morality. Some people come to moral insights and they get passed on to the rest of us. I think slavery is wrong. Do I think slavery is wrong because I worked it out myself? No. I consider it wrong because people say slavery is really wrong, and I picked it up from society.

TS: When you see *Roots* as a kid …

PB: That's right. And I think gay marriage is right probably because everyone around me thinks gay marriage is right, so a lot of this is trickle-down. But this is true for science as well. This is why I think diseases are caused by germs, because people told me. I believe the earth is billions of years old because that's what scientists say.

TS: Right but that doesn't seem analogous to the gay marriage case. Why is the younger generation so much more accepting of gay lifestyles and marriage? It has nothing to do with people telling them homosexuality is OK. It has everything to do with them being exposed to and being around gay people and not having a problem with them. It's just not an issue for my students at all—and I live in Texas!

PB: Let me push the analogy with science. There are two questions that have to be distinguished. The first is, why do so many people now believe in evolution? Not as many as it should be but a lot more than there was 50 years ago. That's question one. Question two is, how do people discover that evolution is true and that species are evolving? It's clear that these are two distinct questions. The former question might be because certain authorities say it's true (and actually most people who believe in evolution have no idea what natural selection is). The second question of how we came to it involves reason, experiment, and argument and so on.

I think it's the same for morality. And so I think that if the question is: why do most people think gay marriage is OK, then the answer is because of the a-rational things we're talking about. But how do we come to appreciate, as a society, that homosexuals have the same rights as heterosexuals? Here, there's a lot of moral argumentation.

TS: You think that argumentation is a real or primary cause of the recognition of gay rights?

PB: Yes I do. I certainly think we're capable of argumentation. You see it all the time, people do it tons. This is where social psychologists get it wrong, because people argue about morality all the time, and we really exercise this capacity of reason. And moral change has a directional property to it. So you look at graphs of acceptances of gay marriage, or interracial marriage, and they just go up and up and up. And I think reason is the only process we know of that has that sort of directional property.

TS: What about familiarity? Couldn't you make the same exact case for familiarity? Whenever there's some sort of stigmatized group, increased familiarity will lead directionally toward a decrease in stigmatization.

PB: Yeah, I don't want to be too quick to argue against that because the consensus probably is due in part to familiarity. You pointed out earlier that arguments in favor of same-sex marriage have been around for a very long time. This existence of these arguments is kind of my point. There are arguments in favor of it, there are reasonable people who deliberate and say that it might seem wrong maybe but it's OK. And there are arguments back and forth. For slavery, there were people arguing that slavery is a good moral system and other people argue that it's bad. And then over time the people who thought it's bad won the day. Then their views spread to the culture at large, and this spread was probably aided by familiarity and other things.

TS: I wonder if there's an empirical question that the debate we're having turns on. Is it "what actually causes people to subscribe to a certain moral views?" Take animal welfare. Would our debate turn on the question of what really caused people to start caring about animal welfare? Was it because of the rational arguments from people like Bentham or Singer? Or was it the pictures in Singer's book *Animal Liberation* that made us say "holy shit, this is what they do in laboratories? That's awful! This is what they do on factory farms? That's disgusting! We have to put a stop to it, I'm outraged!" If the latter is true, I'm right, and if the former is true, you're right?

PB: No, because I think they're both true. There will be a world 50 years from now where factory farming is considered morally repugnant. And we'll look back and say how could people not have known this? I don't think the individuals in the future will have each made a reasoning move that we are now incapable of. They're not smarter or whatever. Similarly there will be a world 50 years from now where everybody will agree about natural selection. So there are social changes that are not driven by reason. But, I think for the moral understanding to occur in the first place there has to be a catalyst or some kind of insight. There was a time when nobody would have thought slavery was wrong, and without the spark of some kind of moral insight or moral argument, we would go on having slavery until the end of time.

TS: So the argument sort of gets the ball rolling. And these other emotions can then be triggered—

PB: —Triggered and exploited. I don't want to be simple-minded about it, because there are cases where you could have moral arguments with bad conclusions. But science can end up giving bad arguments too. There are all these social forces and obstacles. But on the whole both moral reasoning and scientific reasoning leads to progress.

TS: But as you point out, reasoned arguments go both ways. You can reason your way toward conclusions, and the only way you know they're bad conclusions is because of how they feel. Would you agree that our core emotions provide an indispensable check on our reasoning processes? Jonathan Bennett describes a famous case of this with Hermann Goering who intentionally stifled his empathy because he thought it was his moral duty to exterminate the Jews. So Bennett's idea is that you have your morality, your set of moral principles, but your emotions are the ultimate check on these principles.[10]

PB: I strongly disagree with that. There are certain cases we can point to such as Goering, the Nazi doctors, where you have people saying "Wow this feels really repugnant, but I think my argument is sound" and they're just monsters. I agree with that. But from an evolutionary perspective these emotions have evolved from local circumstances. They are reliable to different degrees. I think disgust is not reliable at all and empathy is in between, anger in between. But emotions are always limited, while reason is a ladder you can bring anywhere.

There were people in the 1980s saying "Well, you know, this gay rights issue is all well and good. But if you take their argument to the ultimate conclusion, then you'll have gay people marrying each other. And we know that's wrong, so hold on reason! Let's not be ridiculous." I think that the product of moral progress is that the gut feeling sort of fades, and we get an edifice up that pushes it away.

Now, where's this going to take us? Someone nasty could say to me, what do you think of bestiality? Consensual bestiality doesn't harm animals, but I think that's very gross. Do I think it's wrong? Reason, my utilitarian principles, could speak up to the point where I say certain forms of bestiality aren't wrong. And here I have my gut feeling say "Woah! I better get some better arguments." In the end, though, reason should always win. We should distrust certain gut feelings, and I think our rejection of gay marriage, and before that, interracial marriage, provides perfect examples of gut feelings gone wrong.

TS: But it all has to start with gut feelings at some point, right? Your gut feeling is what tells you that it's bad when people feel pain and good when people feel pleasure.

PB: Yes, that's right.

TS: So it seems like you want to be selective about which gut feelings you accept and which you don't. You might say that reason tells us which of them to accept.

PB: I think for any good moral psychology, there are two types of gut feelings. There are the gut feelings that are the grounds, the foundations of morality. And the truth is there's not much we can do about that. If you don't agree with me that causing unnecessary suffering is wrong we just can't have a moral discussion. A foundational intuition like that has to be taken as a given.

But there are other sorts of gut feelings, like gay marriage is wrong or interracial marriage is wrong. Because they are not primary, you can override them and work around them. This sounds messy, but as you know this is what moral philosophers do all the time. In the end, any decent moral philosophy will have to say "Well, this feels right but actually it's wrong." This process will push us in new directions, but it can't push us too far. If it ended up saying "killing and eating everyone you see is the ultimate moral good" you say "that's not moral, that's nuts."

TS: I agree with you on that. But it does seem somewhat arbitrary what we assign as the *primary* moral feelings and what we assign as expendable. As Jon Haidt loves to point out, for liberals the primary ones are usually the ones that are involved with harm or fairness and equality. Liberals assign the feelings about those categories as primary and consider the other ones to be byproducts, silly, or at best derivative of the harm/fairness feelings. I just don't know how principled that is. Because people who aren't Western liberals regard feelings about family loyalty, group loyalty, respect within a hierarchy, and so forth to be just as deep as our feelings about avoiding pain or treating people equally.

PB: I think that's right as a description of moral rhetoric. My strongly held moral views are foundational and undeniable, yours are sort of things you need to get past. Because mine are self-evident, and yours are just dubious! And I think you're right about the cultural bias. As a liberal, I say we want to be fair to gay couples, who could deny that? And then a conservative might respond, well it violates certain traditions, and I say that's ridiculous. That's just an arbitrary feeling that you can shed. I guess in the end it might turn out to be an empirical question as to which intuitions fall into the different categories.

TS: So how can we make the distinction between what you call "foundational intuitions" and expendable intuitions?

PB: I guess I'd say that making the distinction between the two sorts of intuitions can often be done with common sense. In the end it's an empirical question, but it's an empirical question where sometimes it's obvious what the answer is. So if you tell me you just feel in your heart that school vouchers are immoral, I'm going to say "Look I understand you have that intuition, but that *can't* be a primary intuition. Rather, it has to be derived from other things." Maybe you trust people who say so, or maybe it connects with other feelings—but certainly you wouldn't say "Well the argument has to end there."

But for standard reasons that philosophers point out, there has to be some intuitions that don't derive from other intuitions. And I actually think it's an interesting question whether or not you can talk people out of those. Maybe you can, particularly if they're conflicting. Then the analogy would be to visual illusions. So, you see one line as longer but you're persuaded that your perception is mistaken.

TS: There's a disanalogy there, though, which is that with visual illusions you can show me that I'm wrong. You give me a ruler, I do the measurements, and I say, "Oh you're right, that's an illusion." But there's no analogue for the ruler in ethics, is there? If there are two different intuitions that conflict, two intuitions that people think are foundational, it's not clear at that point which one is the illusion.

PB: I guess it's true. For intuitions of physical space and other things you could appeal to an external reality that you access through science and other forms of observation. You can't do that for morality. So, if you say your moral intuition is that torture is always wrong and I say "Well what if torture saves lives in the long run?" You could say well that's data but that doesn't convince me.

I'm interested in hearing what you have to say about this. What really happens is: we have multiple moral intuitions and then we do this whole reflective equilibrium thing where we coordinate them together and try to resolve inconsistencies. And that's where the argument goes. Often it ends up with one person trying to convince another that their intuition is improperly derived.

TS: But what do you mean by 'improperly derived'?

PB: Hypothetically, let's say I have an intuition that affirmative action is wrong because it is a form of discrimination, and discrimination is wrong. I can imagine someone arguing with me saying, "Well look you don't really believe that discrimination is always wrong." And then giving argument after argument until I concede, "Oh, OK I see some sorts of discrimination are OK."

And that's how moral arguments go. In other cases, moral arguments are plugged into factual considerations. You say "I think abortions are fine because a fetus feels no pain," but then look at this, I'm showing you a fetus *does* feel pain, and this might make you change your mind. A lot of moral arguments are sensitive to issues of consistency and a lot of them are calibrated to facts.

I'm really interested in the case of disgust. Something grosses me out, and I feel it's wrong. And I don't think you can ever really shake that feeling. But I think people could be persuaded that, on balance, disgust is the wrong way to make moral decisions and so is akin to an illusion. The sort of argument you'd make is to say, "Well, people had very strong intuitions, based on disgust, about interracial marriage. But surely you believe interracial marriage isn't wrong." And then this calls into question this mode of moral deliberation. Does that make sense?

TS: Yeah, it does. You can even point this out for intuitions that seem primary. You can point out that it's inconsistent with another intuition they have that may be just as primary. And you can at the very least force them to reconcile it. You might even point to one that they themselves would admit was deeper, an intuition they were more strongly committed to without being aware of it necessarily. Is that the idea?

PB: These are questions I am struggling with. What does seem clear is that we do make moral arguments, we do persuade people morally. And this doesn't seem different in kind from other sorts of arguments people have that sometimes get productively resolved. Of course, there's a whole continuum of things. You and I could disagree about whether it's raining outside and we could go outside and look, that's on one extreme. That's easy. Another extreme is that you say *Straw Dogs* is the best movie ever and I said "meh" and maybe those are harder to resolve.

TS: That might be more in the middle. I was thinking that basic taste judgments are at the other end of the extreme. Like whether eggplant is delicious or horrendous. I think it's horrendous, I hate eggplant. My wife loves it— we're not going to resolve that one.

PB: But that's only a disagreement if you were to argue that eggplant is objectively horrible.

TS: I think eggplant might be objectively horrible but I see your point. You're saying there's a continuum for how objectively we tend to think of moral matters.

PB: Yes. And someone like Sam Harris denies the continuum. I think I'm reading him fairly to say that he believes moral disagreements are just factual disagreements in the end, and that moral views are wrong in the same way that statements of fact are wrong.

TS: But aren't you also committed to that view to some level?

PB: Yeah, to some level. If I think there's moral progress, then I think there has to be moral mistakes and moral truths that we can find through inquiry. But I also think there are points at which we actually can't—which are very hard to resolve that way. Appiah had a very good review of Sam Harris' book,[11] where Appiah says "Look, here are some examples of some things that can't be resolved through scientific argument." And he gives versions of the repugnant conclusion—is it better to raise everybody's happiness a tiny bit while one person's happiness drops a lot? And he points out correctly that there's no factual way to answer this question.

Actually, the examples which strike me the most, as we talked about earlier, are the balance of our obligations toward family and to strangers. So, Harris says, I think correctly, that we care way too much for those close to us and not enough for those in faraway lands. OK, I agree with that. But if you push him, he can't tell us with a scientific analysis exactly how much we should care about people in faraway lands.

TS: He can't even come close, right? That's a great example of something science can barely shed light on.

PB: Right. You can imagine that we have all the data on exactly how happy people will be if you do such and such, how happy my son will be if I send him to a good school, how happy Africans will be if I save their children's lives. Every molecule is known, every data point is exact. Still, I don't know what to do.

TS: Exactly. OK, last question on this, because I'm still trying to figure out ultimately where you stand metaethically, in the debate over whether morality can be objective. Would you call yourself a pluralist? You seem willing to allow for a good amount of flexibility as to what can be called morally good. And everything you've said is consistent with the idea that there are multiple moral truths or moral systems that are jointly incompatible. A single individual could coherently hold any one of them but not all of them.

PB: That's more of a psychological claim than a metaethical claim.

TS: Well, it's metaethical in this sense. If I'm right, there would be no way of (a) persuading a person who embraced a different morality and also (b) providing a principled justification for one over the other. There would be no way to adjudicate between them. You see what I'm saying? It's a psychological question whether they could be convinced one way or the other, but it's a philosophical question whether one is more justifiable than the other.

PB: I honestly don't know. I'm less of a pluralist than someone like Jon Haidt. Jon has all these different moral foundations, and I think his empirical psychological claim is largely true. And then he's a pluralist about it—he thinks that these are different ways to live life well. My own view is that you can look at a moral foundation, a psychologically valid moral foundation, you could track its evolutionary history, developmental history, and then you can say "This really sucks." I think people are often tempted by a version of the naturalistic fallacy, which is that if something evolved through natural selection and cultural selection, then it's somehow good. I again think there are certain moral sentiments which you can look at in a cold-blooded way and say, yeah, it served a function but now it's actually not good, we'd be better off without it. And, here's the controversial point, I think that upon reflection any rational person could come to agree with that.

So, consider female genital mutilation—there's a cultural history, to some extent it might even be a cultural adaptation and thus serves a purpose for having it. But now we can look at it and say that actually it does not make the world better, it makes the world worse. Same for slavery or whatever. More generally, I think the whole foundation of disgust and sanctity is like that.

TS: So you would describe yourself as less of a pluralist than Haidt in that you think there's more work you can do beyond the foundations. But that doesn't mean you're going to arrive at a single truth or single correct moral worldview, right?

PB: That's a really good question, and I just don't know. I'm not just saying I don't know which one is right—consequentialism or all the forms of deontonology or virtue ethics or whatever. What I don't know is whether or not there is any way to make this sort of choice.

TS: What does that depend on, empirically, for you?

PB: My inability to answer that question is why I don't know. So, it goes back to what we were saying about Sam Harris. Not only don't I know how much of my money I should give to charity, I don't even know how I could know.

TS: We can't even conceive of an experiment or any evidence that could answer that question.

PB: Right. Because Harris thinks all you have to do is accumulate data on other people's happiness and your own happiness. But that can't be right. Because even with the full data, you can draw up these different curves of how much happiness I have, my son has, Africans have, and so on, but I still won't know what to do. But it's also because while I think I owe something to strangers, the idea that I don't owe more to my children seems so unnatural that it doesn't seem to be morality at all.

TS: And yet you think an impartiality principle is one of the foundations of morality, right?

PB: Yes I do. But the impartiality principle, I think, is not inconsistent with saying we have different obligations to those close to us and those far away.

TS: It doesn't commit you to favoring everyone's welfare identically?

PB: Right.

TS: So, the empirical question, all this seems to rest on is this: with full information, would a rational person, even one from a different culture with different practices, would that person agree with you?

PB: Yes. And put as a claim about actual people it's probably wrong. I'm a Jew and so if you tell me that male circumcision is stupid, I might say well screw you, you anti-Semite! But that just goes to show that we're not perfectly rational. So I guess maybe my claim is that if we were all perfectly rational, perfectly smart, unbiased, moral agreement would shoot up. But I also can see that it would not perfectly converge. You might think that you should give 40 percent of your money to charity, I think 20 percent. And we might just disagree and not know how to resolve that.

Notes

1 See Chapter 5 (Nancy Sherman) for more on the role of emotions in Aristotelian ethics.
2 See "The War on Reason" *The Atlantic*, March 2014 issue. www.theatlantic.com/magazine/archive/2014/03/the-war-on-reason/357561 and "The Baby in the Well: The Case against Empathy," *New Yorker*, 5/20/13. www.newyorker.com/magazine/2013/05/20/the-baby-in-the-well
3 See especially episodes 24 and 42 for further discussion of issues in this interview.
4 The book, titled *The Monk and the Philosopher*, is a series of dialogues between Ricard and his father Jean-François Revel (New York: Schocken, 1998).
5 Conor Freierdorf has written some excellent pieces critical of our drone policies. See for example "If a Drone Strike Hit an American Wedding, We'd Ground Our Fleet. But after a Dozen or More Deaths at a Yemeni Wedding, Don't Expect Anything to Change." *The Atlantic*, 12/16/13. www.theatlantic.com/politics/archive/2013/12/if-a-drone-strike-hit-an-american-wedding-wed-ground-our-fleet/282373
6 Pereboom is a Cornell philosopher who, like Galen Strawson, denies that blame and punishment can be deserved. Pereboom told me this at a conference, but he may have been quoting another philosopher.
7 See my discussion with Appiah about his book in Chapter 7.
8 See my interview with Singer in Chapter 9 where he does, in fact, say this. We also discuss the mathematics analogy, which Singer offers as support for his moral rationalism.

9 Appiah makes this point about moral revolutions in general—the rational arguments have usually been around for a long time before the progress occurs. Again, see Chapter 7.
10 See Bennett's paper "The Conscience of Huckleberry Finn." *Philosophy* 49 (188): 123–34.
11 Bloom is referring to Harris's book *The Moral Landscape*. David Pizarro and I interviewed Harris twice on our podcast (episodes 59 and 63). See also Appiah's review "Science Knows Best." www.nytimes.com/2010/10/03/books/review/Appiah-t.html?_r=3&scp=1&sq=Sam%20Harris%20moral%20landscape&st=cse

Questions for Discussion

1   What is the difference between empathy and sympathy according to Bloom? Why is this difference important?
2   Why does Bloom think empathy is a bad guide to moral judgment?
3   How does Bloom respond to Sommers' "case against blueberries" comparison?
4   Why does Bloom agree with Pinker that the "manly virtues" often cause more harm than good?
5   What sorts of moral discoveries does Bloom consider similar to the 'discovery of zero'?
6   Why does Sommers think that Bloom's use of *The Cosby Show* and *Will & Grace* examples undermine Bloom's argument that we discover moral truths using reason? How does Bloom respond?
7   Ultimately, does Bloom agree with Singer (see Chapter 9) that morality is objective? Why or why not?

Suggested Reading

Bloom, Paul. "Feeling Sorry for Tsarnaev." *New Yorker*, 5/16/13.
——. "The Baby in the Well: The Case against Empathy." *New Yorker*, 5/20/13.
——. "The War on Reason." *The Atlantic*, March 2014 issue.
Cameron, C. Daryl. "Can You Run Out of Empathy." *Greater Good: The Science of a Meaningful Life*, 5/20/2013. http://greatergood.berkeley.edu/article/item/run_out_of_empathy
Haidt, J. "The Emotional Dog and Its Rational Tail: A Social Intuitionist Approach to Moral Judgment." *Psychological Review* 108 (2001): 814–34.
Revel, Jean François and Matthieu Ricard. *The Monk and the Philosopher: A Father and Son Discuss the Meaning of Life*. New York: Random House LLC, 2011.
Singer, Peter. "Famine, Affluence, and Morality." *Philosophy & Public Affairs* (1972): 229–43.

Assorted Media and Podcast Pairings

"The Origins of Pleasure." TED talk. www.ted.com/talks/paul_bloom_the_origins_of_pleasure

Very Bad Wizards, Episode 28 "The Perils of Empathy (With Paul Bloom)." http://verybadwizards.com/episodes/24

Very Bad Wizards, Episode 42 "Reason, Responsibility, and Roombas (With Paul Bloom)." http://verybadwizards.com/episodes/42

14 Joseph Henrich
Relative Justice

For much of the last century, the dominant economic model of human behavior was known as Homo economicus—a model which predicts that human beings will always act according to their (perceived) rational self-interest. Over the last 20 years, however, researchers in the flourishing field of behavioral economics have challenged this picture of human nature. Through the use of simple but ingenious experiments, these researchers have shown some of the ways that human beings systematically depart from self-interested behavior. The most famous of these experiments is known as the ultimatum game, and it works like this: subjects are randomly assigned into two roles, proposer or responder. Proposers are given $20 and told that they can offer their responder anything between $1 and the whole amount. Responders have two choices: they can accept and walk away with whatever amount the proposer has offered, or they can reject the offer, in which case neither the proposer nor the responder will receive any money at all. That's the whole game.

Now imagine that you're a subject in one of these experiments, and you're the responder. Your proposer is anonymous, but let's call him Doug. If Doug is a member of the species Homo economicus, his only concern will be to walk away with as much money as he can. He'll therefore be tempted to offer only $1 and keep the remaining $19. Doug's only worry is that you'll reject the offer, in which case he will walk away empty-handed. But then Doug would think about it from your perspective. If you're also a member of Homo economicus, you'll accept any offer no matter how low it is. Why? Because $1 is better than nothing, and nothing is what you'll get if you reject. So Doug can safely make the lowest possible offer of $1. And according to the model, you'll accept it.

But consider: how would you really behave in this situation? The choice to make Doug a proposer and you a responder was completely arbitrary. You don't deserve any less money than Doug, do you? The fair thing to do is to split the pot, right? And then he comes up with this insulting offer, $1, 5 percent of the total amount. Is that fair? Are you going to let him get away with that?

If you're like most readers, the answer is likely no. You'll gladly sacrifice the dollar to punish his greed. Nor is it likely that you'd have received such a low offer in the first place. In the experiments conducted in America in the past 20 years, the most common offer proposers make is a full 50 percent of the pot.

And when low or unfair offers do come, responders tend to reject them, even in high-stakes games when the amount is still substantial. Homo economicus may not care about things like fairness, justice, and not getting screwed over. But it seems that we do, even at a cost to our own interests.

So where does Joseph Henrich come into this picture? As a graduate student in anthropology, Henrich was especially attuned to one drawback of these studies: the results were coming from a narrow range of subjects. Since the researchers were economists and psychologists working in universities, their participant pools were comprised almost exclusively of college students, mostly American.[1] Henrich had the brilliant idea of expanding the range of subjects not just demographically, but also culturally. He took the ultimatum game and other experiments to southeastern Peru and ran them with the Machiguenga, a family-centered forager-horticultural society scattered throughout the Peruvian Amazon.

This kind of study was unprecedented in his field. Anthropologists are trained to do ethnography, to observe people in their natural environments and to describe what they see—no controlled experiments allowed. But Henrich went ahead with the study anyway, and he came back with unexpected results. While the Machiguenga people did not behave in line with the Homo economicus model, they didn't behave like Americans either. For one thing, they didn't reject low offers in the ultimatum game. Further studies indicated that Americans and the Machiguenga have strikingly different ideas about fairness and justice, and Henrich's methods allowed him to measure these differences in quantifiable terms.

The study sparked a great deal of interest and led to a large MacArthur Foundation grant. The grant funded a large-scale project to conduct similar experiments in 15 small-scale societies in field sites all across the globe. These studies revealed cross-cultural differences in attitudes about morality and justice in ways that no other analysis has been able to uncover. And by incorporating methodologies from fields as diverse as anthropology, psychology, evolutionary biology, and experimental economics, Henrich and his colleagues paved the way for a revolution in the social sciences, a way of moving past the deep divisions among the disciplines.

Joe Henrich was trained in anthropology at UCLA. He was an associate professor at Emory University before becoming the Canada Research Chair in Culture, Cognition & Evolution at the University of British Columbia in 2006. He is the author, most recently, of Why Humans Cooperate. *I flew out to Vancouver to interview him this past summer, and returned home wondering why anyone would choose not to live in that city.*

June 2008

1 Fear Factor for Anthropologists

TAMLER SOMMERS: You spent a lot of time—well over a year—with the Machiguenga, right? Did you bring back any good stories—especially ones that show some of the different ways in which they view the world?

JOSEPH HENRICH: One thing that really came across, and it happened to be going on while we were there, is this. Missionaries contacted the Machiguenga in the middle of the last century. The missionaries wanted Bible translators, so they tried to get a democratic situation going. And so now each Machiguenga community has an official elected chief. They're in charge of getting development going in the village. The village is really just a cluster of independent families gathered around a school. And then in the rainy season, when school is out of session, everyone disappears to the forest. So there's one elected guy whose job it is to make sure the lawn gets cut and community buildings get built. And we watched day after day as this poor guy tried to get other people to help build the school. He'd blow his horn, no one would come. He'd go around door to door, maybe he'd get one or two people to help for a little while, but then they'd leave and go off to lunch. In the end, the teachers had to force the students to build their own school. And this is contrasted with these villages in Fiji I've been working in the last five years. They have chiefdoms, villages of about the same size, are similarly subsistence-based, on manioc and fish. But there, when the chief asks for help, everyone shows up, the whole situation runs like clockwork. The community buildings get built. Because they have norms about cooperation.

TS: And the Machiguenga just don't.

JH: They're ruggedly independent, to say the least.

TS: Right—in the book you say they would make the cowboy in the American western look like a pathetic conformist.

JH: Yes.

TS: Any interesting anthropologist fish-out-water experiences?

JH: Well, the one I always think of happened when I first got off the plane. I think of it as my first real test as anthropologist. A woman came and saw us and brought out these bowls of *masato*. Traditionally, the Machiguenga would take manioc[2] and chew it up and then spit it into a pot and cook it. And the spit causes it to ferment, turning it into an alcoholic beverage.

TS: Is this the *chicha*?

JH: In other places it's called *chicha*, the Machiguenga call it *masato*. Really it's just chewed up manioc. I knew I'd have to be drinking essentially someone else's saliva. And when they gave it to me, it really smelled like vomit. I was able to sort of hold my breath and get it down.

TS: Sounds like a reality show. It's interesting; spit-based beverages came up in my interview with Steve Stich.[3] He used chicha as an analogy for moral claims, disgustingness claims. He thinks chicha is disgusting, but not that it's objectively true that it's disgusting. The Peruvians aren't wrong when they say that it's tasty. We project the disgustingness onto the world—the disgustingness seems like it's in the chicha, but really the disgust comes from within us. And the same goes for terms like *unfair* or *wrong*.

JH: Yeah, and it reminds me of another Machiguenga example of mine. Evolutionary psychologists often talk about food tastes being the product of evolution. And we might have some food tastes that are a product of evolution, but which foods we eat are much more culturally transmitted. I was hiking with the Machiguenga one time, and we decided to stop for a snack. They rolled over a log and picked up these long, slimy-looking larvae and started eating them. They like them because they're full of fat. I like fat too, but I didn't want to eat the larvae. That taste wasn't culturally transmitted to me.

TS: So the taste for fat in general is universal, but …

JH: Not the larvae.

2   Playing Games with the Machiguenga

TS: What gave you the idea to do the Machiguenga experiment?

JH: I was in graduate school in anthropology at the time. And we were working on a game theory model on the evolution of human cooperation. And repeated interaction models aren't much help in solving the toughest problem: what's called "*n*-person cooperation," a large number of people working together to contribute to some kind of public good.

TS: Because the opportunities to free-ride, to get benefits without paying the costs, are so numerous?

JH: Right. That's why it's a puzzle. But if you introduce punishment into the model, and have punishers who also cooperate, things work a lot better. So we were thinking that in the evolution of human cooperation, punishment is probably important. Rob Boyd, who was my adviser, had been going to interdisciplinary meetings, where he learned about the ultimatum game and behavioral economics. The rejections in the ultimatum game kind of felt like the sort of punishment we thought would be important. So then the idea to take it to the Machiguenga was this: the Machiguenga people live in small independent families scattered throughout the forest. There are no higher-level institutions, not much cooperation. If *they* punish, then we've really got something universal about human nature.

TS: You'd say "even the Machiguenga people" exhibit this kind of behavior.

JH: Right. They would be the toughest test case.

TS: But it turned out that the results were surprising, right?

JH: I wouldn't say that I was *positive* what they were going to do—but when I think about playing the ultimatum game, *I* would reject low offers. So I think I projected my intuitions on to them. I thought they'd reject low offers—they'd be like university students. And the paper I would write when I came back would be confirming the universal human disposition to punish at a cost, in the ultimatum game. But that's not what happened.

TS: I heard that you came back after a few months and told your adviser "I fucked up!" because the data were so out of line with what you were expecting.

JH: Well, I had to modify the protocol of the experiment so that we could run it in that environment, and there was a chance that I'd modified the protocol in some weird way, and that was the cause of the results. And there was also the concern that not only had I gotten the wrong answer but that people would *think* that I had somehow screwed it up. It's a natural assumption—I was an anthropology graduate student doing behavioral economics; it didn't seem like too much of a leap. So the first step in convincing myself was that I used the same protocol with graduate students at UCLA, and in their game the mean offer was 48 percent. So I was able to deal with some of those concerns.

TS: So what exactly were the results with the Machiguenga?

JH: Instead of a mean offer in the high 40s [45–50 percent of the pot]—which you see in America—they had a mean offer of 26 percent. And the modal offer, the most common offer, was 15 percent. And despite all those low offers, no one rejected.

TS: No one rejected?

JH: Well, there was one rejection, of a 25 percent offer, out of the whole sample. And always in my mind I have an asterisk next to that example, because we were looking for subjects to play, and found a Machiguenga woman who had been living in Cuzco [a large city in Peru] and hadn't lived in the village for many years. And she was the one person who rejected.

TS: What's your explanation for the differences in their behavior? Did you do interviews with them?

JH: Yeah, and none of them had the sense that somehow they were being screwed over, or that the first player had an obligation to make a high offer. It seemed quite sensible that they would get a low offer, and then faced with the choice of some money or no money, they took some money.

TS: There was no anger at the proposer because there was no real expectation that they would get a 50–50 offer in the first place?

JH: Right. They kind of hoped maybe to get a little bit more, but they didn't expect to get more. They viewed it more as bad luck to get the role of the responder.

TS: Like losing a coin flip to someone. It's unfortunate but you don't get mad at the person who won the toss.

JH: Exactly.

TS: Okay, so why do you think they have these attitudes?

JH: Well, I can now answer this question after a long time. I couldn't have answered it back when I first did the research. I now think that what we're measuring when we do this with university students and people in industrial societies are culturally evolved norms that have evolved over a long period of the evolution of human societies. And these are norms that allow us to interact in large-scale societies where we have lots of transactions with people we're not related to and won't see again. We don't know where they live, we don't know the names of their children. So we have all these norms that tell us that the right thing to do is split the pot 50–50 and we get mad when people violate that norm. The Machiguenga don't have that norm. And so to them, there's no expectation or rules about money in anonymous situations, and so they just do the self-interested thing, which is not to reject.

TS: You conducted these studies anonymously, right? No one would know who made fair or unfair offers. Do you think the results would have been different if the offers weren't anonymous?

JH: The next year we went—my now-wife (then girlfriend) Natalie and I—we did what are called "public-goods games." In these games, there are four players, and you contribute an amount of your personal allotment to a common pot and then the pot is doubled and divided equally among the group. The fully self-interested thing to do is to give zero. Actually, the way we did it, it's called a common-pool resources game. There are $80 in a common pot, and each player can withdraw between zero and $20. And then whatever you leave in is doubled and then divided equally among the group. What a self-interested person does is withdraw all the money he can and then free-ride, and he still gets his share of what everyone left in the pot.

TS: Because the pot will only be doubled and then divided by four. So you're better off taking out what you can …

JH: Right. So if everyone is self-interested, all the money's gone and nothing doubles. We did this with the Machiguenga and then we also did it with students back in UCLA. The Machiguenga almost always withdraw the whole amount. They leave very little in the pot and very little gets doubled. And university students leave about half in. So there's a big difference there. Then we did two versions of this game among the Machiguenga. One where it was anonymous and one where you had to announce publicly what you were doing. And there was no difference.

TS: Really? Wow.

JH: People have trouble with this because they believe that our way of viewing reputation is the way everyone thinks about reputation. But among the Machiguenga they don't have these kinds of obligations to other families. They have obligations to their extended kin units and that's pretty much it.

TS: I take it there's a big change with university students when the game is not anonymous.

JH: Yes.

TS: So these surprising results led to a wide-ranging research program that examined behavior in 15 small-scale societies, funded by the MacArthur Foundation. How did these studies work?

JH: Everyone did the ultimatum game. Some people did dictator games,[4] and some did public-goods games.

TS: There were two rounds, two generations of this project, correct?

JH: Yeah, so in the second generation, we took all the criticisms we got from the first and tried to address them methodologically. Because that's where we were weakest. There was some uncontrolled methodological variation between the sites. We fixed that up, and did a three-game package. We did a dictator game in every site, an ultimatum game, and a third-party punishment game. We kind of learned how to do it from the first project.

TS: So what's the take-home message from the results of that project?

JH: The take-home message is that there's a lot of variation in behavior. The Machiguenga and groups like the Tsimane in Bolivia, who have a similar lifestyle, hug the bottom end of the distribution, and they don't reject low offers. And then Westerners, especially Americans, are at the high end. We'll punish you if you screw us, and we'll be pro-social (altruistic). Even in the dictator game in America, where the responder has to take the offer no matter what, the most common offer is 50 percent of the pot. The mean is 48 percent. This is incidentally one of the main differences between students and nonstudent adults, the dictator game. Students are much more self-interested.

TS: So depending on your social and cultural environment, your behavior and your ideas about fairness are going to vary.

JH: Our hypothesis is that it has to do with the evolution of societal complexity, in particular—complex markets. One of our measures is the degree of market incorporation the society has. What we think is that you have to have these norms about interacting with strangers in monetary contexts in order to engage with markets. Otherwise, your ability to engage in markets is limited to people you know. So complex large societies that are heavily engaged in markets have these strong fairness norms. And you need the norms to engage the markets. It's a two-way street. So you can live in this society and learn the norms. And the better people learn them, the more the market can be engaged. So this measure predicts the difference in offers.

TS: But there was variation among people who did have similar levels of market incorporation, right?

JH: Yes. Our measures of market integration capture about 50 to 60 percent of the between-group differences in offers. So there's a lot of unexplained variation. But that's still pretty good, given the crudeness of our measures.

3 "We've Found Homo Economicus! He's a Chimp"

JH: You know, we've also done—I don't know if you've seen this work— we've done this with chimps too.

TS: You've done ultimatum games with chimps?

JH: Mike Tomasello and Keith Jensen did the ultimatum game with chimps. And we've done what's called a pro-sociality test, myself and Joan Silk and Dan Povinelli. In our task, chimps have two choices. Choice *a*, they get a food reward and another unrelated chimp gets the same reward. Choice *b*, they get the food reward and the other chimp gets nothing. So if you're purely self-interested, you're indifferent between the two because you get the same reward either way. If you care about others at all, you'll always pick *a*, to deliver the food to the other chimp. And if you're competitive, you'll always pick *a*. And it turns out that chimps are completely indifferent. They don't care.

TS: Huh. That wasn't my impression from *Every Which Way But Loose*.

JH: So I tell my economist friends that we've finally found Homo economicus. He's a chimp!

TS: But with the ultimatum game, you can measure rejection rates with chimps?

JH: Yes, that was the Tomasello experiment, and they never reject.

TS: But now, what about the experiment Frans de Waal and Sarah Brosnan did where the capuchin monkey throws away the cucumber if he sees the other monkey getting a grape?[5] He's mad that the other capuchin got something better; he thinks it's not fair.

JH: Yeah, I wrote a commentary on that for *Nature*, and Sarah Brosnan was a postdoc of mine, so I'm intimately involved with this. The problem with that experiment is that what the capuchins did is the opposite of what humans do. There's another version of the ultimatum game called the impunity game. And it's the same thing, except now if the responder rejects the offer, nothing will happen to the proposer. They keep their money. And when you do that with humans, they never reject. Because the whole point of rejecting is that they want to hurt the proposer, but now the responder can't do that. Now, when you go to the capuchin experiment, the capuchin throws away the cucumber because he wants the grape. But the other capuchin still gets to eat the grape. And we know humans wouldn't do that because this maps onto the impunity game.

TS: So the whole idea of de Waal and Brosnan's experiment was to show that capuchins have a rudimentary standard of fairness resembling ours. And your point is that *humans* don't even have that kind of standard.

JH: Yes. Humans would be grumpy but they'd eat the cucumber. So if it's a standard of fairness, it's one humans don't have.

TS: And, of course, if your work is right, humans have different standards of fairness anyhow.

JH: Yes.

4   Relative Justice?

TS: Let's talk about the philosophical implications of all of this. Do you think your research undermines the idea that certain behavior is universally or objectively fair or just?

JH: Well, yes. I take an evolutionary approach. And from that perspective—I don't know much about philosophy—it's not even clear what an objective notion of fairness would mean.

TS: Just the idea that there's a certain standard of what's *really* fair or unfair, right and wrong. And if people like the Machiguenga violate those standards, they're making a moral mistake. Maybe it's not their fault, but it's a mistake nevertheless—just like being mistaken about the shape of the earth or something. Perhaps they aren't capable of understanding what's really fair and what isn't.

JH: Right. Well, if our theories are right, then beliefs about what you should do in the ultimatum game—and fairness norms in general—are just a product of a particular trajectory of cultural evolution, where you're building large societies in which strangers have to interact. And the other thing is: if you contribute to the group, say, the village or some larger part of society, you're contributing something that you could have been doing for your family. You're doing less for your family, more for everyone else. So one of the things about the evolution of complex societies is that there had to be a shift away from focusing only on your family and your kind, to focusing on these larger groups. So people say they value their families, but actually people in our society value their families a lot less than, say, the Machiguenga—who are entirely devoted to their families and don't allocate labor to society.

TS: So they might be appalled at how little we focus on the welfare of our brothers, sisters, and parents. They would consider *that* immoral. And your view is that there is no one correct answer to who has objectively right norms.

JH: Right.

TS: That's something many philosophers don't want to accept.

JH: So how do philosophers do this? I don't understand where "objectively correct" would come from. Because if I was going to evaluate the Machiguenga as wrong, I would need criteria. Keep in mind, I know nothing about philosophy ...

TS: Well, there's the Kantian notion of the categorical imperative, that acts have to be universalizable.[6] Maybe the Machiguenga wouldn't be able to will that their acts became a universal moral law of nature. Or there's the utilitarian standard—some might argue that their behavior wouldn't result in greater overall happiness. Of course, the tough part is justifying that these principles—utilitarian or Kantian—are indeed objective standards of behavior. I talk about this a lot in my interviews with Steve Stich and with Josh Greene and Liane Young. It seems like the only way to show that these are the universally correct standards is to show that they capture our considered intuitions—our core beliefs, upon reflection. And if your work is on target, it seems like these core intuitions will be different.

JH: Definitely. The deep-seated intuitions are different across cultures.

TS: This reminds me of something [philosopher] Shaun Nichols told me—an interesting story you related to him about your research in Fiji. One of the native helpers where you were staying beat up his—was it his wife, girlfriend?

JH: Yes, his girlfriend, but the mother of his child.

TS: And one of your assistants was talking with the girlfriend and her friends in the tent. And there was no sense that what happened was wrong. Is that accurate?

JH: Yeah, this was really awkward—one of those cultural-relativist moments where I really didn't know what to do. He was working for the project and sleeping in one of my project houses. And one of my graduate students was there. (I had a different sleeping house.) And suddenly she shows up at my door and tells me that Moavu, the guy, is beating up Nakuru, his wife or girlfriend. I knew the norm is that Fijian men can beat their wives; it's perfectly within their province to beat both their kids and their wife. So I made my presence known, and she ended up running by us. He saw us and ended up calming down a little. So I said something like: "Look, this is disgusting to us, so I don't know what I should do; I know that Fijians think differently about this." He decided to stop. But it was a problem, because he was my employee. So of course he stopped.

TS: But not out of any kind of shame.

JH: No.

TS: More like, I'm violating the etiquette of my boss, putting the fork on the wrong side ...

JH: Right, right.

TS: It's an interesting test case for ethical relativism, tougher than these issues about fairness in ultimatum games. Obviously, they have different views about how to treat women. But how comfortable are you with the idea that there is no right or wrong answer about whether you should beat your wife whenever you feel like it? That it just depends on what culture you're in?

JH: My view is that it's wrong to beat your wife, but that there's no objective standard. It's just wrong for me to do it.

TS: So you're willing to say that it's not wrong for Moavu to do it?

JH: Right. Of course, it still disgusts me when he does it. But what I didn't do was go around the village and start preaching to everyone to change to my rules.

TS: That's interesting. Philosophers will go to great lengths to avoid accepting that implication.

JH: That you can't go around telling people what to do?

TS: Not that you can't go around *telling* people what to do exactly. But that it's not *actually wrong* for someone to beat his wife or girlfriend.

JH: The reason why you end up in the spot I'm in is this: once you get an idea about how these norms come about, this is a cultural norm that has a particular cultural evolutionary trajectory. So unless you think our society is on a special cultural trajectory, which I guess would be your out, but ...

TS: You mean that we're on the right trajectory, and they've veered off onto the wrong one?

JH: Or they're stuck in some previous point.

TS: But your point still holds: from what standpoint could we justify the claim that our trajectory is the right one?

JH: Right. But just to finish the story—I wasn't present in the meeting of the girls afterward, but Tanya, my grad student, was. This woman Nakuru was beat up, really hurt, really sad. And so the women all sat around and they were comforting her. And several of them told stories about times they had been beat up. And I was asking Tanya who was mentioned—you know, I knew all the women and I knew all their men. And certain men I figured, there was no *way* that guy would do something like this. And sure enough: their wives had stories about the time these mild-mannered guys beat them up. I was shocked.

TS: And there was no indignation on the part of the women?

JH: Yeah. And the thing that made Tanya mad, I guess, was that Nakuru kept saying: "I should have listened to him. I shouldn't have been so social, talking to those guys."

TS: She was blaming herself …

JH: Right.

TS: Maybe this was an even more difficult test case for Tanya. Was she more tempted to preach about this being wrong?

JH: Yes, it was really hard for her. I told her what I thought, and I think she kept quiet … mostly.

5 Tear Down the Walls!

TS: You have a new book out called *Why Humans Cooperate*, co-authored with your wife Natalie. It focuses on work your wife did with the Chaldeans, an Iraqi immigrant community in metropolitan Detroit.

JH: Yes, it started out as her dissertation, and we decided to transform that into a book incorporating a lot of theory and modeling that comes from evolutionary biology and economics. One reason why it's interesting to wrap the theory part around the anthropological research is that anthropologists typically write about small-scale societies. But here's a case where we find some of the same patterns in middle-class America.

TS: What patterns specifically?

JH: Well, we still find that kinship is important and reciprocity is important. But it manifests itself in different norms. So in a sense, there's this underlying evolved psychology, but it gives rise to interesting cultural variation.

TS: What is the variation as compared with other Americans?

JH: They have an ethnic identity, which is tied to their religion and language. They have strong ties to family and community, and so they have these small grocery stores, which are highly successful. But they avoid hiring non-Chaldeans, average Americans. And they have quite different norms about giving to charity. It's a big reputational hit if you don't give to Iraqi charities. They don't seem to care about other charities.

TS: Is it like with the Machiguenga, where if you give to a non-Chaldean charity that money could be going to help Chaldeans?

JH: Right, so it's actually bad to give to non-Chaldean charities. And they support political candidates who are Chaldean, which goes along with their sense of identity.

TS: A couple things about the book: one is methodological. Your book brings together research from many fields within the sciences—mathematical modeling from evolutionary theory, behavioral experiments in economics, and thick ethnography.[7] This hasn't been done before, has it?

JH: As far as I know, it's not been done. Certainly not the particular combination of things we have. The problem is in the way social science works with the training. If you're trained in anthropology, you're trained how to do thick ethnography. You know zero about how to do experiments. But if you're trained in psychology—I'm in a psychology department right now—you learn how to do laboratory experiments with undergraduate kids, but you learn nothing about how to observe life and make systematic recordings about how people interact in real life. And in neither of those places do you learn much about evolutionary biology and how to make formal models of social interaction. So our effort is to pull all three together and show how each can tell part of the story and work synergistically.

TS: Is this the wave of the future of how to approach the puzzle of human cooperation? Should it be?

JH: Yeah, I think so. Human cooperation and a lot of other puzzles. We need to break down the walls between the social sciences. Everyone should learn multiple methods. And they should focus on problems and draw from whatever techniques and methods they need to solve that particular problem. There should be no reason why a psychologist shouldn't go out and live in a community and do some ethnography that's accompanied by a bunch of experiments.

TS: In philosophy, there's a movement afoot to try to tear down traditional walls between philosophy and the sciences. Philosophers who do this run into a lot of over-the-top hostility and resistance.[8] Do you get that in the social sciences? People trying to defend their turf?

JH: Let's see. There's definitely a core in anthropology who are completely hostile to this approach. They think experiments are unethical.

TS: Why?

JH: That's a good question. I guess they think experiments force people to do things they wouldn't normally do. So you're sort of paying them to be unethical. It's a little bit unformed, but I know about this in particular here at UBC because when I was recruited here, the dean called me up and wanted to hire me. So he figured, this guy's an anthropologist, we'll put him in the anthropology department. I did my talk there and the department pretty much rioted. They said this guy does experiments, this guy does math, and he thinks evolution affects human behavior.

TS: Really? The dominant view in anthropology is still that evolution has no effect on how humans behave.

JH: Yeah. It's fine for talking about stones and bones, but any kind of interesting social behavior—no. This is cultural anthropology. There's also biological anthropology—but there was only one biological anthropologist here at UBC and now there's zero.

TS: And your view is that evolution does play a large role in influencing human behavior, but that it interacts with culture, too, and there's this feedback between the two.

JH: Right, so you need evolution and you need gene-culture co-evolution, which means that part of our genetic evolution has been shaped by culture. And then there's just plain "We're a cultural species, we're heavily reliant on learning from other people." That's just cultural evolution. All of these things play a role in explaining human behavior, and the relative importance depends on the particular problem one is examining.

6 "Why Do You Like Mashed Potatoes?"

TS: Something I found fascinating that came out of my interview with Steve Stich is this: according to Steve, there are many cultures in which people don't feel much of an urge to morally justify their behavior. You talk about this in your book as well.

JH: Yeah, people don't have these elaborate explanations for why they have their beliefs, or why they should do things the way they do them. Sometimes it's even awkward interpersonally, because it's like you asked a stupid question. It's similar to, well, if you like mashed potatoes and I ask, "Well, why do you like mashed potatoes?"

TS: So that's the right analogy. It's like asking them to justify tastes?

JH: That's what it feels like when you're asking them. They have this look: "How am I supposed to know? That's just how it is."

TS: There's a hypothesis that Steve came up with based on this. I'll quote him directly:

> The tradition of trying to justify normative claims in a deep and foundational way, the tradition of trying to provide something like philosophical or argumentative justifications for moral judgments— this is an *extremely* culturally local phenomenon. It's something that exists only in Western cultures and cultures that have been influenced by Western cultures. For much of human history, providing that kind of justification has played no part in normative psychology.

Would you go along with that?

JH: I do think that we have a culture of elaborate post hoc construction. The only thing I'd say is that I'm not sure how much of just a Western phenomenon this is. I have a friend who studies ancient China and it sounds like they have a tradition of this as well—of trying to figure out why we have the beliefs we do. So it could be complex societies that sit around and think about these things. So that's a possible exception, but I'd need to learn more about ancient China before saying anything definite.

TS: Do you think there's some kind of cultural environment that lends itself to this kind of justification?

JH: Well, maybe—this is off the top of my head—it could be that it arises when you have to formalize law. You have judges. So you get into this situation, a legal rhetoric. You've got to explain it, you've got to reapply it, it could be then that you might develop this tradition.

TS: And the cultures that you've found that don't have this tradition of justification—there's no legal system at all?

JH: Well, in places like Machiguenga and Fiji, there's a national legal system which exists somewhere out there, but it doesn't affect day-to-day life. And it's not relevant to things we're asking them about. So I'm trying to think of another analogy. It might be like asking, "Why do you love your children?" The only sensible answer to me would be an evolutionary one.

TS: And that's sort of a different level of explanation.

JH: Right, it doesn't answer why *you* love your children. You just love them, that's all there is to it.

7   Democracy for Everyone? Not So Fast

TS: What do you do when you go on these expeditions? I don't really know the details of how these anthropological studies are conducted. How you interact with the people, what you tell them. For example, your research in Fiji. How does all that work?

JH: When we first arrive, we give a formal presentation to the chief and to the community, and tell them what we're up to. And then we've been living there—well, I have people there now almost full-time. We run interviews, I hire various Fijians from universities there. We do work on a whole bunch of different topics, we're working on lots of different things at the same time. Interviews, experiments, and then just observing daily life.

TS: That's standard procedure? That's what you did with the Machiguenga?

JH: I developed this over the years. The typical anthropological study wouldn't involve many research assistants. So I've developed a kind of corporate version of this. It's on a much larger scale. I use experiments; other anthropologists don't use experiments. We're like psychologists except we do all of this ethnography. We sample people randomly to see what they're doing throughout the day. We study social networks.

TS: Are there conflicts that come up? Resentments, people wondering what you're doing there?

JH: Generally, the community is very supportive of it. It provides a lot of benefits to the community. We do some of the games and people get money, and they love that. We have to buy food when we're there, and that brings benefits. We have had some problems with outsiders, who start up a little trouble when I get some money from the project. So it's not without conflict.

TS: But nothing from inside the community.

JH: No, in fact people really like that we're interested. I've been working on the language, and they love that an outsider can come in and talk to them in their local dialect.

TS: What do you think the social and practical implications of your research are?

JH: One practical implication of all this is that things like formal institutions, legal systems, laws, formal government, they have to be well-fitted to the informal local norms. And so what you can't do is take a formal system from one place and just plop it on top of another place, and expect it to work. Because there's no fit. That seems to have all kinds of implications for economic development, for all kinds of things.

TS: Maybe a certain war we're engaged in? Trying to bring our values, democracy, to a region where it might not fit—is that something you'd think is unwise?

JH: Sure, that definitely comes to mind. Of course, the Iraq situation is just the latest installment of this same notion that happened a lot throughout Africa. Instituting a British parliamentary system or something like that. And it's really hard to get these things to work because it doesn't fit with the local system of values. The idea of doing democracy in a Fijian village, for example, is actually insulting to people there because they have a hierarchy that's based on the chief. And we've been studying why they think the chief has the right to make these decisions. They have an existing system which isn't a democracy, although it does give equal voice to everybody. But it is a decision-making system. If you tried to just stick a democracy in there, I can't imagine what would—things just wouldn't go well.

TS: The norms are too entrenched for that to work.

JH: Yeah. One way to do it would be to start with some area of social life that's not well developed, and try to stick it there. Because people don't have preexisting norms that are being violated. And then maybe gradually you could spread out from there, slowly replacing these other systems.

TS: But aren't their own norms working for them, given their cultural environment? Would it be fair to say that in some types of environment, democracy just isn't suitable?

JH: Yeah. The only way to make it work would be to change the way everyone thinks. And that takes a very long time.

TS: Has your research affected your day-to-day behavior in any way?

JH: Yes. I think having an awareness of the power of culture to shape our brains and our moral beliefs—well, rather than being arrogant about your views, you're more ready to accept that that's what the other guy believes ...

TS: Jon Haidt said something along those lines, that he feels less indignant, even when it comes to political issues.[9]

JH: Yeah, Jon has great examples on this. Because something that hits home for a typical liberal academic would be Republicans, red-state types. I think a lot of my fellow academics think that they've got the right moral values and those people in … rural Missouri have the wrong ones. So once you have this perspective, you might still have your liberal beliefs—I know Jon and I share a bunch of those—but we're not as belittling as some of our colleagues. We don't think people who disagree with us are evil idiots. We understand how you can have these basic differences in how you view the world.

TS: It's interesting that Steve Stich disagreed with that. He said he feels just as strongly about his views, even though he agrees with you on all the empirical issues about the origins of these beliefs. I guess he thinks that some types of moral beliefs involve an attitude that other people should stop doing the practices you find immoral, no matter who they are.

JH: Right. Well, even so, I think with this perspective, the approach you would use to persuade someone to stop would be quite different. If you think they're evil idiots, or just need to be informed or something, that's different than saying they're perfectly well informed and they just have a different interpretation of the facts that we share.

TS: A different interpretation?

JH: Suppose you and another person are viewing a painting. You think it's beautiful and the other person thinks it's ugly. What Jon and I are suggesting is that we've realized that you and the other person may be looking at the same painting through quite different lenses, each distorting the painting in different ways. Your lens distortions lead to a pleasing judgment. You can't remove the lens, or easily see through the other person's, but you can realize we're each using a different lens to judge the same painting. My view is that efforts at persuasion can be fine, by getting others to use your lens. The issue is really about realizing a certain degree of humility with regard to the certainty of our own moral tastes.

Notes

1 This is changing, but slowly. One study was co-authored by the economist Steve Burks, one of my old colleagues at the University of Minnesota, Morris, in 2005. He conducted ultimatum games with adult workers at a publishing company in Kansas City. Steve and his colleagues found that with nonstudent adults, the results tilted even more toward fair offers and 50–50 splits. Joe and Natalie Henrich have found this pattern repeatedly among nonstudents.

2 A root vegetable and staple of the Machiguenga diet.

3 See Chapter 16, p. 272.

4 These are games where the proposer can offer any amount and the responder has to accept. They have no option to turn the money down and send the proposer home with nothing. So the experiment is focused only on the proposer's behavior.

5 In the experiment, when two capuchin monkeys were given cucumbers, they both ate them. But when one capuchin got a grape (which they like much better) instead of a cucumber, the other capuchin refused to eat the cucumber and at times angrily threw

it back in the face of the experimenter. Perhaps the capuchin was angered by the injustice.

6 The Kantian view, roughly, is that only actions whose maxims could be universalized are morally right or permissible. Breaking a promise is therefore forbidden, according to Kant, because if everyone acted on the maxim "Break promises when convenient," the institution of promise-making would collapse. The whole point of promises would be lost.

7 Natalie Henrich spent a year and a half living in Detroit, studying the Chaldean culture—talking to them about their norms, values, behavior. This kind of long-term detailed observation is known as thick ethnography.

8 See the interview with Stephen Stich in Chapter 16 for more about turf wars in philosophy.

9 See Chapter 12, especially sections 3 and 4.

Questions for Discussion

1 What is the Homo economicus view of human nature? How does research in behavioral economics undermine this view?

2 Describe the Ultimatum Game. What initially drove Henrich to bring the game to the Machiguenga? Why did the results of the experiment surprise him?

3 What does Henrich think explains the variations among the 15 sites from the MacArthur study?

4 Does Henrich think there is such a thing as universal or objective justice? Why or why not?

5 Describe the story of the Fijian men who beat their girlfriends. What is Henrich's response to this, and how does this relate to his views about objective justice?

Suggested Readings

Brosnan, Sarah F. and Frans B. M. de Waal. "Monkeys Reject Unequal Pay." *Nature* 425(6955) (2003): 297–99.

Henrich, Joseph. *Foundations of Human Sociality*. New York: Oxford University Press, 2004.

Henrich, Joseph, Robert Boyd, Samuel Bowles, Colin Camerer, Ernst Fehr, Herbert Gintis, Richard McElreath et al. "'Economic Man' in Cross-cultural Perspective: Behavioral Experiments in 15 Small-scale Societies." *Behavioral and Brain Sciences* 28(6) (2005): 795–815.

Henrich, Joseph, Jean Ensminger, Richard McElreath, Abigail Barr, Clark Barrett, Alexander Bolyanatz, Juan Camilo Cardenas et al. "Markets, Religion, Community Size, and the Evolution of Fairness and Punishment." *Science* 327(5972) (2010): 1480–4.

Henrich, Joseph and Natalie Henrich. *Why Humans Cooperate: A Cultural and Evolutionary Explanation*. New York: Oxford University Press, 2007.

Henrich, J., S. J. Heine, and A. Norenzayan (2010). "The Weirdest People in the World." *Behavioral and Brain Sciences* 33(2–3): 61–83

Podcast Pairings

Very Bad Wizards, Episode 17: "Learning about Bushmen by Studying Freshmen."
  http://verybadwizards.com/episodes/17
Very Bad Wizards, Episode 18: "Boy, If Life Were Only Like This (With Joe Henrich)."
  http://verybadwizards.com/episodes/18

15 Alan Fiske and Tage Rai
The Morality of Violence

"A senseless act of violence" is a common phrase but almost never an accurate one. Violence is serious business. People behave violently for reasons. The perpetrators have motives that are strong enough to cause them to act in a way that could easily get them imprisoned or killed. This much is fairly obvious. But what if I told you that violent acts like murder, armed robbery, and sexual assault are not just committed for reasons, but for moral reasons? What if I said that the motives behind these terrible acts tend to be moral ones, and that violent criminals believe they are doing the right thing? Now we're in more controversial territory ...

Fortunately, I don't have to tell you any of this; Alan Fiske and Tage Rai can do it for me. In fact, they already have in their 2015 book Virtuous Violence. *"When people hurt or kill someone," they write, "they usually do so because they feel they ought to: they feel that it is morally right or even obligatory to be violent."[1] They test this claim against a wide range of acts, including gang violence, honor killings, torture, genocide, and rape. They find that even the most gruesome of these acts usually have moral motives behind them.*

Fiske and Rai's views on violence become a little less surprising when considered in the context of their broader approach to moral psychology. In his 1990 book Structures of Social Life: The Four Elementary Forms of Human Relations, *Fiske introduced his Relational Models Theory, which Steven Pinker describes as "the best—indeed the only—overarching theory of social psychology." According to Fiske, human beings across cultures use just four fundamental models to relate to one another and coordinate virtually all aspects of their social lives. There are cross-cultural differences in the way these models are implemented—but the four basic ways of relating are universal. Tage Rai (Fiske's student at the time) then developed and applied Fiske's theory to questions about the causes of moral intuitions, judgments, and behavior. In their co-authored 2011 article in* Psychological Review, *Rai and Fiske defend their "relationship regulation theory" of moral psychology. Morality, they argue, is about regulating the four basic kinds of relationships. The theory rejects the common view that moral intuitions are based entirely on features of the actions—did it cause harm? Was it unfair? Did it violate someone's rights? Rather "any given action will be judged as right, just, fair, honorable, pure, virtuous, or morally correct when it occurs in some social–relational contexts and will be judged as wrong when it occurs in other social–relational contexts."[2]*

*I came across Fiske and Rai's work when teaching a course on moral diversity. It was exciting stuff. I saw their theory as providing a lens through which we could better perceive the roots of moral disagreement across cultures, within cultures, and even within our own conflicted moral minds. When people apply different models to the same situation, they arrive at different moral judgments. In cases of intrapersonal moral conflict, we are often applying two or more different models at once: we are torn about which relationship matters the most. In their new book, Fiske and Rai apply these ideas to acts of violence. Morality is about regulating social relationships. Acts of violence are usually aimed at regulating relationships. Therefore the motives behind them are moral. (Note: Fiske and Rai do **not** believe the acts to be morally right, just morally motivated.)*

Alan Fiske is Professor of Anthropology at UCLA. Tage Rai is a post-doc at MIT's Sloane School of Management. I interviewed both of them over Skype. I began by asking them to describe relationship regulation theory and the four basic relational models.

March 2015

1   Regulating Relationships

ALAN FISKE: Relationship regulation theory is about the ultimate adaptive function of morality but even more it's about the cognitive processes that comprise our moral psychology. It tells us what people are thinking about when they make moral judgments: They're thinking about their relationships and how to make them right.

TAGE RAI: We start from the fundamental assumption that morality has evolved to regulate important social relationships in human lives and communities. And if that's your starting point, that really changes the way you're going to think about our moral psychology.

TAMLER SOMMERS: In what ways?

TR: If you're trying to identify patterns in morality, the relevant questions won't be: 'did that action cause intentional harm? Or 'was it unequal?' Instead you'll look to the social–relational context within which that action took place. In other words, if you're trying to figure out whether an action is deemed right or wrong, it's not going to be based on the *content* of the action, independent of the relational contexts.

TS: So morality isn't about general principles concerning fairness or harm, taken in isolation. These principles may come up, but when they do, they'll have a function—to regulate a certain kind of relationship.

TR: Right, and that way of thinking yields some tractable predictions about moral judgments and other phenomena.

TS: Like what?

AF: Well, if our moral psychology is oriented to regulating relationships then we might ask: are there an infinite number of possible moralities? What are the basic forms of morality that humans draw from? Drawing here on our relational model theory, we say that there are actually only four basic structures. There are only four basic forms of relationships that are being regulated. And particular cultures specify the legitimate ways of regulating those relationships.

TS: So let's go through the different forms of relationships. What's the first?

AF: The first one is a sense of one-ness, a sense of unity, a sense of belonging, where two or more people in the relationship organize what they're doing in terms of some sense of equivalence. That is, they treat the participants in the relationship as equivalent. It doesn't matter who does what. So, if we have a drinking fountain, well, it's just available to everybody to drink from. We don't keep track of who drinks out of it, it's just ours. If there is food in the fridge, well, it's just ours. If there's money in the joint checking account, it's just ours. You see those kinds of relationships both in intense forms—deep love, deep moral commitments, deep commitments in a platoon at war. But you also see them in milder forms.

TS: Players on sports team or something? I guess that can be pretty intense.

AF: Yes, or your identity with the people in your work team, or your university, or your national or ethnic identity (which are often weaker forms of it). It can vary in intensity. So that's what we call the *communal sharing* framework.

TS: And the second?

AF: The second relationship is authority ranking, where people order themselves in a linear hierarchy. People who are at the top are entitled to respect and deference. They have certain prerogatives and priority of access to resources. And those who are below owe their superiors deference and respect. And the people above also have a pastoral responsibility, to care for, look out for, stand up for the people below. They have an obligation to protect and guide, and provide wise leadership to the people lower on the hierarchy. This form of authority ranking exists in many traditional cultures and of course certain aspects of modern ones.

TS: Again, you could think of a sports team. But this time, it's more like the relationship between the players and the head coach.

AF: Yeah, that's right. Or like a military hierarchy or bureaucracy or the relationship between teacher and student.

TS: How about the third form?

AF: The third form of relationship is what we call 'equality matching.' In contrast to the first framework, this is one where people keep track of whether they are equal or what it would take to make them equal. And they may not always be equal but they know exactly what they would have to do to become equal. And that is the reference point to which they try to keep returning.

TS: So in this relationship structure, you don't want one person to be eating twice as much food in the fridge or never buying a round of drinks.

AF: Yes, so you might be taking turns. You might be making equal contributions. You might be taking equal shares in something, it might be tit-for-tat, in-kind reciprocity, one-for-one balance where you give something and get back the same thing. Or there might even be a fair lottery, like a coin flip, where there is an even chance of winning or losing. You see this in the rules of most sports and games around the world. You also see it in eye-for-an-eye vengeance or any kind of tit-for-tat, one-to-one matching relationship.

TS: And the fourth structure?

AF: Now the fourth kind of relationship is what we call 'market pricing.' But we have to be careful about misinterpreting that name because it's not all about markets or economics. These are the relationships that are coordinated by proportionality. There's some ratio or rate or proportion that is socially meaningful. People organize and coordinate the relationship with reference to that.

TS: Can you give some more examples?

AF: It could be of course monetary kinds of things like rents and wages and taxes, tithes, interest rates, and that sort of thing. But it also could be entirely non-monetary things. Any sort of cost–benefit analysis. If you're thinking about whether your girlfriend is too high maintenance and whether it's worth continuing that relationship. If you're thinking about whether a penal sentence is proportional to what somebody did wrong, or if the rewards that people are getting are proportional to their merit. And, more generally, utilitarian moral reasoning is based on a notion that all good and bad consequences can be compared on a ratio scale. Everything can be denominated and proportioned to everything else, and that's how you figure out what's right and wrong. So that's the fourth one, market pricing.

TS: And your view is that morality is largely or entirely about regulating these four different forms of relationships?

AF: The argument is that, across cultures, throughout history, people coordinate virtually all of their social relations using combinations of these four structures. All of them have to be culturally implemented, so they use them in different ways. The structures are not sufficiently specific to tell you what's right and wrong in any particular situation. Not until they are implemented, according to certain cultural precedents and prototypes.

TS: In the article you claim that this account can shed light on moral disagreement.[3]

TR: Yeah, I think so. Take disagreements about, say, distributive justice. If you're Jon Haidt and you say one foundation is 'fairness,' we can still ask: OK, but what's fair? Concretely, fairness can be a number of different things. What we argue is that depending on the relational mode you're working in and its corresponding moral motive, your conception of fairness is going to be very different. If you're motivated by unity in the communal framework, then you're going to be oriented more toward need-based sharing or free sharing without tracking who gets what. If you're motivated by hierarchy, the distributions that you call fair are going to be rank-based. The people at the top are going to be able to distribute the goods however they see fit. And then if we're motivated by equality, we're going to be oriented toward equal division. And if we're motivated by market pricing proportionality, our distributions are going to be based on some sort of merit or equity.

TS: So the disagreements arise when people operating within in different relational modes are making judgments about the same thing?

TR: Yeah so take something like eye-for-an-eye revenge. It's going to make sense if we're using equality, but if we're really relating according to hierarchy then when a superior hits a subordinate, the subordinate is not entitled to hit the superior back. If they were equals they would be.

AF: In the British Navy 200 years ago, if a subordinate struck a superior, the subordinate would be executed. And I just want to emphasize that this is a descriptive account.[4] This isn't our moral view, just an account of what's going on.

2 Conflicting Moral Motives

TS: It would seem like we're often working within multiple relationship structures at once, right? In a lot of situations, we don't just have one moral motive. We might feel the pull of unity and also the pull of equality matching, even though they lead to conflicting judgments.

TR: Sometimes they're going to complement each other and sometimes they are going to be conflicting. If we have rival gangs and one member shoots another member of the other gang, the other gang may feel a desire for eye-for-an-eye revenge. They want to take someone out in that person's gang, but because of unity they don't have to take the shooter out. They can take anyone in that group. So that's a way of combining unity and equality.

TS: Right, the revenge is equality matching, but the selection of the target of the revenge comes from the communal framework. So that's a case where they complement each other. Can you give an example of when they conflict and how your theory makes sense of this?

AF: Let me take that same example. Somebody in your gang kills somebody in my gang. Equality matching demands in a feuding context that we (in some communal way) kill one of yours. But, I may also have a sense of communal connection to the person I have a chance to kill. Maybe he was on my basketball team. Or maybe he was my friend at one point. So in the communal way I feel that I don't want to kill him, but in the equality matching way I feel like I have to kill him. One motive may be stronger than the other. It may be that you don't kill him because he was your friend growing up together. So maybe you don't kill him, or maybe you do, depending on the relative strength of those motives. It depends, in effect, on the relative importance of the relationships.

TR: I think what Alan is saying at the end there is pretty critical. Which relationship motivates you the most? That's how these conflicts are resolved.

TS: I was thinking of an example, say, Sergeant Joe Darby, the whistleblower in the Abu Ghraib scandal. In that case, he felt the pull of unity with his fellow MPs and his larger unit. But that was trumped by … what exactly? What framework is that latter motive in?

AF: He has many motives there. One is having the back of his comrades, loyalty to the service and to his particular unit. But he also has the obligation to obey orders. And he also has moral obligations to the state which has authority over him. And he also has a sense of communal sharing as a citizen of the nation and as a human being. So, he may report it because of what the authorities require, or he may report it out of a sense of compassion. In that case he's thinking, "These are human beings like me who are being humiliated and killed and tortured. And that's a violation of communal sharing because what hurts you hurts me."

TS: So communal sharing can expand to the whole human race at that point? Or even beyond?

AF: Even beyond. People in the Jain religion regard all sentient beings as morally significant. And you wouldn't want to kill or injure any of them.

TR: In the Abu Ghraib case, you can think about the salience of what was happening as a way of strengthening communal ties to the victim. Now we don't typically see this kind of communal connection to abstract others in the world. But when I talk about constituting that relationship, that's exactly what I mean. You're building it through the experience of seeing another suffer, those are the proximate cues we use to constitute relationships.

TS: That's where the relationship is established. Not in the abstract idea of other people. But in the actual experience, when you see a concrete, real person suffering, then you feel communal attachment.

TR: Right, and oftentimes there are going to be huge competing motives across these kinds of things. And that's when we see people in internal conflict. That's when people struggle. Because oftentimes people make a decision that they know is "right" in some sense. But what they really mean is that it is right in terms of one of their relational obligations but wrong in terms of another. And they feel guilty about that.

TS: This is my favorite thing about the theory, what drew me to it originally. It gives us a kind of new lens to see through, a new way of understanding conflict, both between people and within the same person.

3 How Cultures Implement Moral Frameworks

TS: Alan, you mentioned earlier that cultures implement these relationship frameworks in different ways and at different times. Can your theory explain or predict which model a culture will be disposed to implement?

AF: Well, there are huge technical factors in which relational models people use, but there are also social–ecological factors. It can depend on, as Marx said, the system of production, how people are subsisting.[5] Certain relationships will be more or less important, depending on the population density and the ways people need each other just to survive. If you're hunter-gatherers, then you kind of need to be sharing a lot because, well, you know, if you break your leg well who's going to feed you? And if you go out foraging and you don't get much of anything today, you need to count on others to help you.

TR: In environments that are more unpredictable, you're going to have a greater need of those kinds of social insurances. As you gain predictability over your environments, the need to have strong communal ties diminishes to a certain extent. So we also have to consider the costs of these different kinds of relations, the returns on various types of actions in your environment, and the levels of interdependence among your group. Thus, there may be a universal structure to the moral motives people have, but different social conditions will favor the emergence of some motives over others. And these motives which will be implemented in myriad ways, leading to intense diversity across cultures.

TS: Do you have an example of that?

TR: Take norms about private property, which vary across situations and cultures. One of our papers with Daniel Nettle and Karthik Panchanathan suggests that there will be more private property in societies that have a lot of technologies and abilities to reduce the costs of controlling resources through policing. And within a given society, things that are more easily controlled, like tools, will be more likely to be owned, while things that are harder to manage, like land, will be more likely to be communally shared. Here's a situation where a simple parameter like costs helps us understand the evolution of moral norms concerning which things are privately owned and which are communally shared.

AF: That doesn't mean people are thinking about those things consciously, of course. These are more ultimate than proximate factors.[6]

TR: All of these factors get instantiated in the culture and then the culture develops along those lines. Then you get historical changes and eventually you get these kinds of changes across groups.

TS: So you don't expect a perfect match … there's no reason to expect it to be optimal at any given time, but the structure, the ecological–social structure can be broadly predictive of the kinds of models that will be emphasized.

AF: It's no accident that Bentham and Mill developed utilitarianism as a formal moral system at the time that market pricing was becoming the central form of interaction among human beings in England.

4 Is Violence and Even Rape Morally Motivated?

Note: *Some readers may find this section distressing. Please remember that Rai and Fiske are speaking descriptively about violence and sexual assault and do not endorse the motivations behind these actions in any way.*

TS: In your previous work, you stated that a lot of behavior we might think of as amoral or immoral is in fact morally motivated—at least, in the mind of the agent. Your new book *Virtuous Violence* puts this theory to the test. It argues that most violent actions are morally motivated, right?

AF: Right.

TS: So let me begin by asking a methodological question. How do you distinguish actions that truly stem from moral motives versus selfishly motivated actions that are only given post hoc moral justifications.

AF: We were very concerned when we started work on this that all we would find were rationalizations and justifications. But there are several things that show us that this isn't the case. One is that people often explain what they've done in a way that makes perfect sense to them and to their peers— but it doesn't exculpate them in the least.

TS: You mean from an outsider's perspective?

AF: Right, the explanation can even make their situation worse from the point of view of the legal system, or the other consequences that are going to befall them. A rapist says, well, you know, I raped these women because my girlfriend was disrespectful to me and she didn't give me sex when I wanted it. I couldn't get at my girlfriend, but I killed these other women to get back at women for disrespecting me. And we think "whoa, that isn't going to get your sentence reduced!"

TS: So we can be confident that it's their real motive rather than a post hoc justification, because there's no benefit to them for giving it. And there may be a cost.

AF: Yes. And the other thing is that often people tell you about their motives beforehand. And what they tell you about their motives is completely in line with the beliefs of their subculture, their reference group, friends, and family. In many cases the larger society says, "Good on you, that was the right kind of violence to do, of course you should do that." And the community applauds them. People say, "That's exactly what I would do in the same circumstance. And by the way I actually did that a few years ago ..."

TS: So the outsider can discern the motives behind the action from how it's regarded within perpetrator's larger community.

TR: And again, that may not be exculpatory for the community either. They may be putting themselves in harm's way by offering support for the agent of violence. And that tells us a lot. So while we can't exactly get at the internal psychology of a perpetrator in all cases, the justifications they provide are still quite informative. For example, a person might kill somebody and then go back to their neighborhood and brag about it to everyone. That's not going to keep them from getting caught. But it potentially reveals to us the standards of that neighborhood community.

TS: So let's take the most controversial case in your book, in the case of rape.

TR: Rape is the most controversial case—you think?[7]

TS: It's ironic in a way because probably the most horrific practice you talk about in the book is honor killings.[8] But it seems less controversial to say that honor killings are morally motivated. In so many honor killings, the perpetrators have no desire to kill their daughter or sister. It pains them. They feel tremendous grief, they hate themselves afterwards, but they still think they did the right thing. From their perspective, it was a moral obligation. Of course, we think the morality that grounds the practice is horribly misguided. But it is a kind of morality. On the other hand, in the case of rape it seems harder to view the motivations as moral in any recognizable sense of the word.

AF: Well first of all let me say, I found writing this book to be an upsetting and unpleasant job in many ways. And this part was some of the worst. When we started looking at this, we didn't know what we would find. We looked at each kind of violence and asked "is this kind of violence morally motivated?" And we looked at different practices in different cultures.

TS: So you were open to the answer being no.

AF: Yeah, well you have to be.

TS: Of course.

AF: And it wasn't obvious to me when I looked at rape whether we would find moral motives. But almost all the research on rape shows that sex is very rarely the deciding motive. There may be cases where people are motivated by sex, especially in partner rape. But in a huge number of cases, probably the majority although we don't know the exact statistics, what men are trying to do when they rape women is to show that they are entitled to, and *have*, authority over women. They're trying to show that women are subordinate and should do what they are told. And having forcible sex is a way of asserting what the perpetrator genuinely believes is his legitimate authority.

TS: So according to your view, the framework and corresponding motive for sexual assault is authority ranking and hierarchy? The rapists are asserting their authority and making sure that their "subordinates" submit in the proper way?

AF: One way to think about it is this. Until a generation or so ago, there was no crime of spousal rape. In most states in the US, if a man wanted to have sex with his wife and she refused, he was entitled to use force to have sex with her. She couldn't bring a case of "rape" against her husband because there was no such thing. Your husband couldn't rape you because he was morally and legally entitled to force you to have sex.

Many men still adhere to that idea. Most rapists seem to think that this is not just true between spouses, it's true of all men and all women in certain circumstances. In their view, women who are dressed a certain way have given permission and given license, and if they resist well that's just their fault. They have it coming because of the way they're dressed or if they're in a certain place in a certain time. Moreover, coercive sex is a way of asserting the superiority that men are rightly entitled to.

TS: Which would count as morally motivated?

AF: Yes. Now there is a second motive as well. You find this in gang rape, and sometimes perhaps rape in war, although rape in war may have other motives as well. Rape in war is often done to humiliate the other side and assert status. Not so much over the women but over the defeated fighters who can't protect their women. And gang rape seems to be motivated most often, primarily, by a communal sharing motive—to be one of the guys rather than one of the people who fails to participate. It's almost like having a meal together, or something, sharing a beer or something, sharing in the woman is ... I mean, it's so awful I can't talk about it.

TS: It's a way of reinforcing or cementing the bonds of the group.

AF: That's right. And the fact that there is a body and bodily substance involved in communal sharing makes it even more powerful. So sharing bodily substances, in this case mixing up your semen inside this woman, is a way of very deeply bonding. And when somebody is there who doesn't participate, they're harassed by the other guys who say "what, aren't you one of us? What's the matter?" And there's also a status thing because then they're going to be humiliated as un-masculine and un-male and wimpy if they don't do it.

TR: So, in the case of gang rape, the relationship to the victim is not what's important.

AF: That's right. There may be no relationship with the victim. Often it's just a null relationship. She is not treated as a human being. But there is a very strong relationship among the rapists. And again, I just can't emphasize enough that I'm talking descriptively and I find this absolutely unthinkably horrific.

TR: Here's a simple prediction that I have no idea how to test. I'm sure there are ways though. You might predict that dehumanization as a facilitator of violence would be greater in gang rape cases than in other rape cases.

TS: Because when the rapist is just one person, the goal would be more focused on the rapist's relationship to the victim.

AF: If the victim isn't a person, then there's no relationship and nothing is being achieved.

TR: Here's another mid-tier case. Think of the kinds of sexual conquests that groups of men cheer on among one another. If a guy is going out there and successfully having sex with a number of high-status women and that man comes back to his social group, the actions are treated as virtuous within that group. He's admired, he's elevating his own status.

TR: Tamler, you said earlier that it's easier to see honor killings as morally motivated than it is with rape, right?

TS: Morally motivated but of course not morally correct.

TR: Yes. The reason for that might be that within our folk morality, we have this idea that restoring honor or status is within the moral sphere, but that enhancing honor proactively shouldn't count. Enhancing status or esteem shouldn't count as moral. But I don't see any logical reason why that should be the case.

TS: Why not?

TR: Why should we only count it as moral when you return yourself to your prior state? If you've been shamed or shunned and you take certain actions to redeem yourself, then it counts. But if you proactively go out and try to enhance your honor in the group, that doesn't count. That doesn't make any sense from my perspective.

AF: And we know that there are all kinds of contests of violence, from football to jousting to Sir Lancelot killing every other knight he ran into, to Billy the Kid, and John Dillinger. People get status from violence, and violence is used as a way of saying "look, I'm better than you."

TS: I see what you're saying. According to your view, if your action gets you a bump in status, it counts as morally motivated.

TR: Well it can if that was the motivation in the perpetrator's mind.

AF: And if the perpetrator believes that this is legitimate—a legitimate means of enhancing status.

TR: This is getting to what I was talking about before. One thing our theory does is expand the sphere of the moral. It expands it well beyond what a lot of people are comfortable with. Things like increasing status, etiquette violations, various cases where being highly skilled in certain domains are important. And accidents, non-intentional actions, can still have moral significance.

5 Implications for Blame and Punishment

TS: I want to jump to the legal and moral implications in whatever time we have left. Let's start with the legal implications. One thing you bring up is the *mens rea* (or 'guilty mind') principle which states that in order for people to be culpable for a crime, they have to know that what they're doing is wrong. One way to interpret your theory is that it reduces the number of cases in which people acted with *mens rea*, and therefore the number of cases in which people are legally culpable. In fact, if most people regard their violent acts as morally right, that would mean that there are very few cases of actual *mens rea*. Is that an interpretation you endorse?

AF: Well at least we want to raise the issue. The notion of moral wrongdoing or culpability is based in Anglo-Saxon law. It is based on this notion of *knowing* wrongdoing, intending to do wrong, intending evil. And we argue that people are very rarely intending to do evil. They are intending to do what they think is the right thing. Now, they may be aware that there are competing codes. They may be aware that the legal system regards what they're doing as wrong. But nevertheless they think that their more important relationships require the action to be performed.

So then the question is, well, what is the meaning of punishing somebody who thinks they did the right thing? Is the punishment going to have any effect? Why are we punishing them? We might abhor what they do, we might want to prevent them from ever doing it again, but what is the meaning of punishing somebody for something they were sure was right?

TS: Isn't a more plausible reading of *mens rea* that they only need to know their action was (a) illegal, and (b) against the conventional moral codes of the society they're living in? Does *mens rea* really require that there was no moral motive behind the action? Let's take a nice case, given all the ugly cases we've been talking about, civil disobedience. In acts of civil disobedience, you deliberately break the law. You're clearly doing what you think is right, and at the same time accept a kind of legal responsibility.

AF: But the whole idea of civil disobedience is that it can be acceptable. Almost everyone would agree that crimes that are motivated by civil disobedience should probably get a lighter sentence than crimes performed for selfish reasons, right?

TS: That's true, but that may be because it comes from motives that we approve of as a society. It seems unfair to conflate acts of civil disobedience with acts that try to increase our own status at the expense of somebody else's. Both count as morally motivated on your view, but I guess …

TR: But oftentimes civil disobedience is about increasing our own group's status, right?

AF: Yeah, exactly.

TR: If we look at the civil rights movement that's exactly what it was, it was about increasing their status.

TS: Or restoring their status, or bringing it up to par.

TR: Sure, but again you're drawing a distinction between bringing up to equal versus taking equal and moving up higher. And I don't see what logically distinguishes these two cases. From our perspective, the only reason they *feel* different is because you're implicitly using an equality framework to understand how ethnic groups should relate. But for people using an authority framework, they might see civil rights protests as an illegitimate crime, no different than any illegal theft of something that does not belong to you. And indeed I suspect this is how many southern whites and their legal systems perceived blacks and the civil rights movement.

AF: Let me give you another example, Tamler. A guy is brought to trial for assault, OK? He was hitting somebody and hitting him and finally hitting him so hard the other guy was knocked unconscious and couldn't get up. But suppose we find out that actually this happened in an organized boxing match. In general, abstractly, one might say it doesn't matter what it was, you were hitting him. You knew you were hurting him. And you knew you were knocking him unconscious and that was your goal. But if it's a boxing match we usually say well, OK, no penalty.

TS: That's not a fair analogy because …

AF: Why isn't it a fair analogy?

TS: Because the boxers know that what they're doing is both legal and accepted within the norms of their society. It's not like the boxers just thought they were pummeling someone but lucked out because they found themselves in a boxing ring.

AF: I'm not talking about the perpetrator. I'm talking about us, as a legal system. Why do we say it's OK to knock somebody unconscious in a boxing match but it's not OK to knock somebody unconscious if they disrespect you?

TS: Well that's just the law. I mean, if you want to challenge the law that's fine. But that's a different question than the question of legal responsibility once the law is in place, right?

AF: First of all let me say I don't have a position on this *mens rea* issue, I'm just raising the issue of what it might mean to discover that people who are intending to commit acts of violence are usually intending to do right. What is the implication for our legal system? And in particular, should we be punishing people as opposed to other approaches, such as truth and reconciliation, apology, or something like that.

TS: Some sort of restorative approach.

AF: Yes, some kind of restorative justice approach, maybe. We need to ask: what are we doing when we punish people for doing something they thought was right?

TR: So when I hear your question Tamler it strikes me that you're asking something that's slightly different from how Alan is responding. You're asking, legally, can it just be the case that the perpetrator needs only to know the cultural norms of the legal governing body in order to justify punishment? I think that's fine, and potentially true. But I don't think psychologically that's what people are doing. Psychologically, what's going on (and this has become very salient to me as the book has come out and people have gotten upset over it) is that people want to live in a world where we all agree about what is right and wrong. Because then, when somebody does something wrong, they did it even though they believed it was wrong. And then it's easier for us to blame and punish them, right?

TS: I see what you're saying. We feel better about our retributive impulses in those cases.

TR: As soon as we introduce the idea that the perpetrator disagrees with us about the wrongness of the action, then we start to ask the questions that Alan was asking. And that's uncomfortable. People have a very strong desire to be able to blame and punish.

TS: People want criminals to commit crimes because they're just inherently bad, or inherently selfish.

TR: They want it to be true that the defendant himself agrees with the rule and violated it anyway. And we're saying in the book that this is rarely the case. And that makes blame and punishment far less satisfying. And in some of the cases, as Alan suggested, that could potentially lead people to punish less.

TS: Or to punish in a different way—a restorative model maybe, which seems to fit really nicely with your theory. I think you're onto something with that diagnosis. People are uncomfortable with moral disagreement in cases of punishment. They're more comfortable punishing people who agree about the moral codes and are just acting from immoral motives. So let me ask you then: do you think another source of discomfort is that genuine moral disagreement calls into doubt whether certain acts "really" are morally right and certain things really are wrong.

TR: Sure. People want a realist world, they want an objective basis for morality. They want a tablet out there that has commandments on it.

TS: But you both resist the idea that this sort of fundamental disagreement has anti-realist implications in metaethics. You say "we're just giving you this descriptive story." We talked about this on the podcast a little bit,[9] but I wonder if people are right about the implications of your theory. In other words, if your theory is true, then it's harder to morally condemn the practices of other cultures or groups, at least in a philosophically justifiable way.

TR: So you're suggesting that if we're right, when we're condemning another group, we're really just imposing our group's views on the other one, right? And the more powerful group will win out, essentially.

TS: Right, I do think it's a legitimate source of concern for people who want an objective morality.

AF: One way of thinking about the book is that it just takes the fundamental axiom of anthropology and applies it to violence. The fundamental axiom of anthropology is: if you want to understand something that somebody is doing, look at it from their point of view—which means within the framework of their culture and the culturally defined circumstances that they find themselves in.

So, the problem that you're talking about is the same problem that we face in general with regard to other cultures. What they're doing may look foolish, abhorrent, irrational, and so forth from our point of view, but that's because we're looking at it from our point of view. Most of what people are doing makes perfect sense within their culture, within their social–relational context. And that's true of violence just like everything else.

TS: So are you saying that there's no view from nowhere—no unbiased perspective that can adjudicate between these two sets of inconsistent moral systems?

AF: Well I don't know if there's a view from nowhere, but everyone has to live a life, you have to take some view. But I think that it's important before you take that view to understand that other people have other views. From other perspectives, those people are not simply being evil or stupid or whatever. What they're doing makes sense from within their framework. However, once you've really, really taken that to heart, you *don't* have to say "OK, just go ahead, do whatever your culture dictates." I don't know the detailed ethnography of ISIS, but I believe that probably the ISIS people are doing what they think is morally right. There may be a few psychopaths there but that's the exception. And it doesn't mean that I say "well, OK, ISIS, go ahead and kidnap, rape, execute, torture people, burn them alive, that's fine." So even if it makes sense to them, even if drawing and quartering made moral sense to the people who did it in medieval Europe, *I* say, it's a good thing they stopped—and *I'm* committed to stopping anyone from torturing or killing.

TS: And you're saying that from your point of view. And that's what we all have to do—make judgments from our own point of view. What about you, Tage? Do you want to take any metaethical stand here? Do you think your descriptive account undermines the prospects of moral objectivism?

TR: I suppose it depends on the kind of moral objectivism/realism you mean. If you mean realism in the sense that moral claims like 'killing is wrong' have the same truth value as '$2 + 2 = 4$'—meaning that the moral claim would be true even if human beings and their evolutionary and cultural history never existed, then no, our theory doesn't undermine that kind of realism because the idea is already patently absurd. I'm always floored when an academic asks me if our theory implies that nothing is 'really' wrong, as if such a thing was possible in the first place. If you are a scientist doing science, then you have to regard moral claims as preferences, they simply don't have the same truth value as facts. On my reading of the history of philosophy, moral philosophers who subscribe to this strain of moral realism have just been engaged in a long, sad game of motivated reasoning since the Enlightenment. They desperately want morality to have an objective basis, but they don't want that objectivity to be derived from God. So they have spent hundreds of years jumping through hoops to try to argue for an objective basis to morality grounded in logic. And to top it off, they invariably find that in fact, thanks to happy coincidence, the correct moral rules are those generally held by likeminded Western academics. On the list of ideas that are ready to die, moral realism (and the contemporary moral philosophy that supports it) would be near the top. The only way to have a realist basis to morality is to draw on the supernatural.

Now, I think a more interesting question is this. Given the kinds of preferences that people naturally have, are there better or worse ways to live that we can confidently prescribe? I think the short answer is that you have to make decisions in the world. Even not making a decision is still a decision. People look at our work and say "oh, you're relativists." No, I believe people can be wrong. We could look carefully at a cultural practice in theory, like female genital mutilation, and get a deep understanding of what those cultural groups are trying to achieve through the practice. And it could be that there are alternative ways to achieve that same thing that would lead people to be more satisfied. But if that's our approach, then knowing about these kinds of relational models and moral motives is going to help us to make those kinds of prescriptive judgments, even if we are imposing them on others sometimes. But practically, that's going to be really difficult, just to be clear, right?

TS: Sure. You don't focus on this much in your work, but your account doesn't rule out that some moral disagreement is rooted in empirical disagreement. Even in cases where people are morally motivated, they could be working from a false set of empirical assumptions. Maybe an implausible religious commitment or a false belief about the effect of their action on a particular relationship.

TR: That's right. In the article, though, we were suggesting that people have gone too far with this idea. They think whenever there's a moral disagreement, it's always just a misunderstanding or an empirical mistake on one side or something. But sometimes there are just values that are incommensurate against each other. It's not always just a factual disagreement.

6   Starting a New Morality? Here's What You Need to Know

TS: Alan, if you had to describe your philosophical view, what would you call yourself?

AF: I'm a naturalist. And also, I'm a … I'm not sure what the philosophical term is …

TR: Pluralist maybe?

AF: Yeah, in the sense that I believe that for the human mind and human minds in concert, there really are these four basic moral motives. People find love, care, compassion, a sense of mutual responsibility, the idea that have each other's back, they find all of that deeply powerful. They find communal sharing relationships enormously meaningful for their own sake, not just as means to survival but just for their own sake. And although this isn't a popular idea in the West maybe, everywhere else in the world has taken for granted that people find good hierarchical relations to be worthwhile. Of course, any kind of relationship can be exploited or violated, but people find having a place in the hierarchy enormously meaningful, as long as the people above them are looking out for them, guiding them and not exploiting them. And maybe the Pope or God or the chief of the village, he's entitled to more than you. But he also has much more responsibility than you.

TS: Right.

AF: And people everywhere in some contexts seek equality, fairness, evenness, and also proportionality. So if these empirical descriptions are correct, if people really do have these moral frameworks built into them, then in the context of prescriptive morality, you can't just pick any moral system and expect people to adhere to it. These frameworks offer goods that people find to be goods. And the goods are not restricted to getting enough to eat and not suffering pain. There are goods in having solidarity, having respect and deference, having equal matching, and having proportionality. And these goods are intrinsic to human nature. So whatever your prescriptive morality, it has to take human nature into account. And human nature is not simply or purely oriented toward individual maximization of security and pain avoidance.

TS: So based on what you just said, I take it that, for example, utilitarianism doesn't come out so well.

AF: Well utilitarianism is, in a sense, market pricing applied to morality.

TS: So you'd say that it doesn't take the other three frameworks into account, not enough anyway. It doesn't regard them as intrinsically good. It only honors them insofar as they lead to a net increase in utility.

AF: That's right. Utilitarianism gives you one moral answer, but obedience and deference and filial piety and doing God's work or whatever gives you another answer. (I'm an atheist, but I'm speaking descriptively here.) Utilitarianism doesn't honor the idea that people in some cases might sometimes want things to be even and fair even if the total welfare was less than it would be if it was uneven.

TR: So if we're taking a naturalistic approach, then the relational models are really good candidates for figuring out what which kinds of goods people are predisposed toward pursuing. If we're talking prescriptively, our account suggests that there won't necessarily be an optimal balance of these things that will be true everywhere.

TS: But there will be better or worse ways of achieving the goods.

TR: Right, and when they get extremely out of balance, then a social group might have a problem and want to change that. To make this a little more concrete, we can think of those Hippie communes that really tried to push pure communal sharing in every aspect of life. That didn't work. They had to introduce at least some forms of bureaucracy, tracking of contributions, and other market principles in order to survive. Meanwhile, a lot of philosophical approaches try to emphasize intense equality where you treat everyone exactly the same regardless of your relationship ... people won't do it. Same for intense utilitarianism, or dictatorships that only have hierarchy and nothing else. You do need some sort balance but not all groups are going to be falling within this balance comfortably.

TS: And it can be calibrated differently.

TR: Right, there can be different calibrations. So unless it's way out of whack, we won't necessarily want to intervene and change that culture even when they're doing things that might be morally offensive to our sensibilities. It won't be possible to maximize all of the moral goods because the motives are incommensurate. But I suspect that there is a wide range of combinations that cultures will find satisfying.

AF: Yeah, and I think that you're going to find that there's moral conflict both within and between people in terms of which relational model they think they should be applying. Because culture doesn't determine the only ways we can think about things. And culture is polymorphous, there are many different prototypes and precedents within the culture for how to organize any particular interaction. There isn't only one way of doing things, even within a single culture.

   In one sense, our theory offers a pessimistic view because it says there is always going to be room for debate and disagreement. But on the other hand, maybe that's not a bad thing. Maybe the fact that we can constantly reconsider the ways we want to relate is not a bad thing. Maybe that's something that we should keep open.

Notes

1 *Virtuous Violence*, p. xxii, Cambridge University Press. 2015.
2 "Moral psychology is relationship regulation: moral motives for unity, hierarchy, equality, and proportionality." *Psychological Review* 118(1) (Jan. 2011): 57–75.
3 I'm referring to their well-known 2011 article cited above (n. 2).
4 By 'descriptive,' Fiske means that he is only trying to explain why moral disagreement occurs. He is not making a moral judgment that endorses any particular side.
5 Very roughly, Karl Marx argued that the economic structure of a given society determined which moral and political principles it embraced rather than the other way around.
6 In this context, a proximate factor is the immediate (even conscious) mechanism behind a cultural norm. An ultimate factor is a reason for why the moral norm evolved in a given society.
7 Not surprisingly, Fiske and Rai have taken some heat for their view that sexual assault can be morally motivated. Again, they are giving a purely descriptive account of the psychology behind this act. They do not regard their theory as a defense or justification of rape in any way.
8 An honor killing is the murder of a female family member because she is suspected of having extra-marital sex. This murder is committed to restore the honor of the family in the eyes of the larger community. See also Chapters 6 (Miller) and 7 (Appiah).
9 In episodes 31 and 32 of the Very Bad Wizards podcast, Pizarro and I talk about Fiske and Rai's theory and its implications for metaethics.

Questions for Discussion

1 What are the four elemental forms of relationships in Fiske's theory?
2 How might values like fairness change depending on which relational framework the agents are in? What frameworks were influencing Joe Darby's decision to blow the whistle at Abu Ghraib? In general, what determines which framework wins out?
3 How might factors like predictability of environment or ability to control resources affect the frameworks people may use?

4   How does Fiske and Rai's theory help us better understand moral disagreement?

5   What do Fiske and Rai mean when they claim that most violent actions—even acts like murder and sexual assault—are morally motivated? What are some examples that they use to support their claim?

6   Why does Fiske and Rai's theory raise questions about the *mens rea* requirement for legal culpability?

7   How might the recognition most people are morally motivated make us question our impulses to blame or punish?

8   What is the fundamental axiom of anthropology? How is it relevant to the metaethical issues that we discuss in section 5?

9   Why might moralities that focus on only one relational framework (like hippies and communal sharing or utilitarians and market pricing) be doomed to fail?

Suggested Readings

Fiske, Alan and Tage Rai. *Virtuous Violence: Hurting and Killing to Create, Sustain, End, and Honor Social Relationships*. Cambridge: Cambridge University Press, 2014.

Rai, Tage. "How Could They? People Do Violence Because Their Moral Codes Demand It." *aeon magazine* June, 2015. http://aeon.co/magazine/philosophy/people-do-violence-because-their-moral-codes-demand-it

Rai, Tage and Alan Fiske. "Moral Psychology Is Relationship Regulation: Moral Motives for Unity, Hierarchy, Equality, and Proportionality." *Psychological Review* 118(1) (2011): 57–75.

Assorted Media and Podcast Pairings

Fiske, Alan and Tage Rai. "Killing for good? 'Virtuous Violence' Examines Morality in Violence." Interview at AirTalk (Jan. 15, 2015): www.scpr.org/programs/airtalk/2015/01/15/41125/killing-for-good-virtuous-violence-examines-morali

——. "When Good People Kill." Interview at the Brian Lehrer Show, WNYC (Jan. 15, 2015): www.wnyc.org/story/when-good-people-kill

Very Bad Wizards, Episode 31 "An Anthropologist's Guide to Moral Psychology." http://verybadwizards.com/episodes/31

Very Bad Wizards, Episode 32 "Disagreeing about Disagreement." http://verybadwizards.com/episodes/32

Very Bad Wizards, Episode 39 "How Many Moralities Are There? (Part 1)." http://verybadwizards.com/episodes/39

Very Bad Wizards, Episode 40 "How Many Moralities Are There? (Part 2—with Jesse Graham)." http://verybadwizards.com/episodes/40

16 Stephen Stich

"I Walk the Line"

Of all the stereotypes about philosophers, perhaps the most durable is the one about how we spend our days in armchairs, content to expound about the laws of the universe, gazes securely affixed to navels. (Sometimes there's a pipe and a tweed jacket with elbow patches thrown into the mix as well.) The idea behind this picture is that there's a sharp distinction between philosophers on the one hand, and scientists—those people who think you actually have to leave their armchairs to observe the world if they're going to learn anything about it—on the other. Like many stereotypes, this one contains more than a kernel of truth; indeed, many philosophers would embrace it. But there are and always have been exceptions: philosophers who have devoted their careers to blurring or obliterating the line between philosophical and scientific inquiry. Stephen Stich—Board of Governors Professor at Rutgers University—is perhaps the most prominent contemporary example of this kind of philosopher. Beginning with his groundbreaking work on cross-cultural diversity in beliefs about knowledge and truth, and continuing with his more recent work in ethics, Dr. Stich has revealed the vital importance of taking an empirically informed approach to age-old philosophical problems.

Bringing science into philosophy may not seem all that controversial, but many philosophers treat this idea as pure poison. No area in the field generates as much hostility. Philosophers are part of the academy, after all, and will go to great lengths to defend their turf. But after publishing four books and a list of articles far too numerous to mention, as well as winning several prestigious lifetime-achievement awards in philosophy, Stich has been able to carve a place for empirically informed philosophy from the inside of the academic establishment. As much as anyone else in the world right now, Stich has made working on the vague boundary between philosophy and science a respectable endeavor, something you can get paid to do. For this, many young philosophers will forever be in his debt.

Our interview took place in the park outside of the Minneapolis Museum of Art, and then in the coffee shop upstairs. After talking about empirically informed philosophy in general, our discussion turned to how this approach sheds light on crucial problems in ethics. The view that emerges is not quite

*moral relativism, not quite moral nihilism or skepticism, but something stranger
and harder to pin down.*

May 2008

1 Experimental Philosophy: A Contradiction in Terms?

TAMLER SOMMERS: You came to my university this spring for our lecture
    series, and gave a talk called "Why Experimental Philosophers Are Not
    Oxymorons." First, what is experimental philosophy, exactly?

STEPHEN STICH: Well, there's an important sense in which experimental
    philosophy is a very old idea. If you go back to the seventeenth and
    eighteenth centuries, the great philosophical figures of that period were not
    only informed about the empirical sciences but in many cases contributed
    to the empirical sciences. Descartes, Berkeley, and many others. That's a
    tradition that has waxed and waned over the centuries. It certainly hasn't
    been popular in the second half of the twentieth century. As I conceive of
    it—and many other people have different accounts—experimental
    philosophy is simply using experimental and more broadly scientific
    techniques and methods to answer questions that are important in
    philosophical discussion and debate.

TS: Can you give an example?

SS: Sure. Characterized in that way, lots of non-philosophers do experimental
    philosophy. My favorite example is the work of Daniel Batson who, as I
    see it, is one of the great experimental philosophers. He's interested in the
    traditional debate that goes all the way back to Hobbes, some would say all
    the way back to Plato, about whether human beings can be *genuinely*
    altruistic. Batson has designed experiments to try to demonstrate that the
    answer is yes. In doing this, he's addressing a traditional philosophical
    question, a debate that's really quite central in ethics, using experimental
    means.

TS: Do you have a favorite of these experiments that you can describe?

SS: Batson's strategy is to divide and conquer. The debate in this area is
    between those who believe in human altruism on the one hand and the
    "psychological egoists" on the other. Psychological egoists are people who
    say that of course human beings *help* other people—no one has seriously
    denied that—people help each other even at a cost to themselves. But the
    deep question is: what is their motive? The psychological egoists say that
    their motive is always self-interested in one way or another. Batson's
    strategy is to look at each of the traditional self-interested explanations of
    helping behavior and try to design experiments where you pit an altruistic
    explanation and an egoistic explanation against each other.

       The goal is to design experiments that will enable you to rule out one or
    the other. Perhaps his most famous series of experiments looks at one
    egoist idea, a particularly popular one, both traditionally, going all the way
    back to Hobbes, and also in the contemporary literature, particularly in the

social sciences. He gives this idea an unfortunate name: "the aversive-arousal reduction hypothesis."

TS: Unfortunate, to say the least …

SS: Batson is a great psychologist but his nomenclature leaves something to be desired. What this unfortunate name refers to is the egoistic hypothesis that says you help people because seeing their distress, being aware of their distress, causes *you* to be distressed. And your motive in helping people, the deep motive, the underlying motive, is to alleviate your own distress— your "aversive-arousal."

TS: It's worth helping people so that you can stop feeling their pain.

SS: Yes. So, simplifying a little bit, Batson set up situations in which an experimental participant can either help someone or simply leave. And he manipulates whether it's easy or hard to leave. The idea here is if you're genuinely altruistically motivated, if your ultimate motivation is to help the target person, the person who needs the help, then you should help whether leaving is easy or hard.

TS: How was all this measured—by whether it was easy or hard to leave?

SS: Well, let me describe the situation. In one famous experiment, participants *believe*—there's a certain amount of deception here—they *believe* they're seeing another participant over closed-circuit TV. (It's actually a video tape.) And they believe that their job is to watch and evaluate the other participant as she does a learning experiment that requires her to get mild electric shocks. But she's having evident distress at the electric shocks, though they're supposed to be relatively mild. She explains to the experimenter that because of a childhood trauma, she is particularly sensitive to relatively mild electric shocks, and so she's finding this really distressing. Then the experimenter on the tape says, "Okay, well maybe the other participant (who is the real experimental subject here) would be willing to change places with you." At this point, the tape stops, and the real experimental subject is asked whether he or she would be willing to change places with the person being shocked. The manipulation on "easy to escape" versus "hard to escape" is that in one case, the subjects are told that if they choose not to change places with the other participant, then they are free to go. The other group of people are told, "Well, if you choose not to change places with the woman getting the shocks, then you have to continue the experiment and watch eight more trials." So they would have to watch her getting shocked a number of additional times. Now, suppose you're motivated by "aversive-arousal reduction"—that is to say, the desire to stop the unpleasant reaction you're having because you see this other person getting shocked. If that's your motivation, then in one experimental condition you can simply walk out and not have to worry about that anymore. However, if you have to endure eight more trials of watching the person get shocked, then, well—

TS: —You'd be more motivated to switch places, according to the egoistic theory.

SS: Right. And so what happens is—it's slightly complicated— there's another manipulation to affect the extent to which the participant empathizes with the person being shocked. Batson's hypothesis is that you do get real altruism, but only in high-empathy conditions. And in fact participants in the high-empathy condition did agree to switch places with the person getting shocked, whether leaving was easy or hard.

TS: Whether or not they would have to stay and watch more shocks.

SS: Yes. So I think that Batson's work really does move the egoism versus altruism debate forward, which is why it's my parade case for the success of experimental philosophy. You can find the aversive-arousal reduction hypothesis—not under that horrible label, of course—in Hobbes. People have been debating the idea for centuries, and there hasn't been much progress! And here's Batson saying, Look, this doesn't establish that we are genuinely altruistic, of course, but it does establish that if you pit altruism against this particular version of the egoistic hypothesis, this egoistic hypothesis turns out to be untenable; it's not what's happening.

2 "Large Parts of What Philosophers Have Done Are Not Worth Doing"

TS: All this sounds wonderful. So why, in your judgment, have philosophers been so resistant—hostile, really—to experimental or empirically informed approaches to our subject?

SS: Good question, and I'm sure I can't give you a complete answer. You're certainly right about the hostility out there. I think that there are a couple of factors that can partially explain it. The first is suggested by one of my favorite quotes, a passage in "Fin de siècle Ethics," which is an essay written by three of the most eminent moral theorists of our time, Allan Gibbard, Peter Railton, and Stephen Darwall. In the passage that I particularly like, they say that too many philosophers—and parenthetically they add "We don't exempt ourselves"—are content to simply *invent* the facts when they need factual claims to buttress their philosophical arguments. Think about this for a moment: it's a very shocking observation. Philosophers—and I think this was particularly rampant in the last 50 years of the previous century, and still to a very considerable extent in this century—philosophers have gotten into a pattern of simply declaring various sorts of things to be the case, things that are clearly empirical matters, *without a shred of evidence for it*! There's something deeply intellectually disreputable about simply inventing the facts.

TS: So philosophers see this movement as a threat to their unrespectable habits?

SS: Well, the contrast is that the experimental philosophers are standing off to the side saying, "Look, if you're going to make an empirical claim, particularly one that it isn't obviously true, you need some *evidence.*" Inventing the facts is not a respectable activity. In many other areas of the academic world, inventing the facts would get you fired! *Disreputable* is a very mild term for it. This practice of making claims about the nature of human motivation, or about what all people would agree to, or about what people think, and pulling these facts—these putative facts—out of thin air is really something of an intellectual disgrace.

TS: But in their own minds, they're not saying, "Hey, these experimental philosophers are preventing us from continuing our disgraceful practices!" Right? So this would have to be sort of an unconscious motive for the hostility, no?

SS: Perhaps, perhaps. One of my favorite quotes is from Newton, who said "*hypotheses non fingo*"—I don't feign hypotheses. In this area, I'm just not at all sure what people are thinking. But work in experimental philosophy certainly poses a threat to those traditions in philosophy where people make clearly factual claims with no evidence. Now, I said there were two reasons that I could come up with for the controversial nature of the experimental approach. One is that it underscores the lamentable practice of inventing empirical facts to suit your theory. The other is that some of us, some experimental philosophers—and I suppose I've been one of the principal offenders—some of us have suggested that findings in experimental philosophy undermine a *major* methodology that philosophers have been using for a very long time. Arguably, this methodology goes all the way back to Socrates or Plato. It's the method of supporting philosophical theories by using intuitions.

TS: Where intuitions means …

SS: Well, of course it's complicated and controversial, but to simplify a bit: an intuition is a spontaneous judgment about whether a particular case should be classified in one way or another. So going back to Plato, it's a judgment about whether a particular case counts as an instance of justice or an instance of piety, or in the contemporary literature, it's asking whether a person in a specified situation really has knowledge of something or not. The method of attempting to capture the intuitions and supporting your theory on the basis of these intuitions is a venerable one in philosophy. It's not the only method, but it's one of the most central and most widely used methods. Now, what I've been arguing for a long time actually, and have recently begun backing up empirically, is that this entire tradition rests on a very problematic bet. It's a bet that until recently hasn't been acknowledged. It's the bet that there isn't substantial *variation* in philosophically important intuitions. In particular, that there is no cross-cultural variation.

TS: Philosophers are assuming that these intuitions are universally shared?

SS: Well, "universally" may be too strong. But they are betting that there is not a lot of cross-cultural variation. Even many proponents of this method, like my colleague Ernie Sosa, concede that if there is indeed significant intergroup variation in these intuitions—whether there is an empirical question and a hard one—then the use of these intuitions in philosophy—this whole methodology—is undermined. And if that's the case, if philosophers lose their bet, what I've been arguing is that a vast amount of what philosophers have done recently, but also going all the way back to antiquity, belongs in the rubbish bin.

So not surprisingly—if the question is why do people get their backs up about experimental philosophy—that might be a principal reason. If in fact intuitions are culturally variable, or vary by socioeconomic status, or vary in other kinds of ways, then many sorts of philosophical theories based on intuition simply are not to be trusted, and large parts of what philosophers have done are not worth doing.

TS: So for many philosophers, experimental philosophy poses a challenge not just to their own methodology, but to the history of philosophy, or at least large sections of it. I can see how that would arouse a bit of ill will.

SS: Yes. Another thing I've said—perhaps unwisely—is that philosophers typically use the doubly dubious technique of basing their theories on *their own* intuitions along with (as Alison Gopnik once put it)[1] the intuitions of the six white guys down the hall. But until very recently there has been no serious attempt to justify the technique—perhaps none since Plato. Plato at least had a theory to justify this technique. It was his theory of recollection, which says that our souls knew the truth before we were born, and that we forgot most of it when our souls got trapped in our bodies. So intuition is just a sort of recollection. Now I've never met anyone who took this theory seriously. I'm not sure Plato took it seriously. But at least he had the intellectual honesty to present a theory to justify the technique. In the time since Plato, almost no one has tried to give a theory to tell us why we should rely on intuition—why this is a good thing to do—until the last few years, when Tim Williamson, Ernie Sosa, and others have tried to address the issue. For centuries, philosophers have been basing their theories on intuition without ever having asked why that's a legitimate thing to do. So for 2,400 years we've had a methodology that had no justification. The thrust of recent work in experimental philosophy is that there are important cross-cultural and interpersonal differences in intuition. And if that's right, then providing a justification for this sort of "intuition mongering" will be much harder. I want to stress that the evidence we now have is far from conclusive; but most of the straws in the wind are pointing in the same direction. And if there are significant demographic differences in intuition, then the method of basing philosophical theories on intuition may have to be thrown out.

3 Taking on Moral Realism

TS: Of course, this challenge has serious implications for theories about the nature of knowledge and the proper way to acquire it. But I should move on to how empirical work in the sciences bears on issues in ethics. (Although of course these notions are related.) Many of your recent articles argue that work in the sciences undermines the metaethical theory of "moral realism."[2] First, for the non-philosophers out there, and maybe some of the philosophers, too, what exactly is moral realism?

SS: The term "moral realism" is used in many different ways. As I use it, it is a label for a family of theories. What they have in common is the view that moral judgments or moral beliefs are either true or false, correct or incorrect, and that some moral beliefs at least are true. My work has focused on a subset of moral realists, who argue that we should expect *convergence* or agreement in moral judgment under some type of idealized condition, like full agreement over relevant *nonmoral* facts. So for example, you and I might disagree about a moral matter if we disagree on a factual matter; we might disagree on the right policy for dealing with global warming if we also disagree about what's causing global warming. One important group of moral realists, which includes many of the moral theorists associated with Cornell University, believe that if you were to completely eliminate all factual disagreement, you'd eliminate most moral disagreement as well.

TS: To take another example, over something like gay marriage, these theorists would say that once all the relevant facts were known—the effects of gay marriage on heterosexual marriage, for example, or the effects on children, and maybe some religious issues too—then there would no longer be disagreement over whether it was morally right to allow people of the same sex to marry. And according to these theorists, whatever everyone would agree upon under these idealized conditions is morally right, objectively speaking. It's the morally *correct* view.

SS: Yes, right. The central idea is that morality is in some important ways analogous to science. In science, one expects there to be plenty of disagreement on the hard questions, but one also expects convergence over time on an increasingly large number of issues. That, of course, is what we've seen in disciplines like astronomy, chemistry, and biology, and it's what moral realists expect in morality as well. And it's here that I think that the empirical evidence is crucially important. Because what my collaborators and I have been arguing is that this isn't true. Our view is that of course you'd eliminate *some* moral disagreement if you eliminated factual disagreement, but there would still be a great deal of moral disagreement left, because moral disagreement does not arise only from disagreement over nonmoral facts. So these are the targets that we have taken aim at, these so-called "convergentist moral realists." We think that empirical work tends to undermine the claim that convergentists make, although of course the issue is far from settled.

TS: Can you give a good example of where empirical work has undermined the idea that moral views would converge under idealized circumstances?

SS: Well, I think the focus has to be on an empirically supported theory about what moral judgments are *like*. That theory has to specify what the psychological mechanisms underlying moral judgments are; it also has to provide both a developmental and an evolutionary account of why we have those psychological mechanisms. Obviously, a theory of that sort will be very complex. No single experiment or empirical observation could come close to establishing such a theory. And since it is the theory that poses the greatest challenge to moral realism, no single experiment can undermine moral realism. At best, individual studies can lend support to the theory, or to aspects of the theory.

TS: Without going into the kind of detail that would take up the rest of our time, can you describe this theory that you believe undermines moral realism of this kind?

SS: That's a tall order! The work supporting it is drawn from a lot a different areas, some of it exploring cross-cultural differences in moral judgments that don't look like they can be easily explained by differences in factual judgment.

TS: Maybe start with an example of some that work?

SS: Well, one nice example emerged in work that I have been doing in collaboration with John Doris, Kaiping Peng, and others on moral dilemmas like "the Magistrate and the Mob." As you know, the problem posed in the Magistrate and the Mob is whether the judge and the chief of police in a town should falsely accuse and convict an innocent person in order to prevent a mob from rioting and causing a lot of damage and suffering to the townspeople.

TS: This is the scenario philosophers use to pit the utilitarian principle (go with action that produces that greatest good for the greatest number) against the Kantian or deontological principle that you should never knowingly punish an innocent person, no matter how much good it will lead to.

SS: Yes, and the evidence indicates that there is a quite dramatic cross-cultural difference between Chinese and American people on these kinds of issues.

TS: The Chinese come to the more utilitarian conclusion that it's okay to convict an innocent person in order to prevent the rioting. And the Americans don't.

SS: Yes, although that's not to say they're more utilitarian. They just happen to agree with the utilitarian here. We suspect that the real explanation is that they are more communitarian. Of course, with any given result, one could worry that there is some sort of factual assumption in the background on which the two groups differ, but we argue that this is unlikely to be the case here or in a number of other cases that have been studied. What's much more likely to be the case is that there is a difference in the underlying system of norms that is more *community*-focused in Chinese culture, and more *individually* focused in the American case.

TS: And therefore that greater knowledge about other facts, or improved rationality of some kind, wouldn't resolve this moral disagreement.

SS: Yes, though that requires a considerable leap from data to theory. It would be preposterous to make that leap based on a small number of studies. But what I've tried to do, in collaboration with Chandra Sripada, is assemble a body of data from the literature in anthropology, psychology, neuroscience, experimental economics, and several other domains, to support a theory which claims that a special-purpose part of the human mind is designed to detect and store socially salient norms.

TS: Could you describe what a norm is on this account?

SS: Norms, as we conceive of them, are mentally represented rules specifying how people should or should not behave. They serve to trigger emotions and moral judgments—probably the emotions play a very important role in the production of the judgments. So the crucial bit here is that there is a component of the mind which is in one respect like the language faculty. (Only in one respect, let me stress.) It's an innate part of the mind whose function is to acquire information from the environment and to store it and use it. And we believe that, as in the case of language, once those rules are in place, it is very hard to dislodge them. In particular, learning a bunch of facts is not going to do it. So, to use a crude analogy, when you learned English as a child you internalized a set of rules in the part of the mind devoted to storing language competence. You can learn facts until you're a very old man, but that won't stop you from being an English speaker. Similarly, we claim, once you take on board the norms of the surrounding culture, there are no facts you can learn that will get those norms out of the part of the mind devoted to storing norms.

TS: And these norms are different across cultures, developed as responses to different parts of the social and physical environment.

SS: Absolutely.

TS: So to continue with the crude analogy, would you say that just as it's not more rational or more objectively correct to speak English rather than Chinese—it just depends on the environment you're in—in the same way, there's nothing more rational or objectively correct about having a certain kind of moral belief or moral judgment?

SS: Well, the view is potentially inflammatory and therefore needs to be stated with care. But on the model that Sripada and I develop, it looks to me that the appropriate thing to say about norms and moral judgments is that *they aren't the kinds of things that are correct or incorrect, true or false.* But the crucial point I want to make is that even if by using some clever philosophical tools you could develop an argument to show that moral claims can be true, that some norms are correct and some norms aren't, in an important sense that's neither here nor there. Remember, the moral realist we're focusing on is the one who says that if we just get more rational or learn some new nonmoral facts, then our moral views will converge. And my contention is that this isn't true. The norms you've taken on board are different from those that have been internalized by people in different cultures, and they lead you to make different moral judgments. Those judgments are not likely to converge no matter how many additional facts you learn. So when people in different groups have internalized very different norms, it is very likely that we're stuck with deep moral disagreement.

TS: But now there are two ways of looking at that claim. The first is that certain people, certain cultures, are stuck having false or pernicious moral views. Just like color-blind people are stuck not being able to see the redness of a rose. And that unfortunately there's nothing we can do about it. But the rose is still red. The second is that there *is no fact of the matter* about whether any particular moral belief is true or false. Assuming your work does undermine the type of realist you're targeting, would there be some other way of establishing the truth of moral claims?

SS: That's not a question that admits of a simple answer, since there are lots of ways in which a moral realist might try to establish that some moral claims are true. Some moral realists offer rather surprising and implausible accounts of the *meaning* of moral claims; others develop novel accounts of *truth.* There is plenty of logical and philosophical space for moral realists to explore. But I'm not sanguine about any of these strategies.

TS: Are there other *plausible* ways of establishing the truth of moral claims?

SS: No, I think not.

4 Are Moral Judgments Like *Chicha* Judgments?

TS: So it seems like you're arriving at a kind of moral relativism, which I agree is inflammatory. But, well, the fact that a view is inflammatory doesn't make it false. If a theory is true, it's true—whether op-ed columnists like it or not. So would you characterize the "metaethical" view (as philosophers call it) that you find most plausible as a relativist one? That is, the view that no moral judgment can be true or false objectively, universally, across all cultures?

SS: Well, I don't like to call it moral relativism; I much prefer to call it antirealism. The reason for that is that moral relativists tend to think a given judgment can be correct for one culture and incorrect for another. Whereas my kind of antirealism says no, it's not that judgments can be true in one culture but not in another culture. *None* of them is correct, no matter what culture you're in. So that's why I don't like to call it relativism. In some sense it's more radical than relativism. My view is that norms and the moral judgments to which they lead aren't in the *business* of being true or false.

TS: People certainly seem to *think* that moral judgments can be true, though, right?

SS: Well, it is clear that *some* people think that; certainly some philosophers do. But I don't think we know how widespread this belief is. I've been doing some thinking about this since you sent me your list of questions. I think a really nice analogy, and maybe a psychologically important one, too, is to certain emotions. One particularly useful example is disgust. Commonsensically, people think certain activities or foods are disgusting. My tastes run fairly low on the disgust scale: relatively few things disgust me. But one of the things that does is a South American beverage called *chicha. Chicha* is a fermented beverage, a bit like beer, prepared using human spit. What am I inclined to think about *chicha*? Well, I think it's disgusting. And the phenomenology, how it appears to me, is that the disgustingness is *something about the chicha.* I'm just detecting it. But of course, the people for whom this is a favorite beverage find nothing disgusting about it. So let's look more closely at this. Is it plausible that they're wrong and I'm right? Is there something they're missing here? Are these South Americans just confused somehow, unaware of how disgusting *chicha* is? Well, no, that's not what's going on, in spite of the fact that it seems to me that there's something objectively disgusting about *chicha*.

TS: So, we're projecting our own disgust on to the *chicha*?

SS: Yes. Actually, there are two parts of the story. The first goes back to Hume. Our minds project, they paint various things on the world, and disgustingness is one of those things. The human mind makes some things in the world appear disgusting. And it's very hard to get our heads around the fact that *chicha*, or a baby's pooey diaper, aren't objectively disgusting. The second part of the story comes from the sciences—particularly psychology and anthropology. They find that there is a great deal of cross-cultural variation in what people take to be disgusting. Moreover, there are processes that increasingly we're beginning to understand, which underlie the acquisition of disgust elicitors (or "triggers"), and in many cases those triggers are culturally local. The cultural variation and the processes underlying it make it clear that when we find something disgusting we are not detecting anything objective in the world. That's why I think disgust judgments are a useful analogy for moral judgments. Yes indeed, moral judgments present themselves to us as saying something about the world. Then we do some science on our own judgments and the mechanisms underlying them, and on the cross-cultural facts about the phenomena, and it turns out that the best science tells us that moral judgments are not detecting objective features of the world. If you and an Ecuadorian disagree about the disgustingness of *chicha*, there's nothing that's going to settle that disagreement. And similarly for moral disagreements.

TS: Okay, that's a very nice analogy for your view, but there seems to be something different between taste judgments and moral judgments—I had a similar discussion with Jon Haidt about this issue. I might find *chicha* to be completely nasty, but as soon as I learn that Ecuadorians love it, I'm happy to agree that there's no right or wrong answer about whether or not it's disgusting. In spite of that perceptual experience you talk about, people are more or less willing to be antirealists about taste judgments. By contrast, people are much more resistant to antirealism about moral judgments. Take the examples of genital mutilations or honor killings. Americans think these practices are morally wrong. And even when they learn that these are practices that run deep into the heart of other cultures, that these cultures don't see the issue in the same way we do, the reaction isn't, "Well, okay, let's agree to disagree." In this case, unlike the *chicha* case, we think honor killings or genital mutilation are objectively wrong. We think the people who perform those practices have false moral beliefs. Why would there be that extra bit of resistance when it comes to morality?

SS: Well here I would accuse you of doing what philosophers do rather too much, which is pull facts out of thin air.

TS: A nice way of describing the place I'm pulling facts out of ...

SS: Well, it's far from clear that people *do* react to disagreement in the way you describe, either on the disgust side or the moral side. Nor is it clear that everyone reacts in the same way.

TS: So you don't think that people are more resistant to antirealism about morality than they are to antirealism about taste?

SS: I guess I just don't know what the answer to that question is. It seems to me to be very much an empirical question about which we have precious little evidence.

TS: I'd agree that it's an empirical question. But even the phrase "it's a matter of taste"—that's a metaphor for antirealism, isn't it? That's what people say when they concede that there's no fact of the matter about a certain question.

SS: Well, look: even if it turns out that you're right—and this seems to me to be something that would be intriguing to explore empirically—there might be a range of reasons for that. It may be that the norm system plays an importantly different role and perhaps a much more pervasive role in people's lives than the disgust system. After all, the norm system plays a hugely important role in characterizing *who you take yourself to be*. Disgust plays some role in that, but not nearly as important a role. And there's the issue of motivation as well. Disgust can certainly motivate us, especially when it comes to avoidance. The norm system motivates us to avoid things too, but in addition the norm system can lead sometimes, not always, to punitive motivation.

TS: Actually, I'd like to talk about that. When I interviewed Michael Ruse, he argued that the evolutionary function of moral norms, moral judgments, requires that we see them objectively. In his view, the norms wouldn't function as effectively to motivate adaptive behavior—like punitive behavior—if we didn't see them as corresponding to something objective. Whereas with disgust, if you find something disgusting, that's enough motivation for you to avoid it. You don't need to see it as objectively disgusting. Whereas when we're talking about doing something immoral but very tempting, there might not be enough motivation for you to refrain from doing it unless you thought it was objectively wrong. So maybe that's where the persistent illusion of objectivity lies, in the function of these moral norms and judgments.

SS: I'd be hesitant to endorse that story for two reasons, both of them empirical. First of all, we certainly are far from having a conclusive story about why the norm system evolved. There's plenty of debate about the evolutionary function of this system, assuming the system exists. Another empirical question is: would realizing the nature of the psychology that underlies norms undermine part of your motivation to act on your norms? Here again, the answer is far from clear.

TS: In other words, you're wondering whether understanding the psychology of our norm system, and therefore believing norms not to be objective, would have any effect on our motivation whatsoever.

SS: Right. Thinking about the question makes it clear that there may be real implications of a practical sort in more deeply understanding moral psychology. If the answer is yes—if losing the sense of objectivity would undermine your motivation to act according to norms—that's something to think about when promulgating this view. But it strikes me as far from clear that this is the case. Let's think about disgust. I know a fair amount about the psychology of disgust and how disgust judgments vary across cultures. Does that in any way diminish my avoidance of the things I find disgusting? In most cases, not at all. Certainly my reluctance to drink *chicha* is not in any way diminished by my understanding that there's nothing objective about its disgustingness. Why not? Well, look, you can understand how something works, but it still works. Okay, now what about norms? You raise questions about genital mutilation, or practices in honor cultures, and it seems to me that I can perfectly well be an antirealist from the theoretical perspective, and say that my norms are not more objectively correct than those of an honor culture person. Or suppose I disagree with someone about a political issue like gay marriage, or the appropriate role of women in society. Here again, taking the theoretical perspective, I can be an antirealist and insist that their norms are neither more true nor less true than mine. Norms are just not in that business. Nonetheless, I'm *deeply wedded* to my norms; they play a large role in making me who I am. And in this respect I'm not at all unhappy about who I am. So am I motivated to act on those norms? Yes. Will I act on them? You bet I will!

5 Can Moral Intervention Be Justified? (And Does It Need to Be Justified?)

TS: You say you'll act on your norms. Will you do this even to the point of preventing other people from acting on *their* norms?

SS: Well, of course, not everything I take to be morally wrong is something I'm prepared to try to force people to stop. But in cases like genital mutilation or certain other kinds of treatment of women, the answer is most definitely yes. I recognize that other people have other norms, that there's nothing objective about theirs or mine, but I will still work very hard to try to stop them from engaging in these practices.

TS: But think how inappropriate it would be to go on a campaign, to go on some misguided mission to stop people in Ecuador from drinking *chicha*. There would be something wrong with that, right? They like *chicha*, they enjoy it. Let them drink their *chicha*. Now you used that same analogy for moral judgments—why wouldn't you feel that it's deeply inappropriate for people to be campaigning against genital mutilation or other practices arising from different norms?

SS: The answer there, it seems to me, turns on the differences between disgust psychology and norm psychology. And perhaps the differences in their functions, insofar as we understand anything about their functions. Why? Well, because in the case of norms, in addition to there being compliance motivation, there is also motivation to punish people who are norm violators. And this isn't part of the disgust system. So the psychological systems work differently. That's not surprising, since they evolved for different purposes. So you're quite right that if I find out that someone enjoys *chicha* I'm not inclined to prevent him from or to punish him for drinking it. But the norm system works differently. We *are* inclined to prevent people from violating norms and to punish them when they violate norms. So again, I'm inclined as a theoretician to say: here's how it works. But, of course, that system is still part of me. And I'm perfectly happy with this norm system being part of me. Now I concede that I might be wrong about the disconnect between psychological knowledge and moral motivation. It could turn out that if you think about the psychology of norms long enough or hard enough, that could undermine your motivation to punish norm violators and prevent people from violating your norms. But I don't see why that would happen.

TS: But it's not *just* a question of what we're inclined to do, right? There's also the question of what's *appropriate* to do. And— correct me if I'm wrong— you said that different norm systems have evolved in response to different kinds of environments. So isn't there something deeply inappropriate about converting other people in different environments and therefore with different norms to our value system?

SS: There's a lot packed into that question, so let me start by doing some unpacking. First of all, you've changed the focus a bit by asking about *converting* other people to our value system. It is far from clear to me that this is possible. As I noted earlier, I think the norm system may be a bit like the language system: once a rule is internalized, it may be *very* difficult to change. But now, what about trying to change people's behavior, or punishing them for norm violations? In addition to having norms regulating certain sorts of behavior, we also have norms governing what to do about various sorts of norm violations. So there are things that, if I learn that you've done them, I might condemn you for doing. But a very different issue is whether I should try to stop you from doing these things or whether the state should try to stop you. Those are separate normative questions.

TS: I agree with that, certainly.

SS: For example, suppose I learn that you have been mean to your maiden aunt who took care of you for 20 years. You are not exhibiting the sort of gratitude and concern for her well-being that I think would be appropriate in those circumstances. I think you shouldn't behave that way; you're violating a norm requiring gratitude. If you are a casual acquaintance, I would probably do nothing at all. If you are my friend, I might try to persuade you to change your behavior. But I don't think I should try to force you to behave differently, nor do I think that the state should have laws against ingratitude.

TS: Okay, I agree with that. But what seems to me to be an implication of your view—I guess you don't agree—it seems like considerably more actions would fall into that second category, actions we disapprove of but shouldn't take steps to prevent. It seems inappropriate to punish people for what *you* find to be immoral behavior, because you have to think: maybe they're responding to norms that came out of *their* social and physical environment, and these norms work for them. And since there's no objective fact of the matter about whether their behavior or practice is right or wrong, why would I want to, why *should* I want to, prevent or punish them from doing it? Yes, I understand that my norms, given my environment, lead me to *want* to condemn and in some cases punish those violators, but what possible *justification* could there be for me to prevent people from responding to their norms and engaging in what our norms deem to be immoral practices?

SS: So you're suggesting that if you're an antirealist about morality, there are a variety of arguments you could not give to justify enforcing your own moral view or acting to punish people who violate your values or norms.

TS: Yes …

SS: Well, that's right. There are a variety of such arguments that you could no longer use. But now let me raise a further question: To what extent do those arguments and justifications play a significant role in people's motivations? I'm inclined to think that in our culture they play at most a very limited role, and that in many other cultures they play no role at all. These are empirical claims, of course, and they need much more systematic study. But there are a number of findings that encourage my skepticism about the role of justificatory arguments. The most famous of these is Jon Haidt's work on moral dumbfounding.[3] What Haidt finds is that in at least some cases involving consensual incest, people's justifications play *no role whatsoever* in the formation of their own judgments. Jon doesn't go on to ask his participants whether there should be laws against incest of this sort, but I'm willing to bet that most of them would say that laws against consensual incest were fine, that it's a good thing for the state to prohibit this sort of behavior.

TS: Even in the case of Julie and Mark, where it was consensual, they were happy with it, and the subjects couldn't justify why it was wrong. They would still say there should be a law against it.

SS: Yes, exactly. For many people, the fact that they couldn't come up with justifications wouldn't prevent them from saying that the behavior should be prohibited. Another source of evidence comes from anthropologists who have told me over and over again that when you ask people in small-scale societies to provide justifications for behaving in accordance with their norms, the standard response is: "That's what we do." They don't *have* a justification, they don't care that they don't have one. They're not even sure what you're asking for.

TS: That's really interesting.

SS: One more analogy—again only a crude analogy—is the Müller-Lyer illusion. You know that the lines in the Müller-Lyer illusion are exactly the same length, but they still look to be different.

The analogy I'm suggesting is this: empirically it might be the case that you can know the psychology behind different norm systems—yours, say, or those of a culture-of-honor person—and at the theoretical level you know that there's nothing objectively better about your norm system than theirs. *But that doesn't have much of an effect at all!* You're still motivated to stop them.

TS: Okay, but let me keep playing devil's advocate here. In my interview with Haidt, my last question was: What do you think about Julie and Mark [the incestuous brother and sister]? Was it okay for them to have sex? And he said, "Sure, I'm fine with it." Maybe knowing the psychology behind his model led him to alter his moral judgment. In fact, he said that his model had this kind of practical implication. He said it made him more tolerant of other viewpoints, other political viewpoints. He was influenced to stop trying to impose his own judgments on others, and he was less angry when people disagreed with him. And that was the very result of learning about his moral psychology.

SS: Yes, well, with all due respect to Jon, I'm not sure I believe him. After all, if cognitive science has taught us anything, it's that we are not very good at explaining the causes of our own judgments and attitudes, nor are we very good at explaining why our judgments and attitudes change.

TS: What about Bush? The justification for the Iraq War was often couched in terms of giving the gift of democratic values and freedom to the Iraqi people, and that was how the war was sold in many circles. If I understand your view correctly, if the knowledge of your view was widely disseminated, you couldn't use that kind of justification. That Americans have the right way to live—democracy for everyone.

SS: I'm not sure I follow you. What I've been claiming is that, as a matter of psychological fact, someone could make those moral judgments about the war without thinking that there is some objective way of settling his disagreement with someone who disagreed with him.

TS: How?

SS: Let's consider another example, one that isn't fraught with political considerations. I saw an excellent movie the other night called *Water*, by Deepa Mehta. It takes place in India in 1938. It's about the plight of widows in India who, if they didn't jump on the funeral pyres of their husbands, were required to live apart in widows' ashrams where they supported themselves by begging; some of them were reduced to prostitution. Some of the women in these ashrams were widowed when they were 5 or 6 years old, because child marriage was common. At the end of the movie, there's a scrolling text telling the viewer that there are still many hundreds of thousands or maybe millions of widows in India who endure conditions like the ones depicted. On my view, this is obviously another way of life—another "form of life," as the Wittgensteinians might say. However, it's a form that I take to be bad, and in saying that, I'm making a moral judgment. I think it should change! You might ask: Suppose there's someone who has internalized the cluster of the norms that sustain the widows' ashram system and makes that form of life possible. He (or she!) acquired those norms from his culture just as I acquired most of my norms from my culture. In this case, is there something objectively correct about my norms and incorrect about his? My answer is no.

TS: But then why do you say it *should* change? I guess I don't see what allows you to say that.

SS: I'm not sure what the question means. Why do I have to be allowed?

TS: In the same way that if I said "*Chicha*'s disgusting," you would say, "Well, disgusting to *you.*"

SS: No no, I wouldn't say that. I mean that's just the point. It seems to me that we are inclined to say that *chicha* is disgusting. Period. Full stop.

TS: But not "They should stop drinking *chicha*."

SS: No. But that's a different question. Again, notice that you can pull those issues apart even in cases of morality. You shouldn't be nasty to your kindly maiden aunt, but I'm not going to stop you from doing that.

TS: But you don't even say "They shouldn't be drinking *chicha*."

SS: No, that's because the disgust system and the norm system are different. The disgust system isn't designed to affect your behavior toward other people in the way the norm system is.

TS: Let me take another example, a question from the list I sent you. One of the examples of moral disagreement in your work, something I focus on quite a bit in my own work as well, is on the existence of honor cultures—cultures that place great importance in responding aggressively to insults, especially insults to female chastity and the male's manhood. You discuss Nisbett's experiment, where letters are sent to employers in the South and the North in which the applicant reveals that he has been convicted for manslaughter after someone at a bar claimed to have slept with his fiancée. So here's my question: is it okay to beat the crap out of someone who insults you and your fiancée in South Carolina, but morally wrong to do that in Greenwich Village or Boulder, Colorado?

SS: It's just wrong. Period.

TS: It's just wrong. You're saying that because you're Steve Stich, brought up in New York. But if someone else who was brought up in the South says the opposite, that it's wrong to take that insult without giving the guy a beat-down, they would be equally justified. Both comments are equally justified.

SS: "Justified" is your terminology, not mine.

TS: Okay, right, so both comments are equally … equally what, then?

SS: Both comments are expressing deep facts about our internalized norms, which play an important role in determining who we are, or what kinds of people we are. We are very different kinds of people. But that's the end of it. If the question is, "Are my norms true, and theirs false?" the answer is *no*—norms aren't in that line of work.

TS: So the language is misleading. If the two of you are talking about the same thing, and one of you says "It's wrong" and the other says "It's not wrong," that sounds like a contradiction. But it's not.

SS: That's a traditional feature of any non-cognitivist view.

TS: I guess in the same way that if you say *chicha* is disgusting and a Peruvian says it's not, you aren't contradicting each other, even though the language suggests that you are.

SS: Well, the linguistic issues are complex. It may well be that the appropriate account of the semantics of these sentences maintains that people are assuming a kind of objectivism; they both assume they are attributing an objective property to *chicha*. And if that's the case then they're both wrong.

TS: This is what's so interesting about the empirical work done on that question—on whether people do take morality to be objective. I guess there could be cross-cultural variation even there. It sounds like people in those cultures who don't require a justification for their actions, or even know what you're talking about, are a lot less objectivist in their moral thinking. I've always thought that Haidt's dumbfounding cases are evidence that people *do* believe they're appealing to something more objective when making moral judgments. Otherwise, why do they try so hard to keep justifying the judgments?

SS: Well, you may be right about that. But the part I would jump up and down on is your use of the word *people*.

TS: Sure, people may be different on this …

SS: Here's a hypothesis I've been thinking about lately. I don't know whether it's true, but I do plan to spend some time looking for relevant evidence. What the hypothesis claims is that the tradition of trying to justify normative claims in a deep and foundational way, the tradition of trying to provide something like philosophical or argumentative justifications for moral judgments—this is an *extremely* culturally local phenomenon. It's something that exists only in Western cultures and cultures that have been influenced by Western cultures. In many cultures, and for much of human history, providing that kind of justification has played no part in normative psychology.

TS: That's a fascinating hypothesis! I would love to learn more about that. And then it would be really interesting to learn why that tradition developed.[4]

SS: Yep, I think that's right; it certainly would be. It *might* be the case that the tradition is itself based on a culturally local norm (or a cluster of norms) governing the sorts of things one is allowed or required to say when a normative statement is challenged. That might explain your comment, a while back, when you said, "I don't see what *allows* you to say that." The hypothesis also has some rather provocative implications concerning work in moral psychology. If it's right, then the entire Kohlbergian tradition, which looks at the sorts of justifications that people offer for their moral judgments, may have been focused on a cultural artifact, rather than on universal features of moral development as Kohlberg thought.

TS: So Kohlberg was a great ethnographer, as someone once told Richard Nisbett ...[5]

SS: Um, I'm not sure he was a great one, but yes, he was an ethnographer.

6   Some Illusions Should Not Be Corrected

TS: I think I might already have the answers to my last two questions. I was going to ask about the political implications of your view, how it might affect foreign policy decisions, things like that, but now I imagine you'll say that your view likely has no real implication along those lines.

SS: Right, exactly. It's far from clear to me that my view of the nature of the process underlying moral judgment has any substantive implications about what we should do. When I'm reflecting about what we should do when it comes to foreign policy or domestic policy, I'm being driven by a norm system that I've internalized. And, to be sure, there are lots of intriguing questions we could ask about the ways in which views about the psychology of the norm system might interact with the system itself; there are delicate dialectical issues here. But if the question is: whether my view has implications about the attitude we should have toward genital mutilation, or gay marriage, or feeding the starving in Darfur ... as far as I can see, the answer is no.

TS: This is interesting: here's where you have a real disagreement with Josh Greene, whom I just interviewed. He has a polar-opposite view about the implications of learning about our moral psychology. He thinks that the more we understand about it, the more utilitarian we'll become. And he's an antirealist, but he thinks that utilitarianism is going to start making more sense to everyone after we learn what causes nonutilitarian judgments. I take it that you don't see any reason to think that would happen, or that it ought to happen?

SS: Ah, well, on the "ought to happen," I don't know; I'm not sure what that means. But on the "would happen," I think that's utterly laughable, absolutely laughable.[6] Think about the rough analogy with disgust. Many educated people realize that disgustingness is a property we project on to things. Does that in any way undermine the thought that someone barfing on your shirt is disgusting? No.

TS: So then I imagine you don't think your views on knowledge and morality have had much effect on your more day-to-day behavior, the way you make decisions, in your judgments about other people, fights with colleagues, perhaps ...

SS: Well, my views have certainly led to fights with colleagues, but those are fights over the theories in question. But the answer to the question I think you really had in mind is no. The Müller-Lyer analogy is the right one. One can have theoretical views about how one's mind is working without those views having any significant effect on how the mind works.

TS: And we have no control over changing that? I don't know. Maybe here I'd agree with Josh Greene to some extent. Certainly, I've defended a view—I talked about this in my interview with Galen Strawson—which says that coming to the theoretical conclusion that our views on moral responsibility are untenable *can* have a practical effect on your day-to-day life. It can change the way we treat people and ourselves. Not, maybe, in the most dramatic cases, like when a family member is harmed, but in smaller instances. We become less resentful, less bitter. Less retributive perhaps. Gradually, over time.

SS: Is that a claim about what can happen? Is it a causal claim?

TS: Yes. I'm saying that views about moral responsibility can have that causal effect. I'm not claiming that there's decisive evidence to support that, but ...

SS: Well, taken in one way, what you said is certainly true. It is *possible* that views about moral responsibility could have that effect. But, to be a bit facetious, it is also *possible* that having belly-button lint could have that effect. But why should you think it *would*?

But let me give a more serious answer. In some of the work I've done with Chandra Sripada and Dan Kelly, we've explored what we call the "two sets of books hypothesis." It's an idea inspired, in part, by dual-processing theories that have been widely discussed in cognitive science in recent years. The basic idea is that moral judgments may be influenced by two very different sorts of psychological systems. One of these is what I've been calling the "norm system." It has many of the properties that dual-processing theorists attribute to "type-one" systems—it's fast, automatic, unconscious and cognitively impenetrable, and it has a longer evolutionary history. But in addition to the norm system, rules governing behavior may be stored in other components of the mind, components that have some of the properties usually associated with "type-two" systems. They are slower, evolutionarily newer, more cognitively penetrable, and some of the processing that takes place in them is accessible to consciousness. We know relatively little about the sorts of type-two systems that might store behavior-governing rules; we don't understand how they succeed in generating motivation to comply with the rules they store. Now, if you are right that your views about moral responsibility (or other theoretical issues in moral psychology) have changed the way you treat people, I'd guess these changes are the product of type-two systems. A type-two system might also be involved in the culturally local tradition of providing justifications that we talked about earlier. There might be a rule embedded in a type-two system that said (roughly): If you can't come up with a justification for a certain sort of action, then you shouldn't do it.

TS: And that's another norm ...

SS: Well, the terminology is potentially misleading here. I prefer to use the term *norm* for rules stored in the norm system. And indeed, the "If you can't justify it, don't do it" rule might be a culturally local norm. But if it's the sort of rule that you can be convinced of by philosophical argument or by psychological evidence, then it is probably in a cognitively penetrable type-two component of the mind, *not* in the norm system. And if that's the case, I would not call it a norm.

TS: One last thing about this perceptual–illusion analogy. When you call something an illusion, that means you know it's false, right? You know the lines aren't different lengths, even though they look that way. By analogy, you know that your views on, say, the practices of honor cultures aren't objectively correct, even though they appear that way. To the extent that you can design political institutions to deal with the reality behind moral judgments, rather than our illusions about them, then shouldn't we do that? In other words, to the extent that a given institution—perhaps our system of criminal justice—is based on the illusion of moral objectivity, shouldn't we design a system that corrects for this illusion?

SS: Well, first of all, let's be clear that this is a *moral* question, not a psychological question. And if I understand you correctly, it's a very general question. You're asking whether we should *always* design political institutions in a way that corrects for illusions. That's a question that I find hard to answer because, in many cases, I just don't know what it would be to design or redesign political institutions in a way that "corrects" for psychological illusions. Earlier in our conversation, you seemed to be suggesting that if moral objectivity is an illusion and people became aware of that fact, they might no longer condemn practices like genital mutilation, which accord with the norms of other cultures. Would legalizing genital mutilation be a way of "correcting" for the illusion of objectivity? I don't know, since you haven't explained what "correcting" means. But if the answer is *yes*—if legalizing genital mutilation would be a way of correcting for the illusion—then my answer to your question is a resounding *no*! We most definitely should *not* always design legal systems in a way that corrects for illusions.

Notes

1 Gopnik is a professor of psychology and affiliate professor of philosophy at UC Berkeley.
2 Chapters 8 (Michael Ruse), 17 (Joshua Greene and Liane Young), and 12 (Jonathan Haidt) feature more discussion on moral realism versus moral skepticism and relativism.
3 See Chapter 12.
4 In Chapter 14, Joe Henrich gives a hypothesis for why the tradition of moral justification might develop. He ties it to the existence of a legal system.
5 Nisbett is a well-known psychologist at the University of Michigan. Once, when he was working on a theory that he believed applied universally to human cognition, a

colleague told him that the theory was a great piece of ethnography. (In other words, his theory did a nice job describing features of contemporary Western culture.)
6 Greene's response: "Well, I'm writing a book defending my position on this."

Questions for Discussion

1 What is experimental philosophy? Why isn't it new?
2 Why do philosophers criticize experimental philosophy? Why does Stich criticize intuitions?
3 How do Batson's experiments advance the debate between psychological egoists and altruists?
4 How do cross-cultural studies (e.g. Chinese vs. American responses to the Magistrate and the Mob) show that we may never completely agree about morality?
5 What is the analogy that Stich draws between disgust judgments and moral judgments?
6 What are the implications of Stich's theories for moral and political disagreements?

Suggested Readings

Batson, Daniel. *The Altruism Question: Toward a Social–Psychological Answer*. New York: Psychology Press, 1991.

Doris, J. M. and Alexandra Plakias. "How to Argue about Disagreement: Evaluative Diversity and Moral Realism." In Walter Sinnott-Armstrong (ed.), *Moral Psychology: The Cognitive Science of Morality: Intuition and Diversity*. 2. Cambridge, MA: Bradford Books, 2007, vol. 2, ch. 6.

Doris, J. M. and Stephen Stich. "As a Matter of Fact: Empirical Perspectives on Ethics." *Oxford Handbook of Contemporary Philosophy*. Oxford: Oxford University Press, 2005. www.rci.rutgers.edu/~stich/Publications/Papers/05-Jackson-Chap-05.pdf

Kelly, Daniel and Stephen Stich. "Two Theories about the Cognitive Architecture Underlying Morality." In Peter Carruthers, Stephen Laurence, and Stephen Stich (eds.), *The Innate Mind: Foundations and the Future*. Oxford: Oxford University Press, 2007, vol. 3, ch. 18.

Sripada, Chandra Sekhar and Stephen Stich. "A Framework for the Psychology of Norms." In Peter Carruthers, Stephen Laurence, and Stephen Stich (eds.), *The Innate Mind: Foundations and the Future*. Oxford: Oxford University Press, 2006, vol. 2, ch. 17.

Podcast Pairings

Very Bad Wizards, Episode 25: "Burning Armchairs with Joshua Knobe." http://verybadwizards.com/episodes/25

Very Bad Wizards, Episode 31: "An Anthropologist's Guide to Moral Psychology." http://verybadwizards.com/episodes/31

Very Bad Wizards, Episode 32: "Disagreeing about Disagreement." http://verybadwizards.com/episodes/32

17 Joshua Greene and Liane Young

Trolley Problems

Here's the situation. A trolley is racing down the tracks, out of control, and will kill five unsuspecting workers unless you act. You're standing at a switch that can divert the trolley to a second track where there is only one unsuspecting worker. Should you flip the switch?

Most subjects in studies posing this dilemma say that you ought to flick the switch. The reasoning is simple: if you act, one person will die instead of five—a net gain of four lives. But watch what happens when the scenario is adjusted in one small but apparently significant way: the same trolley with the same dead conductor is barreling down the track, headed for the same five unsuspecting workers, but this time there is only one track, and you are on a footbridge, looking down at the situation. In front of you is an unsuspecting fat man. You know that if you push the fat man over the bridge, his girth will be enough to stop the train. He'll be killed, but the five workers will be saved. Should you push him over the bridge?

The results tell a completely different story from the first scenario. The vast majority of subjects think that it would be morally wrong to push the man in order to stop the runaway trolley. What's puzzling is that in many ways the scenarios are identical. In both cases, your act causes one man to die—who wouldn't otherwise—instead of five others. There's that same net gain of four lives. The only difference is that in case one you're flicking a switch, and in case two you make physical contact with the doomed man. What accounts for the radical difference in our moral intuitions?

Philosophers working in the tradition of Immanuel Kant have one answer. In the footbridge scenario, you would be using the fat man as a "mere means" to save five people; you intend to kill him in order to achieve the desired end. Kant's categorical imperative prohibits you from using another rational human being against his will to achieve an end, no matter how worthy. Each human being (no matter how fat) has infinite worth—dignity—and must be treated as an end in himself. This is Kant's big disagreement with the utilitarians or consequentialists, who believe that acts are morally right insofar as they bring about the best outcome. In the trolley switch case, you're not using the single worker as a means to an end—at least not directly. The death is an unfortunate side effect of your act of flicking the switch. So, many neo-Kantian philosophers would say that we correctly perceive the moral wrongness of pushing the man over the bridge, and this accounts for the near-unanimous intuition that we shouldn't do it.

But there's another angle here, too, and this is where cognitive neuroscientists Joshua Greene and Liane Young come into the picture. Joshua Greene, a philosophy Ph.D. at Princeton before turning to psychology, had a hunch that the reactions to these cases had very little to do with a rational understanding of Kantian imperatives and much more to do with our evolved moral psychology. Greene suspected that certain emotions, which were once adaptive for human beings, motivate the different judgments in these cases and others like them.[1] So as a postdoc at Princeton, he presented these scenarios to subjects in a functional MRI machine (a machine that measures brain activity). The results confirmed his prediction: areas in the brain associated with emotions were activated in the footbridge-style up-close-and-personal cases, but not in the impersonal trolley-switch cases. The thought of pushing someone over a bridge triggers our emotions in a way that flicking a switch does not, even though the end results in terms of loss of life are identical.[2] Greene then developed a dual-process model to account for this. According to the model, our reasoning faculties motivate our utilitarian intuitions, the ones that tell us to perform the act that will produce the greatest happiness or least amount of suffering. And our emotions motivate our deontological judgments: we recoil at intentionally harming someone even if doing so reduces the amount of total suffering. The experiment, along with Greene's fluid writing style and dynamic presentations, launched his career and resulted in his appointment at Harvard where he is now Professor of Psychology and director of the Moral Cognition Lab.

Meanwhile, Liane Young, then a rising star in Harvard's Psychology graduate program—and now an associate professor of psychology at Boston College—was developing her own ingenious career-launching experiment to determine the role of emotion in moral judgment. What's the best way to find out how emotion contributes to moral decision-making? Find subjects who don't have any emotions to contribute! (Well, it's a little more complicated than that, as you'll see ...) I began my interview by asking Young to describe this study, which had recently appeared in the journal Nature.

March 2008

1   To Know But Not to Feel

LIANE YOUNG: The basic idea was to investigate the role of emotion in moral judgment by looking at how patients with severe emotional defects make moral judgments. More specifically, we set out to test a new model of moral judgment that Josh put forth, on the basis of his first two fMRI studies—the dual-process model. Josh found neural evidence for the role of emotion in rejecting harm and the role of "reason" in going for the greater good. So we were able to test Josh's dual-process model by looking at a population of individuals with deficits in emotional processing due to brain damage.

TAMLER SOMMERS: What kind of patients exactly?

LY: When I say "population," I really mean six patients. These patients are quite rare; they have very specific lesions in a part of the brain responsible for emotional processing—but the brain is intact everywhere else, and thus so are their other cognitive functions.

TS: They can still do logic problems, math problems, they can reason about consequences.

LY: Right. The site of their brain damage happens to be in the front of the head, right behind the space in between the eyes, and is known as the ventromedial prefrontal cortex, or VMPFC. The VMPFC, when it's working properly, in healthy individuals, responds robustly to stimuli with social emotional content. Like pictures that instill fear in a majority of people—Sarah Palin as our vice president, for example, or more seriously, war scenes or pornography. Patients with damage to the VMPFC, though, don't produce normal emotional responses to such stimuli. So, for example, if you and I saw pictures of mutilated bodies, our hearts might start racing, our palms might start sweating, and so on. And if we saw a scan of our brains, we would see activity in the VMPFC. But when you give the same emotional stimuli to VMPFC patients, all the measurements—heart rate, skin conductance—appear flat.

TS: So how did examining these subjects test Josh's dual-process model?

LY: We sat participants in front of the computer, and they read and responded to scenarios one by one, the original scenarios constructed by Josh for his fMRI study. Their task was to judge whether they would perform a particular action if placed in the shoes of a character in the scenario. The moral scenarios were divided into two groups: impersonal and personal. Impersonal moral scenarios weren't particularly emotionally salient; the harms were impersonal in nature. Personal moral scenarios were emotionally salient; the harms were, as Josh describes them, "up close and personal." So, for example, a classic impersonal scenario is the trolley problem with the guy at the switch. And the personal scenario is the footbridge case. The difference boils down to flipping a switch versus pushing a man. So what we found was that patients with VMPFC damage produced the same patterns of responses on the impersonal scenarios as people without the damage.

TS: Just as likely to say that they would flip the switch as normal patients …

LY: Yes, but on the personal scenarios, VMPFC patients were more likely to endorse harming one to save many. More likely to say they'd push the man over the bridge, for example. They were more willing to go with the numbers, to go with the consequences. In other words, VMPFC patients showed themselves to be moral utilitarians, maximizing welfare, in line with Josh's dual-process model.

TS: Interesting. Because they didn't have the emotional responses to the direct infliction of harm.

LY: Yes, emotional processes allow us to respond to harms, especially those that are up close and personal, like pushing the man off the bridge. These emotions often cause us to reject these harms. Cognitive processes support abstract reasoning, including utilitarian reasoning—figuring out how to bring about the best outcome. Moral judgment in VMPFC patients is dominated by the cognitive processes, and therefore comes out utilitarian. So Josh's model provided just the right level of detail for systematically testing emotion in specific moral judgments.

TS: Let's turn to that. Josh, how did you come up with your model, and the idea for testing it?

JOSHUA GREENE: In high school, I did a philosophically oriented debate, and I remember thinking that utilitarianism made a lot of sense to me. Someone in a debate round presented me with the transplant problem. So I was arguing that we should always do the greatest good for the greatest number, and someone said: "Oh yeah? Well what about if you could kill one healthy person and give all of their organs to five healthy people who need them? Would that be okay?" And I was stumped. I said, "No, I guess it wouldn't." And I was struck by that. Because I thought that I had a pretty good—well, you know, me and John Stuart Mill—that we had a pretty good theory, and then this person really stumped me.

Then in 1995, I read [Antonio] Damasio's book *Descartes' Error.* I remember the moment. I was in Israel at my sister's bat mitzvah, I was sitting in the hotel room alone reading, and I stood up in my bed, and said "This is it!" That is, I read the description of Phineas Gage—the man who survived a steel rod cutting through his skull and giving him brain damage in regions of the brain associated with emotion. Damasio describes his condition as "to know but not to feel." And I thought: that's what's going on in the footbridge case. There's this feeling that "this is wrong," and that *feeling* is different from the *thought* "I know it makes sense to kill one person to save five." And I immediately thought: I bet if you tested patients with emotional deficits like Gage, they would be more utilitarian. And actually, the first study I had in mind was just like the study Liane described. And then when I was at Princeton I heard there was this new guy in town who set up a brain-imaging center and was interested in talking to philosophers. So I went to see him. He's a very no-nonsense guy. He just sat back and said, "Okay, shoot." I told him about the trolley problem, and Phineas Gage. And he said, "Oh, yeah," and he was on board right away. And that was how I ended up in the Cohen lab.

TS: So your experiment along with Liane's shows how our emotional responses lead us to make anti-utilitarian judgments in these up-close-and-personal cases. How do you think this research bears on the status of those intuitions? In other words, how do these studies bear on the *justification* of utilitarian and Kantian intuitions?

JG: My primary goal was to explain the intuitions, to understand why we say yes sometimes and no other times—

TS: —Without justifying them?

JG: I certainly wasn't interested in justifying the intuitions as they are. If my theory was right, you could interpret the results as debunking the Kantian intuitions.

TS: Can you explain what you mean by *debunk*, exactly?

JG: A debunking explanation is one that explains why we have a belief in a way that makes it unlikely that the belief is true. For example, you might believe that you are having a conversation with a lampshade, and then you might explain away (i.e., debunk) that belief by appealing to the fact that you recently ingested LSD.

TS: And you thought our Kantian emotional responses might be affecting our moral judgments the same way LSD affects our judgments about whether lampshades can talk?

JG: In a very abstract sense, yes. But this analogy has limitations, of course. An LSD trip is an unnatural experience for which our brains were not designed. Moral emotions, in contrast, are part of normal, adaptive brain function. Despite these differences, the idea is that both explanations—you were hallucinating and you were having an emotional response—can undermine judgments made under those circumstances, depending on your assumptions about whether LSD-induced hallucinations or emotional responses are likely to reflect an independent truth.

2 Selective Debunking

TS: This leads to a key question for me about Josh's work, or at least the implications of his work. You say you're a debunker, and you focus on debunking the Kantian intuitions. In the end you want to support the moral theory of utilitarianism. You want to debunk all the intuitions but the utilitarian ones.

JG: Right …

TS: But I never figured out how that fits with your general moral skepticism— your view that no moral beliefs are true, including utilitarian beliefs. I would think that as a moral skeptic you would deny or debunk *all* moral intuitions, not just the intuitions that aren't consistent with your favorite theory.

JG: Well, right, I don't think utilitarianism is the right theory, the *true* theory. But I do have utilitarian values. That is: I think that happiness and suffering are things that matter. They matter to me. I also think everyone's happiness and suffering matters equally. That more suffering is worse than less suffering. That more happiness is better than less happiness. Those are values I can't let go of. And those postulates that lead to utilitarianism, I can't shake them. And I see no reason to shake them. By contrast, the kinds of intuitions that guide Kantian or deontological thinking, like "Well, if you intend to kill all those people, that's really bad; but if you intend something else, while at the same time *knowing* that those people will die as a side effect of your bombing the munitions factory, that's not so bad"—well, *that* I'm skeptical of!

TS: Skeptical in what sense, though?

JG: Look, the people are just as dead! And you know just as much that you're killing them. Why should it matter that you didn't specifically intend for them to die? Why should we care about that distinction? I have the immediate *feeling* that it matters. I have the feeling like other people do. But why does it make it okay to kill people just because it's not what you're going after? Who cares what's going on in your head! They're dead! So I've always been skeptical of those kinds of deontological distinctions that seem bogus. And that's my motivation for studying those stances. Trying to understand them in proximate causal terms (e.g., this is just an emotional response) and—I think this is crucial—in evolutionary terms. Explaining why for *nonmoral* reasons we might have these moral intuitions. And that's where the real debunking happens. And so, to answer your question—how can you be a moral skeptic and a utilitarian at the same time—I don't think utilitarianism is true. I think it's what you're left with after you've disavowed all the stuff that is arbitrary or contingent or not hard to let go of when you understand where it came from.

TS: Liane, you want to break in?

LY: Yes. So, it's also going to be emotional responses to harm and suffering that's leading you to those fundamental principles of utilitarianism, right?

JG: Yep. I have a grad student who's working on finding those emotions right now.

LY: So even though it's not the *same* emotions that are grounding utilitarian intuitions rather than Kantian intuitions, they're still emotions, right? Because I always thought that your debunking account of Kantianism was grounded by the fact that principles were rooted in emotional responses, and that emotion was an unreliable source for moral judgments, that they exert biases in illicit ways. But utilitarian principles are also grounded in emotions, so …

TS: Right, it seems like you could run the same debunking argument on utilitarian principles.

JG: This is really an important and complicated issue. I think that Hume and Liane are right that all moral evaluation has to have some kind of affective or emotional basis. What I would want to focus on, then, are the different kinds of emotions that are involved and what they're sensitive to. In the trolley case that Fiery [Cushman] and Liane did, for example, it turns out that we have different emotional responses to killing someone when our own muscles are involved in moving the person, rather than just relying on gravity. [Subjects find it more wrong to stop the trolley by pushing someone over a bridge than by releasing them via a trapdoor.] And this is where the rubber meets the road. Are emotions sensitive to things that upon reflection we think ought not to matter?

TS: Then the key issue for you is how we regard the emotional responses upon reflection?

JG: Yes. Now, I think that no one would say—I'm sure some philosopher somewhere would, but no sane person would ever say that it's morally important in and of itself whether you touch the person to harm them or use a trapdoor to harm them. But our emotions are sensitive to that difference. And that leads to differences in judgment. By contrast, if I have a sense of sympathy for someone who suffers or a basic feeling of approval when someone becomes happier or has their situation improved, that's not something I'm inclined to disavow after I think about it. So I think what it really comes down to is not "emotions bad; cognition good." It's all emotional on some level. It's rather that some emotions are more rigid and inflexible and sensitive to things that we wouldn't ever think are morally important.

TS: So emotions that you would endorse upon reflection are good (but not true), and emotions that you would not endorse upon reflection are bad (but not false)?

JG: Right—with full information, including scientific information that we're only just beginning to gather. So in a sense, I have a coherentist moral epistemology.[3] I don't think that utilitarianism or any other moral theory comes out of the sky as a correct moral theory. I have certain values, intuitions, and beliefs about how the world is and how the human mind is, and as I reflect about the tensions within my own values and intuitions and try to understand them scientifically, I think that some of those values stand up pretty well to this kind of scrutiny, and others wither. And the more I've learned, the more I've become skeptical about Kantian intuitions, and confident that our utilitarian intuitions are perfectly respectable.

TS: Well, that leads to my next question. Let's say I also have another intuition that it's morally appropriate for me to value my daughter's happiness over the happiness of a total stranger's daughter. It's just as basic as your utilitarian beliefs, and one that I'm just as likely to endorse upon reflection. But this intuition goes against the utilitarian principle that we should value everyone's happiness equally. Why should I junk my intuition in favor of the utilitarian one?

JG: There are two ways to respond to that. One is to say, look, some things are just non-negotiable. Morally speaking, I don't think my child's welfare is morally more important than anyone else's. But I have no illusions about the fact that this is not a bias that I can overcome. And because other people have this bias, it would be disastrous to try to make people overcome it. So from a policy perspective, it would be ludicrous to try to get people to care equally about all children. And from a personal perspective, it would be ludicrous for me to try to talk myself out of that state. So maybe ideally if I was rewriting the species, I'd write out the partial-to-your-children inclination, but I still don't think it's wrong to love my wife and child more than, you know, many other—

LY: —Than you love me and Tamler.

JG: Well, you guys are great …

LY: But fundamentally you've got to accept that there's nothing morally wrong with being partial to your children. Right?

JG: I think we all have that belief. And then we learn about Darwin, about natural selection, and kin selection. And if you're me, you get to the point where you say: "Okay, so maybe that belief isn't ideally morally justified, but it's just a feature of our psychology."

TS: But as you said, there's also an evolutionary story for why we care about anyone at all—why we have an aversion to the suffering of other people, for why we have the utilitarian intuition. Why isn't that just a feature of our psychology? In other words, what I'm still struggling with is: you seem to think that Darwinism debunks my intuition that it's morally justified to value my daughter's happiness over the happiness of somebody else. But natural selection doesn't debunk your utilitarian intuition. It's selective debunking. Why is one principle more debunkable than the other?

JG: Well, that's an interesting question. There's a tension between the utilitarian intuition and the kin-selection, partiality-to-your children principle. In the face of that tension, which does it make more sense, intellectually, to give up? That the most happiness is good? Or that it's good for me to care about my offspring, even if that doesn't produce the most happiness? I don't know if I can spell this out further. Maybe I can, but one seems more basic, more fundamental than the other. You can imagine a world in which everyone cares about each other equally—their own children as much as anyone else's. And everyone was wired that way. That's still a recognizably moral world. Whereas a world in which everyone is indifferent to the happiness of others doesn't strike me as a moral world at all. So maybe therein lies the asymmetry. I'm actually working this out for the first time and I think it's something I need to spell out.

LY: But that's still a value judgment about which world is better. And that's just an appeal to another intuition.

JG: I think it's an appeal to a conceptual notion of morality. You can imagine a world that everyone would term "moral" without one principle: partiality to kin. But you can't imagine a world that anyone would term moral where no one cared whether people suffered or were happy—it was all the same to them. And that's what makes the utilitarian intuition more fundamental. I'm actually really glad this came up, because it's where my [recent] article ends,[4] and I haven't yet tried to formulate this. But in any case, I want to reiterate that there's a difference between these kinds of arguments and what the Kantians do, which is to ignore the scientific explanation for their emotions and pretend that there's some deep reason, some philosophical justification for their intuitions when instead it's just this post hoc cop-out.

TS: But isn't there a third option? To be fully aware of the science behind my intuition? To say, "Look, I know all about why I'm partial to my children, I know all about kin selection. And I don't care!" I stand by that intuition. If that means I have to diverge in some cases from another intuition I have, so be it. Who says there needs to be this one universal principle that guides all my actions anyway?

JG: You don't have to believe there's only one universal principle. But you do want to believe that your moral intuitions aren't arbitrary, right? The problem with the thoroughgoing pluralist view you're defending is that you do take yourself to be acting for reasons. Morality presents itself as objective to us. And if you're admitting that you have this intuition, then you could have had another one, and, well, you're ending up having to accept that morality comes down to a set of whims.

LY: But morality is always going to come down to that in a sense, right? There is no independent way of justifying any principle or theory—whether it's utilitarian or Kantian.

JG: Right. Which is why I'm no longer a moral realist. So now I think the best we can do is try to get to your core bedrock values, the ones that it's inconceivable to give up. And starting with those, make everything as consistent as possible. Both internally consistent and consistent with what we know about how your mind works, how human nature works, and where it comes from.

TS: Okay, let me try to frame my question a different way. Back in the day, when I was denying free will and moral responsibility—

JG: —Always a dangerous thing …

TS: Tell me about it. Inevitably, at some point, people would say: "What if someone harmed your daughter Eliza? You wouldn't think he was morally responsible for doing that?" Well, I had a couple of responses. First, psychologically I wouldn't be able to think that person didn't deserve blame or punishment. In fact, I'd want to give the guy as much punishment as possible with my bare hands. With something like that, your retributive emotions override any kind of theory you have in your head. But then I thought about something else, something that made me question even my theoretical skepticism about free will and moral responsibility.[5] Even if I *could* somehow use my theory to overcome or undermine my retributive hatred of this person, I wouldn't want to. I actually think there'd be something *wrong* with me if I didn't have that irresistible inclination. In other words, it's *not* an ideal version of me that would abandon retributive feelings toward a person who hurt Eliza. And so that makes me think that there is something deeper about our attachment to our children. It's not just something that makes us think, look, we have it, we can't get rid of it, so let's enjoy it. To me, having this attachment is about as deeply right as anything else we could possibly believe.

JG: So is it that you think it's deeply *right* to have that attitude, or that you think it's deeply *you*?

TS: I think something would be wrong with me if I could overcome it. I'll say it like that.

JG: Well, let me put it this way. I don't think it would be wrong of me to rewire my brain so that I became a more perfect utilitarian. Imagine if I could rewire my brain so that all I do is make money and give it away to poor people in an efficient way. Now, would I choose to do that? Well, I wouldn't choose to do that. But that's essentially because I'm partial to *myself.* And part of what it is to be *me* is to have these non-ideal values. So it wouldn't be wrong to rewire myself into a kind of utilitarian saint. But I don't want to. And the reason why I don't want to is that I want to continue to *exist.* Another way to think about it is: Imagine if I could kill myself and bring to life someone who was morally better than myself, according to my criteria. I wouldn't want to do that, because I want to exist as someone recognizably *me* ...

TS: So it's a personal-identity thing. That's interesting.

JG: Yes, it really becomes exactly that: a personal-identity issue. If I were to rewrite my desires, I might come out better according to my own standards, but *I* wouldn't come out.

3 Meta-Metaethics

TS: So Liane, let me ask you—because I know something about Josh's metaethical views, but I don't know about yours—

JG: I don't either, actually. We've never really talked about it.

TS: How have your fMRI studies and your work with patients with emotional deficits affected your view of morality in general?

LY: Hmm. I don't know if I've come to a conclusion like Josh has about what my metaethical views are, based on the data of my experiments and others. I guess my views are still evolving.

TS: What are the candidates?

LY: One possibility is to take a closer look at my intuitions and ensure that I can at least come up with some kind of justification for those intuitions. That seems like a bare minimum, but it clearly isn't enough.

JG: Although it is a substantive test, right? You can't do that with some of those more deontological intuitions, like ones that involve body contact or no body contact.

LY: True, but nor do I want to, in some cases, and that's another interesting thing to think about. In what cases am I motivated to try to come up with a justification for my intuitions, and in what cases am I totally content to dismiss my intuitions? I think one of the reasons I give more weight to certain intuitions than Josh or Singer or other utilitarians is those "meta-intuitions" that tell me when I ought to put in the effort to justify an intuition, and when I should be content to dismiss it as a bias.[6] Or, on the flip side, when I believe that some principles are fundamental, and I should stop looking for justifications. I can't seem to wrap my head around those meta-intuitions. That's not to say I'm going to stop trying, but it seems like there's a whole other layer of intuitions that I don't think we're studying, intuitions that guide our *inquiry* into the intuitions we are studying.

TS: So if I get this right, Josh has a meta-intuition that his intuitions should be as consistent as possible with each other, and they need to come from sources that he trusts. Your meta-intuition is that sometimes it's just okay to have either inconsistent intuitions or intuitions that can't be unified by one principle.

LY: Are you trying to say I'm less coherent than Josh?

TS: Well, maybe I am, but not in a pejorative sense—I have that feeling too, sometimes. Why couldn't you have a general framework that allows for a plurality of different conflicting principles?

LY: It's not exactly that—you say that in Josh's view, the sources of the intuitions matter, and all the intuitions should cohere together nicely, and for me I have intuitions about whether certain sources of moral judgment are legitimate or illicit sources.

TS: Okay—intuitions about what counts as a debunking explanation, and what counts as a plain old explanation.

LY: And it's those intuitions that I don't understand, and therefore think that maybe there's some role for those intuitions in my overall view of morality.

JG: Yeah, so I think Liane and I both want to have a coherent value system, but that maybe we have different starting points. I've been a skeptic my whole life. I'm relatively ready to abandon intuitive common sense beliefs in favor of what I think is better. Whereas other people are going to have a higher standard of evidence required before they jettison something that makes intuitive sense to them.

4 To Push or Not to Push

TS: One question I always like to ask is how you apply your own theories to your everyday life and your research. I'll start with Josh. You accused John Rawls of constructing an entire theory of justice, an entire methodology, just to justify his intuition that utilitarianism was morally objectionable. Well, a much less sympathetic person than I am could say: Josh, look at your story. You started out as a utilitarian as a kid, as a high-school student, and now you've constructed, through your work and your research, a kind of justification of utilitarian principles. Boy, *that* worked out nicely. How *convenient.* How maybe post hoc. Now, I'm not saying you're doing that, but I wonder: do you *worry* that you're doing the same thing that you're accusing Rawls of doing? After all, your own theory—Jon Haidt's theory, too[7]—would predict that you would be doing exactly that.

JG: I think it's a very good question. I've been asked something along those lines before, and I had to admit that the view came first, and the research came later. And I can't help being a little embarrassed by that history, but I think I can be vindicated. I think what's going on—not to sound obnoxious—but I think I'm a pretty insightful person, and I was intuitively skeptical of what one ought to be skeptical of. Certain nonutilitarian intuitions seemed fishy to me—and so I was able to further justify that skepticism. There was a time when I wasn't so confident, like when I got hit with the transplant problem, all the counterexamples to utilitarianism. And so I delved into those counterexamples. It could have happened that I would have found intuitive yet clear and sensible reasoning behind those intuitions, kind of like what Rawls would hope for—these subtle but normatively plausible principles behind them. If that were the case, then I might have said: "There's a wisdom here, à la Leon Kass." But instead what I found were heuristics, biases, and emotions. Along with an evolutionary story that makes the reliability of those emotions questionable. And so I've had an up and down. But now I've arrived at a kind of steady state where I'm comfortable as a subjectivist utilitarian. But the ride to get here wasn't totally smooth.

TS: And you think you've avoided the temptation to cook the books in your own way.

JG: You never know for sure. I've only just gotten started, and it's true that so far I've devoted most of my resources to experiments that show that my theory is right.

TS: What about you, Liane? You haven't been doing this stuff for quite as long, but do you worry about the temptation to use theories—scientific theories— to justify your initial intuitions?

LY: Again, I feel like you always start out with these intuitions, what we value. Josh started out with utilitarian intuitions, I didn't. We had different starting points. Now I've evolved more toward Josh's view, but not all the way. You seem to start out with these priors and then throw out anything you can't come up with good reason to justify. And it seems like the language that we use for deontological intuitions is post hoc rationalization. Mostly. But in the case of utilitarianism, we talk about sensible reasonable accounts rather than rationalization, but I'm not sure if the difference is that stark.

JG: But I don't see how there's any rationalization going on with utilitarianism! Everybody is a utilitarian to some extent. Everyone thinks that outcomes matter.

TS: All things being equal.

JG: Yes, all things being equal, everyone thinks it's better to have less suffering than more suffering. Everyone applies those principles. It's just a question of whether you also have other principles in there to override them.

LY: First, just because everyone does it, that doesn't mean everyone isn't rationalizing. But second, I think there are other non-utilitarian principles that everyone shares and everyone thinks are fundamental. Everyone thinks intentions matter, or more broadly, that what happens in the mind matters, and not just in a utilitarian way. So in the same way that people are utilitarian to some extent, people are all non-utilitarian to some extent. They think people's beliefs and intentions matter independent of the usefulness of taking those things into account. To the same extent that they think that outcome matters.

TS: So then let me ask you, Josh. If you're on the footbridge behind the fat man—do you think you should push him?

JG: Personally, I wouldn't feel comfortable doing it. After all, I'm only human. But if someone else were to do it, and do it for the right reasons, knowing that it would work, I wouldn't condemn it.

TS: Liane?

LY: Well, I've certainly got the easier job here, because for this case at least my squeamishness about pushing people off bridges is supported by my intuition that it's morally wrong to do so. Maybe it's just the emotions talking, but I suspect that there really is more to the moral story than consequences. How the story plays out exactly over the next few decades will be interesting, but my bet is that it'll have something to do with intentions, maybe not in the trolley-problem sense, but generally what's going on in our heads when we act—doing not just the right thing but, like Josh said, for the right reasons. So I guess this is my long way of saying, no, I wouldn't push the man. I think there's more to morality than maximizing consequences.

Notes

1 Greene discusses another, more practical example, one originally developed by the philosopher Peter Unger. If you drove by a bleeding hiker with a broken leg because you didn't want the blood staining your car's leather upholstery, you'd be a moral monster. But spending $400 on leather upholstery rather than donating that money to a charity that could undoubtedly save someone overseas from losing a limb seems perfectly acceptable. What's the morally relevant difference between these two cases?

2 The experiment was celebrated for the insight it offered and also for the new avenues of investigation that it opened. Although the practice is now relatively common, no one before Greene and his colleagues had thought to run brain scans on subjects as they made moral judgments.

3 Roughly, this is a view that the right or most reasonable moral system is one that is the most consistent within itself and with other nonmoral beliefs.

4 Greene is referring to an essay called "The Secret Joke of Kant's Soul," which attempts to expose the emotional basis behind our Kantian judgments.

5 This thought has led to a slight shift in my views on responsibility since my interview with Galen Strawson (Chapter 1) in 2003.

6 This is the key question in the debate between the three of us. How do we know when an intuition is a bias rather than a reflection of a reasonable moral belief?

7 See Chapter 12.

Questions for Discussion

1 How, according to Greene, can learning the psychology behind our moral judgments change our opinion about what they should be?

2 What does Greene's experiment with the trolley problem and Young's experiment with the VMPC patients tell us about emotions and deontological theories in ethics?

3   What is a debunking explanation? Give an example.
4   Why does Greene think his psychological account of moral decision-making can debunk our deontological intuitions? Why do Young and I disagree?
5   How can moral theories fall prey to confirmation bias? Does Greene's theory avoid the problems he accuses Rawls of?

Suggested Reading

Note: Greene's website www.joshua-greene.net/publications provides links to most of his recent articles and media.
Cushman, Fiery and Liane Young. "The Psychology of Dilemmas and the Philosophy of Morality." *Ethical Theory and Moral Practice* 12 (2009): 9–24.
Greene, Joshua. "From Neural 'Is' to Moral 'Ought': What Are the Moral Implications of Neuroscientific Moral Psychology?" *Nature Reviews Neuroscience* 4 (2003): 847–50.
——. "The Secret Joke of Kant's Soul." In *Moral Psychology: The Neuroscience of Morality: Emotion, Brain Disorders, and Development*. Cambridge, MA: MIT Press, 2008, vol. 3, pp. 35–80.
——. *Moral Tribes: Emotion, Reason, and the Gap between Us and Them*. New York: Penguin, 2013.

Assorted Media and Podcast Pairings

"Deep Pragmatism: A Conversation with Joshua D. Greene." Interview, ed. John Brockman. *Edge*, Aug. 30, 2013: edge.org.
Greene, Joshua. "Moral Tribes: Emotion, Reason, and the Gap between Us and Them." Talks at Google, May 19, 2014: www.youtube.com/watch?v=VaoTKurm_1k
Young, Liane. "CPBD 078: Liane Young – How to Change Someone's Moral Judgment with Magnets." Interviewed by Luke Muehlhauser, Nov. 14, 2010: commonsenseatheism.com.
——. "TEDxHogeschoolUtrecht—The Brain on Intention." TEDx Talks, Jan. 9, 2012: www.youtube.com/watch?v=D6XcjuN0sjY Very Bad Wizards, Episode 6 "Trolleys, Utilitarians, and Psychopaths." http://verybadwizards.com/episodes/6
Very Bad Wizards, Episode 20 "Boston, Brains, and Bad Pronunciation (with Molly Crockett)." http://verybadwizards.com/episodes/20
Very Bad Wizards, Episode 36 "An Irresponsible Meta-Book Review of Joshua Greene's *Moral Tribes*." http://verybadwizards.com/episodes/36

Glossary

Note: This is just a brief definition of these terms and concepts, many of which are quite complex. For more detailed accounts, you can refer to the *Routledge Encyclopedia of Philosophy*, *Stanford Encyclopedia of Philosophy*, and *The Internet Encyclopedia of Philosophy*. All three are good resources.

Agency The capacity to deliberate, make choices, and act on those choices.

A priori knowledge Knowledge we can acquire without doing any observations to check whether they're true. For example, I can know that all bachelors are unmarried men without asking every bachelor (or even a representative sample) if they're married. Mathematics and logic are thought to be *a priori* spheres of knowledge.

Cognitive Having to do with reasoning, rationality, and concepts. It's usually (but not always) considered to be in opposition to emotions and desires.

Collectivist Cultures can be placed on a continuum between individualist and collectivist. A collectivist culture tends to emphasize group over individual values. Consequentially, a collectivist culture is more likely to understand an individual's character and behaviors as a reflection of the group (e.g., family, team, village) they belong to.

Counterexample An example or argument used to demonstrate that a general principle is false. For example, someone might say that all Americans love guns. If you could find an American that doesn't love guns, that person would be a counterexample to the general principle, thereby showing that it's false.

Debunking explanation An explanation for a phenomenon that shows why our belief about it is false. The new explanation both explains why we believe the first (false) one and why the new explanation is better.

Deontological ethics Deontology is the study of the nature and duties of obligations. Deontological is often contrasted with utilitarian or consequentialist theories of ethics. While consequentialists think consequences matter most in ethics, deontologists argue that duties and obligations can outweigh even good consequences. Kant is the best-known example of a deontologist (see: http://plato.stanford.edu/entries/ethics-deontological).

Descriptive claim A claim about how the world is (in contrast to *normative claims*, which are claims about how the world ought to be).

Determinism The theory that the future is fixed, because every event has a cause, and the causes stretch back until the beginning of the universe. A determinist believes that if you entered into a super-computer all the laws of physics, all the physical facts about a person, and the world at one point in time, in theory the computer could calculate what that person will do at any point in the future.

Dual-process model A model of the mind that holds that our brain processes can be roughly divided into two categories: fast and slow. The fast ones are rules of thumb that operate unconsciously, but are more susceptible to error. The slow ones are deliberate, conscious, and less likely to lead to errors.

Empathy The ability to take somebody else's perspective and feel, to some degree, what someone else feels. For example, most people wince and turn away when they see Dustin Hoffman having his teeth drilled without anesthetic in *Marathon Man*.

Empirical Refers to claims that have to do with observations about the world. When I make an empirical claim, I make a claim—in principle—about how the world is that can be verified by observation.

Epistemology The branch of philosophy that studies knowledge. Epistemologists try to answer questions like: What does it mean to *know* something? What counts as justification for a belief? What's the difference between merely believing something and knowing it? What sorts of things can we know and not know?

Error theory Metaethical error theorists agree with moral realists that morality presumes the existence of objective moral values. But they also believe that there are no objective values. So all moral claims are false. By analogy, if you lived in seventeenth-century Salem, you might be an error theorist about witches. You would agree that witch discourse presumed the existence of witches. But (as an enlightened person) you would also believe that there are no witches. So when someone stated that "Goodwife Johnson is a witch", they would be making a false claim.

Eudaemonia Often interpreted as 'happiness,' it is better understood as 'flourishing.' A eudaemonic life is one within which an individual comes to develop all their best human qualities. The term is mostly associated with Aristotelian and other virtue ethics traditions.

Expressivism A metaethical theory. In contrast to both moral realists and error theorists, expressivists believe that moral assertions are not propositions with truth values. Rather, they are expressions of approval or disapproval toward actions or states of affairs and a desire for you to share my attitudes. If I tell you that "it's wrong to torture people," I am not making a claim like "the sun is shining." Rather, I'm expressing my deep disapproval of torture and trying to get you to disapprove of it as well.

Expressivist theory of punishment The goal of punishment is not to give people what they deserve, which is hard to make sense of, and not just to deter future crime, but to publicly express condemnation of an act. Punishment is the only way to express moral condemnation of an act or a system.

Fatalism The idea that I don't have control over what happens to me. I have a predetermined fate that cannot be avoided no matter what I do.

Fundamental attribution error Occurs when, in explaining the causes of a behavior, we overestimate the role of the agent's character traits and underestimate the role of environmental and situational forces.

Genetic inheritance The collection of physical, psychological, and behavioral traits that are passed down genetically.

Incommensurable Two things or values are incommensurable when they can't be compared by the same standard of measurement.

Individualist Cultures can be placed on a continuum between individualist and collectivist. An individualist culture tends to emphasize individual over group values. Consequentially, an individualist culture is more likely to understand an individual's attributes and behavior as a reflection of that individual's personal beliefs, values, motives, and character.

Instrumental reason/rationality The kind of reasoning you engage in when you try to figure out how to achieve your goals or satisfy your desires; often called "mean–ends" reasoning. That is, it's the kind of reasoning you use to figure out the best means to attain a particular end or way of reconciling conflicting ends. Some philosophers (such as Hume) think this is the *only* kind of reasoning possible; i.e., reason can't tell us what to value, it can only tell us how to get there. Others (such as Kant and Plato) think that reason can help us decide which *ultimate* goals and intrinsic values we should pursue.

Instrumental value Something has instrumental value if it helps you get the thing or achieve a further good. For example, if you really want to go on vacation then money has instrumental value for achieving your end. It helps you achieve your real goal, which is going on vacation.

Internalize An attitude or behavior gets internalized when it becomes part of one's nature by learning or unconscious assimilation.

Intersubjectivity When something is valued within a group or community, it gains intersubjective value. Think of it as the consequence of adding up everyone's subjective view that some thing has value or is a value. For example, if everyone in a community agreed that doing logic has value, then doing logic is intersubjectively valuable for that community. Intersubjective values enjoy a kind of quasi-objective value. They're objective in the sense that they're objective values for a particular group or community. However, intersubjective values aren't objectively valuable in the sense that they are values for all human beings.

Intrinsic value Something has intrinsic value if it is valuable for no other reason than for its own sake. For example, we want happiness for its own sake, not for any other reason.

Kantian ethics Kant argued that reason can lead us to what we should value and what our values should be. Right and wrong are a matter of following universal rules that can be accessed through reason. When evaluating whether an action is right, Kantians are concerned with intentions and respect for individual autonomy, as opposed to consequences. The opposite view would be Hume's—that we should reflect on our emotions or desires to figure out what to value. (*See*: **deontology.**)

Learned helplessness When, through conditioning, a human or animal stops trying to avoid a harmful stimulus because it has come to believe that avoidance won't change the harmful outcome. More generally, through conditioning you come to believe that your behavior has no effect on what will happen to you.

Mind independence Refers to facts that don't depend on the observer. For example, if I say that the earth is an oblate spheroid the truth of its shape doesn't depend on me. It's an oblate spheroid even if looks flat to me, or a reality TV personality tells me it's flat.

Moral relativism (also **cultural relativism**) Moral relativists believe that the moral rightness or wrongness of an act is relative to the culture in which it takes place. Nothing is objectively right or wrong: it all depends on the values of the culture in which an act takes place. Although the two terms are often used synonymously, cultural relativism is better regarded as a descriptive view that moral attitudes and practices differ across cultures.

Moral responsibility The idea that it's appropriate or that it "makes sense" to blame or praise someone for their actions. Moral responsibility usually implies that the agent could have chosen to act otherwise and that their action is the consequence of their having chosen to act the way they did.

Necessary and sufficient conditions A is a necessary condition for B means that B cannot obtain without A occurring. For example, having four wheels is necessary for being a car. That is, if something doesn't have four wheels it isn't a car. A is a sufficient condition for B means when A obtains it's enough for B to also obtain. For example, wearing a sweater indoors is sufficient for being warm. However, it's not *necessary*. I could get warm many other ways.

Nihilism Nihilists believe that there is no such thing as objective moral values. Although nihilism and anti-realism are substantively identical, nihilists are often thought to take a darker view of the implications of a valueless universe.

Non-cognitivism (metaethics) Non-cognitivism is the view that moral expressions such as 'right', 'wrong', 'good', 'bad' don't have truth values. They aren't the sort of claims that can be true or false. Expressivism is a version of non-cognitivism.

Nonrealist/anti-realist (metaethics) Nonrealists believe that there are no objective moral values. Nonrealists come in a variety of flavors including error theorists, emotivists, and expressivists.

Normative reason One that counts in favor of doing (or abstaining from doing) some act.

Normative theory   Theory that is concerned with how one should act or live. It is often contrasted with a *descriptive theory* of human behavior which is concerned with how people actually do live, not how they ought to live.

Objective value   Something has objective value if its value doesn't depend on facts about you. For example, many people think that happiness, courage, and health are objective values. If you disagreed, you'd just be wrong about their value.

Pluralism (moral)   Moral pluralism is the view that there are various (often competing) moral values or principles that we may consider when making a judgment. Contrast with absolutist theories like utilitarians who argue that only consequences matter or Kantians who argue that universalizability or respect for autonomy are all that matter.

Practical reason   Practical reasoning is the kind of reflective reasoning I engage in when I'm trying to figure out what to do in a particular circumstance or how best to achieve a particular goal. It's also what I do when I try to resolve conflicts between my various goals.

Proximate cause   The immediate cause of some behavior. The proximate cause for me pushing someone might be that he insulted my mother. Contrast this with ultimate cause: I pushed him because evolutionarily those who defended their immediate family from threats had an evolutionary advantage over those that didn't. So, the disposition to respond to the threat to my mother is (ultimately) caused by a long evolutionary story.

Psychological egoism   A descriptive theory that holds human beings have only one ultimate goal: maximizing their own welfare.

Rationalism (moral)   Kant argued that reason can lead us to what we should value and what our values should be. The opposite view would be Hume's: we should reflect on our emotions or desires in order to figure out what to value.

Realist (moral)   A moral realist believes that there are objective moral values. From this it follows that moral assertions can be true or false and that people can be morally right or wrong. (Contrast with **non-cognitivism** and **error theory**.)

Reflective equilibrium   Reflective equilibrium is the process (or state) of balancing our intuitions and considered judgments about particular cases with our intuitions about general principles.

Retributivism   Within theories of punishment, retributivism is the view that punishment is justified only when offenders receive the punishment they deserve. Contrast with utilitarian theories of punishment which hold that punishment is justified by the benefits (like deterrence) it will bring to society.

Sentimentalism   Moral sentimentalists hold that our emotions are an important source of moral judgment and values.

Situationism   The theory that human behavior is determined by surrounding circumstances rather than by personal qualities.

Subjective/subjective value   Something is subjective if its truth or appearance depend on the subject. For example, some people think exercise feels good, others don't. There's no right (i.e., objective) answer. Whether exercise feels good will depend on the individual. Exercise has subjective value if its value depends on facts about the individual who values it (e.g., they enjoy it, it provided a sense of fulfillment). Exercise is *objectively* valuable if we say that it has value regardless of what particular individuals think about it. If someone doesn't value it, they're simply mistaken.

Teleology   The idea that things (and creatures) have a purpose or nature and that we can understand what is good for them in terms of that purpose or nature. For example, on Aristotle's view, 'being political' is an aspect of human nature and so we can assess how good a human is (in that particular respect) to the degree that they successfully engage in political activity.

Theory of mind   A creature with theory of mind is capable of understanding that other people have beliefs, desires, intentions, and perspectives. And they are able to take the perspective and attribute mental state to others. Without theory of mind, one cannot have empathy, because empathy requires the ability to take the perspective of others.

Utilitarianism   A moral theory that states that if you're faced with a situation where you have to choose between competing possible actions, always choose the action that will produce the greatest *net* amount of good for *everyone*. For example, if I have to choose between saving one person or five people, I should save the five people—regardless of how I save them.

Virtue ethics   Associated with Aristotle, virtue ethics is an approach to ethics that focuses on the character rather than the act. It's about the life and the person as opposed to the act (unlike utilitarianism and Kantian ethics). Virtue ethics holds that being virtuous not only helps you achieve a life of happiness but makes up what it is for a human to be happy. That is to say, for a human the *definition* of happiness includes having the various virtues. Also for virtue ethicists, happiness does *not* refer to a feeling or psychological state. It is a way of living, an activity—specifically, the most excellent way a human can live (*see* **eudaemonia**). An approach/theory of ethics.

Index

Page numbers in **bold** indicate glossary items.